U0901367

本书出版得到《大中华文库》出版经费资助

大中华文库

LIBRARY OF CHINESE CLASSICS

大中华文库

汉英对照

LIBRARY OF CHINESE CLASSICS

Chinese-English

汉书选

CHRONICLES OF THE HAN DYNASTY

I

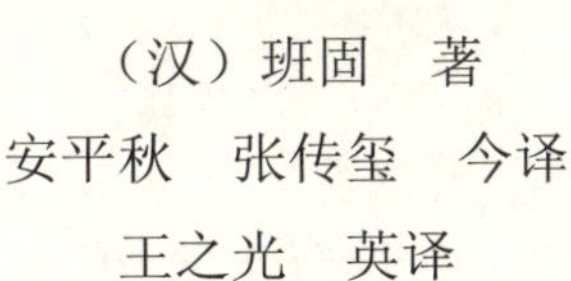

（汉）班固　著

安平秋　张传玺　今译

王之光　英译

Written by Ban Gu (Han Dynasty)

Edited by An Pingqiu, Zhang Chuanxi

Translated by Wang Zhiguang

外文出版社

Foreign Languages Press

First Edition 2015

ISBN 978-7-119-09408-3

Published by Foreign Languages Press Co. Ltd
24 Baiwanzhuang Road, Beijing 100037, China
http://www.flp.com.cn
Email: flp@CIPG.org.cn
Distributed by China International Book Trading Corporation
35 Chegongzhuang Xilu, Beijing 100044, China
P.O. Box 399, Beijing, China
Printed in the People's Republic of China

总　　　序

杨牧之

《大中华文库》终于出版了。我们为之高兴，为之鼓舞，但也倍感压力。

当此之际，我们愿将郁积在我们心底的话，向读者倾诉。

一

中华民族有着悠久的历史和灿烂的文化，系统、准确地将中华民族的文化经典翻译成外文，编辑出版，介绍给全世界，是几代中国人的愿望。早在几十年前，西方一位学者翻译《红楼梦》，将书名译成《一个红楼上的梦》，将林黛玉译为"黑色的玉"。我们一方面对外国学者将中国的名著介绍到世界上去表示由衷的感谢，一方面为祖国的名著还不被完全认识，甚而受到曲解，而感到深深的遗憾。还有西方学者翻译《金瓶梅》，专门摘选其中自然主义描述最为突出的篇章加以译介。一时间，西方学者好像发现了奇迹，掀起了《金瓶梅》热，说中国是"性开放的源头"，公开地在报刊上鼓吹中国要"发扬开放之传统"。还有许多资深、友善的汉学家译介中国古代的哲学著作，在把中华民族文化介绍给全世界的工作方面作出了重大贡献，但或囿于理解有误，或缘于对中国文字认识的局限，质量上乘的并不多，常常是隔靴搔痒，说不到点子上。大哲学家黑格尔曾经说过：中国有最完备的国史。但他认为中国古代没有真正意义上的哲学，还处在哲学史前状态。这么了不起的哲学家竟然作出这样大失水准的评论，何其不幸。正如任何哲学家都要受时间、地点、条件的制约一样，黑格尔也离不开这一规律。当时他也只能从上述水平的汉学家译过去的文字去分析、理解，所以，黑格尔先生对中国古代社会的认识水平是什么状态，也就不难想象了。

中国离不开世界，世界也缺少不了中国。中国文化摄取外域的新成分，丰富了自己，又以自己的新成就输送给别人，贡献于世界。从公元5世纪开始到公元15世纪，大约有一千年，中国走在世界的前列。在这一千多年的时间里，她的光辉照耀全世界。人类要前进，怎么能不全面认识中国，怎么能不认真研究中国的历史呢?

二

中华民族是伟大的，曾经辉煌过，蓝天、白云、阳光灿烂，和平而兴旺；也有过黑暗的、想起来就让人战栗的日子，但中华民族从来是充满理想，不断追求，不断学习，渴望和平与友谊的。

中国古代伟大的思想家孔子曾经说过：“三人行，必有我师焉。择其善者而从之，其不善者而改之。”孔子的话就是要人们向别人学习。这段话正是概括了整个中华民族与人交往的原则。人与人之间交往如此，在与周边的国家交往中也是如此。

秦始皇第一个统一了中国，可惜在位只有十几年，来不及做更多的事情。汉朝继秦而继续强大，便开始走出去，了解自己周边的世界。公元前 138 年，汉武帝派张骞出使西域。他带着一万头牛羊，总值一万万钱的金帛货物，作为礼物，开始西行，最远到过“安息”（即波斯）。公元 73 年，班超又率 36 人出使西域。36 个人按今天的话说，也只有一个排，显然是为了拜访未曾见过面的邻居，是去交朋友。到了西域，班超派遣甘英作为使者继续西行，往更远处的大秦国（即罗马）去访问，“乃抵条支而历安息，临西海以望大秦”（《后汉书·西域传》）。“条支”在“安息”以西，即今天的伊拉克、叙利亚一带，“西海”应是今天的地中海。也就是说甘英已经到达地中海边上，与罗马帝国隔海相望，“临大海欲渡”，却被人劝阻而未成行，这在历史上留下了遗恨。可以想见班超、甘英沟通友谊的无比勇气和强烈愿望。接下来是唐代的玄奘，历经千难万险，到“西天”印度取经，带回了南亚国家的古老文化。归国后，他把带回的佛教经典组织人翻译，到后来很多经典印度失传了，但中国却保存完好，以至于今天，没有玄奘的《大唐西域记》，印度人很难编写印度古代史。明代郑和“七下西洋”，把中华文化传到东南亚一带。鸦片战争以后，一代又一代先进的中国人，为了振兴中华，又前赴后继，向西方国家学习先进的科学思想和文明成果。这中间有我们的领导人朱德、周恩来、邓小平；有许许多多大科学家、文学家、艺术家，如郭沫若、李四光、钱学森、冼星海、徐悲鸿等。他们的追求、奋斗，他们的博大胸怀、兼收并蓄的精神，为人类社会增添了光彩。

中国文化的形成和发展过程，就是一个以众为师、以各国人民为师，不断学习和创造的过程。中华民族曾经向周边国家和民族学习过许多东西，假如没有这些学习，中华民族绝不可能创造出昔日的辉煌。回顾历史，我们怎么能够不对伟大的古埃及文明、古希腊文明、古印度文明满怀深深的感激？怎么能够不对伟大的欧洲文明、非洲文明、美洲文明、澳洲文明，以及中国周围的亚洲文明充满温情与敬意?

中华民族为人类社会曾作出过独特的贡献。在15世纪以前，中国的科学技术一直处于世界遥遥领先的地位。英国科学家李约瑟说：“中国在公元3世纪到13世纪之间，保持着一个西方所望尘莫及的科学知识水平。”美国耶鲁大学教授、《大国的兴衰》的作者保罗·肯尼迪坦言：“在近代以前时期的所有文明中，没有一个国家的文明比中国更发达，更先进。”

世界各国的有识之士千里迢迢来中国观光、学习。在这个过程中，中国唐朝的长安城渐渐发展成为国际大都市。西方的波斯、东罗马，东亚的高丽、新罗、百济、南天竺、北天竺，频繁前来。外国的王侯、留学生，在长安供职的外国官员，商贾、乐工和舞士，总有几十个国家，几万人之多。日本派出“遣唐使”更是一批接一批。传为美谈的日本人阿倍仲麻吕 (晁衡) 在长安留学的故事，很能说明外国人与中国的交往。晁衡学成仕于唐朝，前后历时五十余年。晁衡与中国的知识分子结下了深厚的友情。他归国时，传说在海中遇难身亡。大诗人李白作诗哭悼:“日本晁卿辞帝都，征帆一片远蓬壶。明月不归沉碧海，白云愁色满苍梧。”晁衡遇险是误传，但由此可见中外学者之间在中国长安交往的情谊。

后来，不断有外国人到中国来探寻秘密，所见所闻，常常让他们目瞪口呆。《希腊纪事》 (希腊人波桑尼阿著) 记载公元2世纪时，希腊人在中国的见闻。书中写道：“赛里斯人用小米和青芦喂一种类似蜘蛛的昆虫，喂到第五年，虫肚子胀裂开，便从里面取出丝来。”从这段对中国古代养蚕技术的描述，可见当时欧洲人与中国人的差距。公元9世纪中叶，阿拉伯人来到中国。一位阿拉伯作家在他所著的《中国印度闻见录》中记载了曾旅居中国的阿拉伯商人的见闻：

——一天，一个外商去拜见驻守广州的中国官吏。会见时，外商总盯着官吏的胸部，官吏很奇怪，便问："你好像总盯着我的胸，这是怎么回事?"那位外商回答说："透过你穿的丝绸衣服，我隐约看到你胸口上长着一个黑痣，这是什么丝绸，我感到十分惊奇。"官吏听后，失声大笑，伸出胳膊，说："请你数数吧，看我穿了几件衣服?"那商人数过，竟然穿了五件之多，黑痣正是透过这五层丝绸衣服显现出来的。外商惊得目瞪口呆，官吏说："我穿的丝绸还不算是最好的，总督穿的要更精美。"

——书中关于茶 (他们叫干草叶子) 的记载，可见阿拉伯国家当时还没有喝茶的习惯。书中记述："中国国王本人的收入主要靠盐税和泡开水喝的一种干草税。在各个城市里，这种干草叶售价都很高，中国人称这种草叶叫'茶'，这种干草叶比苜蓿的叶子还多，也略比它香，稍有苦味，用开水冲喝，治百病。"

——他们对中国的医疗条件十分羡慕，书中记载道："中国人医疗条件很好，穷人可以从国库中得到药费。"还说："城市里，很多地方立一石碑，高10肘，上面刻有各种疾病和药物，写明某种病用某种药医治。"

——关于当时中国的京城，书中作了生动的描述：中国的京城很大，人口众多，一条宽阔的长街把全城分为两半，大街右边的东区，住着皇帝、宰相、禁军及皇家的总管、奴婢。在这个区域，沿街开凿了小河，流水潺潺；路旁，葱茏的树木整然有序，一幢幢宅邸鳞次栉比。大街左边的西区，住着庶民和商人。这里有货栈和商店，每当清晨，人们可以看到，皇室的总管、宫廷的仆役，或骑马或步行，到这里来采购。

此后的史籍对西人来华的记载，渐渐多了起来。13 世纪意大利旅行家马可·波罗，尽管有人对他是否真的到过中国持怀疑态度，但他留下一部记述元代事件的《马可·波罗游记》却是确凿无疑的。这部游记中的一些关于当时中国的描述使得西方人认为是“天方夜谭”。总之，从中西文化交流史来说，这以前的时期还是一个想象和臆测的时代，相互之间充满了好奇与幻想。

从 16 世纪末开始，由于航海技术的发展，东西方航路的开通，随着一批批传教士来华，中国与西方开始了直接的交流。沟通中西的使命在意大利传教士利玛窦那里有了充分的体现。利玛窦于 1582 年来华，1610 年病逝于北京，在华二十余年。除了传教以外，做了两件具有历史象征意义的事，一是 1594 年前后在韶州用拉丁文翻译《四书》，并作了注释；二是与明代学者徐光启合作，用中文翻译了《几何原本》。

西方传教士对《四书》等中国经典的粗略翻译，以及杜赫德的《中华帝国志》等书对中国的介绍，在西方读者的眼前展现了一个异域文明，在当时及稍后一段时期引起了一场“中国热”，许多西方大思想家的眼光都曾注目于中国文化。有的推崇中华文明，如莱布尼兹、伏尔泰、魁奈等，有的对中华文明持批评态度，如孟德斯鸠、黑格尔等。莱布尼兹认识到中国文化的某些思想与他的观念相近，如周易的卦象与他发明的二进制相契合，对中国文化给予了热情的礼赞；黑格尔则从他整个哲学体系的推演出发，认为中国没有真正意义上的哲学，还处在哲学史前的状态。但是，不论是推崇还是批评，是吸纳还是排斥，中西文化的交流产生了巨大的影响。随着先进的中国科学技术的西传，特别是中国的造纸、火药、印刷术和指南针四大发明的问世，大大改变了世界的面貌。马克思说："中国的火药把骑士阶层炸得粉碎，指南针打开了世界市场并建立了殖民地，而印刷术则变成了新教的工具，变成对精神发展创造必要前提的最强大的杠杆。"英国的哲学家培根说：中国的四大发明"改变了全世界的面貌和一切事物的状态"。

三

大千世界，潮起潮落。云散云聚，万象更新。中国古代产生了无数伟大的科学家：祖冲之、李时珍、孙思邈、张衡、沈括、毕昇……产生了无数科技成果：《齐民要术》、《九章算术》、《伤寒杂病论》、《本草纲目》……以及保存至今的世界奇迹：浑天仪、地动仪、都江堰、敦煌石窟、大运河、万里长城……但从15世纪下半叶起，风水似乎从东方转到了西方，落后的欧洲只经过400年便成为世界瞩目的文明中心。英国的牛顿、波兰的哥白尼、德国的伦琴、法国的居里、德国的爱因斯坦、意大利的伽利略、俄国的门捷列夫、美国的费米和爱迪生……光芒四射，令人敬仰。

中华民族开始思考了。潮起潮落究竟是什么原因？中国人发明的火药，传到欧洲，转眼之间反成为欧洲列强轰击中国大门的炮弹，又是因为什么？

鸦片战争终于催醒了中国人沉睡的迷梦，最先"睁眼看世界"的一代精英林则徐、魏源迈出了威武雄壮的一步。曾国藩、李鸿章搞起了洋务运动。中国的知识分子喊出"民主与科学”的口号。中国是落后了，中国的志士仁人在苦苦探索。但落后中饱含着变革的动力，探索中孕育着崛起的希望。“向科学进军”，中华民族终于又迎来了科学的春天。

今天，世界毕竟来到了21世纪的门槛。分散隔绝的世界，逐渐变成联系为一体的世界。现在，全球一体化趋势日益明显，人类历史也就在愈来愈大的程度上成为全世界的历史。当今，任何一种文化的发展都离不开对其他优秀文化的汲取，都以其他优秀文化的发展为前提。在近现代，西方文化汲取中国文化，不仅是中国文化的传播，更是西方文化自身的创新和发展；正如中国文化对西方文化的汲取一样，既是西方文化在中国的传播，同时也是中国文化在近代的转型和发展。地球上所有的人类文化，都是我们共同的宝贵遗产。既然我们生活的各个大陆，在地球史上曾经是连成一气的“泛大陆”，或者说是一个完整的“地球村”，那么，我们同样可以在这个以知识和学习为特征的网络时代，走上相互学习、共同发展的大路，建设和开拓我们人类崭新的“地球村”。

西学仍在东渐，中学也将西传。各国人民的优秀文化正日益迅速地为中国文化所汲取，而无论西方和东方，也都需要从中国文化中汲取养分。正是基于这一认识，我们组织出版汉英对照版《大中华文库》，全面系统地翻译介绍中国传统文化典籍。我们试图通过《大中华文库》，向全世界展示，中华民族五千年的追求、五千年的梦想，正在新的历史时期重放光芒。中国人民就像火后的凤凰，万众一心，迎接新世纪文明的太阳。

1999年8月　北京

PREFACE TO THE *LIBRARY OF CHINESE CLASSICS*

Yang Muzhi

The publication of the *Library of Chinese Classics* is a matter of great satisfaction to all of us who have been involved in the production of this monumental work. At the same time, we feel a weighty sense of responsibility, and take this opportunity to explain to our readers the motivation for undertaking this cross-century task.

1

The Chinese nation has a long history and a glorious culture, and it has been the aspiration of several generations of Chinese scholars to translate, edit and publish the whole corpus of the Chinese literary classics so that the nation's greatest cultural achievements can be introduced to people all over the world. There have been many translations of the Chinese classics done by foreign scholars. A few dozen years ago, a Western scholar translated the title of *A Dream of Red Mansions* into "A Dream of Red Chambers" and Lin Daiyu, the heroine in the novel, into "Black Jade." But while their endeavours have been laudable, the results of their labours have been less than satisfactory. Lack of knowledge of Chinese culture and an inadequate grasp of the Chinese written language have led the translators into many errors. As a consequence, not only are Chinese classical writings widely misunderstood in the rest of the world, in some cases their content has actually been distorted. At one time, there was a "*Jin Ping Mei* craze" among Western scholars, who thought that they had uncovered a miraculous phenomenon, and published theories claiming that China was the "fountainhead of eroticism," and that a Chinese "tradition of permissiveness" was about to be laid bare. This distorted view came about due to the translators of the *Jin Ping Mei (Plum in the Golden Vase)* putting one-sided stress on the raw elements in that novel, to the neglect of its overall literary value. Meanwhile, there have been many distinguished and well-intentioned Sinologists who have attempted to make the culture of the Chinese nation more widely known by translating works of ancient Chinese philosophy. However, the quality of such work, in many cases, is unsatisfactory, often missing the point entirely. The great philosopher Hegel considered that ancient China had no philosophy in the real sense of the word, being stuck in philosophical "prehistory." For such an eminent authority to make such a colossal error of judgment is truly regrettable. But, of course, Hegel was just as subject to the constraints of time, space and other objective conditions as anyone else, and since he had to rely for his knowledge of Chinese philosophy on inadequate translations it is not difficult to imagine why he went so far off the mark.

China cannot be separated from the rest of the world; and the rest of the world cannot ignore China. Throughout its history, Chinese civilization has enriched itself by absorbing new elements from the outside world, and in turn has contributed to the progress of world civilization as a whole by transmitting to other peoples its own cultural achievements. From the 5th to the 15th centuries, China marched in the front ranks of world civilization. If mankind wishes to advance, how can it afford to ignore China? How can it afford not to make a thoroughgoing study of its history?

2

Despite the ups and downs in their fortunes, the Chinese people have always been idealistic, and have never ceased to forge ahead and learn from others, eager to strengthen ties of peace and friendship.

The great ancient Chinese philosopher Confucius once said, "Wherever three persons come together, one of them will surely be able to teach me something. I will pick out his good points and emulate them; his bad points I will reform." Confucius meant by this that we should always be ready to learn from others. This maxim encapsulates the principle the Chinese people have always followed in their dealings with other peoples, not only on an individual basis but also at the level of state-to-state relations.

After generations of internecine strife, China was unified by Emperor

Qin Shi Huang (the First Emperor of the Qin Dynasty) in 221 B.C. The Han Dynasty, which succeeded that of the short-lived Qin, waxed powerful, and for the first time brought China into contact with the outside world. In 138 B.C., Emperor Wu dispatched Zhang Qian to the western regions, i.e. Central Asia. Zhang, who traveled as far as what is now Iran, took with him as presents for the rulers he visited on the way 10,000 head of sheep and cattle, as well as gold and silks worth a fabulous amount. In 73 D.C., Ban Chao headed a 36-man legation to the western regions. These were missions of friendship to visit neighbours the Chinese people had never met before and to learn from them. Ban Chao sent Gan Ying to explore further toward the west. According to the "Western Regions Section" in the *Book of Later Han*, Gan Ying traveled across the territories of present-day Iraq and Syria, and reached the Mediterranean Sea, an expedition which brought him within the confines of the Roman Empire. Later, during the Tang Dynasty, the monk Xuan Zang made a journey fraught with danger to reach India and seek the knowledge of that land. Upon his return, he organized a team of scholars to translate the Buddhist scriptures, which he had brought back with him. As a result, many of these scriptural classics which were later lost in India have been preserved in China. In fact, it would have been difficult for the people of India to reconstruct their own ancient history if it had not been for Xuan Zang's *A Record of a Journey to the West in the Time of the Great Tang Dynasty*. In the Ming Dynasty, Zheng He transmitted Chinese culture to Southeast Asia during his seven voyages. Following the Opium Wars in the mid-19th century, progressive Chinese, generation after generation, went to study the advanced scientific thought and cultural achievements of the Western countries. Their aim was to revive the fortunes of their own country. Among them were people who were later to become leaders of China, including Zhu De, Zhou Enlai and Deng Xiaoping. In addition, there were people who were to become leading scientists, literary figures and artists, such as Guo Moruo, Li Siguang, Qian Xuesen, Xian Xinghai and Xu Beihong. Their spirit of ambition, their struggles and their breadth of vision were an inspiration not only to the Chinese people but to people all over the world.

Indeed, it is true that if the Chinese people had not learned many things from the surrounding countries they would never have been able to produce the splendid achievements of former days. When we look back upon history, how can we not feel profoundly grateful for the legacies of the civilizations of ancient Egypt, Greece and India? How can we not feel fondness and respect for the cultures of Europe, Africa, America and Oceania?

The Chinese nation, in turn, has made unique contributions to the community of mankind. Prior to the 15th century, China led the world in science and technology. The British scientist Joseph Needham once said, "From the third century A.D. to the 13th century A.D. China was far ahead of the West in the level of its scientific knowledge." Paul Kennedy, of Yale University in the U.S., author of *The Rise and Fall of the Great Powers*, said, "Of all the civilizations of the pre-modern period, none was as well-developed or as progressive as that of China."

Foreigners who came to China were often astonished at what they saw and heard. The Greek geographer Pausanias in the second century A.D. gave the first account in the West of the technique of silk production in China: "The Chinese feed a spider-like insect with millet and reeds. After five years the insect's stomach splits open, and silk is extracted therefrom." From this extract, we can see that the Europeans at that time did not know the art of silk manufacture. In the middle of the 9th century A.D., an Arabian writer includes the following anecdote in his *Account of China and India*:

"One day, an Arabian merchant called upon the military governor of Guangzhou. Throughout the meeting, the visitor could not keep his eyes off the governor's chest. Noticing this, the latter asked the Arab merchant what he was staring at. The merchant replied, 'Through the silk robe you are wearing, I can faintly see a black mole on your chest. Your robe must be made out of very fine silk indeed!' The governor burst out laughing, and holding out his sleeve invited the merchant to count how many garments he was wearing. The merchant did so, and discovered that the governor was actually wearing five silk robes, one on top of the other, and they were made of such fine material that a tiny mole could be seen through them all! Moreover, the governor explained that the robes he was wearing were not made of the finest silk at all; silk of the highest grade was reserved for the garments worn by the provincial governor."

The references to tea in this book (the author calls it "dried grass") reveal that the custom of drinking tea was unknown in the Arab countries at that time: "The king of China's revenue comes mainly from taxes on salt and the dry leaves of a kind of grass which is drunk after boiled water is poured on it. This dried grass is sold at a high price in every city in the country. The Chinese call it 'cha.' The bush is like alfalfa, except that it bears more leaves, which are also more fragrant than alfalfa. It has a slightly bitter taste, and when it is infused in boiling water it is said to have medicinal properties."

Foreign visitors showed especial admiration for Chinese medicine. One wrote, "China has very good medical conditions. Poor people are given money to buy medicines by the government."

In this period, when Chinese culture was in full bloom, scholars flocked from all over the world to China for sightseeing and for study. Chang'an, the capital of the Tang Dynasty was host to visitors from as far away as the Byzantine Empire, not to mention the neighboring countries of Asia. Chang'an, at that time the world's greatest metropolis, was packed with thousands of foreign dignitaries, students, diplomats, merchants, artisans and entertainers. Japan especially sent contingent after contingent of envoys to the Tang court. Worthy of note are the accounts of life in Chang'an written by Abeno Nakamaro, a Japanese scholar who studied in China and had close friendships with ministers of the Tang court and many Chinese scholars in a period of over 50 years. The description throws light on the exchanges between Chinese and foreigners in this period. When Abeno was supposedly lost at sea on his way back home, the leading poet of the time, Li Bai, wrote a eulogy for him.

The following centuries saw a steady increase in the accounts of China written by Western visitors. The Italian Marco Polo described conditions in China during the Yuan Dynasty in his *Travels*. However, until advances in the science of navigation led to the opening of east-west shipping routes at the beginning of the 16th century Sino-Western cultural exchanges were coloured by fantasy and conjecture. Concrete progress was made when a contingent of religious missionaries, men well versed in Western science and technology, made their way to China, ushering in an era of direct contacts between China and the West. The experience of this era was embodied in the career of the Italian Jesuit Matteo Ricci. Arriving in China in 1582, Ricci died in Beijing in 1610. Apart from his missionary work, Ricci accomplished two historically symbolic tasks — one was the translation into Latin of the "Four Books," together with annotations, in 1594; the other was the translation into Chinese of Euclid's *Elements*.

The rough translations of the "Four Books" and other Chinese classical works by Western missionaries, and the publication of Père du Halde's *Description Geographique, Historique, Chronologique, Politique, et Physique de l'Empire de la Chine* revealed an exotic culture to Western readers, and sparked a "China fever," during which the eyes of many Western intellectuals were fixed on China. Some of these intellectuals, including Leibniz, held China in high esteem; others, such as Hegel, nursed a critical attitude toward Chinese culture. Leibniz considered that some aspects of Chinese thought were close to his own views, such as the philosophy of the *Book of Changes* and his own binary system. Hegel, on the other hand, as mentioned above, considered that China had developed no proper philosophy of its own. Nevertheless, no matter whether the reaction was one of admiration, criticism, acceptance or rejection, Sino-Western exchanges were of great significance. The transmission of advanced Chinese science and technology to the West, especially the Chinese inventions of paper-making, gunpowder, printing and the compass, greatly changed the face of the whole world. Karl Marx said, "Chinese gunpowder blew the feudal class of knights to smithereens; the compass opened up world markets and built colonies; and printing became an implement of Protestantism and the most powerful lever and necessary precondition for intellectual development and creation." The English philosopher Roger Bacon said that China's four great inventions had "changed the face of the whole world and the state of affairs of everything."

3

Ancient China gave birth to a large number of eminent scientists, such as Zu Chongzhi, Li Shizhen, Sun Simiao, Zhang Heng, Shen Kuo and Bi Sheng. They produced numerous treatises on scientific subjects, including *The Manual of Important Arts for the People's Welfare, Nine Chapters on the Mathematical Art, A Treatise on Febrile Diseases* and *Compendium of Materia Medica*. Their accomplishments included ones whose influence has been felt right down to modern times, such as the armillary sphere, seismograph, Dujiangyan water conservancy project, Dunhuang Grottoes, Grand Canal and Great Wall. But from the latter part of the 15th century, and for the next 400 years, Europe gradually became the cultural centre upon which the world's eyes were fixed. The world's most outstanding scientists then were England's Isaac Newton, Poland's Copernicus, France's Marie Curie, Germany's Rontgen and Einstein, Italy's Galileo, Russia's Mendelev and America's Edison.

The Chinese people then began to think: What is the cause of the rise and fall of nations? Moreover, how did it happen that gunpowder, invented in China and transmitted to the West, in no time at all made Europe powerful enough to batter down the gates of China herself?

It took the Opium War to wake China from its reverie. The first generation to make the bold step of "turning our eyes once again to the rest of the world" was represented by Lin Zexu and Wei Yuan. Zeng Guofan and Li Hongzhang started the Westernization Movement, and later intellectuals raised the slogan of "Democracy and Science." Noble-minded patriots, realizing that China had fallen behind in the race for modernization, set out on a painful quest. But in backwardness lay the motivation for change, and the quest produced the embryo of a towering hope, and the Chinese people finally gathered under a banner proclaiming a "March Toward Science."

On the threshold of the 21st century, the world is moving in the direction of becoming an integrated entity. This trend is becoming clearer by the day. In fact, the history of the various peoples of the world is also becoming the history of mankind as a whole. Today, it is impossible for any nation's culture to develop without absorbing the excellent aspects of the cultures of other peoples. When Western culture absorbs aspects of Chinese culture, this is not just because it has come into contact with Chinese culture, but also because of the active creativity and development of Western culture itself; and vice versa. The various cultures of the world's peoples are a precious heritage which we all share. Mankind no longer lives on different continents, but on one big continent, or in a "global village." And so, in this era characterized by an all-encompassing network of knowledge and information we should learn from each other and march in step along the highway of development to construct a brand-new "global village."

Western learning is still being transmitted to the East, and vice versa. China is accelerating its pace of absorption of the best parts of the cultures of other countries, and there is no doubt that both the West and the East need the nourishment of Chinese culture. Based on this recognition, we have edited and published the *Library of Chinese Classics* in a Chinese-English format as an introduction to the corpus of traditional Chinese culture in a comprehensive and systematic translation. Through this collection, our aim is to reveal to the world the aspirations and dreams of the Chinese people over the past 5,000 years and the splendour of the new historical era in China. Like a phoenix rising from the ashes, the Chinese people in unison are welcoming the cultural sunrise of the new century.

August 1999 Beijing

前　言

东汉初大史学家班固（公元32–92年）撰成的《汉书》，是与司马迁（公元前145/公元前135–前90年)《史记》相并称的史学巨著，因其杰出的成就，两千年来被人们世代传诵不衰。

（一）

班固字孟坚，扶风安陵（今陕西咸阳东北）人。班固生活的时代，东汉王朝（公元25–220年）国力处于上升时期，生产发展，社会安定，为学术的发展提供了良好的条件。班固著史又有深厚的家学渊源。父亲班彪曾任东汉朝廷司徒府的属官。他官职虽低，但“才高而好著述”，认为《史记》成就很高，而其续作者所写的一些片断文字质量低下，与《史记》太不相称。他搜集整理史料，撰写了《史记》后传数十篇。班彪对《史记》的续作，就成为班固著史的先声。

班固于16岁入洛阳太学，用功苦读，“无不穷究”。父亲卒后，他随母亲回原籍安陵居住，遂决心继承父志，撰修《汉书》。公元63年（永平五年），因被人告发“私修国史”，被逮入狱。其弟班超驰赴洛阳，上书汉明帝，陈述父兄著书心志，扶风郡也将书稿送至。明帝见而奇其书，任他为兰台令史，参与修撰《东观汉纪》。升为郎官，典校皇家藏书，明帝勉励他最终完成《汉书》的著述。汉章帝也很欣赏班固的文学才能，“朝廷有大议，使难问公卿，辩论于前”。公元89年，他以中护军随大将军窦宪出兵匈奴。公元92年，窦宪因罪自杀，班固为仇家借机罗织罪名被捕，死于洛阳狱中。班固撰修《汉书》，约自公元一世纪50年代至80年代，历时二十余年。

（二）

《汉书》的内容，上起刘邦起义、建立汉朝，下迄王莽篡汉失败，完整地记述西汉一朝（公元前206年–公元23年）230年的盛衰兴亡。全书共一百篇，80余万字，由“纪”、“表”、“志”、“传”四部分构成。十二篇“纪”，记述了高帝、惠帝、吕后、文帝、景帝、武帝、昭帝、宣帝、元帝、成帝、哀帝、平帝十二世的大事，作为全书的纲领。其中，《高帝纪》等四篇跟《史记·高祖本纪》等篇相关，而《汉书》补充了许多重要内容，更能显示出西汉前期上升、兴盛的历史局面。八篇“表”，其中有六篇王侯表是在《史记》有关各表基础上作分合增减，《百官公卿表》、《古今人表》是班固新创。十篇“志”，为《律历志》、《礼乐志》、《刑法志》、《食货志》、《郊祀志》、《天文志》、《五行志》、《地理志》、《沟洫志》、《艺文志》，是在《史记》“八书”的基础上大大发展了。七十篇“传”，详细记载了西汉一代各方面代表人物的活动，围绕十二篇“纪”展开，具体诠释了历史盛衰的内涵。其中包括了陈胜、项籍、张耳、陈馀等秦汉之际的起义人物，有韩信、张良、萧何、晁错、张骞、苏武、霍光、赵充国等汉代将相名卿，有荆燕吴楚等同姓王侯，有文学家、思想家、经师、说士、循吏、酷吏、货殖、游侠等人物，以及记载国内外少数民族活动等。

班固在《汉书·司马迁传》中高度评价司马迁的史学成就，赞誉他：“有良史之材”，“善序事理”，“不虚美，不隐恶，故谓之实录”。表明班固本人同样以“不虚美，不隐恶”，写出“实录”式的史书作为自己治史的准则。西汉前期的历史，班固大量地以《史记》的记载为依据，这是事理的自然。而同时，他又精心地搜集新的史料，作了许多有价值的补充。《惠帝纪》及王陵、吴芮、蒯通、伍被、贾山、东方朔、李陵、苏武诸传，都是新增的篇目。特别是张骞事迹，《史记》是在《大宛列传》中叙述的，并非人物传记。《汉书》特为张骞立专传，给了他应有的历史地位。有关班固对西汉前期重要史实的增补，如高帝、文帝、景帝三篇纪中，补充了大量有关社会经济和重要事件、政令的材料。又在《萧何传》中增记项羽负约，封沛公于巴蜀为汉王，汉王怒，欲攻羽，萧何力言不可，乃至汉中就国，然后积蓄实力，伺机再起。《韩信传》中的史实也有重要补充。班固还申明，对确凿有据的史实才作增补，否则阙疑，表明他确实发扬了司马迁的实录精神。

实录精神和历史见识，使班固能够较深入地考察历史进程，对于一些问题提出了经得起时间检验的精辟见解。藩国问题是西汉史一大课题。《汉书·诸侯王表》序中肯地论述了中央与藩国势力作斗争所经历的主要阶段，至武帝以后，“诸侯唯得衣租食税，不与政事”，标志着严重的藩国问题得到解决。班固的论述提纲挈领，成为后人论述西汉藩国问题最权威的依据。

武帝时期（公元前141－前87年），何以能出现鼎盛局面？班固对此也有精辟的论述。《公孙弘兒宽卜式传·赞》中说，武帝时期的鼎盛局面集中体现在两项，一是开拓边境，奠定版图，二是建立一套礼仪、政治、法律制度。“上方欲用文武，求之如不及，群士慕向，异人并出。……汉之得人，于兹为盛。”时代需要大量非凡人才，人才便成批涌现出来。班固一连举出当时大批杰出人才，如董仲舒、公孙弘、兒宽、韩安国、司马迁、司马相如、桑弘羊、张骞、卫青、霍去病等。依靠这些人物，使武帝时代达到极盛，“是以兴造功业，制度遗文，后世莫及”。而在《西域传》中又记载：由于武帝连年对边境大规模用兵，耗费了大量人力、物力，至其晚年，国库空虚，社会动荡。面对如此严重局面，武帝终于醒悟过来，吸收秦朝灭亡的教训，实行政策转变，罢兵息民，挽救了危机。于征和四年（公元前89年），特地下诏书，“陈既往之悔”。此后昭帝、宣帝即继续沿着这一罢兵力农的路线走下去，因而出现了“中兴”局面。

《汉书》对西汉时代的历史功绩如实地予以大量记载，同时对于西汉社会的阴暗面也直书无隐。《汉书》中对于西汉时期贵族、豪强大量兼并土地、造成平民“贫无立锥之地”，对于朝廷和地方官吏刑罚的严酷，对于诸侯王悖逆不法，穷奢极欲，以骇人听闻的手段，残害无辜百姓的犯罪行为，对于匡衡、张禹等一批以儒学大师担任显赫职位的人物，其实质却是庸碌自私、虚伪贪婪、专事谄媚、贻误国政之徒，都以确凿的史实无情地予以揭露。这些，都足以为班固的“实录”精神和高尚史德提供有力的证明。

（三）

以上《汉书》对西汉一代盛衰的忠实记载和深刻总结，是与其在历史编纂和历史叙事的出色成就互为表里、完美地相统一的，因而成为历代“正史”编纂的典范之作。

“历史编纂”是指历史学家为再现客观历史而为其史著构建恰当的总体格局、框架结构，并将其史学思想贯穿于全书之中的综合能力。它为史书的丰富内容提供了合适的载体，史家的史识、史学、史才在此得到集中的体现，历史知识的传播也由此得以实现。重视历史编纂的技巧，是中国史学重要的民族特色，从《左传》、《史记》开始就形成了优良传统，班固将之发扬光大。《汉书》历史编纂的成就，主要有三项。

一是断代为史，开创了著史的新格局。《史记》上起黄帝，下迄司马迁所生活的武帝时期，是通史体裁。由于《史记》取得了巨大的成功，后人仰慕不已，纷纷续作，写出片断篇章附于其后，据《史通》等书记载，续作者有褚少孙、刘向、扬雄、刘歆、班彪等十七人之多。这样做，只限于修修补补，其结果，除了褚少孙和班彪所记片断文字留下来外，其余统统湮灭无闻。这就成为司马迁以后一百多年间历史编纂的一大难题，若不解决，则“保持历史记载连续不断”的目的就不能达到。班固则有气魄、有能力将西汉一代独立撰成一史，上起高祖，下迄王莽，构建了著史的新格局，把历史编纂大大向前推进。班固所创立的断代史体裁，是对《史记》的继承，又是影响极为深远的创造。因此，刘知幾在《史通·六家》篇中评价说：“如《汉书》者，究西都之始末，穷刘氏之废兴，包举一代，撰成一书。言皆精练，事甚该密，故学者寻讨，易为其功。自尔迄今，无改斯道。”以后二十二部“正史”的体裁都效法《汉书》，沿用不改。班固虽然“断汉为史”，但他又有贯通古今的“通史”精神，许多篇章都体现出历史发展前后相互联系，不能割断。还有一点值得注意的，据《论衡》记载，东汉初年俗儒头脑中充满尊古卑今的意识，不重视汉代功业。班固及时撰成《汉书》，以“宣扬汉德”为宗旨，就有破除当时复古倒退思想的积极意义。

二是大大拓宽了历史记载的范围，囊括了社会生活的丰富内容。这在十篇“志”中表现得最为突出。十志在《史记》八书的基础上加以发展，将书志体完善起来。如白寿彝教授在《司马迁与班固》一文中说，十志包含了自然的社会的学问，自古以来的典章制度都囊括进来了，从而为法律史、经济史、历史地理学、学术史等分支学科提供了开创性著作。如《食货志》，它比《史记·平准书》在内容上和认识上都有重大的发展。全志扩充为“食”、“货”两个部分，“食”指农业生产，包括土地问题；“货”指布、丝织品和商业货币，包括商业交换活动。认为这两项是国家富强和社会发展的基础。在内容上，班固增写了先秦至汉初的史实，续写了武帝晚年至王莽灭亡一百七八十年间的经济措施和经济状况。篇中对于重要的制度和在历史上影响较大的政策主张，必求记载明晰。篇末更以确凿的史实载明，王莽政权灭亡的根本原因，正是由于其种种倒行逆施的政策，造成了经济的混乱，“农商失业，食货俱废，民涕泣于市道”。其统治也注定必然覆亡。《刑法志》则系统记述秦汉刑法制度的沿变，肯定汉朝刑法比起周、秦取得很大进步，同时又据实批评封建皇朝法律的残酷。篇末，更用长段议论，大声疾呼删除繁苛的旧刑律，制定简明而能便民的新律令。这些记述和痛切的议论，表明班固具有深刻的观察力和对民众疾苦的同情心。《地理志》、《艺文志》也都是影响深远的名篇。

三是体例组织严密合理。特别是在七十篇列传的编排上，做到了历史联系与逻辑联系相一致。为了避免零散纷繁、漫无头绪，班固成功地采用了专传与合传相结合的形式，作了周密安排。专传，是为记载人物事迹多者而设。合传，是将人物事迹联系密切，或是人物身份行为相近似者，合在一起记载。合传的设立，极具匠心，把二百多人物组织到四十七篇合传之中，显得眉目清楚，线索分明。而从现代观点看，设置合传，可以突出某一类型人物的行为和思想特征，以群体的形象出现，有利于反映社会历史情状。

班固又富有文学才华，所作《两都赋》、《幽通赋》，是汉赋名篇。《汉书》的历史叙事，更是历史与文学相结合的典范。班固笔下的许多人物和场景写得栩栩如生，他熟练地运用了多种叙事技巧，如：用对话刻划人物性格；借细节描写反映人物的心理；对比手法；精心描写场面、情景，作有力的烘托等。特别是《苏武传》，历来评价为写得“慷慨悲凉，极其精彩”。为了表现苏武的民族气节和刚强不屈的性格，从其八十多岁的一生中，重点描述其出使、羁留匈奴十九年的艰苦经历；而在十九年岁月中，又仅仅选择诱降迫降、幽禁断食、流放牧羊、李陵苦劝等典型性事件，作了细致刻画，因而使苏武的形象生动传神，其艺术感染力千百年来不曾泯灭。《汉书》又多载有用之文。如西汉一代公卿名臣的重要论议，思想家的出色政论，文学家的辞赋华章，皆尽收书中。宋代文学家黄庭坚（公元1045－1105年），和他的朋友们经常以聚集在一起诵习的方式来研读《汉书》，从中吸取思想营养，并有“不读《汉书》则俗”的感叹。《汉书》的典雅文字如何受到历代文人学者的宝爱，由此可见一斑。

（四）

《汉书》撰成后，自魏晋至唐初六百年间，有众多学者“共行钻仰”，作注释者多达二十五家，形成了专门之学。唐初颜师古(公元581年－645年)，在此基础上，撰成《汉书注》，内容详审，成为注释《汉书》的集大成之作。至晚清，王先谦（公元1842–1917年），又撰有《汉书补注》，系主要采集清代考证学家研究《汉书》的成果，也甚便读者参考。《汉书》作为一部中国古代史学名著，早已传播到海外。10世纪初，日本皇宫中的讲书仪式就有《汉书》的内容，日本古代正史《日本书纪》（成书于720年）和朝鲜高丽王朝官修《三国史记》（始修于1145年）都仿照了《汉书》编纂的体裁、体例。欧美学者对《汉书》的译介始于19世纪后半叶。至20世纪，英国、美国、法国、加拿大等国有更多的学者相继完成了选译和研究《汉书》的著作，为《汉书》向西方传播作出贡献。今天，《大中华文库》出版《汉书选》，精选出《汉书》中的名篇，由知名学者译成忠实、优美的文字，正是符合当前加强各国间文化交流需要的极有意义的工作，定将受到各国读者的欢迎，成为进一步了解和研究《汉书》的必读之书。

北京师范大学
教　　授　**陈其泰**

写于2012年12月

Introduction

Ban Gu (AD 32-92), a great historian of the early Eastern Han Dynasty (AD 25-220), wrote the *Chronicles of the Han Dynasty*, a masterpiece to rival the *Records of the Grand Historian* by Sima Qian (c. 145-87 BC) of the Western Han Dynasty (202 BC-AD 9). As a result of its outstanding quality, the *Chronicles of the Han Dynasty* have passed down through the ages to modern times.

I

Ban Gu, courtesy name Mengjian, a native of Anling, Fufeng County (now northeast of Xianyang, Shaanxi Province), lived in the Eastern Han Dynasty at a time when its strength was rising, its agricultural production was improving, and its society was stable. Ban Gu's times provided excellent conditions for academic development. His enthusiasm for historical writing could also be attributed to his family background. His father, Ban Biao, served as a petty official in the court's *Situfu*, or the Office of Prime Minister, but he had a great talent and loved to write books. He thought that fragments added by later writers to the *Records of the Grand Historian* had spoiled it in terms of quality. He therefore collected further materials and wrote dozens of additions. Ban Biao's supplements to the *Records of the Grand Historian* became the inspiration for Ban Gu's own historical writing.

At the age of 16, Ban Gu entered the imperial college, where he spared himself no effort in his studies. After the death of his father, Ban Gu followed his mother back to Anling. He decided to continue his father's work on the *Chronicles of the Han Dynasty*. In AD 63, accused of privately revising the national history, Ban Gu was arrested and imprisoned. His younger brother, Ban Chao, traveled rapidly on horseback to Luoyang and presented a letter to Emperor Mingdi explaining how his father and brother had aspired to extend the book. The book draft was also sent to the emperor by Fufeng County officials. After reading the draft the emperor was impressed, and he made Ban Gu a palace secretary (*lantailingshi*) working on the *Dongguan Hanji*, a history from Eastern Han Emperor Guangwu to Emperor Lingdi. Ban Gu was later promoted to be *langguan*, an official of the emperor's retinue responsible for proofreading royal books. Emperor Mingdi encouraged him to complete the *Chronicles of the Han Dynasty*. Emperor Zhangdi also appreciated his literary talent, asking him to resolve difficult problems and join debates at major court meetings. In AD 89, appointed as an army supervisor, Ban Gu accompanied General Dou Xian in an attack on the Xiongnu. In AD 92, when Dou Xian was forced to commit suicide, Ban Gu was also framed by his rival and arrested; he died in prison in Luoyang. Ban's work on the *Chronicles of the Han Dynasty* lasted more than 20 years, from the 5th to the 8th decade of the first century.

II

The *Chronicles of the Han Dynasty* record the rise and fall of the Western Han Dynasty. It starts from the Liu Bang uprising which founded the Han Dynasty, and ends with Wang Mang's failure to usurp imperial power. The book consists of 100 volumes of more than 800,000 characters, entitled "*Ji* (annal)", "*Biao* (chronological table)", "*Zhi* (treatise)", and "*Zhuan* (biography)". In 12 volumes, *Ji* offers a chronological overview of the most important events during the reigns of Emperors Gaozu, Huidi, Wendi, Jingdi, Wudi, Zhaodi, Xuandi, Yuandi, Chengdi, Aidi and Pingdi as well as Empress Lü. Among these, four annals – including the "Annals of Emperor Gaodi" – are related to the "Annals of Emperor Gaozu" under the *Records of the Great Historian*, and the *Chronicles of the Han Dynasty* added much important content to the flourishing period of the early Western Han Dynasty. *Biao* contains eight volumes, of which six were completed on the basis of the *Records of the Grand Historian*, and the other two – the "Table of Nobility Ranks and Government Offices" and the "Prominent People from the Past Until the Present" – were created by Ban Gu. Based on eight *Shu* (treatise) of the *Records of the Grand Historian*, *Zhi* consists of ten volumes – "Treatise on Rhythm and the Calendar", "Treatise on Rites and Music", "Treatise on Punishment and Law", "Treatise on Food and Commodities", "Treatise on Sacrifices", "Treatise on Astronomy", "Treatise on the Five Elements", "Treatise on Geography", "Treatise on Rivers and Canals", and "Treatise on Literature." In 70 volumes *Zhuan* describes activities of representative people in all areas that elaborate on characters portrayed in the 12 volumes of *Ji*, in an effort to present the rise and fall of the Western Han Dynasty. These include leaders of the uprisings such as Chen Sheng, Xiang Yu, Zhang Er, Chen Yu and others who were active between the period of the Qin (221-206 BC) and Han (202 BC-AD 220) dynasties, and Han Xin, Zhang Liang, Xiao He, Chao Cuo, Zhang Qian, Su Wu, Huo Guang, Zhao Chongguo and other generals, ministers and nobles, as well as the princes of Jing, Yan, Wu and Chu. They also include literary writers, thinkers, teachers of Confucian classics, lobbyists, upright officials, cruel officials, and traders and knights-errant, and also records of the activities of the peoples in or beyond the imperial borders.

In the "Biography of Sima Qian" of the *Chronicles of the Han Dynasty*, Ban Gu offered high praise to Sima Qian's achievements in historiography. He considered Sima to be a gifted historian, skilled in lucid narration, who neither exaggerated beauty nor concealed evil – thereby exemplifying the principles required for presenting factual records. Ban Gu adopted and abided by these principles in his own treatment of history. Concerning the history of early Western Han Dynasty, Ban Gu based his writing largely on the *Records of the Grand Historian*, while searching for sources of additional information. The "Annals of Emperor Huidi", as well as the biographies of Wang Ling, Wu Rui, Kuai Tong, Wu Bei, Jia Shan, Dongfang Shuo, Li Ling, and Su Wu were all new volumes. In particular, the story of Zhang Qian, originally narrated in the "Biography of Da Yuan" of the *Records of the Grand Historian*, became an individual biography in the *Chronicles of the Han Dynasty*, which gave Zhang Qian his due place in history. In the annals of Emperors Gaodi, Wendi and Jingdi, Ban Gu added new information about society, the economy, major events, and government orders. In the "Annals of Xiao He", Ban Gu provided supplementary information explaining how Xiang Yu failed to fulfill a promise to Liu Bang, and instead ordered him to become King Han in Bashu. Liu Bang was angered by the order and planned to attack Xiang Yu, but he was persuaded by Xiao He to go to Hanzhong, expand his strength, and wait for the opportune moment. Significant supplements were also added to the "Annals of Han Xin" .

Ban Gu declared that he would not accept supplementary materials unless he was sure of their reliability. He refrained from passing judgment on matters that were unclear. In this way he remained true to Sima Qian's spirit in his presentation of factual records.

This shared spirit and historical understanding enabled Ban Gu to produce a penetrating analysis of the historical process and to offer profound insights into some issues, which can be attested by time. Vassal states had been a major problem for the Western Han Dynasty. The preface of the "Table of Nobles Related to the Imperial Clan" modestly elaborates on the imperial court's main struggles with its vassal states. It was after Emperor Wudi that such problems were resolved, for "the vassal kings were content with their rents and tax revenues, they were no longer involved in political matters." Ban Gu's account became the authoritative basis for later generations to discuss the vassal states of the Western Han Dynasty.

Why did the country become strong during the reign of Emperor Wudi (141 BC-87 BC)? Ban Gu gave a detailed analysis. In the "Biographies of Gongsun Hong, Bu Shi and Ni Kuan", it was said that Emperor Wudi concentrated on two things: one was the expansion of his territory, and the other was the establishment of a series of ritual, political and legal systems. The court had great need of a company of civil and military people of distinction, and these emerged in great numbers in response to the court's call. These distinctive talents included Dong Zhongshu, Gongsun Hong, Ni Kuan, Han Anguo, Sima Qian, Sima Xiangru, Sang Hongyang, Zhang Qian, Wei Qing, and Huo Qubing. They helped Emperor Wudi's reign to reach its peak, with outstanding civil and military achievements that were hardly rivaled by later generations.

The "Annals of the Western Regions" records: Owing to Emperor Wudi's military campaigns along the borders, his dynasty expended great quantities of manpower and materials. In his later years, his military actions led to an empty state treasury and social turmoil. Confronted with serious crises, Emperor Wudi came to his senses. He drew the lesson of the Qin Dynasty's fall and changed his policy, putting a stop to military campaigns and thereby placating the common people. He thus avoided the likely consequences of the crises. In AD 89 he issued an imperial edict stating his regrets for past errors. Subsequently, Emperors Zhaodi and Xuandi continued his policy of avoiding warfare and supporting agriculture, which resulted in a period of plenty.

The *Chronicles of the Han Dynasty* do not gloss over the dark side of the Western Han Dynasty, while extensively and accurately recording its accomplishments. It reveals that the aristocrats and despots annexed land, driving the common people into poverty; that imperial and local officials adopted cruel measures against the common people while dukes and princes broke the laws and imposed horrific oppression on innocent people; and that a number of masters of Confucianism including Kuang Heng and Zhang Yu held important posts but were of limited ability, selfish, hypocritical, greedy, and obsequious in their attitude to particular high officials, thereby having a detrimental effect on government affairs. These candid records testify to Ban Gu's historical ethics.

III

The faithful records and profound summary of the Western Han Dynasty in the *Chronicles of the Han Dynasty* represent an ideal combination of historical compilation and narration, becoming a model for later imperial works of history.

"Historical compilation and narration" refers to the ability of a historian to construct a proper overall framework for his or her work in order to present an objective history, and implement his or her historiographical thought in the work. It provides a suitable carrier for rich historical material, a physical manifestation of the historian's learning and talent, and a dissemination of historical knowledge. Highlighting the skill of historical compilation and narration is a significant feature of China's historiography. This skill began with the *Chronicle of Zuo* and the *Records of the Grand Historian* and was developed by Ban Gu. The *Chronicles of the Han Dynasty* represented the following three achievements:

The first was an innovative approach to the writing of history. The *Records of the Grand Historian*, a comprehensive history, recounted Chinese history from the time of the Yellow Emperor to the period of Emperor Wudi, when Sima Qian lived. Owing to its tremendous success, the *Records of the Grand Historian* motivated many people of later generations to continue to add to it. According to the *Shitong* (*All about Historiography*) (AD 710) and other books, more than 17 authors including Chu Shaosun, Liu Xiang, Yang Xiong, Liu Xin and Ban Biao wrote supplements, but only the texts by Chu Shaosun and Ban Biao survived. This posed a problem for historians during more than a century following Sima Qian. If the problem remained unresolved, the objective of keeping continuous historical records could not be attained.

Ban Gu was able enough to record the history of the Western Han Dynasty, starting from Emperor Gaozu, founder of the Han Dynasty, and concluding with Wang Mang, founder of the short-lived Xin Dynasty. Ban Gu advanced historical writing by making dynastic history a genre, and his work was both a legacy of the *Records of the Grand Historian* and an important and profound innovation. As Liu Zhiji commented in "Liujia" ("Six Historiographical Traditions") of *All about Historiography*, "The *Chronicles of the Han Dynasty* wrote about one dynasty by studying the beginning and end of the Western Han Dynasty and the vicissitudes of the Liu family. The book's concise wording and comprehensive details made it easy for researchers to search and discuss. From that time until the present, no book has challenged this approach to writing a history."

Subsequently, 22 "official histories" followed the practice of the *Chronicles of the Han Dynasty*. Although Ban Gu wrote a dynastic history for the Western Han Dynasty, he still made many chapters interconnected. Another aspect worthy of note is that according to *Lun Heng*, people of the early Eastern Han Dynasty respected ancient values while playing down the importance of the Han's own accomplishments. Ban Gu wrote the *Chronicles of the Han Dynasty* with the intention of promoting Han virtues and sweeping away retrogressive ideas.

Ban's second achievement was to greatly expand the scope of historical records, extending their remit to include various aspects of social life. This practice is most strikingly reflected in the ten *Zhi*, which, based on eight *Shu* (treatise) of the *Records of the Grand Historian*, improved the genres of *Zhi* and *Shu*. As Professor Bai Shouyi's *Sima Qian* and *Ban Gu* says, the ten *Zhi* include information on nature and society, as well as the past decrees and laws, therefore providing an innovative example for such branches of science as histories of laws, economy and academic learning, as well as history and geography.

For example, the "Treatise on Food and Commodities" represents an improvement in terms of its content and knowledge compared with "Equalization" of the *Records of the Grand Historian*. The whole treatise was expanded into two parts – food, and commodities and money. The former covers agricultural production including land issues, while the latter includes cloth, textiles, commercial coinage and trading activities. These two items laid the foundations for national strength and social advancement. In terms of content, Ban Gu supplemented the history between pre-Qin and early Han, and continued to write on the economic measures and status quo over the 170-180 years from the late period of Emperor Wudi to the fall of Wang Mang.

There was a need for clarification in terms of the major institutions and historically significant policies. At the end of the treatise, solid facts show that the fall of Wang Mang's regime could be attributed to the perverse policies that led to complete economic chaos – rising unemployment in agriculture and commerce, the abolition of food and monetary systems, and people suffering on the streets. His rule was doomed.

The "Treatise on Punishment and Law" systematically describes the evolution of the Qin and Han criminal laws, affirming that the Han criminal law made greater progress than that of the Zhou and Qin dynasties. At the same time the treatise provides a factual critique of the cruelty of feudal imperial law. At the end of the treatise, a lengthy paragraph was dedicated to a call for the abolition of old criminal laws and the formulation of new ones that would be concise and adapted to the lifestyle of the public. Such descriptions and pointed arguments manifest Ban Gu's profound insight into the suffering of the ordinary people and his sympathy for their plight. The treatises on geography and literature are also renowned for their profound and long-lasting influences.

Ban's third achievement was his rational and structured editing style. The editing of 70 biographies achieved a successful reconciliation between historical and logical relations. To avoid random arrangement of historical characters, Ban Gu adopted individual and integrated biographies. Individual biographies were dedicated to characters of particular import, while integrated ones were designed for those whose deeds were in some way related, or those with similar identities. Painstaking structuring of the integrated biographies organized more than 200 people into 47 sections which were narrated with clarity and had comprehensible story lines. From a modern perspective, integrated biographies could throw into prominence the deeds and thoughts of a particular type of characters. Dealing with characters in groups could help reflect social and historical conditions.

Possessed of a great literary talent, Ban Gu also wrote two odes – the "Ode to Two Capitals" and the "Ode to *Youtong*" (an understanding of gods and Nature). To vividly describe characters and scenes, he employed many narrative skills, portraying characters through dialogue, reflecting psychology through detail, and highlighting situations through analogy. For example, to manifest

Su Wu's moral integrity and unyielding character, Ban Gu chose some typical events from his life, among which his life as a 19-year detainee in the Xiongnu, after having been dispatched there as an envoy, was highlighted. During his stay in the Xiongnu camp Su Wu refused to surrender despite the use of enticement, force, solitary confinement, deprivation of food, exile to grazing pastures, and cajolement on the part of his friend Li Ling. By means of such details Su Wu's vivid image was strengthened, creating a legacy of great artistic appeal that endured for thousands of years.

The *Chronicles of the Han Dynasty* also carried some useful articles such as coverage of major discussions among ministers and nobles, outstanding arguments by thinkers, and poems and odes by writers. Huang Tingjian (AD 1045-1105), a man of letters of the Song Dynasty (960-1279), studied the *Chronicles of the Han Dynasty* by reciting it along with his friends. They drew intellectual nourishment from the activity, feeling that a person who did not read the work would become vulgar. This shows that writers and scholars loved the *Chronicles of the Han Dynasty*'s elegant language.

IV

Following its completion, the *Chronicles of the Han Dynasty* were studied by a number of scholars over the Wei-Jin period (AD 220-420). There were as many as 25 annotated editions, forming special categories of study. Based on these, Yan Shigu (AD 581-645) of the Tang Dynasty (618-907) completed *An Annotation of the Chronicles of the Han Dynasty*, adding further detail. In the late Qing Dynasty (1644-1911), Wang Xianqian (1842-1917) also wrote *Supplemented Notes to the Chronicles of the Han Dynasty*, collecting textual research on the book by Qing experts, and facilitating the use of the book as a reference work. As an iconic element of ancient China's historiography, the *Chronicles of the Han Dynasty* have long been disseminated overseas. In the early 10th century, New Year's lectures in the Japanese royal court included the *Chronicles of the Han Dynasty*. The official ancient history of Japan, the *Chronicles of Japan*, completed in AD 720, as well as the official *Historical Records of Three Kingdoms*, started in 1145 during the Korean Koryo Dynasty (918-1392), both imitated the genre and editing styles of the *Chronicles of the Han Dynasty*. US and European scholars began the translation and introduction of the *Chronicles of the Han Dynasty* in the late 19th century. By the 20th century, many scholars from the UK, the US, France, Canada and other countries had completed works of translation and research relating to the book, making due contribution to disseminating it in the West. Now the Great China Library series is publishing *A Selection of the Chronicles of the Han Dynasty*, translated by renowned scholars. This work will be of significance in strengthening cultural exchange between countries and should be welcomed by international readers – it will be a must-read for further understanding of and research into the *Chronicles of the Han Dynasty*.

Professor Chen Qitai
Beijing Normal University
December 2012

目　录

CONTENTS

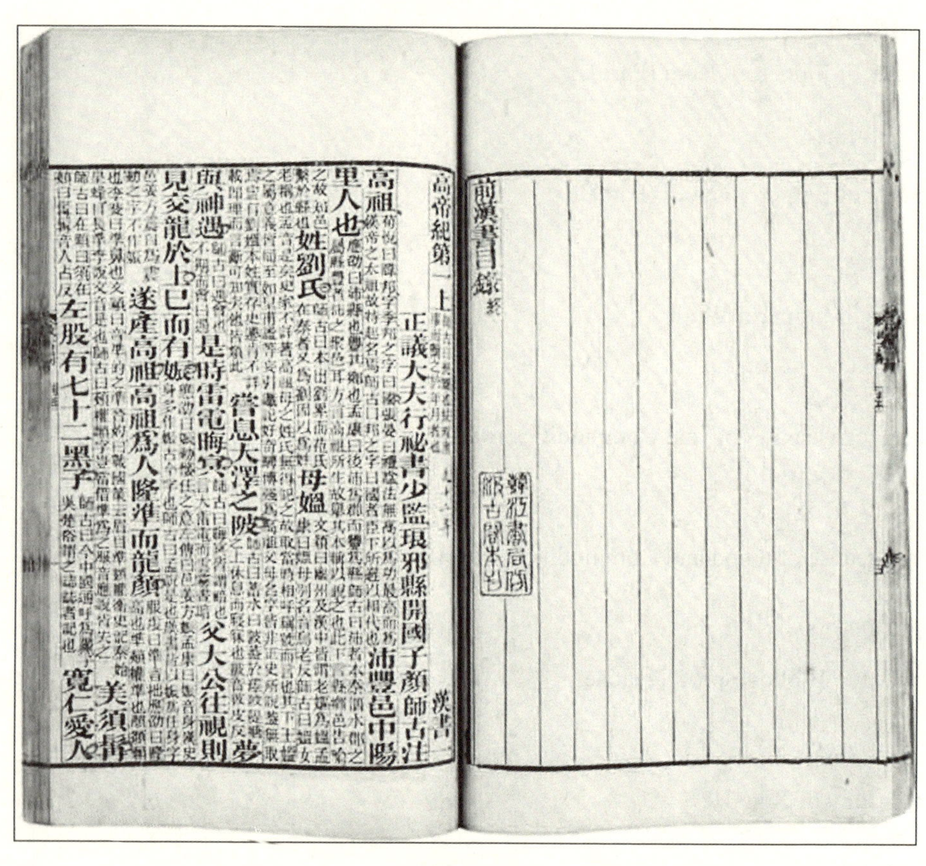

《汉书》书影

A copy of a passage from the *Chronicles of the Han Dynasty*

班固（公元32—92年）

Ban Gu（AD 32–92）

高帝纪（上）

【原文】

高祖，沛丰邑中阳里人也，姓刘氏。母媪尝息大泽之陂，梦与神遇。是时雷电晦冥，父太公往视，则见交龙于上。已而有娠，遂产高祖。

高祖为人，隆准而龙颜，美须髯，左股有七十二黑子。宽仁爱人，意豁如也。常有大度，不事家人生产作业。及壮，试吏，为泗上亭长，廷中吏无所不狎侮。好酒及色。常从王媪、武负贳酒，时饮醉卧，武负、王媪见其上常有怪。高祖每酤留饮，酒雠数倍。及见怪，岁竟，此两家常折券弃责。

高祖常繇咸阳，纵观秦皇帝，喟然大息，曰："嗟乎，大丈夫当如此矣！"

单父人吕公善沛令，辟仇，从之客，因家焉。沛中豪杰吏闻令有重客，皆往贺。萧何为主吏，主进，令诸大夫曰："进不满千钱，坐

【今译】

汉高祖，沛县丰邑中阳里人，姓刘。他的母亲曾在湖岸上休息，梦中与神相交遇。当时雷电交加，天空阴暗，他的父亲太公前往看视，就看见蛟龙伏在他的母亲身上，此后怀孕，便生下了高祖。

高祖这个人，高鼻梁，龙形的眉宇，漂亮的胡须，左腿有七十二颗黑痣。生性宽仁爱人，心地开阔，不拘小节。不肯干家里人的生产活计。到了壮年试用为官吏，当上泗上亭长，与官府的官吏们都混得很熟。又嗜酒好色。常到王老太、武大娘酒店赊酒吃，时常醉卧不起，武大娘、王老太见高祖身上常有怪异。高祖每次来店中饮酒，店家就多售酒好几倍。在看到怪异之后，年终，这两家总是毁掉欠债契券，不向高祖要债。

高祖曾经去咸阳服役，在观看秦始皇出行时，叹息说："唉呀，大丈夫就应当这样威风啊！"

单父人吕公与沛县县令是好友，避仇家，初来作客，后就安了家。沛中豪杰、官吏听说县令有贵客，都前往相贺。萧何任县廷功曹，主管接收馈赠礼品钱财，向客人们宣布："贺钱不满一千的，

Chapter 1

Annals of Emperor Gaodi, Part I

The Han Emperor Gaozu, surnamed Liu, alias Ji, was from Zhongyang neighborhood, in Feng Town of Pei County. His mother was sleeping by the lake shore, and dreamed she encountered a god. There was thunder and lightning, so his father went to have a look under the dark sky, and he saw a flood dragon lying on top of her who, soon pregnant, gave birth to Gaozu. This Gaozu had a high nose, a dragon-shaped forehead, a beautiful beard, and 72 moles on his left leg. Benevolent by nature, he was open-minded. He did not care for menial tasks, but was always ready for something important. In his prime years, he became a village chief on Sishui River, when he got over-familiar with all officials in the county. He was very fond of the drink, and of sex too. Often he went to drink on tick at Granny Wang's, or Aunt Wu's pub, and would get too drunk to stand up. The women saw something out of the ordinary on him, and each time he came drinking, they earned several times more from selling wine. After seeing the strange sights, at the end of the year, the two always destroyed his drink tab and canceled what he owed.

Gaozu once went to the capital Xianyang to serve as a corvee laborer. Seeing the Emperor Qin Shihuang in a procession, he sighed and said: "Oh, a real man should be awesome like this!" Mr. Lü of Shanfu County was good friend with the Magistrate of Pei, and had come here initially as a guest so as to avoid his enemy, but later he settled here as his home. The gallants and officials in Pei, learning of the magistrate's important guest, came to pay respects. Xiao He, a section chief, was in charge of receiving money gifts and to

【原文】

之堂下。”高祖为亭长，素易诸吏，乃给为谒曰“贺钱万”，实不持一钱。谒入，吕公大惊，起，迎之门。吕公者，好相人，见高祖状貌，因重敬之，引入坐上坐。萧何曰：“刘季固多大言，少成事。”高祖因狎侮诸客，遂坐上坐，无所诎。酒阑，吕公因目固留高祖。竟酒，后，吕公曰：“臣少好相人，相人多矣，无如季相，愿季自爱。臣有息女，愿为箕帚妾。”酒罢，吕媪怒吕公曰：“公始常欲奇此女，与贵人。沛令善公，求之不与，何自妄许与刘季？”吕公曰：“此非儿女子所知。”卒与高祖。吕公女即吕后也，生孝惠帝、鲁元公主。

高祖尝告归之田。吕后与两子居田中，有一老父过请饮，吕后因餔之。老父相后曰：“夫人天下贵人也。”令相两子，见孝惠帝，曰：“夫人所以贵者，乃此男也。”相鲁元公主，亦皆贵。老父已去，高祖适从旁舍来，吕后具言客有过，相我子母皆大贵。高祖问，曰

【今译】

坐在堂下。”高祖任亭长，向来轻视诸官吏，在拜帖上伪称说“贺钱一万”，实际上不带一钱。传报进去，吕公大惊，站起迎接到门口。吕公这人，喜欢为人相面，见高祖相貌，便敬重他，请他坐上座。萧何说：“刘季从来多说大话，很少办成事。”高祖因轻视诸客人，便坐在上座，无所退让。饮酒的客人多数退席之后，吕公暗示高祖留下。饮酒完毕后，吕公说：“我少年时喜好给人相面，相的人很多，没有你这相貌的，希望你自爱。我有一个亲生女儿，愿意作你的打扫房间的妾。”酒宴过后，吕婆对吕公发怒说：“你当初称女儿是宝贝，欲许配贵人。沛令待你很好，向你求婚，你不给，为什么你把女儿随便许给刘季？”吕公说：“这不是女人所能知道的。”终于许给高祖。吕公女就是后来的吕后，生孝惠帝、鲁元公主。

高祖曾请假回家到田中。吕后与两个孩子住在田舍，有一老父路过要点水喝，吕后随即招待饭食。老父给吕后相面说：“夫人是天下贵人。”让相两个孩子，看见孝惠帝，说：“夫人所以当贵，就是因为这个男孩子。”相鲁元公主，也都主贵。老父已走，高祖正好从别的屋子过来，吕后说出过路客人相我母子都有大贵的事。高祖问，回

the guests he announced: "He who presents less than 1,000 cash, sit below in the hall." Gaozu as a chief never had much respect for officials, so he made the false claim on his name card of "10,000 cash in congratulation" without, in fact, bringing any money at all. When he was announced, Mr. Lü was shocked, and rose to greet him at the door. Lü was good at physiognomy, and when he saw Gaozu's looks, he respected him and ushered him to take the seat of honor. Xiao He said: "Liu is all talk but no action." Gaozu, lacking respect for the guests, took the VIP seat without any polite protestations of refusal. When many of the guests finished drinking and were leaving, Lü hinted that Gaozu should stay. When they had done drinking, Lü said: "Your humble servant has been an adept of physiognomy since a teenager, and I have seen many faces, but never one like yours. I hope you will uphold self-love. I have a cherished daughter, who is willing to clean your room as a concubine."

After the banquet, Mrs. Lü berated her husband: "You always said you'd hold this girl precious, so as to marry her to a man of eminence. The Magistrate of Pei is so good to you, and has asked you for her hand, but you did not give it. How can you casually promise her to Liu Ji?" Lü said: "This is not something womenfolk can understand." And finally he did promise her to Gaozu. Miss Lü was later the Empress, the mother of Emperor Huidi and Elder Princess of Lu.

Gaozu once asked for leave to return home. Empress Lü was living with two children in a farm hut, when an old man passed by and asked for a drink of water. Empress Lü treated him to a meal. The old man read her fortune from her face and said: "Madame is the most noble person in the world." Asked to read the faces of the two children, he saw the future Emperor Huidi, and said: "Madame is noble because of this boy." Princess of Lu also looked noble. When Gaozu happened to come out from another hut, the old man had already left but Empress Lü told him every detail about the visit

【原文】

“未远”。乃追及，问老父。老父曰：“乡者夫人儿子皆以君，君相贵不可言。”高祖乃谢曰：“诚如父言，不敢忘德。”乃高祖贵，遂不知老父处。

高祖为亭长，乃以竹皮为冠，令求盗之薛治，时时冠之，及贵常冠，所谓“刘氏冠”也。

高祖以亭长为县送徒骊山，徒多道亡。自度比至皆亡之，到丰西泽中亭，止饮，夜皆解纵所送徒。曰：“公等皆去，吾亦从此逝矣！”徒中壮士愿从者十馀人。高祖被酒，夜径泽中，令一人行前。行前者还报曰：“前有大蛇当径，愿还。”高祖醉，曰：“壮士行，何畏！”乃前，拔剑斩蛇，蛇分为两，道开。行数里，醉困卧。后人来至蛇所，有一老妪夜哭。人问妪何哭，妪曰：“人杀吾子。”人曰：“妪子何为见杀？”妪曰：“吾子，白帝子也，化为蛇，当道，今者赤帝子斩之，故哭。”人乃以妪为不诚，欲苦之，妪因忽不见。

【今译】

答说：“去不远。”便去赶上，问老父。老父说：“刚才相过的夫人儿子都因您的缘故大贵，您的相貌贵不可言。”高祖致谢说：“真如老父所说，决不会忘记您的大德。”到高祖富贵时，就不知老父在什么地方。

高祖任亭长后，便用竹皮作冠，让求盗小吏去薛县为他制作，常常戴着。到显贵时还常戴，这就是所谓的“刘氏冠”。

高祖以亭长身份为县里押送犯人前往骊山劳动，犯人在路上多逃走。他估计到了骊山就跑光了，行至丰西泽中亭，停下喝酒，夜间全部释放了所送犯人。说：“诸位都走吧，我也从此逃跑啦！”犯人中的壮士愿跟随他的有十几人。高祖带着酒气夜间从泽中小道穿行，让一人在前边探路。探路的人回报说：“前面有大蛇横在路中，请回去吧。”高祖带着醉意说：“壮士走路，怕什么！”便前去，拔剑斩蛇，蛇分为两段，道路通了。走了数里，醉困而卧。后面的人来到蛇死之处，有一老妇夜间哭泣。人们问老妇为什么哭，老妇说：“有人杀了我儿。”人们说：“老婆婆的儿子为何被杀？”老妇说：“吾儿是白帝子，变为蛇，躺在路中间，今天让赤帝子杀了，因此才哭。”人们以为老妇不说实话，想让她吃点苦头，老妇忽然不见。后面的人

and that he had identified the mother and children as noble. Gaozu asked for him, and she replied: "He's not gone far." He caught up with the old man, who said: "A moment ago, I found Madame and the son are noble because of you, but your facial features are as noble as I can possibly say." Gaozu thanked him: "If what you say is true, I shall not dare to forget your great favor." When Gaozu did come to the throne, he just did not know the old man's whereabouts.

As a chief, he told his sheriff clerk to have a crown made of bamboo bark in neighboring Xue County, and wore it frequently. As Emperor he often wore this as "Crown of the Liu Clan."

As chief, he was charged by the county with escorting convict laborers to Lishan Mountains to work, but many of the convicts escaped en route. Reckoning that all of them would have escaped before reaching the destination, he stopped to drink at Zezhong village to the west of Feng Town, and released all the remaining convicts during the night. He told them: "You may all run, gentlemen, and I will also abscond forthwith!" But a dozen stout convicts were willing to follow him. Gaozu, drunk, went along a marsh track at night, having ordered one person to go ahead and scout the way. The scout returned to say: "There's a big snake lying across the road ahead. Please go back." Gaozu, being drunk, said: "The brave soldier walking, has nothing to fear!" Then he went forward, drew his sword to cut the snake, severing it in two and opening up the way. Several *li* later, drunk and tired, he lay down. Later, some people came along to the dead snake and find an old woman sobbing at night. When asked the reason for her tears, the woman said: "Someone killed my son." The people asked: "Why was the old lady's son killed?" The woman said: "My son was son of the White Emperor, transformed into a snake lying across the road, so that Red Emperor's son killed him today. That is why I cry." They thought the woman was not telling the truth, and wanted to punish her, but she suddenly disappeared. When the men reached Gaozu, he

【原文】

后人至，高祖觉，告高祖。高祖乃心独喜，自负。诸从者日益畏之。

秦始皇帝尝曰“东南有天子气”，于是东游以猒当之。高祖隐于芒、砀山泽间，吕后与人俱求，常得之。高祖怪，问之，吕后曰：“季所居上常有云气，故从往常得季。”高祖又喜。沛中子弟或闻之，多欲附者矣。

秦二世元年秋七月，陈涉起蕲，至陈，自立为楚王，遣武臣、张耳、陈馀略赵地。八月，武臣自立为赵王。郡县多杀长吏以应涉。九月，沛令欲以沛应之。掾、主吏萧何、曹参曰：“君为秦吏，今欲背之，帅沛子弟，恐不听。愿君召诸亡在外者，可得数百人，因以劫众，众不敢不听。”乃令樊哙召高祖。高祖之众已数百人矣。

于是樊哙从高祖来。沛令后悔，恐其有变，乃闭城城守，欲诛萧、曹。萧、曹恐，逾城保高祖。高祖乃书帛射城上，与沛父老曰：

【今译】

到了，高祖也醒了，便告诉刚才之事，高祖心中暗自高兴，十分得意。随从的人日益怕他。

秦始皇曾说“东南有天子气”，于是东游以压服此气。高祖隐藏在芒、砀山泽之间，吕后同别人一起来找他，常能找见。高祖奇怪地问她，吕后说：“你所住的地方上空常有云气.所以按着云气方向总能找到你。”高祖又很高兴。沛县的青年有人听说此事，很多愿意追随他了。

秦二世元年秋七月，陈涉在蕲县起义。后到陈县，自立为楚王，派武臣、张耳、陈馀攻占赵地。八月，武臣自立为赵王。各郡县百姓多杀其官吏响应陈涉起义。九月，沛县令想在沛县响应起义。主吏萧何、掾属曹参说：“君为秦官，今天想背叛朝廷，率领沛子弟，恐怕不会有人从命。希望您召回各位逃亡在外的人，可以得到几百人，用来威胁众人，众人不敢不听。”县令便让樊哙召回高祖。这时高祖手下已有几百人。

不久，樊哙与高祖回来。沛令后悔起来，害怕发生变故，便关闭城门据守，想杀掉萧何、曹参。萧何、曹参恐惧，翻城投靠高祖。高祖便写信射至城上，对沛县父老说：“天下都被秦朝坑害很久了。今

woke up and heard all, much to his private pride and pleasure. His entourage increasingly feared him.

The First Emperor of Qin once said: "In the southeast there is the emanation of a Son of Heaven," and so he marched east to suppress this emanation. Gaozu hid himself among the mountains and marshes of Mang and Dang, but when Empress Lü and others looked for him together, they were able to find him. When the amazed Gaozu questioned her, Lü said: "There is cloudy emanation over the place you live. Therefore we followed it to find you." Gaozu was again very happy. When the youth of Pei heard this, many of them wanted to align themselves with him.

In the seventh moon of year one of the second Qin Emperor (209 BC), Chen She revolted in Qi County. When he arrived at Chen, he enthroned himself as King of Chu, sending Wu Chen, Zhang Er, and Chen Yu to attack and occupy Zhao. In the eighth moon, Wu Chen enthroned himself as King of Zhao. In various prefectures and counties, people killed their chief officials to mirror Chen She's revolt. In the ninth moon, the Magistrate of Pei wanted to do likewise in Pei County. The section chief Xiao He, and aide Cao Can said: "Mr. Magistrate is a Qin official, but today you want to turn your back on the Dynasty, and lead the Pei youths. Perhaps they will not obey orders. We recommend that you recall those fugitives outside Pei, perhaps several hundred will come. With them you can intimidate the people who would not then dare to disobey." The magistrate then told Fan Kuai to recall Gaozu, who by now had several hundred people under him.

Soon, Fan Kuai returned with Gaozu, but the magistrate started to get cold feet, and for fear of unforeseen developments, he closed the gates guarding the city, planning to execute Xiao He and Cao Can. These two became afraid and climbed the wall to throw in their lot with Gaozu. Gaozu then wrote a letter on silk, which was shot onto the city wall, telling the Pei elders: "The world has suffered

【原文】

“天下同苦秦久矣。今父老虽为沛令守，诸侯并起，今屠沛。沛今共诛令，择可立立之，以应诸侯，即室家完。不然，父子俱屠，无为也。”父老乃帅子弟共杀沛令，开城门迎高祖，欲以为沛令。高祖曰：“天下方扰，诸侯并起，(令)[今]置将不善，一败涂地。吾非敢自爱，恐能薄，不能完父兄子弟。此大事，愿(吏)[更]择可者。”萧、曹（等）皆文吏，自爱，恐事不就，后秦种族其家，尽让高祖。诸父老皆曰：“平生所闻刘季奇怪，当贵，且卜筮之，莫如刘季最吉。“高祖数让，众莫肯为，高祖乃立为沛公。祠黄帝，祭蚩尤于沛廷，而衅鼓旗。帜皆赤，由所杀蛇白帝子，（所）杀者赤帝子故也。于是少年豪吏如萧、曹、樊哙等皆为收沛子弟，得三千人。

是月，项梁与兄子羽起吴。田儋与从弟荣、横起齐，自立为齐王。韩广自立为燕王。魏咎自立为魏王。陈涉之将周章西入关，至戲，秦将章邯距破之。

【今译】

父老虽然替沛令守城，但诸侯都起兵，将要杀光城里的人。沛县众人今天同杀县令，选择可以立为首领的人拥立起来，以响应诸侯，就可以保全家室性命。不然，父子都将被杀，是白送死。”父老便率子弟同杀沛令，开城门迎高祖，想立他为沛令。高祖说：“天下正在骚动，诸侯都起兵，如立头领不好，会一败涂地。我不是顾惜自己，恐怕能力薄弱，不能保全父兄子弟。此是大事，希望另选可以胜任的。”萧何、曹参都是文官，很顾惜自己，担心事不成功，以后让秦朝诛杀全家，也都推让高祖。诸父老都说：“平常听说刘季不同寻常，当为贵人，又去占卜算卦，都不如刘季最吉利。”高祖再三推让，众人没有愿意干的，高祖便立为沛公。在沛县大堂祭祀黄帝和蚩尤，用牲畜血染旗帜和战鼓。旗帜都是红的，这是因杀了白帝子，杀者是赤帝子的缘故。于是年轻能干的官吏像萧何、曹参、樊哙等都去招收沛县青年，共收了三千人。

这一月，项梁与兄子项羽在吴县起兵。田儋与堂弟田荣、田横在齐地起兵，自立为齐王。韩广自立为燕王。魏咎自立为魏王。陈涉部将周章西入关，至戏水，秦将章邯率军击败周章。

under the Qin for a very long time. Although the elders now defend this city for the magistrate, the feudal lords have all sent troops into battle, going to kill off everybody in this town. If the people of Pei today kill the magistrate, and choose a worthy leader to mirror the actions of the feudal lords, they may preserve the lives of their families. Otherwise, the fathers and sons are to be killed, and will die in vain." The elders then led the juniors to kill the magistrate and open the gate to Gaozu, ready to make him magistrate. Gaozu said: "The world is in tumult, and the feudal lords all send troops into battle. Without an able general we may get wiped out. Without being self-serving, I fear my ability is too weak to preserve the fathers and juniors. This is an important matter, and I hope you will select someone more competent than I." Xiao He and Cao Can were both civil officials, and self-serving; they were concerned that if this venture failed the Qin would put their entire families to death, so they both proposed Gaozu. The various elders said: "We have often heard the strange things about Liu Ji, so he should be a noble person. Then we practiced divination, and, according to the trigrams, Liu Ji is the most auspicious." Gaozu declined over and over again, but no one was willing to step up, so he then was hailed as Magistrate of Pei. In the county hall they held sacrificial offering to Yellow Emperor and Chi You, anointing their flags and battle drums with the blood of the animal sacrifices. Their flags were all red, because the White Emperor's child had been killed by the Red Emperor's son. Therefore, the young gallant officials like Xiao He, Cao Can, and Fan Kuai recruited the Pei youths, altogether mobilizing 3,000 people.

In this month, Xiang Liang and his nephew Xiang Yu revolted in Wu. Tian Dan and his cousins Tian Rong and Tian Heng staged an armed rebellion in Qi, proclaiming himself the King of Qi. Han Guang proclaimed himself King of Yan, and Wei Jiu proclaimed himself King of Wei. Chen She's general Zhou Zhang crossed the

【原文】

秦二年十月，沛公攻胡陵、方与，还守丰。秦泗川监平将兵围丰二日，出与战，破之。令雍齿守丰。十一月，沛公引兵之薛。秦泗川守壮兵败于薛，走至戚，沛公左司马得杀之。沛公还军亢父，至方与。赵王武臣为其将所杀。十二月，楚王陈涉为其御庄贾所杀。魏人周市略地丰沛，使人谓雍齿曰："丰，故梁徙也，今魏地已定者数十城。齿今下魏，魏以齿为侯守丰；不下，且屠丰。"雍齿雅不欲属沛公，及魏招之，即反为魏守丰。沛公攻丰，不能取。沛公还之沛，怨雍齿与丰子弟畔之。

正月，张耳等立赵后赵歇为赵王。东阳甯君、秦嘉立景驹为楚王，在留。沛公往从之，道得张良，遂与俱见景驹，请兵以攻丰。时章邯从陈，别将司马尼将兵北定楚地，屠相，至砀。东阳甯君、沛

【今译】

秦二年十月，沛公攻占胡陵、方与两县，回兵守丰邑。秦泗川御史平率军围丰邑。第二天，义军出兵交战，击破秦军。命雍齿守丰。十一月，沛公率军到薛县。秦泗川守壮兵败薛县，逃往戚县，被沛公左司马得杀死。沛公还军亢父，到了方与。赵王武臣被其部将所杀。十二月，楚王陈涉被其车夫庄贾杀害。魏人周市攻略丰、沛，派人对雍齿说："丰是原魏都梁迁徙的地方，今魏地已平定了几十城。你今天降魏，魏封你为侯并驻守丰；不降，我们就攻破丰并杀光城内的人。"雍齿平素就不愿属沛公，到魏招降时，就降魏并替魏守丰。沛公攻丰，不能攻取，就返回沛县，怨恨雍齿与丰的青年人叛变。

正月，张耳等拥立赵国后代赵歇为赵王。东阳人宁君、秦嘉拥立景驹为楚王，驻在留县。沛公前往投靠景驹，途中得张良，于是与张良一同见景驹，请派兵攻丰。这时章邯攻打陈县，别将司马尼率军北面平定楚地，在相县大肆屠杀，到达砀县。东阳宁君、沛公率兵向

Pass and reached Xishui River where he was defeated by the Qin general Zhang Han.

In the 10th moon of year two of the second Qin Emperor, Gaozu (now Magistrate of Pei) captured Huling and Fangyu, and brought his soldiers back to defend Feng Town. Governor Ping of Sichuan led his Qin army to besiege Feng. The next day, the rebels broke out and defeated the besieging army. Yong Chi was ordered to defend Feng. In the 11th moon, the Magistrate of Pei marched his army to Xue County. Zhuang, the Qin commander of Sichuan, was defeated at Xue, and fled to Qi, only to be captured and killed by the Left Commander of Magistrate of Pei. The Magistrate of Pei returned to Kangfu with his army and arrived at Fangyu. Wu Chen, the King of Zhao was killed by one of his officers. In the 12th moon, Chen She, the King of Chu, was killed by his charioteer Zhuang Jia. Zhou Shi of Wei attacked Feng and Pei, and sent someone to persuade Yong Chi: "Feng is the resettlement area of the original Wei capital Liang. Now Wei has occupied dozens of its cities. If you surrender to Wei, Wei will make you a marquis stationed in Feng. If you do not surrender, we will turn the city to ruin and kill every person in it." Initially Yong Chi was unwilling to align himself to the Magistrate of Pei, so he surrendered to become Wei's general at Feng. The Magistrate of Pei did attack Feng, but failed to take it, so they returned to Pei, full of hatred for Yong Chi and the mutinous young people of Feng.

In the first moon, Zhang Er and others enthroned Zhao Xie as King of Zhao who was a descendant of the Zhao kings. Ning Jun and Qin Jia from Dongyang enthroned Jing Ju as King of Chu, and stationed in the Liu County. Magistrate of Pei went to attach himself to King Jing, and met Zhang Liang on the way, so they went together to ask Jing Ju for troops to attack Feng. At that time Zhang Han attacked Chen, and Detached General Sima Yi led his army north to conquer Chu, inflicting a great massacre in Xiang County,

【原文】

公引兵西，与战萧西，不利，还收兵聚留。二月，攻砀，三日拔之。收砀兵，得六千人，与故合九千人。三月，攻下邑，拔之。还击丰，不下。四月，项梁击杀景驹、秦嘉，止薛，沛公往见之。项梁益沛公卒五千人，五大夫将十人。沛公还，引兵攻丰，拔之。雍齿奔魏。

五月，项羽拔襄城还。项梁尽召别将。六月，沛公如薛，与项梁共立楚怀王孙心为楚怀王。章邯破杀魏王咎、齐王田儋于临济。七月，大霖雨。沛公攻亢父。章邯围田荣于东阿。沛公与项梁共救田荣，大破章邯东阿。田荣归，沛公、项羽追北，至城阳，攻屠其城。军濮阳东，复与章邯战，又破之。

章邯复振，守濮阳，环水。沛公、项羽去，攻定陶。八月，田荣立田儋子市为齐王。定陶未下，沛公与项羽西略地至雍丘，与秦军战，大败之，斩三川守李由。还攻外黄，外黄未下。

【今译】

西，与秦军在萧县西交战，失利，收兵在留县聚集。二月，攻砀县，三天攻占。收砀县兵，得到六千人，与原有人马合为九千人。三月，攻占下邑。回军攻丰不下。四月，项梁击杀景驹、秦嘉，驻军薛县，沛公前往相见。项梁增兵给沛公五千人及五大夫爵位的将领十人。沛公返回，带兵攻破丰县。雍齿逃往魏。

五月，项羽攻占襄城，返回。项梁尽召别将。六月，沛公到薛，与项梁共同拥立楚怀王之孙心为楚怀王。章邯破杀魏王魏咎、齐王田儋于临济。七月，连日大雨。沛公攻亢父。章邯包围田荣于东阿。沛公与项梁同救田荣，在东阿大败章邯。田荣回齐，沛公、项羽追击章邯败军，追至城阳，屠城。然后驻扎濮阳县东，又与章邯交战，再败秦军。

章邯重新整军，固守濮阳城，环水防御。沛公、项羽离开濮阳，攻打定陶县。八月，田荣立田儋的儿子田市为齐王。定陶未攻下，沛公与项羽向西略地至雍丘，与秦军交战，大败秦军，斩三川守李由。回军攻外黄，未攻下。

and reached Dang. Ning Jun and Magistrate of Pei marched west, and gave battle to Qin in the west of Xiao, but getting the worst of the fight they withdrew their troops to Liu. In the second moon, they attacked Dang, and captured it in three days. They recruited 6,000 Dang soldiers to their cause, bolstering their numbers to 9,000 troops. In the third moon, they captured Xiayi. They returned to Feng, but still could not conquer it. In the fourth moon, Xiang Liang killed Jing Ju and Qin Jia, so Magistrate of Pei went up to see him at his garrison in Xue, where he received 5,000 soldiers to reinforce his army, including ten generals with *wudafu* title. Magistrate of Pei came back and his troops broke Feng. And Yong Chi fled to Wei.

In the fifth moon, Xiang Yu captured the City of Xiang and returned. Xiang Liang summoned all the detached generals. In the sixth moon, Magistrate of Pei came up to Xue, and together with Xiang Liang crowned Xin, the grandson of King Huai of Chu, as the new King Huai of Chu. At Linji, Zhang Han routed and killed Wei Jiu the King of Wei and Tian Dan the King of Qi. In the seventh moon, there were days of heavy rain. Magistrate of Pei attacked Kangfu. Zhang Han surrounded Tian Rong in Dong'e. Magistrate of Pei, working with Xiang Liang, came to Tian Rong's rescue and destroyed Zhang Han at Dong'e. Tian Rong returned to Qi, while Magistrate of Pei and Xiang Yu chased the defeated enemy to Chengyang, and massacred everyone in it. Then they made camp in eastern Puyang, and fought with Zhang Han again, inflicting defeats on the Qin soldiers.

But Zhang Han rallied his army, tenaciously defending Puyang City and digging a moat around it. Magistrate of Pei and Xiang Yu left Puyang, turning their attack on Dingtao. In the eighth moon, Tian Rong crowned Tian Shi the son of Tian Dan as King of Qi. With Dingtao not captured, Magistrate of Pei and Xiang Yu marched west to Yongqiu to fight the Qin army. They inflicted a total defeat

【原文】

项梁再破秦军，有骄色。宋义谏，不听。秦益章邯兵。九月，章邯夜衔枚击项梁定陶，大破之，杀项梁。时连雨自七月至九月。沛公、项羽方攻陈留，闻梁死，士卒恐，乃与将军吕臣引兵而东，徙怀王自盱台都彭城。吕臣军彭城东，项羽军彭城西，沛公军砀。魏咎弟豹自立为魏王。后九月，怀王并吕臣、项羽军自将之。以沛公为砀郡长，封武安侯，将砀郡兵。以羽为鲁公，封长安侯。吕臣为司徒，其父吕青为令尹。

章邯已破项梁，以为楚地兵不足忧，乃渡河北击赵王歇，大破之。歇保钜鹿城，秦将王离围之。赵数请救，怀王乃以宋义为上将，项羽为次将，范增为末将，北救赵。

【今译】

项梁两次打败秦军，有骄傲之色。宋义劝说，不听。秦为章邯增兵。九月，章邯夜间率士兵衔枚至定陶偷袭项梁，大败项梁军，项梁被杀。当时连绵阴雨从七月下到九月。沛公、项羽正攻陈留，听到项梁战死，士卒惊恐，便与将军吕臣率兵向东，从盱台县迁走怀王，定都于彭城。吕臣驻扎城东，项羽驻扎城西，沛公驻扎砀县。魏咎弟魏豹自立为魏王。闰九月，怀王合并吕臣、项羽军，亲自统率。任沛公为砀郡郡长，封武安侯，统领砀郡兵。任项羽为鲁公，封长安侯，吕臣任司徒，他的父亲吕青任令尹。

章邯大败项梁后，以为楚地兵不足以担忧，便渡河北上攻击赵王赵歇，大败赵军。赵歇退守巨鹿城，秦将王离包围巨鹿。赵王多次求救，怀王便以宋义为上将，项羽为次将，范增为末将，北上救赵。

on the Qin army and killed Li You the Governor of Sanchuan. Then they turned their armies around to attack Waihuang, but without success.

With two victories over the Qin, Xiang Liang became very proud, and was deaf to Song Yi's attempts to admonish him. The Qin reinforced Zhang Han's troops, and in the ninth moon, he ordered his soldiers on a night march, each with a wooden stick in the mouth to ensure silence, to attack Xiang Liang at Dingtao. Xiang Liang was killed in their overwhelming victory.

It rained continuously from the seventh to ninth moon. Magistrate of Pei and Xiang Yu were attacking Chenliu when the news of Liang's death reached them. Their soldiers were shocked and afraid, so they marched east with General Lü Chen, removed King Huai of Chu from Xuyi, and made Pengcheng the new capital. Lü Chen was stationed east of the city, Xiang Yu to the west, and Magistrate of Pei was encamped in Dang. Wei Jiu's brother Wei Bao made himself the King of Wei. In the intercalary ninth moon, King Huai of Chu merged the armies of Lü Chen and Xiang Yu, taking personal command of the new force. He appointed Magistrate of Pei as Governor of Dang, granting him the title of Marquis of Wu'an, commanding the Dang soldiers. He also made Xiang Yu Magistrate of Lu, with the title Marquis of Chang'an; appointed Lü Qing as Lingyin (premier) and his son Lü Chen as Minister of Land and People.

After Zhang Han crushed Xiang Liang, the Chu soldiers were no longer a concern, and he progressed north across the river to attack King Zhao Xie. They defeated Zhao, who retreated to the city Julu, at the time surrounded by Wang Li from Qin. Zhao repeatedly asked for help, so King Huai of Chu sent an army north to rescue him. At their head was Song Yi as the General in Chief, with Xiang Yu as his second in command, and Fan Zeng as the third.

【原文】

初，怀王与诸将约，先入定关中者王之，当是时，秦兵强，常乘胜逐北，诸将莫利先入关。独羽怨秦破项梁，奋势，愿与沛公西入关。怀王诸老将皆曰："项羽为人慓悍祸贼，尝攻襄城，襄城无噍类，所过无不残灭。且楚数进取，前陈王、项梁皆败，不如更遣长者扶义而西，告谕秦父兄。秦父兄苦其主久矣，今诚得长者往，毋侵暴，宜可下。项羽不可遣，独沛公素宽大长者。"卒不许羽，而遣沛公西收陈王、项梁散卒。乃道砀至(阳城)[城阳]与杠里，攻秦军壁，破其二军。

秦三年十月，齐将田都畔田荣，将兵助项羽救赵。沛公攻破东郡尉于成武。十一月，项羽杀宋义，并其兵渡河，自立为上将军，诸将黥布等皆属。十二月，沛公引兵至栗，遇刚武侯，夺其军四千馀人，并之，与魏将皇欣、武满军合，攻秦军，破之。故齐王建孙田安下济

【今译】

当初，怀王与诸将订立盟约，先攻占关中者为关中王。当时秦军强大，常乘胜追击败军，诸将领没有把先入关视为有利之事。只有项羽怨恨秦杀项梁，愤激之下，愿与沛公一道西入关中。怀王诸老将都说："项羽性情慓悍好杀，曾攻占襄城，襄城被杀得没留下活人，所过之地生灵无不遭残害灭绝。况且楚多次进兵，前有陈王、项梁都遭失败，不如另派长者扶义西进，告谕秦地父兄。秦地的父老兄弟被其主的暴政苦害很久了，今要是能派长者前往，不侵扰残暴，应该是能攻下来的。项羽不可以派遣，只有沛公向来是宽厚大度的长者。"最后没有答应项羽西进的要求，而派遣沛公向西收编陈王、项梁的散亡兵卒。沛公于是取道砀县至城阳与杠里，进攻秦军壁垒，击破二县秦军。

秦三年十月，齐将田都叛田荣，率军助项羽救赵。沛公攻破东郡尉于成武。十一月，项羽杀宋义，合并其军渡漳河，自立为上将军，诸将黥布等都归属项羽。十二月，沛公率兵至栗县，遇刚武侯，夺其军四千余人归于自己统率，与魏将皇欣、武满军联合攻破秦军。原齐

Earlier, King Huai of Chu had made a covenant with the generals that the first of them to take Guanzhong would be made the king there. At that time, the Qin army was strong and often went in pursuit of the defeated, so many generals did not think being the first to enter Guanzhong as necessarily benefiting them. Only Xiang Yu hated Qin so much for killing his uncle Xiang Liang that, his rage untamed, he was quite eager to go west and enter it with Magistrate of Pei. The veteran generals of King Huai of Chu said: "Xiang Yu's nature is ferocious and blood-thirsty. When he captured Xiangcheng, the slaughter stopped only once there was nobody left breathing. Wherever he goes, not a living soul on the land escapes extinction. Moreover, Chu has repeatedly attacked, and both King Chen and Xiang Liang met with failure. We would do better to send a respected elder to the west, pleading our cause before the fathers and brothers of Qin. The Qin elders have suffered under their tyrant for a long time. If we are able to send this gentleman there, without resorting to invasion or atrocity, we should be able to capture it. We cannot send Xiang Yu, and only Magistrate of Pei has always been a magnanimous leader." In the end, they did not agree to Xiang Yu's demand to go westward, instead sending Magistrate of Pei to assemble King Chen and Xiang Liang's scattered soldiers. He marched up to Chengyang and Gangli via Dang, attacked Qin defenses, defeating Qin troops in the two counties.

In the 10th moon of year three of the second Qin emperor, Qi general Tian Du rebelled against Tian Rong, leading his army to help Xiang Yu rescue Zhao. Magistrate of Pei defeated the commandant of Dongjun Prefecture at Chengwu. In the 11th moon, Xiang Yu killed Song Yi, merged their two forces and crossed the Zhang River, setting himself up as General Superior, in command over Tattooed Bu and other generals. In the 12th moon, Magistrate of Pei marched to Li County, and met Marquis of Gangwu whose 4,000-strong army he annexed to his own command. He cooperated with

【原文】

北，从项羽救赵。羽大破秦军钜鹿下，虏王离，走章邯。

二月，沛公从砀北攻昌邑，遇彭越。越助攻昌邑，未下。沛公西过高阳,郦食其为里监门，曰：“诸将过此者多，吾视沛公大度。”乃求见沛公，沛公方踞床，使两女子洗。郦生不拜，长揖曰：“足下必欲诛无道秦，不宜踞见长者！”于是沛公起，摄衣谢之，延上坐。食其说沛公袭陈留。沛公以为广野君，以其弟商为将，将陈留兵。三月，攻开封，未拔。西与秦将杨熊会战白马，又战曲遇东，大破之。杨熊走之荥阳，二世使使斩之以徇。四月，南攻颍川，屠之。因张良遂略韩地。

时赵别将司马卬方欲渡河入关，沛公乃北攻平阴，绝河津。南，战雒阳东，军不利，从轘辕至阳城，收军中马骑。六月，与南阳守齮战犨东，（大）破之。略南阳郡，南阳守走，保城守宛。沛公引兵过

【今译】

王田建之孙田安攻下济北，随从项羽救赵。项羽在巨鹿城下大败秦军，俘获王离，赶跑章邯。

二月，沛公从砀县北攻昌邑，路遇彭越。彭越助攻昌邑，未攻下。沛公向西到高阳邑，郦食其为里门卒，说：“诸将路过此地的有很多，我看沛公度量大。”便求见沛公。沛公正坐在床上，让两女子洗脚。食其不叩拜，作一个长揖说：“足下必想诛灭无道的秦朝，不应坐着接见长者！”于是沛公起身，提衣谢罪，请至上座。郦食其劝沛公袭陈留城。沛公任食其为广野君，他的弟弟郦商为将军，率领陈留兵。三月，攻开封，未攻下。向西与秦将杨熊会战于白马，又战于曲遇东，大破秦军。杨熊败走荥阳，秦二世派使者斩杨熊示众。四月，沛公南攻颍川，屠城。在张良帮助下攻占了韩地。

当时赵别将司马卬正欲渡黄河入关，沛公便北攻平阴，堵绝了黄河的渡口。沛公向南与秦军战于雒阳东，失利，从轘辕山到阳城，收集军中战马。六月，与南阳守齮交战于犨东，大破秦军。攻略南

the Wei armies of Huang Xin and Wu Man to defeat the Qin army. Tian An, grandson of the original King of Qi Tian Jian, took over Jibei, and followed Xiang Yu to save Zhao. Xiang Yu defeated the Qin army under the walls of Julu, capturing Wang Li, and driving Zhang Han away.

In the second moon, Magistrate of Pei marched north from Dang to attack Changyi, and met Peng Yue, who assisted him. but they failed to capture it. Then they went west to Gaoyang. Li Yiji, as a soldier guarding the inner door, said: "Generals come and go through here a lot, but to my mind the Magistrate is the most magnanimous." So he asked to see the Magistrate of Pei. The Magistrate was sitting on the bed with two maids washing his feet. Mr. Li did not kneel to him, but just made a long bow and said: "If you are to overthrow the unprincipled Qin Dynasty, you should not remain seated when meeting with your senior!" Magistrate of Pei immediately stood up, and, holding up the skirt of his robe, apologized, ushering him to a superior seat. Li Yiji advised him to raid Chenliu for its grain warehouse. Magistrate of Pei appointed him as Lord Guangye, and his younger brother Li Shang as general of the Chenliu soldiers. In the third moon, they attacked Kaifeng, but could not take it. Then they met Qin general Yang Xiong in the west and fought a battle at Baima; the war spread to the east of Quyu, where they smashed the Qin army. Yang fled to Xingyang, and was publicly executed by an emissary from the Qin Emperor. In the fourth moon, Magistrate of Pei attacked Yingchuan in the south, and massacred its people. With Zhang Liang's help they captured the Han territory.

At that time, Sima Ang, a detached general of Zhao, tried to cross the Yellow River to enter the Pass, so Magistrate of Pei attacked Pingyin in the north, to block the Yellow River crossing. Then he fought the Qin army in the south, east of Luoyang; frustrated of victory, he marched from the Huanyuan Mountains to Yangcheng to collect army horses. In the sixth moon, east of Chou,

【原文】

宛西。张良谏曰："沛公虽欲急入关，秦兵尚众，距险。今不下宛，宛从后击，强秦在前，此危道也。"于是沛公乃夜引军从他道还，偃旗帜，迟明，围宛城三匝。南阳守欲自刭。其舍人陈恢曰："死未晚也。"乃逾城见沛公，曰："臣闻足下约先入咸阳者王之，今足下留守宛。宛郡县连城数十，其吏民自以为降必死，故皆坚守乘城。今足下尽日止攻，士死伤者必多；引兵去宛，宛必随足下。足下前则失咸阳之约，后有强宛之患。为足下计，莫若约降，封其守，因使止守，引其甲卒与之西。诸城未下者，闻声争开门而待足下，足下通行无所累。"沛公曰："善。"七月，南阳守齮降，封为殷侯，封陈恢千户。引兵西，无不下者。至丹水，高武侯鳃、襄侯王陵降。还攻胡阳，遇番君别将梅锠，与偕攻析、郦，皆降。所过毋得卤掠，秦民

【今译】

阳郡，南阳守败走，退守宛城。沛公率兵过宛城而西。张良劝谏说："沛公虽想赶快入关，但秦兵尚众，又据险防守。今天不攻下宛城，宛守军从后攻击，强秦在前，这是危险之道。"于是沛公夜间引军从另一条道路返回，偃旗息鼓，将近天明时，包围宛城三重。南阳守想自刎，舍人陈恢说："还没到死的时候。"便越城来见沛公，说："臣听说足下约定先入咸阳者称王关中，今足下留攻宛城。宛郡县连城数十座。这里的官吏人民自认为投降必死，因此都登城坚守。今足下天天进攻宛城，士兵死伤必定很多；率兵离开宛，宛城秦军必定追击足下。足下前面失去咸阳盟约，后面有强宛之患。为足下考虑，不如约宛受降，封赏郡守，使他守宛，收编他的甲卒与他们一同向西进军。这样，诸城未攻下的，闻声争相开门而等待足下的到来，足下通行没有阻碍。"沛公说："好计。"七月，南阳守齮投降，封为殷侯，封陈恢为千户。带兵西行，沿途没有不投降的。到丹水，高武侯鳃、襄侯王陵投降。回军攻胡阳，遇番君吴芮的别将梅锠，与他协力

he fought against the Governor of Nanyang and destroyed the Qin army. He raided Nanyang Prefecture, whose governor was defeated and retreated to Wancheng. Magistrate of Pei passed Wancheng on his march west, but Zhang Liang remonstrated: "Although you are eager to get through the Pass, the Qin army are still plenty, and they hold a strategic defensive point. If you do not take Wancheng today, its defenders may attack you from behind, and this is dangerous since the strong Qin troops lie ahead." So Magistrate of Pei ordered his army back by night, taking a different route and without flags or fanfare. By dawn they had three rings of troops surrounding Wancheng. Nanyang Governor wanted to cut his own throat, but his aide Chen Hui said: "This is not yet the time to die." He then climbed the wall to see the Magistrate, saying: "Your servant understands that you have a covenant to make King of Guanzhong the first who step into Xianyang. Now you remain here to attack Wancheng. There are dozens of counties under its jurisdiction. Since the officials and people think that surrender will inevitably mean annihilation they will all climb the wall and resolutely defend the city. If you stay and attack the city every day, certainly many of your soldiers will be killed or injured; when you leave, the Qin army here will pursue you. You will both lose the Xianyang covenant, and will worry about the strong Wancheng troops at your rear. It would serve you better to negotiate Wancheng's surrender, and appoint its governor to defend Wancheng. You can incorporate his soldiers with your own and march west together. Thus, those towns not yet captured will open their gates at the news and wait for your arrival. Then your passage will not be hindered." Magistrate of Pei said: "Good plan." In the seventh moon, Nanyang Governor Yi surrendered, to be appointed Marquis of Yin, and Chen Hui was given a fief of 1,000 households. The troops marched west, and no one refused to surrender along the way. At Danshui, Sai the Marquis of Gaowu and Wang Ling the Marquis of Xiang surrendered. They

【原文】

喜。遣魏人甯昌使秦。是月章邯举军降项羽，羽以为雍王。瑕丘申阳下河南。

八月，沛公攻武关，入秦。秦相赵高恐，乃杀二世，使人来，欲约分王关中，沛公不许。九月，赵高立二世兄子子婴为秦王。子婴诛灭赵高，遣将将兵距峣关。沛公欲击之，张良曰："秦兵尚强，未可轻。愿先遣人益张旗帜于山上为疑兵，使郦食其、陆贾往说秦将，啖以利。"秦将果欲连和，沛公欲许之。张良曰："此独其将欲叛，恐其士卒不从，不如因其怠懈击之。"沛公引兵绕峣关，逾蒉山，击秦军，大破之蓝田南。遂至蓝田，又战其北，秦兵大败。

元年冬十月，五星聚于东井。沛公至霸上。秦王子婴素车白马，

【今译】

攻析、郦二城，二城降。所经过之处禁止掳掠，秦民喜悦。沛公派魏人宁昌为使者到秦都。这月章邯举军降项羽，项羽以章邯为雍王。瑕丘人申阳攻下河南郡。

八月，沛公攻武关，进入秦地。秦相赵高惊恐，就杀秦二世，派人来，想约定分割关中，沛公不许。九月，赵高立秦二世哥哥的儿子子婴为秦王。子婴诛杀赵高，遣将率兵据守峣关。沛公想攻击峣关，张良说："秦兵还很强大，不可轻敌。希望先派人在山上多举旗帜作为疑兵，派郦食其、陆贾前去劝秦将，用利引诱。"秦将果然想联合，沛公想答应。张良说："这仅仅是秦将要叛变，恐怕其士卒不从，不如乘他们懈怠的机会攻击他们。"沛公引兵绕过峣关，越过蒉山，击秦军，在蓝田南大败秦军。接着到了蓝田，又在蓝田北面交战，秦兵大败。

汉元年冬十月，五星聚于东井星。沛公到霸上。秦王子婴乘坐素

turned back to attack Huyang, and met Detached General Mei Xuan, in the service of Wu Rui, Lord of Po. Together with him, they attacked Xi and Li, both of which surrendered. Wherever they went, looting was prohibited, much to the Qin people's joy. Magistrate of Pei sent Ning Chang from Wei as messenger to the Qin capital. This month, all troops under Zhang Han surrendered to Xiang Yu, who made Zhang Han King of Yong. Shen Yang from Xiaqiu attacked and took Henan.

In the eighth moon, Magistrate of Pei attacked Wuguan Pass, attacking Qin on its own territory. Zhao Gao, the Prime Minister of Qin, panicked and killed the Emperor. He sent a messenger to negotiate terms, splitting Guanzhong area, but Magistrate of Pei rejected the approach. In the ninth moon, Zhao Gao made Ziying, the Emperor's nephew the King of Qin, Ziying then killed Zhao Gao and sent a general and troops to dig in at Rao Pass. Magistrate of Pei wanted to attack this pass, but Zhang Liang advised against it: "The Qin army is still strong, and we cannot underestimate them. I hope you will agree to send troops into the mountains, brandishing our banners in their thousands. While this deceptive deployment is going on, send Li Yiji and Lu Jia to persuade the Qin general, tempting him with the prospect of gain." The Qin general did indeed agree to join hands, and Magistrate of Pei wanted to promise him, but Zhang said: "This is just the Qin general's intention to mutiny, but I fear his soldiers will not obey. It is better to take the opportunity of their being off guard to attack them." Magistrate of Pei led his troops to bypass Rao Pass, cross Kuishan Mountains and defeat the Qin army south of Lantian. They went directly to Lantian and joined battle again north of Lantian, destroying the Qin army.

In the tenth moon of year one of the Han Dynasty (206 BC), the five planets gathered near the dongjing constellation in Gemini. Magistrate of Pei arrived at Bashang. Ziying the King of Qin surrendered at Zhidao, riding a simple chariot pulled by white

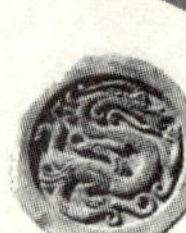

【原文】

系颈以组，封皇帝玺符节，降枳道旁。诸将或言诛秦王，沛公曰：“始怀王遣我，固以能宽容，且人已服降，杀之不祥。”乃以属吏。遂西入咸阳，欲止宫休舍，樊哙、张良谏，乃封秦重宝财物府库，还军霸上。萧何尽收秦丞相府图籍文书。十一月，召诸县豪桀曰：“父老苦秦苛法久矣，诽谤者族，耦语者弃市。吾与诸侯约，先入关者王之，吾当王关中。与父老约，法三章耳：杀人者死，伤人及盗抵罪。馀悉除去秦法。吏民皆按堵如故。凡吾所以来，为父兄除害，非有所侵暴，毋恐！且吾所以军霸上，待诸侯至而定要束耳。”乃使人与秦吏行至县乡邑告谕之。秦民大喜，争持牛羊酒食献享军士。沛公让不受，曰：“仓粟多，不欲费民。”民又益喜，唯恐沛公不为秦王。

或说沛公曰：“秦富十倍天下，地形强。今闻章邯降项羽，羽号

【今译】

车白马，用丝带拴着脖子，封裹着皇帝玉玺、虎符和节，在枳道旁投降。诸将有人说应杀死秦王，沛公说：“当初怀王派我，本来是由于我能宽容，况且人家已经服罪请降，杀他不吉利。”便交由部下看管。于是西入咸阳，并想留宿宫中。樊哙、张良劝阻，才把秦重宝财物封存在府库中，还军驻扎霸上。萧何尽收秦丞相府地图、户籍、档案文书。十一月，召集各县豪杰说：“父老受秦苛法之苦很久了，诽谤者灭族，偶语者处死于街头。我与诸侯定约，先入关者称王，我当在关中为王。与父老约法三章：杀人者偿命，伤人及盗抵罪。其余的秦法全部废除。官吏百姓原来的情况不变。我入关的目的，是为父老兄弟们除害，不是为了掠夺施暴行的，不要恐惧！我之所以驻扎霸上，是为了等诸侯到来再定约束。”于是派人与秦吏到县乡邑告谕百姓。秦民大喜，争相带上牛羊酒食献给官兵享用。沛公推让不受，说：“仓库中粟米很多，不想花费百姓的。”百姓更加高兴，惟恐沛公不当秦王。

有人劝沛公说：“秦地富有十倍于天下，地形强固。今听说章邯

were resolved, for "the vassal kings were content with their rents and tax revenues, they were no longer involved in political matters." Ban Gu's account became the authoritative basis for later generations to discuss the vassal states of the Western Han Dynasty.

Why did the country become strong during the reign of Emperor Wudi (141 BC-87 BC)? Ban Gu gave a detailed analysis. In the "Biographies of Gongsun Hong, Bu Shi and Ni Kuan", it was said that Emperor Wudi concentrated on two things: one was the expansion of his territory, and the other was the establishment of a series of ritual, political and legal systems. The court had great need of a company of civil and military people of distinction, and these emerged in great numbers in response to the court's call. These distinctive talents included Dong Zhongshu, Gongsun Hong, Ni Kuan, Han Anguo, Sima Qian, Sima Xiangru, Sang Hongyang, Zhang Qian, Wei Qing, and Huo Qubing. They helped Emperor Wudi's reign to reach its peak, with outstanding civil and military achievements that were hardly rivaled by later generations.

The "Annals of the Western Regions" records: Owing to Emperor Wudi's military campaigns along the borders, his dynasty expended great quantities of manpower and materials. In his later years, his military actions led to an empty state treasury and social turmoil. Confronted with serious crises, Emperor Wudi came to his senses. He drew the lesson of the Qin Dynasty's fall and changed his policy, putting a stop to military campaigns and thereby placating the common people. He thus avoided the likely consequences of the crises. In AD 89 he issued an imperial edict stating his regrets for past errors. Subsequently, Emperors Zhaodi and Xuandi continued his policy of avoiding warfare and supporting agriculture, which resulted in a period of plenty.

The *Book of Han* does not gloss over the dark side of the Western Han Dynasty, while extensively and accurately recording

【原文】

曰雍王，王关中。即来，沛公恐不得有此。可急使守函谷关，毋内诸侯军，稍征关中兵以自益，距之。”沛公然其计，从之。十二月，项羽果帅诸侯兵欲西入关，关门闭。闻沛公已定关中，羽大怒，使黥布等攻破函谷关，遂至戏下。沛公左司马曹毋伤闻羽怒，欲攻沛公，使人言羽曰：“沛公欲王关中，令子婴相，珍宝尽有之。”欲以求封。亚父范增说羽曰：“沛公居山东时，贪财好色，今闻其入关，珍物无所取，妇女无所幸，此其志不小。吾使人望其气，皆为龙，成五色，此天子气。急击之，勿失。”于是飨士，旦日合战。是时，羽兵四十万，号百万。沛公兵十万，号二十万，力不敌。会羽季父左尹项伯素善张良，夜驰见张良，具告其实，欲俱与去，毋特俱死。良曰：

【今译】

降项羽，项羽封他为雍王，在关中为王。就要来了，沛公恐怕不能得到此地。可赶快派将守住函谷关，不要让诸侯军入关，可征调关中兵加强军力，以便能抗拒项羽。”沛公听从此计。十二月，项羽果然率诸侯兵打算向西入关，关门已闭。听说沛公已平定关中，项羽大怒，派黥布等攻破函谷关，遂到达戏下。沛公左司马曹毋伤听说项羽发怒，想进攻沛公，就派人对项羽说：“沛公想当关中王，让子婴为相，珍宝尽归己有。”想以此得到项羽封赏。亚父范增劝项羽说：“沛公住在山东时，贪财好色。今天听说他入关，珍宝无所取，妇女无所爱，他的这一志向不小。我派人望其气，都成龙，有五彩之色，此即天子气。赶快攻击，勿失良机。”于是犒劳士兵，次日天明交战。这时，项羽兵四十万，号称百万。沛公兵十万，号称二十万，力不能抵。正好项羽叔父左尹项伯平时与张良友善，夜间急来见张良，全告诉了实情，劝他一同离去，不要白白送死。张良说：“我替韩王

richer than the rest of the empire, with rugged terrain and robust strongholds. I heard that Zhang Han has surrendered to Xiang Yu, who has made him King Yong ruling in Guanzhong. He is coming, so I'm afraid, Sire, that you cannot win that place. It is advisable to dispatch a general quickly to defend Hangu Pass, preventing the troops of vassal kings from crossing the border, and soldiers can be mobilized here in Guanzhong to strengthen military forces in order to resist Xiang Yu." Magistrate of Pei took this advice. In the 12th moon, Xiang Yu sure enough intended to lead the vassal kings' troops west through the Pass, but it was sealed. Hearing that Magistrate of Pei was in control of Guanzhong, XiangYu was furious and sent Tattooed Bu to break Hangu Pass, and they marched to Xixia. Hearing of Xiang Yu's rage, Cao Wushang, the Left Commander of Magistrate of Pei, wanted to turn on the Magistrate, so, with the ambition of winning a fiefdom from Xiang Yu, he sent him a messenger saying: "The Magistrate intends to be the King of Guanzhong, make Ziying the prime minister, and keep all the treasures for himself." Fan Zen ig, a senior advisor to Xiang Yu, said: "Magistrate of Pei was greedy and lustful when he was staying cast of the mountains, but I heard that since entering the Pass he is no longer greedy for the treasures or lustful for women. His ambition is not small, and I have sent someone to look at his emanation, a many-colored mist in the form of a dragon, namely, the cloud of the Son of Heaven. Quickly attack him, lest we miss the opportunity." Then they rewarded their soldiers with good food, and were to launch their attack at dawn the next day.

At this time, Xiang Yu commanded 400,000 soldiers, claiming them to be a million strong. Magistrate of Pei was outnumbered, commanding 100,000 while claiming 200,000. It so happened that Xiang Bo, Xiang Yu's Deputy Premier and junior uncle, was on good terms with Zhang Liang, and he hurried to see Zhang by night, gave him the full military picture, and urged him to leave together,

【原文】

“臣为韩王送沛公，不可不告，亡去不义。”乃与项伯俱见沛公，沛公与伯约为婚姻，曰：“吾入关，秋豪无所敢取，籍吏民，封府库，待将军。所以守关者，备他盗也。日夜望将军到，岂敢反邪！愿伯明言不敢背德。”项伯许诺，即夜复去。戒沛公曰：“旦日不可不早自来谢。”项伯还，具以沛公言告羽，因曰：“沛公不先破关中兵，公巨能入乎？且人有大功，击之不祥，不如因善之。”羽许诺。

沛公旦日从百馀骑见羽鸿门。谢曰：“臣与将军戮力攻秦，将军战河北，臣战河南，不自意先入关，能破秦，与将军复相见，今者有小人言，令将军与臣有隙。”羽曰：“此沛公左司马曹毋伤言之，不然，籍何以(生)[至]此？”羽因留沛公饮。范增数目羽击沛公，羽不应。范增起，出谓项庄曰：“君王为人不忍，汝入以剑舞，因击沛公，杀之。不者，汝属且为所虏。”庄入为寿。寿毕，曰：“军中无

【今译】

送沛公，不能不告诉，不说而逃是不义的。”于是张良与项伯同见沛公。沛公与项伯约为婚姻，说：“我入关，秋毫没有敢私取，登记户口，查封府库，等待将军。之所以派人守关，是为了防盗。日夜盼望将军到来，岂敢反叛呀！愿项伯说明不敢违背将军对我的好处。”项伯答应，当夜返回，行前告诫沛公说：“明晨不能不早点亲自来认错。”项伯回去，把沛公所言全都告诉项羽，并说：“沛公不先破关中兵，你能入关吗？况且人家有大功，攻击他是不吉利的，不如就此善待他。”项羽许诺。

沛公清晨带百余骑去鸿门拜见项羽，说：“臣与将军并力攻秦，将军战河北，臣战河南，没想到会先一步入关，能破秦，与将军再相见。今天有小人进谗言，让将军与臣产生嫌疑。”项羽说：“这是沛公左司马曹毋伤说的，不然，我怎么会这样？”项羽于是就留沛公饮酒。范增几次用眼睛暗示项羽击杀沛公，项羽没有反应。范增起身，出外对项庄说：“君王为人心慈，你入帐舞剑，乘机击沛公，杀死

rather than dying for no purpose. Zhang said: "Your servant was sent by the the King of Hann to accompany Magistrate of Pei, so I cannot leave without telling him, for it would not be righteous." Thus, Zhang Liang and Xiang Bo went together to see Magistrate of Pei. The Magistrate agreed to a marriage alliance with Xiang Bo, saying: "I crossed the border, but I did not dare take anything away for private purposes. I registered the population accounts, closed the repository, waiting for the General. The reason why I sent soldiers to guard the Pass was to keep off thieves. Day and night I'm looking forward to the arrival of General. How dare I rebel! I hope Xiang Bo will explain that I would not go against his beneficence." Xiang Bo promised and returned that night, warning as he left: "Tomorrow morning, first thing you have to apologize." Xiang Bo came back to tell his nephew what had been said, adding: "If the Magistrate had not first crushed the army in Guanzhong, how could you enter it? Moreover, it would be unlucky to attack one who has done a great merit. It would be best to show him leniency." Xiang Yu agreed to this.

Early next morning, Magistrate of Pei rode with a hundred men to see Xiang Yu at Hongmen, and he apologized: "The General and your servant joined forces to attack Qin, with the General fighting in the north of the River, and I in its south, but I did not expect to be inside the Pass a step earlier, to break Qin and then meet with the General again. Petty men now slander me, to cause the General to suspect me." Xiang Yu said: "The slander came from your own Left Commander Cao Wushang. How else would I be thus toward you?" Xiang Yu then invited Magistrate of Pei to stay and drink wine and ignored Fan Zeng's repeated winks to strike his rival. Fan Zeng rose, went out, and said to Xiang Zhuang: "Our master is too soft-hearted. Go inside the tent and take out your sword and take your chance to strike and kill the Magistrate. Otherwise, you and yours will soon be captured." So Xiang Zhuang entered to propose a toast.

【原文】

以为乐，请以剑舞。”因拔剑舞。项伯亦起舞，常以身翼蔽沛公。樊哙闻事急，直入，怒甚。羽壮之，赐以酒。哙因谯让羽。有顷，沛公起如厕，招樊哙出，置车官属，独骑，与樊哙、靳彊、滕公、纪成步，从间道走军，使张良留谢羽。羽问：“沛公安在？”曰：“闻将军有意督过之，脱身去，间至军，故使臣献璧。”羽受之。又献玉斗范增。增怒，撞其斗，起曰：“吾属今为沛公虏矣！”

沛公归数日，羽引兵西屠咸阳，杀秦降王子婴，烧秦宫室，所过无不残灭，秦民大失望。羽使人还报怀王，怀王曰：“如约。”羽怨怀王不肯令与沛公俱西入关，而北救赵，后天下约。乃曰：“怀王者，吾家所立耳，非有功伐，何以得专主约！本定天下，诸将与籍也。”春正月，阳尊怀王为义帝，实不用其命。

【今译】

他。不这样的话，你们不久就被俘了。”项庄进帐祝酒。礼毕之后说：“军中没有可以取乐的，请让我舞剑。”于是拔剑起舞。项伯也起舞，总是用身体掩护沛公。樊哙听说事急，直入帐中，很忿怒。项羽视之为壮士，赐酒给樊哙。樊哙就势责问项羽。不一会儿，沛公起身去厕所，招樊哙出来，留下车马从属，自己骑马，让樊哙、靳强、滕公、纪成步行，从小道回营，让张良留下谢项羽。项羽问：“沛公在何处？”张良说：“听说将军有意督责他，他脱身已去，从小道回到军中了，因此让臣献上玉璧。”项羽接受下来。又献给范增玉斗.范增发怒，撞碎玉斗，站起来说：“我们要成为沛公的俘虏了！”

沛公回到军中几天后，项羽带兵西入咸阳进行大肆屠杀，杀死秦降王子婴，烧毁秦宫室，所到之处无不毁灭，秦民非常失望。项羽派人还报楚怀王，楚怀王说：“当初盟约不变。”项羽怨恨怀王不肯让他与沛公同时西向入关，而让他北上救赵，使他未先入关，便说：“怀王是我家所立，没有功绩，凭什么能主盟约！本来平定天下的，是诸将和我项籍。”春正月，表面上尊怀王为义帝，实际上不听他的命令。

After performing the rite, he said: "We have little entertainment in the army, so please allow me to perform a sword dance." So he drew his sword and danced. But so too did Xiang Bo, always shielding the Magistrate with his own body. When Fan Kuai heard about the danger, he rushed in, very angry. Xiang Yu regarded Fan Kuai as a hero, and presented wine to him. Fan Kuai closely questioned Xiang Yu on the situation. After a while, the Magistrate rose to go to the toilet, and called Fan Kuai out. He rode off, leaving behind his entourage and his chariot. Fan Kuai, Jin Qiang, Magistrate of Teng, and Ji Cheng followed on foot, taking a path back to their camp. He had Zhang Liang stay behind to thank Xiang Yu.

When Xiang Yu asked: "Where is the Magistrate?" Zhang replied: "He heard the General is minded to hold him responsible for errors, so he has left, taking a path back to his army, but he has commanded your servant to offer the insignia of jade." Xiang Yu accepted it. And a jade cup was then dedicated to Fan Zeng, who, incensed, smashed it to smithereens. He rose up, crying out: "We shall all become the Magistrate's prisoners!"

A few days after this, Xiang Yu took his troops west, massacring Xianyang people, killing the surrendered King of Qin Ziying, burning down the Qin palaces, destroying everything wherever he went, to the great dismay of the Qin people. Xiang Yu reported back to King Huai of Chu, who said: "Abide by the covenant." Resenting that the king had refused to let him march west through the Pass with Magistrate of Pei, sending him north to save Zhao instead and making him late for the covenant, Xiang Yu said: "King Huai of Chu was established by my family. He has no merit, by what right can he control the covenant! It is my generals and the Xiang clan who have conquered the world." In the first moon, though he made a pretense of enthroning King Huai of Chu as Emperor Yi, Xiang Yu did not, in fact, obey his orders .

In the second moon, Xiang Yu crowned himself Hegemon

【原文】

二月，羽自立为西楚霸王，王梁、楚地九郡，都彭城。背约，更立沛公为汉王，王巴、蜀、汉中四十一县，都南郑。三分关中，立秦三将：章邯为雍王，都废丘；司马欣为塞王，都栎阳；董翳为翟王，都高奴。楚将瑕丘申阳为河南王，都洛阳。赵将司马印为殷王，都朝歌。当阳君英布为九江王，都六。怀王柱国共敖为临江王，都江陵。番君吴芮为衡山王，都邾。故齐王建孙田安为济北王。徙魏王豹为西魏王，都平阳。徙燕王韩广为辽东王。燕将臧荼为燕王，都蓟。徙齐王田市为胶东王。齐将田都为齐王，都临菑。徙赵王歇为代王。赵相张耳为常山王。汉王怨羽之背约，欲攻之，丞相萧何谏，乃止。

夏四月，诸侯罢戏下，各就国。羽使卒三万人从汉王，楚子、诸侯人之慕从者数万人，从杜南入蚀中。张良辞归韩，汉王送至褒中，

【今译】

二月，项羽自立为西楚霸王，领有梁、楚地区九个郡，定都彭城。又违背盟约，改立沛公为汉王，领有巴、蜀、汉中三郡四十一县，定都南郑。三分关中，立秦三降将：章邯为雍王，定都废丘；司马欣为塞王，定都栎阳；董翳为翟王，定都高奴。楚将瑕丘人申阳为河南王，定都洛阳。赵将司马印为殷王，定都朝歌。当阳君英布为九江王，定都六。怀王柱国共敖为临江王，定都江陵。番君吴芮为衡山王，定都邾。战国末年齐王田建之孙田安为济北王。徙魏王魏豹为西魏王，定都平阳。徙燕王韩广为辽东王。燕将臧荼为燕王，定都蓟。徙齐王田市为胶东王。齐将田都为齐王，定都临菑。徙赵王赵歇为代王。赵相张耳为常山王。汉王怨项羽背弃盟约，想进攻项羽，丞相萧何劝阻，才作罢。

夏四月，诸侯离开项羽麾下，各回本国。项羽只拨卒三万人随汉王，楚国人、诸侯国人仰慕汉王而随从他的有数万人，从杜县南进蚀

of Western Chu, commanding nine prefectures in the regions of Liang and Chu, with his capital in Pengcheng. And contrary to the Covenant, he changed the position of Magistrate of Pei to that of King of Han, commanding forty-one counties in three prefectures of Ba, Shu, and Hanzhong, with his capital in Nanzheng. Guanzhong was divided into three portions, for the three Qin generals: Zhang Han as King Yong, with his capital in Feiqiu; Sima Xin as King of Sai, with his capital in Liyang; and Dong Yi as King of Di, with his capital in Gaonu. The Chu general Shen Yang from Xiaqiu was made King of Henan, with his capital in Luoyang. The Zhao general Sima Ang was made King of Yin, with his capital in Zhaoge. Lord Ying Bu of Dangyang was made King of Jiujiang, with his capital in Liu. Gong Ao (King Huai of Chu's top general) was made King of Linjiang, with his capital in Jiangling. Lord of Po Wu Rui was made King of Hengshan, with Zhu as his capital. Tian An, the grandson of the former King of Qi Tian Jian was made King of Jibei. Wei Bao, King of Wei, was moved to be King of Western Wei, with his capital in Pingyang. Han Guang, King of Yan, was moved to be King of Liaodong. Zang Tu, a Yan general, was made King of Yan, with his capital in Ji. Tian Fu, King of Qi, was moved to be King of Jiaodong. Qi general Tian Du was made King of Qi, with his capital in Linzi. Zhao Xie, King of Zhao, was moved to be King of Dai. Zhao's premier Zhang Er was made King of Changshan. The King of Han blamed Xiang Yu for betraying the covenant, and wanted to attack him, but his prime minister Xiao He dissuaded him.

In the fourth moon, the vassal kings returmed to their respective kingdoms. Xiang Yu allocated only 30,000 people to follow the King of Han, but many more tens of thousands swelled the number of his followers, including Chu people, and other admirers. He traveled south from Du to enter Shi. The King accompanied Zhang Liang as far as Baozhong to bid him farewell as Zhang returned to his own Kingdom of Hann. Zhang advised the King to burn down the plank

【原文】

因说汉王烧绝栈道，以备诸侯盗兵，亦视项羽无东意。

汉王既至南郑，诸将及士卒皆歌讴思东归，多道亡还者。韩信为治粟都尉，亦亡去，萧何追还之，因荐于汉王，曰："必欲争天下，非信无可与计事者。"于是汉王齐戒设坛场，拜信为大将军，问以计策。信对曰："项羽背约而王君王于南郑，是迁也。吏卒皆山东之人，日夜企而望归，及其锋而用之，可以有大功。天下已定，民皆自宁，不可复用。不如决策东向。"因陈羽可图、三秦易并之计。汉王大说，遂听信策，部署诸将。留萧何收巴蜀租，给军[粮]食。

五月，汉王引兵从故道出袭雍。雍王邯迎击汉陈仓，雍兵败，还走。战好畤，又大败，走废丘。汉王遂定雍地。东如咸阳，引兵围雍王废丘，而遣诸将略地。

田荣闻羽徙齐王市于胶东而立田都为齐王，大怒，以齐兵迎击田

【今译】

中。张良辞汉王归韩国，汉王送他至褒中，他劝汉王烧毁栈道，以防各诸侯偷袭，也向项羽表示无东向之意。

汉王已至南郑，诸将及士卒都唱歌，思念东归，不少人中途逃回去。韩信任治粟都尉，也逃走了，萧何追还韩信，随即推荐给汉王，说："必想争天下，除了韩信再没有可以与之谋划的人了。"于是汉王斋戒设坛场，拜韩信为大将军，询问争天下的计策。韩信对答说："项羽背弃盟约而让君王在南郑称王，是左迁。官兵皆山东人，日夜企望东归，利用这种锋锐之气，可以成大功。天下已平定，人民皆自安宁，不可再用。不如决策东向。"于是讲述了项羽可打败、三秦易兼并之计。汉王很高兴，就听从韩信计策，部署诸将。留下萧何征收巴、蜀地区租税，供给军粮。

五月，汉王率兵从故道县出兵袭雍国。雍王章邯在陈仓迎击汉王，雍兵大败，后退；在好畤再战，又大败，逃回废丘。汉王便平定雍地。东往咸阳，引兵把雍王包围在废丘，然后遣诸将略地。

田荣听说项羽把齐王田市迁往胶东，而立田都为齐王，大怒，带

bridges, in order to prevent any sneak attack by the vassal kings and also to demonstrate to Xiang Yu that he had no intention to move east. By the time the King of Han arrived in Nanzheng, his officers and soldiers were singing about missing the east, and many people had fled along the way. His Grain Captain Hann Xin also fled, but was chased and brought back by Xiao He, who then recommended him to the King: "If you will contest for the world, you could get no better strategist than Hann Xin." Therefore, the King of Han fasted and set up an altar, ordaining Hann Xin as Great General, asking for his plan to conquer the world. Hann Xin replied: "Xiang Yu abandoned the covenant and demoted the King to rule in Nanzheng. Your men and officials are from east of the mountains, waiting day and night to return east. Take advantage of this cutting edge, and you will achieve a great cause. The world has calmed down, and the people peaceably settled, no longer available to fight. The best course is to decide to march east." Then he demonstrated how Xiang Yu could be overcome, and the areas controlled by the three former Qin generals easily annexed. Overjoyed, the King of Han adopted Hann Xin's plan, deploying all the generals. Xiao He was left behind to collect the revenues from Ba and Shu, for the supply of rations.

In the fifth moon, the King of Han retraced his steps, leading troops to attack Yong, engaging Zhang Han the King Yong at Chencang. Yong was defeated and withdrew, but in Haozhi he stopped his retreat and rejoined battle, only to lose again before fleeing to Feiqiu. Thus the King of Han conquered Yong territory. Proceeding east toward Xianyang, he led his troops to surround King Yong at Feiqiu, and then sent his generals to occupy the territory.

When Tian Rong heard about Xiang Yu removing Qi's King Tian Fu to Jiaodong, and replacing him with Tian Du, he was outraged. He led his Qi soldiers to attack Tian Du, who was defeated and surrendered to Chu. In the sixth moon, Tian Rong killed Tian Fu and made himself King of Qi. At the time, Peng Yue was in Juye,

【原文】

都，都走降楚。六月，田荣杀田市，自立为齐王。时彭越在钜野，众万馀人，无所属。荣与越将军印，因令反梁地。越击杀济北王安，荣遂并三齐之地。燕王韩广亦不肯徙辽东。秋八月，臧荼杀韩广，并其地。塞王欣、翟王翳皆降汉。

初，项梁立韩后公子成为韩王，张良为韩司徒。羽以良从汉王，韩王成又无功，故不遣就国，与俱至彭城，杀之。及闻汉王并关中，而齐、梁畔之，羽大怒，乃以故吴令郑昌为韩王，距汉。令萧公角击彭越，越败角兵。时张良徇韩地，遗羽书曰："汉欲得关中，如约即止，不敢复东。"羽以故无西意，而北击齐。

九月，汉王遣将军薛欧、王吸出武关，因王陵兵，从南阳迎太公、吕后于沛。羽闻之，发兵距之阳夏，不得前。

二年冬十月，项羽使九江王布杀义帝于郴。陈馀亦怨羽独不王

【今译】

领齐兵迎击田都。田都败走降楚。六月，田荣杀田市，自立为齐王。当时彭越在巨野，有众万余人，无所归属。田荣授彭越将军印，令他在梁地反项羽。彭越击杀济北王田安，田荣便兼并了三齐之地。燕王韩广也不肯迁往辽东。秋八月，臧荼杀韩广，兼并其地。塞王司马欣、翟王董翳皆降汉。

当初。项梁立韩国之后公子成为韩王，张良任韩司徒。项羽认为张良已跟从汉王，韩王成又无功，所以不让韩王成回本国，把他带到彭城，杀掉。当听到汉王占领关中，齐、梁背叛，项羽大怒，就以从前的吴县令郑昌为韩王，率兵拒汉王。令萧公角击彭越，彭越击败萧公角兵。当时张良略取韩地，写信给项羽说："汉王想得到关中，只要实现了盟约即止兵，不敢东进。"项羽因此没有向西之意，于是北上击齐。

九月，汉王遣将军薛欧、王吸出武关，依靠王陵之兵，从南阳去沛县迎太公、吕后。项羽听说此事后，就发兵在阳夏阻挡，不得前往。

汉二年冬十月，项羽派九江王英布至郴县杀义帝。陈馀也怨恨项

commanding 10,000 people, but uncommitted to any vassal king.

Tian Rong granted Peng Yue a seal of general with orders to rebel against Xiang Yu in the area of Liang. When Peng Yue attacked and killed Tian An King of Jibei, Tian Rong united three territories of Qi. Hann Guang, the King of Yan, also refused to move to Liaodong. In the eighth moon, Zang Tu killed him and annexed his territory. Sima Xin King of Sai and Dong Yi King of Di both submitted to Han.

Earlier, Xiang Liang had set up Cheng, a prince of the Hann line, as the King of Hann, and Zhang Liang as Hann's Minister over the Masses. Xiang Yu thought that Zhang had aligned with the King of Han, and that Cheng had not performed service, so he did not permit Cheng to return to his own kingdom, instead taking him to Pengcheng and killing him. When he heard that the King of Han had reunited Guanzhong, and that Qi and Liang had changed sides, Xiang Yu was furious. He made Zheng Chang, the former magistrate of Wu, the King of Hann, oppose the King of Han. He ordered Magistrate Xiao Jiao to attack Peng Yue, but Xiao's soldiers were beaten.

Now Zhang Liang had subjugated Hann territory, and he wrote to Xiang Yu: "The reason the King of Han wanted Guanzhong was to fulfill the covenant and move his troops no further; he would not dare venture east." Thus persuaded, Xiang Yu was not minded to march west, and attacked Qi in the north instead.

In the ninth moon, the King of Han sent Generals Xue Ou and Wang Xi out of Wuguan Pass, relying on Wang Ling's soldiers, in order to fetch his father and Empress Lü from Pei via Nanyang. When Xiang Yu heard this, he sent his troops to block their passage at Yangxia.

In the 10th moon of year two of Han, Xiang Yu sent Ying Bu the King of Jiujiang to kill Emperor Yi at Chen. Chen Yu also harbored a grudge against Xiang Yu for making him alone not a

【原文】

已，从田荣藉助兵，以击常山王张耳。耳败走降汉，汉王厚遇之。陈馀迎代王歇还赵，歇立馀为代王。张良自韩间行归汉，汉王以为成信侯。

汉王如陕，镇抚关外父老。河南王申阳降，置河南郡。使韩太尉韩信击韩，韩王郑昌降。十一月，立韩太尉信为韩王。汉王还归，都栎阳，使诸将略地，拔陇西。以万人若一郡降者，封万户。缮治河上塞。故秦苑囿园池，令民得田之。

春正月，羽击田荣城阳，荣败走平原，平原民杀之。齐皆降楚，楚焚其城郭，齐人复畔之。诸将拔北地，虏雍王弟章平。赦罪人。二月癸未，令民除秦社稷，立汉社稷。施恩德，赐民爵。蜀汉民给军事

【今译】

羽惟独不封他为王，就向田荣求援兵，去击常山王张耳。张耳败走降汉，汉王以礼厚待。陈馀迎代王赵歇返回赵，赵歇立陈馀为代王、张良自韩从小道前来归汉，汉王封张良为成信侯。

汉王到陕县，安抚关外的父老。河南王申阳降汉，设立河南郡。派韩太尉韩信击韩，韩王郑昌降。十一月，汉王立韩太尉韩信为韩王。汉王回关中，定都栎阳，派诸将攻城略地，攻下陇西郡。汉王提出率一万人或一郡来降者，封万户侯。整修河上郡边塞。开放秦原有苑林园池，让百姓去耕种。

春正月，项羽在城阳击田荣，田荣败走平原郡，被平原民杀死。齐地都降楚，楚烧毁其城郭，齐人又叛离。汉诸将攻下北地郡，俘获雍王弟章平。赦免罪人。二月二十日，令百姓拆除秦的社稷，立汉社稷。施行恩德，赏赐百姓爵位；蜀郡、汉中郡百姓供给军粮军需很劳

king, so he took reinforcement troops from Tian Rong in order to attack Zhang Er, the King of Changshan. Defeated, the King of Changshan submitted to Han, whose king treated him favorably. Chen Yu welcomed Zhao Xie King of Dai to return to Zhao, but Zhao made Chen Yu King of Dai instead. Zhang Liang came from Hann via byways to join Han, and the King of Han made him Marquis of Chengxin.

The King of Han came to Sha'an, to pacify the elders outside the Pass. Shen Yang King of Henan submitted, hence the establishment of Henan Prefecture. The King of Han sent Hann Xin, Hann's Defender-in-Chief to attack Hann, whose king Zheng Chang yielded.

In the 11th moon, the King of Han made Hann Xin King of Hann. He came back to Guanzhong, made his capital Liyang, and sent his generals to occupy more territory, thus bringing Longxi under his rule. It was decreed that a fief of 10,000 households would be awarded to anyone submitting with 10,000 people or a prefecture. Repair of the fortress at Heshang was ordered. The imperial gardens and lakes closed off by the Qin Dynasty were opened for the people as farmland.

In the first moon, Xiang Yu attacked Tian Rong at Chengyang, who was defeated and fled to Pingyuan, only to be killed by the local people. The lands of Qi fell to Chu, but when Chu burned down their city walls, the Qi people rose in revolt.

Han generals conquered Beidi and captured Zhang Ping, brother of King Yong. Prisoners were pardoned. On the 20th day of the second moon, the people were ordered to replace the Qin altars to grain and earth gods with those of Han. A policy of benevolence was instituted, with rewards of civilian rank titles; the people of Shu and Hanzhong had undergone great hardship providing military rations and supplies, so they were exempted from land taxes for two years; the families of soldiers from Guanzhong were excused taxes and

【原文】

劳苦，复勿租税二岁。关中卒从军者，复家一岁。举民年五十以上，有修行，能帅众为善，置以为三老，乡一人。择乡三老一人为县三老，与县令丞尉以事相教，复勿繇戍。以十月赐酒肉。

三月，汉王自临晋渡河，魏王豹降，将兵从。下河内，虏殷王印，置河内郡。至脩武，陈平亡楚来降。汉王与语，说之，使参乘，监诸将。南渡平阴津，至洛阳，新城三老董公遮说汉王曰："臣闻'顺德者昌，逆德者亡'，'兵出无名，事故不成'。故曰：'明其为贼，敌乃可服。'项羽为无道，放杀其主，天下之贼也。夫仁不以勇，义不以力，三军之众，为之素服，以告之诸侯，为此东伐，四海之内莫不仰德，此三王之举也。"汉王曰："善，非夫子无所闻。"于是汉王为义帝发丧，袒而大哭，哀临三日。发使告诸侯曰："天

【今译】

苦，免除两年赋税；关中从军兵卒，免除家中租税、劳役一年；推举年五十岁以上、品行好、能率众作善事的庶民为三老，每乡一人；选乡三老一人为县三老，为县令县丞县尉进行政事的顾问，免除徭役。每年十月赐给三老酒肉。

三月，汉王从临晋渡黄河。魏王魏豹降，率兵跟从汉王。攻下河内，俘虏殷王司马印，设河内郡。至修武县，陈平离楚降汉。汉王与陈平谈话，很高兴，让他为汉王参乘，监督诸将。南渡平阴津，到了洛阳，新城三老董公拦住汉王说："臣听说'顺行德义者昌盛，违背德义者灭亡'，'师出无正义之名，军事因此不会成功'。所以说：'指明他是逆贼，敌人才可征服。'项羽行事暴虐无道，流放杀死他的君主，是天下之逆贼。仁爱不靠武勇，正义不靠暴力，汉王三军众士，应为义帝穿孝服，告谕诸侯，为义帝被杀而东伐项羽，四海之内，无不仰慕汉王之德。这是三王实行过的正义之举。"汉王说："太好了。不是先生听不到这些高见。"于是汉王为义帝发丧，袒露左臂大哭，公祭三日。派出使臣通告诸侯说："天下共立义帝，北

labor service for one year; there would be a selection of Elders, one per village, from civilians over the age of 50, men of good character and ability to mobilize people to do good; also the county-level Elders, eligible for counseling political affairs with the magistrate and aide and sheriff, also exempt from corvee and military service. In the 10th moon every year, the Elders were granted wine and meat.

In the third moon, the King of Han crossed the Yellow River at Linjin Ferry. Wei Bao the King of Wei submitted, and joined his expedition. They captured Henei, taking prisoner Sima Ang King of Yin, and establishing Henei Prefecture. They reached Xiuwu, where Chen Ping defected from Chu to Han. The King of Han talked happily with Chen Ping, and made him his chariot-companion in charge of supervising the generals. They crossed Pingyin Ford, southward to Luoyang, but Mr. Dong, the Elder of Xincheng, stopped the King there: "Your servant heard 'Those who follow virtue will prosper, and those who violate moral codes shall perish; military ventures not in the name of justice will fail.' So I say to you: 'The enemy who is identified as usurper will be overcome.' Xiang Yu is brutal and unprincipled. He expelled and killed his own lord, and now he usurps the empire. Benevolence does not depend on military valor, and justice need not use force. Han's troops should wear mourning for Emperor Yi, thereby declaring to the vassal kings that you march east in order to avenge his death and take Xiang Yu. Proceed thus and, within the four seas, all will admire your virtue. This was just what the Three Kings practiced in the ancient times." The King of Han said: "Excellent. Without you, master, I could not have heard such lofty advice." Thus, the King proclaimed mourning for Emperor Yi, weeping, baring his left arm, in a public memorial ceremony that lasted three days. Envoys were sent to notify the vassal kings: "Emperor Yi was enthroned by all of us, we all declared allegiance to His Majesty. Now Xiang Yu exiled and killed our Emperor in the south. That's regicide and treason! I personally

【原文】

下共立义帝，北面事之。今项羽放杀义帝江南，大逆无道！寡人亲为发丧，兵皆缟素。悉发关中兵，收三河士，南浮江汉以下，愿从诸侯王击楚之杀义帝者！”

夏四月，田荣弟横收得数万人，立荣子广为齐王。羽虽闻汉东，既击齐，欲遂破之而后击汉，汉王以故得劫五诸侯兵，东伐楚。到外黄，彭越将三万人归汉，汉王拜越为魏相国，令定梁地。汉王遂入彭城，收羽美人货赂，置酒高会。羽闻之，令其将击齐，而自以精兵三万人从鲁出胡陵，至萧，晨击汉军，大战彭城灵壁东睢水上，大破汉军，多杀士卒，睢水为之不流。围汉王三匝。大风从西北起，折木发屋，扬砂石，昼晦，楚军大乱，而汉王得与数十骑遁去。过沛，使人求室家，室家亦已亡，不相得。汉王道逢孝惠、鲁元，载行。楚骑

【今译】

面称臣供职。今项羽流放杀害义帝于江南，大逆无道！寡人亲自为义帝发丧，士兵都穿白色丧服。我要征发全部关中兵，收编三河地区士卒，南自江、汉以下，愿意跟从诸侯王们讨伐楚国杀害义帝的凶逆！”

夏四月，田荣之弟田横收编数万人，立田荣之子田广为齐王。项羽虽听说汉王东进，但他已经出兵击齐，便打算破齐之后再去击汉，汉王因此得以强率魏王、河南王、韩王、殷王、常山王五诸侯之兵，东伐楚。到达外黄后，彭越率三万人归汉。汉王拜彭越为魏相国，让他平定梁地。汉王接着进入彭城，缴获项羽的美人珍宝，设宴聚会大贺。项羽闻知，命部将击齐，而自率精兵三万人从鲁地出胡陵县，到达萧县，天亮击汉军，在彭城灵壁东的睢水上与汉军大战，大败汉军，杀伤极多，睢水被尸体堵塞而不流。包围汉王的楚军有三层。忽然，大风从西北刮起，折树倒屋，飞沙走石，白天昏暗，楚军大乱，汉王得以趁机与数十骑逃走。过沛县，派人找家眷，家眷也已逃亡，没找到。汉王路上遇见孝惠帝、鲁元公主，同车逃走。楚骑兵追汉王，

proclaimed a funeral for His Majesty, and my soldiers wore white mourning. My intention now is to send all the troops in Guanzhong, incorporating soldiers from the three He areas, southward down Yangtze and Hanjiang rivers. We are willing to follow the vassal kings' crusade against the atrocious regicide of the Emperor in Chu!"

That summer, in the fourth moon, Tian Heng, the younger brother of Tian Rong incorporated tens of thousands into his forces and made Tian Guang, the son of Tian Rong, the King of Qi. Although Xiang Yu had heard of Han's march east, he had sent troops against Qi, so he intended to go after Han once Qi had been broken. Therefore the King of Han was able to compel five vassal kings (Wei, Henan, Hann, Yin and Changshan) on an eastbound expedition against Chu. When they reached Waihuang, Peng Yue's 30,000 soldiers joined Han. The King made Peng Yue premier of Wei, with orders to conquer Liang. The King of Han then entered Pengcheng, captured Yu's beauties and treasures, and hosted a grand celebration banquet. When XiangYu heard about this, he left his generals to attack Qi, and led his 30,000 crack troops from Lu via Huling to Xiao, and attacked the Han forces at first light. A great battle took place on Suishui River east of Lingbi in Pengcheng, with the Han forces overwhelmed, and so many soldiers killed that the river was blocked by corpses. The King of Han was encircled, three lines deep. Suddenly, a gale rose up from the northwest, breaking trees and sweeping away huts, hurling sand and rocks, and turning daylight to dusk. With the Chu army in disarray the King of Han and dozens of riders seized this opportunity to escape. Passing through Pei, he sent to find his family members, but they too had fled, and were nowhere to be found. On the road, he met future Emperor Huidi and Elder Princess Lu, escaping on a shared chariot. The Chu cavalry chased the King, who, desperate, pushed the two children off the chariot but Magistrate Teng (Xiahou Ying) brought them back

【原文】

追汉王，汉王急，推堕二子。滕公下收载，遂得脱。审食其从太公、吕后间行，反遇楚军，羽常置军中以为质。诸侯见汉败，皆亡去。塞王欣、翟王翳降楚，殷王卬死。

吕后兄周吕侯将兵居下邑，汉王往从之。稍收士卒，军砀。

汉王西过梁地，至虞，谓谒者随何曰：“公能说九江王布使举兵畔楚，项王必留击之。得留数月，吾取天下必矣。”随何往说布，果使畔楚。

五月，汉王屯荥阳，萧何发关中老弱未傅者悉诣军。韩信亦收兵与汉王会，兵复大振。与楚战荥阳南京、索间，破之。筑甬道，属河，以取敖仓粟。魏王豹谒归视亲疾。至则绝河津，反为楚。

六月，汉王还栎阳。壬午，立太子，赦罪人。令诸侯子在关中者皆集栎阳为卫。引水灌废丘，废丘降，章邯自杀。雍(州)[地]定，八十

【今译】

汉王情急，把两个孩子推下车。滕公夏侯婴又把他们拉上车，才得脱险。审食其跟从太公、吕后从小道逃走，反而遇上楚军而被俘去，被项羽安置在军中作为人质。诸侯见汉王大败，都四散逃走。塞王司马欣、翟王董翳降楚，殷王司马卬死。

吕后兄周吕侯率兵驻下邑县，汉王前往投奔。稍稍收集了一些士卒，驻扎砀县。

汉王西过梁地，到虞县，对谒者随何说：“你能劝九江王英布让他举兵叛楚，项王必留下攻击英布。如果他能停留数月，我就一定能夺取天下。”随何前往劝说英布，果然使他背叛了楚国。

五月，汉王驻屯荥阳，萧何征发关中的老弱和未达兵役登记年龄的人全到军中报到。韩信也收集士兵与汉王会师，汉军士气又大振。与楚军在荥阳南的京、索一带交战，打败楚军。汉筑甬道，通到黄河，以取敖仓粮食。魏王魏豹请假探视亲属疾病。一到家便断绝黄河渡口，反汉降楚。

六月，汉王返回栎阳。十九日，立太子，赦罪人。命关东人在关中从军的都集合起来任栎阳卫士。汉兵引水灌废丘，废丘降汉，章邯

aboard and they got away. Shen Yiji followed the King's father and Empress Lü in their flight along a back road, only to be captured by Chu troops and placed in the camp by Xiang Yu as hostages. When the vassal kings saw the King of Han totally beaten, they scattered to the four winds. The King of Sai Sima Xin and the King of Di Dong Yi surrendered to Chu, and the King of Yin Sima Ang died.

Empress Lü's brother Marquis of Zhoulü was stationed at Xiayi, where the King of Han took refuge. They gathered together a few stray soldiers, and made camp in Dang.

The King of Han went west via Liang to Yu, and said to his go-between Sui He: "If you, sir, could persuade Ying Bu King of Jiujiang to rebel against the Chu, King Xiang Yu would stay to attack him, and if he could keep him occupied for a few months, we should be able to win the empire." Sui He went over to persuade Ying Bu, who did indeed betray Chu.

In the fifth moon, the King of Han was garrisoned in Xingyang, and Xiao He mobilized all the old or feeble and those as yet unregistered for military corvee to report to the army. Hann Xin also collected soldiers and joined forces with the King of Han, and the morale of Han troops was boosted. They fought and defeated Chu in the south of Xingyang between Jing and Suo. Han built a walled corridor to the Yellow River so as to transport grain from the Aoshan Hill granary. King Wei Bao asked leave to visit a sick parent, but as soon as he arrived, he cut off the Yellow River crossing, defecting from Han to Chu.

In the sixth moon, the King of Han returned to Liyang. On the 19th day, he named his Crown Prince and issued an amnesty. All the sons of the vassal kings who were in Guanzhong were ordered together at Liyang to be guards. The Han soldiers diverted water to flood Feiqiu, which surrendered and Zhang Han committed suicide. The Yong area was put under Han rule, including 80-plus counties, zoned into Heshang, Weinan, Zhongdi, Longxi, and Shangjun

【原文】

馀县，置河上、渭南、中地、陇西、上郡，令祠官祀天地四方上帝山川，以时祠之。兴关中卒乘边塞。关中大饥，米斛万钱，人相食。令民就食蜀汉。

秋八月，汉王如荥阳，谓郦食其曰："缓颊往说魏王豹，能下之，以魏地万户封生。"食其往，豹不听。汉王以韩信为左丞相，与曹参、灌婴俱击魏。食其还，汉王问："魏大将谁也？"对曰："柏直。"王曰："是口尚乳臭，不能当韩信。骑将谁也？"曰："冯敬。"曰："是秦将冯无择子也，虽贤，不能当灌婴。步卒将谁也？"曰："项它。"曰："是不能当曹参，吾无患矣。"九月，信等虏豹，传诣荥阳。定魏地，置河东、太原、上党郡。信使人请兵三万人，愿以北举燕赵，东击齐，南绝楚粮道。汉王与之。

三年冬十月，韩信、张耳东下井陉击赵，斩陈馀，获赵王歇。置常山、代郡。甲戌晦，日有食之。十一月癸卯晦，日有食之。

【今译】

自杀。雍地平定，有八十余县，设河上、渭南、中地、陇西、上郡五郡。命祠官祭天地四方上帝山川诸神，按时祭祀。征发关中兵卒守边塞。关中发生饥荒，米一斛值万钱，人吃人。汉王命人民到蜀郡、汉中谋生。

秋八月，汉王前往荥阳，对郦食其说："婉言劝告魏王魏豹，能劝说成功，把魏地万户封给先生。"食其前往，魏豹不听。汉王任韩信为左丞相，与曹参、灌婴同击魏。食其返回，汉王问："魏大将是谁？"回答说："柏直。"汉王说："乳臭未干，不能抵挡韩信。骑将是谁？"回答说："冯敬。"汉王说："是秦将冯无择之子，虽贤能，不能抵挡灌婴。步将是谁？"回答说："项它。"汉王说："他不能抵挡曹参，我没有可怕的了。"九月，韩信等捉到魏豹，押送到荥阳。平定魏地，设河东、太原、上党三郡。韩信派人请求增兵三万，愿率兵北取燕、赵，东击齐，南断楚粮道交通。汉王如数给韩信增兵。

三年冬十月，韩信、张耳东下井陉，击赵，斩代王陈馀，俘虏赵王赵歇。设常山郡和代郡。甲戌晦，日食。十一月癸卯晦，有日食。

prefectures. Sacrifice officials were ordered to make offerings to Heaven, Earth, Four Directions, Supreme God, gods of rivers and mountains, keeping specific times. Guanzhong soldiers were mobilized to guard the frontier. There was famine in Guanzhong, so bad that one *hu* of husked millet cost 10,000 cash, and cannibalism was rife. The King ordered people to make their way to Shu and Hanzhong prefectures to make a living there.

In autumn, in the eighth moon, he went to Xingyang, and said to Li Yiji: "You'll politely advise King Wei Bao. If you persuade him successfully, I'll present 10,000 households in Wei area to you." Li Yiji went, but Wei Bao did not listen. The King made Hann Xin Left Prime Minister, and sent him to attack Wei together with Cao Can and Guan Ying. When Li Yiji returned, the King asked: "Who is Wei's Chief General?" He replied: "Bai Zhi." The King said: "Wet behind the ears, he can't stand up to Hann Xin. Who is their cavalry general?" He replied: "Feng Jing." The King said: "He is the son of Qin general Feng Wuze. Though virtuous and able, he cannot resist Guan Ying. Who is the infantry general?" He replied: "Xiang Ta." The King said: "He is no match for Cao Can, so I have nothing to fear." In the ninth moon, Hann and others caught Wei Bao, and escorted him to Xingyang. Wei was pacified, and Hedong, Taiyuan and Shangdang prefectures were set up. Hann Xin sent a request for 30,000 additional troops so as to take Yan and Zhao in the north, attack Qi in the east, and cut off Chu's grain supply routes in the south. The King of Han gave him everything he wanted.

In the 10th moon of year three, Hann Xin and Zhang Er marched east to Jingxing to attack Zhao, killing Dai's king Chen Yu, and capturing Zhao's king Zhao Xie. Changshan and Dai prefectures were established. On the 30th day of that moon, there was a solar eclipse. On the 29th day of the 11th moon, there was a solar eclipse.

Sui He successfully persuaded Tattooed Bu to rebel against the Chu. Chu sent Xiang Sheng and Long Qie to attack him, and

【原文】

随何既说黥布，布起兵攻楚。楚使项声、龙且攻布，布战不胜。十二月，布与随何间行归汉。汉王分之兵，与俱收兵至成皋。

项羽数侵夺汉甬道，汉军乏食，与郦食其谋桡楚权。食其欲立六国后以树党，汉王刻印，将遣食其立之。以问张良，良发八难。汉王辍饭吐哺，曰："竖儒几败乃公事！"令趋销印。又问陈平，乃从其计，与平黄金四万斤，以间疏楚君臣。

夏四月，项羽围汉荥阳，汉王请和，割荥阳以西者为汉。亚父劝项羽急攻荥阳，汉王患之。陈平反间既行，羽果疑亚父，亚父大怒而去，发病死。

五月，将军纪信曰："事急矣！臣请诳楚，可以间出。"于是陈平夜出女子东门二千馀人，楚因四面击之。纪信乃乘王车，黄屋左纛，曰："食尽，汉王降楚。"楚皆呼万岁，之城东观，以故汉王得

【今译】

随何劝英布成功，英布起兵攻楚。楚派项声、龙且进攻英布，英布战败。十二月，英布与随何经小道归汉。汉王分给他兵卒，与他一同收集散兵到了成皋。

项羽多次侵夺汉的粮道，汉军缺粮，汉王与郦食其谋划削弱楚的力量。食其主张立六国后裔为王，以树立盟军，汉王已刻了玺印，要派食其去封王。他又问张良，张良提出八条反对意见。汉王吐出口中的饭，说："臭书生几乎坏了老子的大事！"下令赶快销毁玺印。又问陈平，便听从他的计策，交给他黄金四万斤，用来离间楚君臣。

夏四月，项羽包围汉王于荥阳，汉王请和，割荥阳以西的土地属汉。范增劝项羽尽快攻击荥阳，汉王十分忧虑。陈平反间计已经奏效，项羽果然怀疑范增。范增大怒而去，发病死于途中。

五月，将军纪信说："事情紧急！臣请求去欺骗楚军，君王可以寻机出走。"于是陈平乘夜从东门放出二千多女子，楚军四面攻击。纪信便乘上王车，黄缯车盖，左竖羽幢，说："军粮吃光了，汉王降楚。"楚兵皆呼万岁，都到城东观看，汉王乘机与数十骑出西门逃

defeated him. In the 12th moon, Bu and Sui He returned by back roads to Han. The King of Han allocated troops to Bu, and together they gathered stray soldiers at Chenggao.

Xiang Yu made repeated incursions on the Han army's food channels, creating a food shortage among their troops. The King of Han and Li Yiji planned to weaken Chu's strength. Yiji proposed establishing the descendants of the former six kingdoms as kings, so as to make military allies of them. The King had had the official seals engraved, ready to send Yiji to confer them, before asking Zhang Liang for his view. Zhang raised a string of objections. The King of Han spat out the rice in his mouth, saying: "That naive bookworm almost destroyed our cause!" He ordered the immediate destruction of the seals. He then accepted advice from Chen Ping, giving him 40,000 catties of gold, which he used to drive a wedge between Chu's lord and his court officials .

In the fourth moon, Xiang Yu besieged the King of Han at Xingyang, who sued for peace, suggesting demarcating the land west of Xingyang as Han territory. Fan Zeng advised Xiang Yu to lose no time in attacking Xingyang. The King of Han was greatly worried. However, Chen Ping's stratagem of sowing discord had been so effective that Xiang Yu really suspected Fan Zeng, who got furious and rushed away, but he fell ill and died on the way.

In the fifth moon, General Ji Xin said: "Things are critical! Your servant requests to deceive the Chu, so the King can slip away." Chen Ping then released by night over 2,000 women from the east gate, and Chu soldiers attacked them from every direction. Then Ji Xin boarded the royal chariot, with its yellow silk canopy and upright plume on the leftside, saying: "Our food is exhausted. The king submits to the Chu." The Chu soldiers all cheered, dashing to the east side to watch, thereby allowing the King of Han to escape via the unguarded west gate, accompanied by dozens of horsemen. He left Censor-in-Chief Zhou Ke, Wei Bao, and Mr. Zong in charge

【原文】

与数十骑出西门遁。令御史大夫周苛、魏豹、枞公守荥阳。羽见纪信，问："汉王安在？"曰："已出去矣。"羽烧杀信。而周苛、枞公相谓曰："反国之王，难与守城。"因杀魏豹。

汉王出荥阳，至成皋。自成皋入关，收兵欲复东。辕生说汉王曰："汉与楚相距荥阳数岁，汉常困。愿君王出武关，项王必引兵南走，王深壁，令荥阳成皋间且得休息。使韩信等得辑河北赵地，连燕齐，君王乃复走荥阳。如此，则楚所备者多，力分。汉得休息，复与之战，破之必矣。"汉王从其计，出军宛叶间，与黥布行收兵。

羽闻汉王在宛，果引兵南，汉王坚壁不与战。是月，彭越渡睢，与项声、薛公战下邳，破杀薛公。羽使终公守成皋，而自东击彭越。汉王引兵北，击破终公，复军成皋。六月，羽已破走彭越，闻汉复军

【今译】

遁。让御史大夫周苛、魏豹、枞公守荥阳。项羽见纪信，问："汉王在何处？"回答说："已经出城走了。"项羽烧死纪信。周苛、枞公相互商量说："背叛过汉王的魏王赵豹，很难与他同守城池。"于是就杀死魏豹。

汉王逃出荥阳，到成皋。从成皋入关，想招兵再东进。辕生劝汉王说："汉与楚相持荥阳多年，汉常常困迫。希望君王出武关，项王必引兵南去，王深挖濠沟高筑壁垒，坚守不出战，让荥阳、成皋间暂且得到休息。韩信等要是平定了河北赵地，联合燕、齐，君王就再去荥阳。这样，楚所防备的地方就增多，兵力分散。汉得到休息，再与之交战，必定败楚。"汉王听从此计，出军宛、叶之间，与英布一面行军一面招兵扩军。

项羽听说汉王在宛，果然引兵向南，汉王坚壁不交战。这月，彭越渡睢水，与项声、薛公在下邳交战，破杀薛公。项羽派终公守成皋，亲自东击彭越。汉王带兵北上，击破终公军，再次驻军成皋。六月，项羽已经击破并赶走彭越军，听说汉又占领成皋，便引兵向西攻

of Xingyang. When Xiang Yu saw Ji Xin, he asked: "Where is your King?" Ji said: "Gone from here." Xiang Yu had him burned to death. Meanwhile Zhou Ke discussed with Mr. Zong: "Wei Bao, who betrayed our Han state can hardly guard the city with us." So they killed him.

When the King of Han escaped from Xingyang, he went into the Pass at Chenggao, intent on recruiting soldiers and then marching east again. Master Yuan advised him: "There has been stalemate between Han and Chu at Xingyang for many years, and Han is often hard pressed. My advice is that you go out from Wuguan Pass, which would make King Xiang lead his troops south. Then you dig deep trenches and build up high ramparts, defending it stoutly without making sorties, so that the area between Xingyang and Chenggao can remain in peace for a while. If Hann Xin and others subjugate the area of Zhao north of the River, in collaboration with Yan and Qi, then you could return to Xingyang. This way, there will be more places where Chu is on the defensive, which would fragment their forces. Han would be able to recuperate, before reopening the fight with Chu, which, rested, we would certainly win." The King of Han took this advice, and marched between Wan and She, marching with Tattooed Bu whilst recruiting to expand his army.

When Xiang Yu heard that the King was in the Wan area, he did lead his troops south, but the King strengthened his defenses, not engaging in battle. This month, Peng Yue crossed Sui River, and fought Xiang Sheng and Magistrate Xue at Xiapi, defeating and killing the latter. Xiang Yu assigned the defense of Chenggao to Magistrate Zhong, whilst attacking Peng Yue in the east himself. The King of Han marched north, smashing Zhong and garrisoning once more in Chenggao. In the sixth moon, Xiang Yu had broken and driven off Peng Yue's troops, and when he heard of Han stationing at Chenggao again he led his troops westward to invade Xingyang. There Zhou Ke was taken alive and Xiang Yu made him an offer: "Be

【原文】

成皋，乃引兵西拔荥阳城，生得周苛。羽谓苛："为我将，以公为上将军，封三万户。"周苛骂曰："若不趋降汉，今为虏矣！若非汉王敌也。"羽亨周苛，并杀枞公，而虏韩王信，遂围成皋。汉王跳，独与滕公共车出成皋玉门，北渡河，宿小脩武。自称使者，晨驰入张耳、韩信壁，而夺之军。乃使张耳北收兵赵地。

秋七月，有星孛于大角。汉王得韩信军，复大振。八月，临河南乡，军小脩武，欲复战。郎中郑忠说止汉王，高垒深堑勿战。汉王听其计，使卢绾、刘贾将卒二万人，骑数百，渡白马津入楚地，佐彭越烧楚积聚，复击破楚军燕郭西，攻下睢阳、外黄十七城。九月，羽谓海春侯大司马曹咎曰："谨守成皋。即汉王欲挑战，慎勿与战，勿令得东而已。我十五日必定梁地，复从将军。"羽引兵东击彭越。

汉王使郦食其说齐王田广，罢守兵与汉和。

【今译】

取荥阳城，生擒周苛。项羽对周苛说："当我的将，让你任上将军，封三万户。"周苛骂道："你不赶快降汉，今天就成俘虏了！你不是汉王对手。"项羽烹杀周苛，同时杀死枞公，又俘韩王韩信，接着包围成皋。汉王逃走，只与滕公同车出成皋玉门，北渡黄河，宿于小修武邑。自称使者，早晨驰入张耳、韩信壁垒，夺得了他们的军队。就派张耳北去赵地招兵。

秋七月，在大角星区出现彗星。汉王得到韩信军，又大振军威。八月，临黄河南向，驻扎小修武，想再战。郎中郑忠劝止汉王，高垒深堑，不要去交战。汉王听从此计，派卢绾、刘贾率军二万人，骑兵数百，渡白马津进入楚地，帮助彭越烧楚军粮，在燕县城西再次击败楚军，攻下睢阳、外黄十七城。九月，项羽对海春侯大司马曹咎说："谨守成皋。即使汉王要挑战，也要谨慎守城，不要交战，不让汉东进就可以了。我十五天必平定梁地，再会合将军。"项羽引兵东击彭越。

汉王派郦食其劝齐王田广，撤去防守士兵，与汉和好。

my general. I will make your honor Superior General, with a fief of 30,000 households." But Zhou Ke cursed him: "If you do not hurry and submit to Han, you will be captured today! You are no match for the the King of Han." In response, Xiang Yu had Zhou Ke boiled alive, killed Mr. Zong, and took King Hann Xin prisoner. Then he surrounded Chenggao. The King fled out of Chenggao's north gate, with just the Magistrate of Teng on the same chariot. He crossed the Yellow River northward, and stationed at Little Xiuwu. In the guise of a messenger, he galloped into the strongholds of Zhang Er and Hann Xin in the early morning, and snatched their troops. He sent Zhang Er north to recruit in Zhao.

In the seventh moon, a comet appeared over the Arcturus constellation. The King of Han took over Hann Xin's troops, thereby boosting his military strength. In the eighth moon, he marched south toward the Yellow River, and stationed at Little Xiuwu, minded to fight another battle. Attendant Zheng Zhong dissuaded him, urging him to avoid battle but to dig in behind high walls and deep trenches. The King followed his advice, and sent Lu Wan and Liu Jia with 20,000 infantry, plus hundreds of cavalry, across White Horse Ford into Chu, to help Peng Yue burn the Chu grain stores. They inflicted further defeats on the Chu army west of the walls of Yan, capturing 17 towns in all, including Suiyang and Waihuang. In the ninth moon, Xiang Yu told Cao Jiu, Marquis of Haichun and Commander-in-Chief: "Defend Chenggao carefully. Even if the King of Han makes a challenge, be cautious, do not engage. Just do not allow him to move east. I will recover the Liang area in 15 days, and then I will join you." He led his troops to attack Peng Yue in the east.

The King of Han sent Li Yiji to persuade the King of Qi Tian Guang into withdrawing the defending soldiers, and to be on good terms with Han.

In the 10th moon of year four, Hann Xin used Kuai Tong's stratagem and raided Qi. The King of Qi boiled Li Yiji alive and fled

【原文】

四年冬十月，韩信用蒯通计，袭破齐。齐王亨郦生，东走高密。项羽闻韩信破齐，且欲击楚，使龙且救齐。

汉果数挑成皋战，楚军不出，使人辱之数日，大司马咎怒，渡兵汜水。士卒半渡，汉击之，大破楚军，尽得楚国金玉货赂。大司马咎、长史欣皆自刭汜水上。汉王引兵渡河，复取成皋，军广武，就敖仓食。

羽下梁地十馀城，闻海春侯破，乃引兵还。汉军方围钟离眛于荥阳东，闻羽至，尽走险阻。羽亦军广武，与汉相守。丁壮苦军旅，老弱罢转饷。汉王、羽相与临广武之间而语。羽欲与汉王独身挑战，汉王数羽曰："吾始与羽俱受命怀王，曰先定关中者王之。羽负约，王我于蜀汉，罪一也。羽矫杀卿子冠军，自尊，罪二也。羽当以救赵还报，而擅劫诸侯兵入关，罪三也。怀王约入秦无暴掠，羽烧秦宫室，掘始皇帝冢，收私其财，罪四也。又强杀秦降王子婴，罪五也。诈坑

【今译】

四年冬十月，韩信用蒯通之计，袭破齐。齐王烹杀郦食其，东走高密。项羽听说韩信破齐，而且还想击楚，就派龙且救齐。

汉军果然多次在成皋挑战，楚军不出战。汉派人辱骂数日，楚大司马曹咎大怒，就率兵渡汜水。士兵半渡，汉军发起攻击，大破楚军，尽获楚国金玉宝货。大司马曹咎、长史司马欣都自杀在汜水上。汉王引兵渡河，再取成皋，驻军广武，用敖仓粮供军。

项羽攻下梁地十余城，得知海春侯军败的消息，便引兵返回。汉军正包围钟离眛于荥阳东，闻听项羽到，都转占险要地区。项羽也驻军广武，与汉军相持。壮丁苦于军事征战，老弱疲于运送军饷。汉王、项羽在广武之间对话。项羽想与汉王单身交战，汉王责备项羽说："我与你当初同时受命怀王，说先定关中者称王关中。你违约，让我去蜀汉为王，此为罪一。你假藉王命杀死卿子冠军宋义，自立为上将军，此为罪二。你应当救赵后还报覆命，却擅自胁迫诸侯兵入关，此为罪三。怀王约定入关不得施暴掠抢，你烧秦宫室，掘始皇帝墓，私吞所取财物，此为罪四。又强杀秦降王子婴，此为罪五。在新

east to Gaomi. When Xiang Yu heard that Hann Xin had conquered Qi, and wanted to attack Chu, he sent Long Qie to help Qi.

Sure enough, at Chenggao Han did try repeatedly to provoke the Chu army, but they did not take the bait until, after being harangued and insulted for days by Han messengers, Cao Jiu became furious and led Chu troops across Sishui River. With half their number across, Han attacked, destroying the Chu army, and looting all the Chu's treasures and goods. Cao Jiu and Secretary General Sima Xin cut their own throats in the river. The King of Han led his victorious troops across the river, and retook Chenggao. They garrisoned in Guangwu Mountains, supplied from the Aocang grain store.

Xiang Yu had taken a dozen towns in Liang, but he led his troops back at the news of Marquis of Haichun's military debacle. Han was surrounding Zhongli Mo east of Xingyang, and moved to high ground when they heard that Xiang Yu was coming. Xiang Yu also camped in Guangwu in a stand-off with Han. Young soldiers suffered from the military campaigns; the elderly and weak struggled to transport their pay. The King of Han had a dialogue across Guangwu with Xiang Yu, who suggested they fight in single combat. The King berated him: "Both you and I received orders from King Huai of Chu that the first person to conquer Guanzhong would be its king. But you reneged on that, and made me king in Shu and Han; this is your first crime. You killed Song Yi, the General of Generals under the guise of royal order, making yourself Superior General; this is crime two. You should have reported back after saving Zhao, but you forced the army of vassal kings inside the Pass without authorization; this is crime three. King Huai of Chu made a covenant that prohibited atrocities or looting after entering Qin, but you burnt the Qin palaces, and dug into the tomb of Emperor Shihuang, misappropriating Qin property; this is crime four. You insisted on killing Ziying, the toppled King of Qin; this is crime five. In Xin'an, you entrapped and buried alive 200,000 Qin

【原文】

秦子弟新安二十万，王其将，罪六也。皆王诸将善地，而徙逐故主，令臣下争畔逆，罪七也。出逐义帝彭城，自都之，夺韩王地，并王梁楚，多自与，罪八也。使人阴杀义帝江南，罪九也。夫为人臣而杀其主，杀其已降，为政不平，主约不信，天下所不容，大逆无道，罪十也。吾以义兵从诸侯诛残贼，使刑馀罪人击公，何苦乃与公挑战！”羽大怒，伏弩射中汉王。汉王伤胸，乃扪足曰：“虏中吾指！”汉王病创卧，张良强请汉王起行劳军，以安士卒，毋令楚乘胜。汉王出行军，疾甚，因驰入成皋。

十一月，韩信与灌婴击破楚军，杀楚将龙且，追至城阳，虏齐王广。齐相田横自立为齐王，奔彭越。汉立张耳为赵王。

汉王疾瘉，西入关，至栎阳，存问父老，置酒。枭故塞王欣头栎阳市。留四日，复如军，军广武。关中兵益出，而彭越、田横居梁地，往来苦楚兵，绝其粮食。

【今译】

安县欺诈坑杀秦子弟二十万，封其将为王，此为罪六。你的部将皆封在肥美之地，却赶走原来的君王，让臣下争权叛主，此为罪七。从彭城赶走义帝，你自为都城；夺韩王地，兼并梁、楚，多留给自己，此为罪八。派人暗杀义帝于江南，此为罪九。为人臣而杀其君主，杀已降之人，执政不平和，君主订约而不信守，天下所不容，大逆不道，此为罪十。我率正义之师跟诸侯一同诛灭凶残逆贼，让刑余的罪人打击你就行了，老子何必与你挑战！”项羽大怒，埋伏的弩射中汉王。汉王伤胸，却去摸脚说：“奴虏射中了我的脚趾！”汉王受伤卧床，张良强请汉王起身去慰劳士兵，以安定军心，不让楚军乘机取胜。汉王出来巡行军中，病重，随即驰入成皋。

十一月，韩信与灌婴击破楚军，杀楚将龙且，追击败军到城阳，俘虏齐王田广。齐相田横自立为齐王，逃奔彭越。汉王立张耳为赵王。

汉王伤口痊愈，西行入关，到栎阳，慰问父老，设酒款待。在栎阳街市挂起原塞王司马欣的头。留住四日，又回到军中，驻广武。关中为汉增加兵员，而彭越、田横占据梁地，来往骚扰楚军，断绝楚军粮饷补给。

descendants, and made kings of their former generals; this is crime six. You gave your generals fiefs in fertile areas, but you drove away the original kings, making your subject compete rebelliously; this is crime seven. You drove Emperor Yi away from Pengcheng, making it your own capital; you snatched the King of Hann's territory, and annexed Liang and Chu, keeping most of it for yourself; this is crime eight. You sent men to assassinate Emperor Yi south of the Yangtze; this is crime nine. You, a subject, killed your lord, and killed those who had surrendered. You rule without practicing justice, without honoring the imperial covenant, and the empire will not tolerate it. You are treasonous and immoral; this is crime ten. I command the army of righteousness along with the vassal kings to eliminate the cruel usurper. It would be in order simply to let the condemned prisoners strike you down. What need do I have to challenge you to single combat!" Xiang Yu was furious, and a crossbow arrow hit the King of Han in the chest. But he touched his foot, and said: "Son-of-a-bitch shot me in the toe!" The injured King lay in bed, but Zhang Liang urged him up to reward the soldiers as a way of restoring morale, so that Chu could not take advantage. The King came out to patrol the army. Now gravely ill, he rushed to Chenggao.

In the 11th moon, Hann Xin and Guan Ying broke the Chu army, killing its general Long Qie and giving chase as far as Chengyang and capturing the King of Qi Tian Guang. Qi's prime minister Tian Heng made himself King of Qi, and fled to Peng Yue. The King of Han made Zhang Er King of Zhao. The King's wound healed, and he marched westbound inside the Pass, to Liyang. By way of greeting the elders, he prepared a wine reception. The severed head of the former King of Sai, Sima Xin, was dangled in the market of Liyang. After staying four days, he went back to the army in Guangwu. Additional soldiers were dispatched from Guanzhong, and Peng Yue plus Tian Heng occupied Liang, harassing the Chu army to and fro, cutting off its food supplies.

【原文】

韩信已破齐，使人言曰："齐边楚，权轻，不为假王，恐不能安齐。"汉王怒，欲攻之。张良曰："不如因而立之，使自为守。"春二月，遣张良操印，立韩信为齐王。秋七月，立黥布为淮南王。八月，初为算赋。北貉、燕人来致枭骑助汉。汉王下令：军士不幸死者，吏为衣衾棺敛，转送其家。四方归心焉。

项羽自知少助食尽，韩信又进兵击楚，羽患之。汉遣陆贾说羽，请太公，羽弗听。汉复使侯公说羽，羽乃与汉约，中分天下，割鸿沟以西为汉，以东为楚。九月，归太公、吕后，军皆称万岁。乃封侯公为平国君。羽解而东归。汉王欲西归，张良、陈平谏曰："今汉有天下太半，而诸侯皆附，楚兵罢食尽，此天亡之时，不因其几而遂取之，所谓养虎自遗患也。"汉王从之。

——卷一上《高帝纪》第一上

【今译】

韩信已破齐军，派人对汉王说："齐靠近楚，我权威轻，不代理齐王，恐不能安定齐地。"汉王大怒，想伐韩信。张良说："不如就势立韩信为齐王，让他自己坚守一方。"春二月，派张良带上王印，立韩信为齐王。秋七月，立英布为淮南王。八月，开始征收成人丁口税。北貉、燕人赠送勇猛的骑兵助汉。汉王下令：士卒不幸死亡的，官吏给制衣衾棺殓，转送回家。四方民心归附。

项羽自知缺少援助，军粮用尽，韩信又进兵击楚，项羽惧怕起来。汉派了陆贾劝说项羽，请接回太公，项羽不同意。汉又派侯公劝说项羽，项羽才与汉约定，中分天下，割鸿沟以西为汉，以东为楚。九月，送回太公、吕后，汉军齐呼万岁。于是封侯公为平国君。项羽罢军东归。汉王想西归，张良、陈平劝阻说："今汉有天下大半，诸侯又都归附，楚兵疲劳食尽，这是天亡项羽的时候，不乘其危机而消灭之，就是养虎自留祸害。"汉王听从了这一劝告。

Hann Xin, having smashed Qi, sent a messenger saying: "Qi borders on Chu, but I am lightly authorized. I fear I cannot stabilize Qi unless with the status and authority of king." The King of Han was furious, tempted to attack him. But Zhang Liang said: "Why not make him the King of Qi as he wishes, and have him defend it for his own sake?" In the second moon, the King sent Zhang to confer the seal on Hann Xin as King of Qi. In the seventh moon, Tattooed Bu was made King of Huainan. In the eighth moon, Han began to levy suan, a poll tax on adults. People of Beihe and Yan presented intrepid cavalry to help Han. The King decreed: "When soldiers have the misfortune to die, officials shall provide shrouds and coffins and transfer them to their hometown for their burial." Allegiance became universal.

Aware of his own shortage of food and aid, and that Hann Xin was marching on Chu, Xiang Yu became worried. Han sent Lu Jia to persuade him, wanting the return of the King's captured father, but Xiang Yu did not agree.

Han then sent Mr. Hou to negotiate, and agreement was reached to carve the empire in the middle, with lands west of Honggou Canal to belong to Han, and those east of it to Chu. In the ninth moon, the King's father and Empress Lü were returned, and Han soldiers sang out "Long live the King." Mr. Hou was appointed as Lord Pingguo. Xiang Yu withdrew his troops and returned east. The King of Han was about to return west, but Zhang Liang and Chen Ping argued against that course of action: "Han occupies more than half of the empire today, and you have the allegiance of all the vassal kings, while the Chu troops are exhausted and hungry. This is the day destined for Xiang Yu's demise. If we do not take advantage of his crisis to destroy him, it will be like rearing a tiger to court disaster." The King followed this advice.

高帝纪（下）

【原文】

五年冬十月，汉王追项羽至阳夏南止军，与齐王信、魏相国越期会击楚，至固陵，不会。楚击汉军，大破之。汉王复入壁，深堑而守。谓张良曰：“诸侯不从，奈何？”良对曰：“楚兵且破，未有分地，其不至固宜。君王能与共天下，可立致也。齐王信之立，非君王意，信亦不自坚，彭越本定梁地，始君王以魏豹故，拜越为相国。今豹死，越亦望王，而君王不早定。今能取睢阳以北至穀城皆以王彭越，从陈以东傅海与齐王信，信家在楚，其意欲复得故邑。能出捐此地以许两人，使各自为战，则楚易败也。”于是汉王发使使韩信、彭越。至，皆引兵来。

十一月，刘贾入楚地，围寿春。汉亦遣人诱楚大司马周殷。殷畔楚，

【今译】

五年冬十月，汉王追击项羽至阳夏南，停止前进，与齐王韩信、魏相国彭越约定会师击楚，到固陵，未能会师。楚军出击，大破汉军。汉王退回壁垒，深挖堑濠坚守。汉王对张良说：“诸侯不来会师，怎么办？”张良回答说：“楚军将要失败，诸侯没有得到封地，他们不来会师是理所当然的。君王若能与他们共有天下，可立即来会师。齐王韩信之立，并不是君王本意，韩信也感到自己的地位不巩固。彭越本来平定梁地，当初君王因魏豹的缘故，拜彭越为相国。今魏豹已死，彭越也想称王，而君王却没有早日决定封王。今能取睢阳以北到谷城都给彭越封他为王，从陈县以东至沿海地区给齐王韩信，韩信家在楚，他很愿意再得到故乡之地。如能捐弃这些地区封给这两个人，让他们各自为战，那么楚就容易灭亡。”于是汉王派出使臣到韩信、彭越处。使臣一到，果然，韩、彭二将都引兵来会战。

十一月，刘贾进入楚地，包围寿春。汉也派人诱降楚大司马周殷。周殷叛楚，用驻舒之兵对六县进行屠城，率九江兵迎接英布，

Chapter 2

Annals of Emperor Gaodi, Part II

In the 10th moon of year five, the King of Han in pursuit of Xiang Yu halted to the south of Yangxia, and agreed with the King of Qi Hann Xin and Wei's Prime Minister Peng Yue to join forces to attack Chu. But they were unable to join forces at Guling. Chu attacked and destroyed Han troops. The King of Han got back behind high barriers and deep trenches to defend himself. He asked Zhang Liang: "The vassal kings will not follow me. What's to be done?" Zhang replied: "The Chu army is going to fall, but no fiefs have yet been distributed; no wonder they do not come. If the King is able to share the empire, they can be tempted immediately to the rendezvous. Hann Xin was made King of Qi, against your own inclinations, so he feels his status is shaky. Peng Yue settled Liang, but for the sake of Wei Bao, the King made Yue its Prime Minister. With Wei Bao now dead, Peng Yue too wishes to make himself king, but Your Majesty has delayed any decision. Suppose you make Peng Yue king of the lands north of Suiyang up to Gucheng, and allocate the area from Chen to the east coast to the King of Qi Hann Xin. His hometown is in Chu, and he is very keen to get back his homeland. If these areas can be put aside for these two individuals, this will make them fight on their own account, and then it will be easy to break up Chu." So the King sent envoys to Hann Xin and Peng Yue. Sure enough, both generals led their troops to battle on his behalf.

In the 11th moon, Liu Jia entered Chu, and surrounded Shouchun. Han also sent someone to tempt the Chu Commander-in-Chief Zhou Yin into surrender. Zhou Yin betrayed Chu and with his

【原文】

以舒屠六，举九江兵迎黥布，并行屠城父，随刘贾皆会。

十二月，围羽垓下。羽夜闻汉军四面皆楚歌，知尽得楚地，羽与数百骑走，是以兵大败。灌婴追斩羽东城。楚地悉定，独鲁不下，汉王引天下兵欲屠之，为其守节礼义之国，乃持羽头示其父兄，鲁乃降。初，怀王封羽为鲁公，及死，鲁又为之坚守，故以鲁公葬羽于榖城。汉王为发(葬)[丧]，哭临而去。封项伯等四人为列侯，赐姓刘氏。诸民略在楚者皆归之。汉王还至定陶，驰入齐王信壁，夺其军。初项羽所立临江王共敖前死，子尉嗣立为王，不降。遣卢绾、刘贾击虏尉。

春正月，追尊兄伯号曰武哀侯。下令曰："楚地已定，义帝亡后，欲存恤楚众，以定其主。齐王信习楚风俗，更立为楚王，王淮

【今译】

并屠杀城父县，然后跟随刘贾会师。

十二月，项羽被围在垓下。他夜间听到汉军四面皆唱楚歌，知道汉已全部占领楚地，他与数百骑逃走，所以楚军大败。灌婴追击至东城，斩项羽。楚地完全平定，只有鲁地没有攻下。汉王引天下兵打算屠杀鲁城，因为鲁是讲气节守礼义之国，便拿项羽之头让父老兄弟观看，鲁才降汉。当初，怀王封项羽为鲁公，到他死后，鲁人还为他坚守封地，故以鲁公之礼葬项羽于谷城。汉王为他发丧，痛哭离去。汉王封项伯等四人为列侯，赐姓刘。各地百姓被掳掠至楚的都返回故乡。汉王回定陶，驰入齐王韩信军营，夺其军权。当初项羽所封立的临江王共敖已经死去，其子共尉嗣立为王，不降汉。汉王派遣卢绾、刘贾攻打并俘虏了共尉。

春正月，汉王追尊兄刘伯号武哀侯。下令说："楚地已平定，义帝无后继人，我想安抚楚民众，要为他们立一个君主。齐王韩信熟习楚风俗，改立为楚王，封地为淮北，定其都在下邳。魏相国建城侯彭

soldiers stationed in Shu he massacred Liu County, and led Jiujiang soldiers to meet Tattooed Bu. Having put Chengfu to the slaughter, he joined forces with Liu Jia.

In the 12th moon, Xiang Yu was surrounded at Gaixia. Right through the night he could hear Han soldiers on all sides chorusing Chu folk songs, and realized that all of Chu was occupied. He took flight with hundreds of riders, so his army was completely defeated. Guan Ying chased him to Dongcheng, where he decapitated him. Thus, all of Chu was completely subjugated, the sole exception being Lu, which would not surrender. The King of Han brought troops from across the empire, intending to put Lu to the slaughter. However, since Lu was a land of integrity and propriety, they simply took Xiang Yu's head so that the Lu elders and brothers could see it, thus convincing them to surrender to Han. Earlier, King Huai of Chu had made Xiang Yu Magistrate of Lu, and after his death, his people still adhered to his fief. Therefore, Xiang Yu was buried in Gucheng as Magistrate of Lu. The King of Han arranged his funeral, where he led the ceremony weeping and then left. He made Xiang Bo and others adjunct marquises, and bestowed on all four the new surname Liu. The people held in captivity in Chu were returned to their homes. The King of Han went back to Dingtao, marched into the King of Qi Hann Xin's barracks, and appropriated its military strength. Gong Ao, whom Xiang Yu had made King of Linjiang, had died, succeeded by his son Gong Wei, who did not surrender. The King of Han sent Lu Wan and Liu Jia to attack and capture Gong Wei.

In the first moon of the next year, the King posthumously honored his elder brother Liu Bo as Marquis of Wuai.

He decreed: "Chu has been subjugated, but Emperor Yi has no successor. We wish to be solicitous for the people of Chu, and fix upon a king for them. The King of Qi Hann Xin is familiar with Chu customs, so we make him King of Chu, ruling over the north of Huai

【原文】

北，都下邳。魏相国建城侯彭越勤劳魏民，卑下士卒，常以少击众，数破楚军，其以魏故地王之，号曰梁王，都定陶。"又曰："兵不得休八年，万民与苦甚，今天下事毕，其赦天下殊死以下。"

于是诸侯上疏曰："楚王韩信、韩王信、淮南王英布、梁王彭越、故衡山王吴芮、赵王张敖、燕王臧荼昧死再拜言，大王陛下，先时秦为亡道，天下诛之。大王先得秦王，定关中，于天下功最多。存亡定危，救败继绝，以安万民，功盛德厚。又加惠于诸侯王有功者，使得立社稷。地分已定，而位号比拟，亡上下之分，大王功德之著，于后世不宣，昧死再拜上皇帝尊号。"汉王曰："寡人闻帝者，贤者有也，虚言亡实之名，非所取也。今诸侯王皆推高寡人，将何以处之哉？"诸侯王皆曰："大王起于细微，灭乱秦，威动海内。又以辟陋之地，自汉中行威德，诛不义，立有功，平定海内，功臣皆受地食

【今译】

越为魏民勤劳，亲近士卒，经常以少击众，多次击破楚军，应以魏国原来的封地立他为王，号梁王，其都定在定陶。"又说："战争八年不得休止，万民苦难深重，如今天下的战事结束，赦免天下死罪以下的犯人。"

这时诸侯上疏说："楚王韩信、韩王信、淮南王英布、梁王彭越、原衡山王吴芮、赵王张敖、燕王臧荼冒死再拜说，大王陛下：以前秦行无道，天下诸侯起而诛灭它。大王先俘得秦王，平定关中，对天下功劳最多。保存了危亡者，救助了败绝者，安定万民，功德盛大。又加恩惠于诸侯王有功之人，让他们建立封国。封地已经划定，大王与别人的号位相同，无上下之分，大王功德显著，没有宣明后世。冒死再拜献上皇帝尊号。"汉王说："我听说帝是有贤德之人才有的尊号，虚言无实之名号，不可取。今诸侯王都推崇寡人，将怎样处理呢？"诸侯王都说："大王出身地位卑微，诛灭暴乱的秦朝，威势震动海内。又在僻陋之地，从汉中推行威德，诛杀不义之徒，封立

River, with the capital at Xiapi. Wei's Prime Minister Peng Yue, Marquis of Jiancheng, has toiled diligently for the people of Wei and consorted humbly with his soldiers. He would attack superior forces, and, though outnumbered, frequently broke the Chu troops. It is fitting for him to be made king on the Wei's original fief, and called King of Liang, with the capital at Dingtao." He then said: "This war has dragged on without end for eight years, bringing great suffering to the people, and now the events under heaven are concluded, so let there be an amnesty for all prisoners except for capital crimes."

Then the vassal kings presented a petition, saying: "Hann Xin King of Chu, Hann Xin King of Hann, Ying Bu King of Huainan, Peng Yue King of Liang, Wu Rui formerly King of Hengshan, Zhang Ao King of Zhao, and Zang Tu King of Yan, make bold to advise Your Majesty by making repeated obeisance. In former times, Qin ruled with utter disregard for morality, so all under heaven rose to destroy it. The Great King was the first to take prisoner the King of Qin, and subjugate Guanzhong, performing the greatest meritorious deeds under heaven. The King has saved a nation in its time of peril, rescued a lost world, and settled peoples, which is a grand contribution and great virtue. Moreover the benefits have been shared with the meritorious vassal kings, delineating their fiefdoms. But the King has the same title as the rest, with no distinction of superiority and inferiority. The King's achievements are plain to all, but no such proclamation is made to later generations. We make bold to present the respected title of Emperor." The King of Han responded: "I heard that 'Emperor' is the honorable appellation of the virtuous person, but I cannot take an empty word without substance. Now the vassal kings have highly exalted me, but how will we handle it?" They replied: "The King was born humble, but destroyed the violent and unjust Qin, to exercise power and influence within the seas. From the remote and desolate Hanzhong you also spread military virtue. You eliminated the unrighteous,

【原文】

邑，非私之也。大王德施四海，诸侯王不足以道之，居帝位甚实宜，愿大王以幸天下。”汉王曰：“诸侯王幸以为便于天下之民，则可矣。”于是诸侯王及太尉长安侯臣绾等三百人，与博士稷嗣君叔孙通谨择良日二月甲午，上尊号，汉王即皇帝位于汜水之阳。尊王后曰皇后，太子曰皇太子，追尊先媪曰昭灵夫人。

诏曰：“故衡山王吴芮与子二人兄子一人，从百粤之兵，以佐诸侯，诛暴秦，有大功，诸侯立以为王。项羽侵夺之地，谓之番君。其以长沙、豫章、象郡、桂林、南海立番君芮为长沙王。”又曰：“故粤王亡诸世奉粤祀，秦侵夺其地，使其社稷不得血食。诸侯伐秦，亡诸身帅闽中兵以佐灭秦，项羽废而弗立。今以为闽粤王，王闽中地，勿使失职。”

帝乃西都洛阳。夏五月，兵皆罢归家。诏曰：“诸侯子在关中者，复之十二岁，其归者半之。民前或相聚保山泽，不书名数，今天

【今译】

有功之人，平定海内，功臣都有封地食邑，没有私自独占。大王之德施于四海，诸侯王无法与之相比，大王居帝位很符合实际，希望大王君临天下。”汉王说：“各诸侯认为是便于天下之民，那就这样吧。”于是诸侯王及太尉长安侯卢绾等三百人，与博士稷嗣君叔孙通选择吉日，定在二月甲午日，敬上尊号，汉王在汜水之北即皇帝位。尊王后曰皇后，太子曰皇太子，追尊先母曰昭灵夫人。

诏书说：“原衡山王吴芮与子二人、兄子一人，率领百粤之兵帮助诸侯，诛灭暴秦，立有大功，诸侯立他为王。项羽侵夺他的土地，称之为番君。今以长沙、豫章、象郡、桂林、南海五郡立番君吴芮为长沙王。”又说：“原粤王亡诸世代祭祀粤人先祖，秦侵夺其地，使他的社稷再也得不到祭祀。后来诸侯伐秦，亡诸亲率闽中兵帮助灭秦，项羽不立他为王。今立他为闽粤王，以闽中为封地，不要使他失职。”

高皇帝于是西都洛阳。夏五月，士兵都复员回家。高帝下诏说：“诸侯后代在关中的，免赋役十二年，回乡的减一半。以前有的民众

gave fiefs to the deserving, pacified the interior, and endowed the heroes with fiefs, rather than monopolizing everything. The King has practiced virtue across the land, and we vassal kings cannot be compared. So it is in accordance with reality that you take the position of Emperor. We hope His Majesty will rule the empire." This was his reply: "If the vassal kings deem it beneficial for the people, then so be it." Then the vassal kings, Defender-in-Chief Lu Wan Marquis of Chang'an and 300 more, together with Erudite Lord Jisi Shusun Tong, selected an auspicious date, the third day of the second moon in 202 BC. Thcy sincerely recommended the respectful appellation. The King of Han was enthroned as Emperor north of the Sishui River. The Queen was honored as Empress, the Crown Prince as Imperial Prince, and his late mother given the posthumous title of Lady Zhaoling. The Imperial Edict read: "The former King of Hengshan Wu Rui and two sons, and a nephew, led soldiers from various Yue areas to help the vassal kings. He earned great merit in destroying the despotic Qin, so the vassal kings made him king. Xiang Yu encroached upon his land, calling him Lord Bo. Hereby we decree to confer upon Lord Bo Wu Rui the title of King of Changsha, with dominion over Changsha, Yuzhang, Xiang, Guilin, and Nanhai Prefectures. The Imperial Edict also said: "The former King of Yue Wu Zhu for generations worshiped Yue ancestors, but Qin infringed upon their land, so that his altar of land and grain could not be worshiped. Later, the vassal kings rebelled against Qin, and Wu Zhu led Minzhong soldiers to help destroy Qin, but Xiang Yu did not establish him as a king. Hereby we make Wu Zhu King of Min-Yue, ruling over Minzhong. Let him not neglect their care."

Now, as Emperor, he went west to declare Luoyang his capital. In the fifth moon, the soldiers were all demobilized. The Imperial Edict declared: "The descendants of vassal kings remaining in Guanzhong shall be exempt from tax or labor service for 12 years, or for half that period if they return to their homelands. Those who

【原文】

下已定，令各归其县，复故爵田宅，吏以文法教训辨告，勿笞辱。民以饥饿自卖为人奴婢者，皆免为庶人。军吏卒会赦，其亡罪而亡爵及不满大夫者，皆赐爵为大夫。故大夫以上赐爵各一级，其七大夫以上，皆令食邑，非七大夫以下，皆复其身及户，勿事。”又曰：“七大夫、公乘以上，皆高爵也。诸侯子及从军归者，甚多高爵，吾数诏吏先与田宅，及所当求于吏者，亟与。爵或人君，上所尊礼，久立吏前，会不为决，甚亡谓也。异日秦民爵公大夫以上，令丞与亢礼。今吾于爵非轻也，吏独安取此！且法以有功劳行田宅，今小吏未尝从军者多满，而有功者顾不得，背公立私，守尉长吏教训甚不善。其令诸吏善遇高爵，称吾意。且廉问，有不如吾诏者，以重论之。”

【今译】

聚集躲藏在山泽中，没有户籍，今天下已安定，让他们各回原县，恢复原来的爵位田宅，官吏讲解法律条文分辨义理，使百姓明白，不得鞭打羞辱。民众因饥饿自卖为别人的奴婢者，都免为平民。军官士兵遇到大赦，无罪而无爵及虽有爵位但不到大夫的，一律赐给大夫爵位。原有大夫以上爵的各赐爵一级，七大夫以上，都受食邑，不是七大夫以下，都免自身及一户的赋役，不事差役。”又说：“七大夫、公乘以上的，都是高级爵位。诸侯后代及从军回乡的，有很多高爵，我多次下诏官吏先给他们田宅，还有他们向官吏请求应当得到的，要从速办理。爵位高的称人君，都是被天子尊敬礼遇的，有些长时间摆在官吏面前的事，不给解决，真是不足为训。过去秦民爵在公大夫以上，就与县令、丞行平等礼节。今天我对爵位并不轻视，为什么官吏敢这样对待爵位！况且法律规定有功劳的给田宅，今小吏未曾从军者多自满足，而有功者反而得不到，背公立私，郡守、郡尉、县令、县长管教得很不好。今命令官吏们都要很好地对待高爵，让我满意。今后将要察访，有不按我诏书办理的官吏，从重论处。”

went into hiding, gathering in mountains and marshes, without residence registration, shall all go back to their original counties, since the world is pacified today. Let them recover their original titles, fields and houses. Officials shall explain the law to distinguish and make moral principles understandable to the people, but shall not whip or humiliate them. People who sold themselves into slavery because of hunger shall be freed as commoners. Former officers and soldiers in receipt of pardon, those innocent but without a title, and those with a title below grand master level shall be given that title. Those whose original titles were above grand master level shall be upgraded one degree; those above seventh level grand master shall be entitled to fiefs; those below seventh level shall be exempted from tax and labor service for themselves and their own households, with no forced labor service to local offices." It went on, "Titles above seventh level grand master or Public Charioteer are senior titles. Among the returned descendants of vassal kings and the military veterans, there are many senior titles. I have repeatedly ordered the officials to give them priority when allocating fields and houses. If they request the official to give them their entitlement, this shall be speedily expedited. Those with a high title are lords of men, all respected by the Emperor and treated with due courtesy; but that some things remain unsolved by the officials for a long time is far from exemplary. In the past, Qin people with titles higher than that of universal grand master had equal status as magistrate and ceremonial aide. Today if I do not treat the titles lightly, how can officials dare to do so! Furthermore, the law has it to grant fields and houses to the meritorious; but now it is the petty clerks who never served in the army who get satisfaction, and not the meritorious. This is favoring private interest at the expense of public service, and is poor discipline on the part of governors and magistrates or lieutenants. Let it be ordered that the various officials treat the high-title grandees well, to my satisfaction. There will be inspections

【原文】

帝置酒雒阳南宫。上曰："通侯诸将毋敢隐朕，皆言其情。吾所以有天下者何，项氏之所以失天下者何？"高起、王陵对曰："陛下嫚而侮人，项羽仁而敬人，然陛下使人攻城略地，所降下者，因以与之，与天下同利也。项羽妒贤嫉能，有功者害之，贤者疑之，战胜而不与人功，得地而不与人利，此其所以失天下也。"上曰："公知其一，未知其二。夫运筹帷幄之中，决胜千里之外，吾不如子房；填国家，抚百姓，给饷餽，不绝粮道，吾不如萧何；连百万之众，战必胜，攻必取，吾不如韩信。三者皆人杰，吾能用之，此吾所以取天下者也。项羽有一范增而不能用，此所以为我禽也。"群臣说服。

初，田横归彭越。项羽已灭，横惧诛，与宾客亡入海。上恐其久为乱，遣使者赦横，曰："横来，大者王，小者侯；不来，且发兵加诛。"横惧，乘传诣雒阳，未至三十里，自杀。上壮其节，为流涕，发卒二千人，以王礼葬焉。

【今译】

高皇帝设宴于雒阳南宫。他说："通侯各将不要隐瞒我，都要讲实情。我之所以能得天下的原因是什么？项羽之所以失天下的原因是什么？"高起、王陵对答说："陛下轻慢而对人不尊重，项羽仁爱而敬重人。然而陛下派人攻城略地，有所降服，给与赏赐，与将士同享其利。项羽妒贤嫉能，对有功的人妒忌，对贤能的人猜疑，战胜者不记功劳，夺得地盘的不给赏赐，这些就是他失天下的原因。"皇上说："你们知其一，不知其二。运筹帷幄之中，决胜千里之外，我不如张子房；安定国家，安抚百姓，供给粮饷，不绝于道，我不如萧何；统领百万大军，战必胜，攻必取，我不如韩信。三人皆人杰，我能任用，这是我所以取天下的原因。项羽有一个谋士范增而不能用，这是他被我擒获的原因。"群臣心悦诚服。

起初，田横归附彭越。项羽已灭，田横害怕被杀，与宾客逃到海中。皇上恐怕他们日久叛乱，派使者前往赦免田横，并对他说："田横回来，大首领可封王，小首领可封侯；不来，马上发兵诛灭。"田横害怕，乘官车前往雒阳，在离雒阳不到三十里处自杀。皇上很称赞他的气节，为他流泪，派士兵两千人按王礼将他埋葬。

in the future, and those who have not fulfilled my edict shall be severely punished."

At a banquet hosted by the Emperor in the South Palace of Luoyang, he said: "The marquises and generals shall not hide anything from us. All must tell the truth as they see it. Why was I able to win the world? Why did the house of Xiang lose it?" Gao Qi and Wang Ling responded: "Your Majesty did not treat people with due respect, while Xiang Yu was benevolent and respected people. But Your Majesty sent people to conquer territory, and rewarded the attackers with what they seized, thus sharing the benefit more widely. Xiang Yu was envious of people of worth and ability, persecuting the meritorious and suspicious of the intelligent. He did not acknowledge the credit of the victors, or reward the winner of cities, and for this reason he lost the world."

The Emperor said: "You know one aspect, but not the other. I am no match for Zhang Liang, who contrived strategic plans at headquarters to assure victory 1,000 *li* away; I am not as good as Xiao He in stabilizing the state to keep the people content, in ensuring supplies of pay and provisions, and keeping the supply routes open; nor am I as good as Hann Xin in commanding millions of troops, winning every battle, and taking in every attack. These three were all outstanding men, and it is because I could employ them, that I took the world. Xiang Yu had one counselor Fan Zeng, whom he could not use; this is the reason that he was captured by me." The ministers were convinced totally.

Initially, Tian Heng had showed allegiance to Peng Yue. When Xiang Yu was eliminated, Tian Heng feared this meant death for him, and fled into the sea along with his entourage. The Emperor, suspecting they would rebel in the long run, sent a messenger to pardon Tian Heng, and said: "If Tian Heng comes back, the great leader can be king, and the lesser one a marquis; otherwise, I will immediately send troops to wipe you out." Tian Heng feared, and

【原文】

戍卒娄敬求见，说上曰："陛下取天下与周异，而都雒阳，不便，不如入关，据秦之固。"上以问张良，良因劝上。是日，车驾西都长安。拜娄敬为奉春君，赐姓刘氏。六月壬辰，大赦天下。

秋七月，燕王臧荼反，上自将征之。九月，虏荼。诏诸侯王视有功者立以为燕王。荆王臣信等十人皆曰："太尉长安侯卢绾功最多，请立以为燕王。"使丞相哙将兵平代地。

利幾反，上自击破之。利幾者，项羽将。羽败，利幾为陈令，降，上侯之颍川。上至雒阳，举通侯籍召之，而利幾恐，反。

后九月，徙诸侯子关中。治长乐宫。

六年冬十月，令天下县邑城。

【今译】

戍卒娄敬求见皇上，劝皇上说："陛下夺取天下与周朝不同，却建都洛阳，不合适，不如入关，占据旧秦的险固地区。"皇上问张良，张良也趁机劝说皇上。当日，皇上起驾西行建都长安。拜娄敬为奉春君，赐姓刘。六月二十九日，大赦天下。

秋七月，燕王臧荼反叛，皇上亲自率兵征讨。九月，俘虏臧荼。下诏征询诸侯王选有功者立为燕王。荆王臣信等十人都说："太尉长安侯卢绾功劳最多，请立为燕王。"派丞相樊哙率兵平定代地。

利幾反，皇上亲自率兵击破叛军。利幾原是项羽部将。项羽败时，利幾任陈县令，降汉，封颍川侯。皇上到洛阳，按通侯名册召见，利幾恐惧，因此反叛。

闰九月，调关东青年到关中。修建长乐宫。

六年冬十月，皇上命天下的县邑都筑城墙。

took the official carriage to Luoyang, but committed suicide less than 30 *li* away from the capital. The Emperor praised his integrity, shed tears for him, sent 2,000 troops and buried him according to the rites of a king.

Frontier soldier Lou Jing asked for an audience, and persuaded the Emperor: "Your Majesty won the world in a different way than the Zhou dynasty, but took the same capital - Luoyang. But Luoyang is unsuitable; it would be better to relocate inside the Hangu Pass, occupying Qin's solid impregnable stronghold." The Emperor asked Zhang Liang, who also took the opportunity to urge this course of action. That very day, the Emperor moved west to the capital Chang'an. He named Lou Jing as Lord Fengchun, bestowing the surname Liu. On the third day of the sixth moon, he declared amnesty.

In the seventh moon, King of Yan Zang Tu rebelled, and the Emperor himself led troops against him, capturing the rebel in the ninth moon. He decreed that the vassal kings should recommend a meritorious person to become the King of Yan. King Liu Jia and 10 others said: "Defender-in-Chief and Marquis of Chang'an Lu Wan is most meritorious, and we request he be made the King of Yan." Prime Minister Fan Kuai was sent to subjugate the area of Dai.

When Li Ji, a former general under Xiang Yu, rebelled, the Emperor personally routed the rebels. When Xiang Yu was defeated, Li was the county magistrate of Chen, but when he submitted to Han, the Emperor made him Marquis of Yingchuan. When the Emperor moved to Luoyang, he summoned him under the marquis register, but Li feared, and rebelled.

In the intercalary ninth moon, the youth of the vassal kings were transferred to Guanzhong. Construction of Changle Palace was completed.

In the 10th moon of year six of his reign, the Emperor Gaozu ordered the building of defensive walls around counties and towns

【原文】

人告楚王信谋反，上问左右，左右争欲击之。用陈平计，乃伪游云梦。十二月，会诸侯于陈，楚王信迎谒，因执之。诏曰："天下既安，豪桀有功者封侯，新立，未能尽图其功。身居军九年，或未习法令，或以其故犯法，大者死刑，吾甚怜之。其赦天下。"田肯贺上曰："甚善，陛下得韩信，又治秦中。秦，形胜之国也，带河阻山，县隔千里，持戟百万，秦得百二焉。地势便利，其以下兵于诸侯，譬犹居高屋之上建瓴水也。夫齐，东有琅邪、即墨之饶，南有泰山之固，西有浊河之限，北有勃海之利。地方二千里，持戟百万，县隔千里之外，齐得十二焉。此东西秦也。非亲子弟，莫可使王齐者。"上曰："善。"赐金五百斤。上还至雒阳，赦韩信，封为淮阴侯。

甲申，始剖符封功臣曹参等为通侯。诏曰："齐，古之建国也，

【今译】

有人告楚王韩信谋反，皇上问左右的人，左右的人争相请求去攻击韩信。皇上用陈平之计，伪装到云梦巡游。十二月，在陈县会见诸侯，楚王韩信迎接拜见皇上，被武士乘机捆绑起来。下诏说："天下已经安定，豪杰有功者封为侯，因新当皇帝，还没有来得及把有功的人员都考虑进去。在军队十九年，有的没有学过法令，有的犯了法，罪大的判了死刑，我很怜悯。今赦免天下罪人。"田肯祝贺皇上说："事情办得很好，陛下抓了韩信，又建都关中。秦地，是以形势之利取胜之地，山河险阻，与诸侯相隔千里，如用百万士卒来攻，秦只用百分之二的兵力就能抵御。地势便利，如向关东发兵对付诸侯，就像在高屋之上用瓶子倒水。齐国，东有琅邪、即墨之丰富资源，南有泰山之险固，西有浊河阻隔，北有渤海之利。地方二千里，如有百万士卒来攻，相隔在千里之外，齐只用十分之二的兵力就能抵御。这就是东西两个秦国。如果不是皇上的亲子弟，不可在齐为王。"皇上说："很好。"赐黄金五百斤。皇上还至洛阳，赦免韩信，封为淮阴侯。

二十八日，开始剖符封功臣曹参等为通侯。下诏说："齐，古代

throughout the realm. Someone reported that the King of Chu Hann Xin was planning to rebel, and when the Emperor asked his courtiers, they vied with each other to attack Hann. The Emperor, acting on Chen Ping's stratagem, pretended to inspect Yunmeng. In the 12th moon, he met with the vassal kings at Chen, and when Hann Xin came to kowtow, he was grabbed and tied up. An edict was issued: "Peace has been restored to the land, and the meritorious gallants have been made marquises. Newly established, I have not been able to consider all those with military merits. Nine years in the army, and some people have not learned the law, and some have broken it, sometimes committing a major crime punishable by death. But I am merciful. Let there be a general amnesty." Tian Ken congratulated him: "Your Majesty has made a wise decision, You have apprehended Hann Xin, and now rule from Qin's Guanzhong. The land of Qin is favored by its terrain, a land of mountains and rivers forming natural barriers, and keeping the vassal kings off a thousand *li* away. If even a million soldiers were to attack, they could be quelled using just 20,000 of the Qin troops. Our terrain is advantageous, so that if we send troops against the vassal kings, it will be like pouring water off a steep roof – sweeping down irresistibly from a commanding height. As for Qi, it is surrounded in the east by the rich resources of Langya and Jimo, in the south by the bastion of Mount Tai, in the west by the barrier of the turbid Yellow River, and in the north by the boon of the Bohai Sea. Its area is 2,000 *li* square. If attacked with a million soldiers, it would need just 20 percent of Qi troops to resist, since it is over a thousand *li* from here. This is something like the eastern and western states of Qin. Nobody can be made king in Qin if not the Emperor's siblings or children." The Emperor said: "I approve," and gifted him 500 catties of gold. The Emperor returned to Luoyang, and pardoned Hann Xin, making him Marquis of Huaiyin.

On the 28th day, the Emperor began to split the tallies of

【原文】

今为郡县，其复以为诸侯。将军刘贾数有大功，及择宽惠修絜者，王齐、荆地。”春正月丙午，韩王信等奏请以故东阳郡、鄣郡、吴郡五十三县立刘贾为荆王，以砀郡、薛郡、郯郡三十六县立弟文信君交为楚王。壬子，以云中、雁门、代郡五十三县立兄宜信侯喜为代王，以胶东、胶西、临淄、济北、博阳、城阳郡七十三县立子肥为齐王，以太原郡三十一县为韩国，徙韩王信都晋阳。

上已封大功臣(三)[二]十馀人，其馀争功，未得行封。上居南宫，从復道上见诸将往往耦语，以问张良。良曰：“陛下与此属共取天下，今已为天子，而所封皆故人所爱，所诛皆平生仇怨。今军吏计功，以天下为不足用遍封，而恐以过失及诛，故相聚谋反耳。”上曰：“为之奈何？”良曰：“取上素所不快，计群臣所共知最甚者一

【今译】

建立了国家，今为郡县，应恢复为诸侯国。将军刘贾多次立大功，还要选择性情宽厚品德纯洁的，封在齐、荆地为王。”春正月十三日，韩王信等奏请把原东阳郡、鄣郡、吴郡五十三县封给刘贾为荆王，把砀郡、薛郡、郯郡三十六县封给弟文信君刘交为楚王。十九日，把云中、雁门、代郡五十三县封给兄宜信侯刘喜为代王，把胶东、胶西、临淄、济北、博阳、城阳郡七十三县封给长子刘肥为齐王，把太原郡三十一县划为韩国，迁徙韩王信的国都至晋阳。

皇上已封大功臣二十余人，其余的因争功，未能进行封赏。皇上住在南宫，从复道经过，常常看到诸将三三两两在一起小声议论，就询问张良。张良说：“陛下与这些人同取天下，今陛下已为天子，而已经封赏的都是老朋友和所爱之人，所杀的都是平生有仇有怨的人。今天军吏计算军功，认为天下土地少，不足以人人都封侯，又恐怕因过被杀，因此相聚商议谋反。”皇上说：“这事怎么办？”张良说：“选皇上向来不喜欢的，估计群臣都知道最严重的一人，先封他以示

authority, assigning Cao Can and other meritorious courtiers to the ranks of marquises or grandees of the highest order. An edict was issued saying: "Of old, Qi used to be a State in its own right, but now it is a collection of counties and prefectures. It should be restored as a princedom. General Liu Jia repeatedly rendered outstanding service, and we will also select people of generous nature and moral purity to be kings in Qi and Jing."

On the 13th day of the first moon next spring, Hann Xin King of Hann and others petitioned as follows: that 53 counties in the original Dongyang, Zhang, and Wu prefectures be given over to Liu Jia, as King of Jing; that a fiefdom of 36 counties in Dang, Xue and Tan prefectures be given to Hann's younger brother Lord of Wenxin, Liu Jiao as the King of Chu. On the 19th day, they made his elder brother Liu Xi the Marquis of Yixin the King of Dai, with a fiefdom of 53 counties in Yunzhong, Yanmen, and Dai prefectures; his son Liu Fei became King of Qi, governing 73 counties in Jiaodong, Jiaoxi, Linzi, Jibei, Boyang, and Chengyang prefectures; 31 counties of Taiyuan Prefecture were assigned to Hann, moving the capital to Jinyang.

The Emperor had given fiefdoms to over 20 of the meritorious, but had held off the rest due to the mad contention for reward. The Emperor lived in the South Palace, and from the upper passage, he often saw the generals whispering together, so he asked Zhang Liang. Zhang said: "Your Majesty won the empire with these people. But now that you have become Emperor, you have given fiefdoms to your old friends and loved ones, whereas those you killed are those you bore a grudge against in your life. Now the military clerks have calculated the martial merits, and find that there is not enough land in the whole empire to give fiefs to everyone, and the generals fear they may be put to death because of faults, so they gather together to discuss rebellion." The Emperor said: "What is to be done about it?" Zhang's reply was: "Choose one for whom your dislike is known to

【原文】

人，先封以示群臣。”三月，上置酒，封雍齿，因趣丞相急定功行封。罢酒，群臣皆喜，曰：“雍齿且侯，吾属亡患矣！”

上归栎阳，五日一朝太公。太公家令说太公曰：“天亡二日，土亡二王。皇帝虽子，人主也；太公虽父，人臣也。奈何令人主拜人臣！如此，则威重不行。”后上朝，太公拥彗，迎门却行，上大惊，下扶太公。太公曰：“帝，人主，奈何以我乱天下法！”于是上心善家令言，赐黄金五百斤。夏五月丙午，诏曰：“人之至亲，莫亲于父子，故父有天下传归于子，子有天下尊归于父，此人道之极也。前日天下大乱，兵革并起，万民苦殃，朕亲被坚执锐，自帅士卒，犯危难，平暴乱，立诸侯，偃兵息民，天下大安，此皆太公之教训也。诸王、通侯、将军、群卿、大夫已尊朕为皇帝，而太公未有号。今上尊太公曰太上皇。”

【今译】

意于群臣。”三月，皇上设宴，封雍齿，随即催促丞相尽快确定功劳等次进行封赏。宴后，群臣都很高兴，说：“雍齿尚且封侯，我们就不必发愁了！”

皇上返回栎阳，五天一谒见太公。太公家令劝太公说：“天无二日，土无二王。皇帝虽是你的儿子，却是人主；太公虽是皇上的父亲，却是人臣。怎么能让人主拜人臣！这样，皇上的威权就不能体现。”后来皇上谒见太公，太公握帚，在门口迎接退行，皇上大惊，下车扶太公。太公说：“帝是人主，怎么能因我而乱天下大法！”于是皇上心里称赞家令之言，赐黄金五百斤。夏五月十三日，下诏书说：“人之最亲的人，没有亲过父子的，因此父有天下传归于子，子有天下尊归于父，这是人道的最高原则。过去天下大乱，战火四起，万民遭殃，朕身披铠甲，手执锐器，亲自统率士卒，救护危难，平定暴乱，封立诸侯，停止战争，休养百姓，使天下太平，这都是太公教训的结果。诸王、通侯、将军、群卿、大夫已尊朕为皇帝，而太公没有名号。今敬尊太公为太上皇。”

one and all. Make him the first to receive a fiefdom as a signal to the rest." In the third moon, the emperor hosted a banquet to present a fief to Yong Chi, at which he urged the prime minister to determine others contribution as soon as possible. After the dinner, the courtiers were very pleased, and said: "If even Yong Chi is a marquis, so we do not have to worry about it!"

The Emperor returned to Liyang, and paid homage to his father every five days. The father's butler advised his master: "There is no second sun in the heaven, nor a second sovereign in the land. Although the Emperor is your son, he is the lord of man; although you are the Emperor's father, you are his subject. How can we make the lord kowtow to the subject! This way, his majesty and authority cannot be manifested." After that, when the Emperor came to pay homage, his father simply greeted him at the gate with a broom to sweep the steps, and backed away slowly. This disconcerted the Emperor, who got off his chariot to support his father. His father said: "The Emperor is the lord. How can you disrupt the fundamental law of the world because of me!" So the Emperor thought the words of the butler praiseworthy, and granted him 500 catties of gold. On the 23rd day of the fifth moon, his edict said: "There is no closer relationship than that of father and son. It is the highest principle of humanity that if a father has the world, he passes it on to his son, and if the son has the world he respects his father. In the past there was chaos in the world, with wars everywhere, and the people suffered, so I donned my armor and took up my weapons, personally commanded my troops, braved dangers to put down the tyrannous and rebellious, established vassal kings to stop the war, give the people respite so that peace and harmony might reign; and this is the result of lessons learned from my father. Kings, marquises, generals, courtiers and grand masters have enthroned me as Emperor, but my father does not have a title. Today we will respect this father as Super-Emperor."

【原文】

秋九月，匈奴围韩王信于马邑，信降匈奴。

七年冬十月，上自将击韩王信于铜鞮，斩其将。信亡走匈奴，(与)其将曼丘臣、王黄共立故赵后赵利为王，收信散兵，与匈奴共距汉。上从晋阳连战，乘胜逐北，至楼烦，会大寒，士卒堕指者什二三。遂至平城，为匈奴所围，七日，用陈平秘计得出。使樊哙留定代地。

十二月，上还过赵，不礼赵王。是月，匈奴攻代，代王喜弃国，自归雒阳，赦为合阳侯。辛卯，立子如意为代王。

春，令郎中有罪耐以上，请之。民产子，复勿事二岁。

二月，至长安。萧何治未央宫，立东阙、北阙、前殿、武库、大仓。上见其壮丽，甚怒，谓何曰："天下匈匈，劳苦数岁，成败未可知，是何治宫室过度也！"何曰："天下方未定，故可因以就宫室。

【今译】

秋九月，匈奴在马邑包围韩王信，韩王信降匈奴。

七年冬十月，皇上率军在铜鞮击韩王信，斩其部将。韩王信逃往匈奴，他的部将曼丘臣、王黄共立原赵国之后赵利为王，收韩王信散兵，与匈奴共同抵抗汉军。皇上从晋阳连续作战，乘胜追击至楼烦，遇上大冷天，士卒冻掉手指的有十分之二三。随即到了平城，被匈奴包围七天，用陈平秘计才得解围。派樊哙留下平定代地。

十二月，皇上返回时，经过赵国，不以礼接见赵王。这月，匈奴攻代，代王刘喜弃国逃跑，自回洛阳，皇上赦免他降为合阳侯。二十八日，封儿子如意为代王。

春，令郎中判有耐罪以上的，要先请示。百姓生儿子，免除二年差役。

二月，皇上到长安。萧何建未央宫，正东阙、北阙、前殿、武库、大仓。皇上认为太壮丽了，很生气，对萧何说："天下喧扰不安，劳苦多年，成败尚不可知，为什么建造宫室这样过度奢丽！"萧何说："天下还没有平定，因此就要造宫室。况且天子以四海为家，

In the ninth moon, the Huns surrounded King Hann Xin at Mayi, He surrendered to them.

In the 10th moon of year seven, the Emperor led his army and attacked Hann Xin at Tongdi, and killed his general. Hann Xin fled to the Huns, and his generals Man Qiuchen and Wang Huang set up Zhao Li, a descendant of the former King of Zhao, as king, rallying Hann stragglers, and tried to resist the Han army in collaboration with the Huns. The Emperor fought all the way from Jinyang, and pushed on to Loufan in the flush of victory, but got caught in a cold snap, and two or three out of every ten officers and soldiers lost fingers. Then they retreated to Pingcheng, to be besieged by the Huns for seven days, freeing themselves by means of a secret plan by Chen Ping. Fan Kuai was left behind to conquer Dai.

In the 12th moon, the Emperor returned via Zhao, without paying any courtesy call on its king. This month, the Huns attacked Dai, whose king Liu Xi abandoned it to come back to Luoyang on his own accord, throwing himself on the Emperor's mercy, and being demoted to Marquis of Heyang. On the 11th day of the first moon, the Emperor made his son Liu Ruyi the King of Dai.

In spring, it was decreed that for a gentleman of the interior charged with a crime punishable by removal of whiskers and above, his sentence was to be examined first. People having a new baby son were exempted from two years of labor service.

In the second moon, the Emperor went to Chang'an. Xiao He had built Weiyang Palace, with a watchtower facing due east, a north watchtower, front hall, arsenal, and imperial treasury. Seeing its magnificence, the Emperor exploded to Xiao: "The empire is in turmoil. We have toiled for many years, but who knows whether success or failure will be ours! Why build such a palace of such reckless extravagance!" Xiao said: "Since the world is not yet subjugated, we can thus build palaces. Moreover, the Son

【原文】

且夫天子以四海为家，非令壮丽亡以重威，且亡令后世有以加也。”上说。自栎阳徙都长安。置宗正(宫)[官]以序九族。夏四月，行如雒阳。

八年冬，上东击韩信余寇于东垣。还过赵，赵相贯高等耻上不礼其王，阴谋欲弑上。上欲宿，心动，问：“县名何？”曰：“柏人。”上曰：“柏人者，迫于人也。”去弗宿。

十一月，令士卒从军死者为槥，归其县，县给衣衾棺葬具，祠以少牢，长吏视葬。十二月，行自东垣至。

春三月，行如雒阳。令吏卒从军至平城及守城邑者，皆复终身勿事。爵非公乘以上毋得冠刘氏冠。贾人毋得衣锦绣绮縠絺纻罽，操兵，乘骑马。秋八月，吏有罪未发觉者，赦之。九月，行自雒阳至，淮南王、梁王、赵王、楚王皆从。

【今译】

不壮丽就不能加重声威，只是让后世不要超过这种壮丽就是了。”皇上很高兴。从栎阳迁都长安。设置宗正官以谱序九族。夏四月，前往洛阳。

八年冬，皇上率军在东垣击韩王信的残部。返回时经过赵国，赵相贯高等因为皇上不礼待赵王而感到耻辱，阴谋刺杀皇上。皇上想留宿，心中一动，问该县叫什么名，回答说：“柏人。”皇上说：“柏人者，迫于人也。”于是离开该县。

十一月，下令为从军战死的士卒做小棺，送归本县，县给制衣衾棺椁葬具，用羊和猪祭祀，长吏视葬。十二月，从东垣返回京师。

春三月，前往雒阳。下令让从军去平城的官兵及守城邑的人，都免赋役终身。爵不在公乘以上，不得戴刘氏冠。商人不得穿锦绣绮縠絺纻罽制的衣服、携带兵器、乘车骑马。秋八月，官吏有罪没有发觉的，赦免。九月，从洛阳返回京师，淮南王、梁王、赵王、楚王都跟从而来。

of Heaven has the world as his home, and cannot emphasize his authority without such magnificence, so that future generations should not surpass this magnificence." The Emperor was happy at this and moved the capital from Liyang to Chang'an. The position of Chamberlain for the Imperial Clan was established to examine the genealogy of the imperial clan. In the fourth moon, he inspected Luoyang.

In the winter of year eight of his reign, the Emperor led his troops east to attack the remnants of Hann Xin's army at Dongyuan. He returned via Zhao, where Zhao's prime minister Guan Gao and others felt the humiliation of the Emperor's impolite treatment of their ruler, so they conspired to assassinate the Emperor. The Emperor wanted to lodge here but suddenly felt his heart lurch, and so asked: "What is the name of the county?" And the attendant replied: "Boren." The Emperor said: "Boren means being bothered by someone." He left the county without spending the night there.

In the 11th moon, he decreed that soldiers who died in war be given a small coffin and be returned to their county of origin, which was to provide a quilt and shroud in an outer coffin, together with a sheep and pig sacrifice, and senior officials were to preside over the burial. In the 12th moon, he returned from Dongyuan to the capital.

In the third moon, he went to Luoyang. He decreed that officers and soldiers who were dispatched to military posts in Pingcheng and the town guards would be exempt from corvee labor for life.

Those with titles below that of Public Charioteer were not allowed to wear the caps of the Liu clan. Merchants might not wear beautiful clothes made of embroidery, colored silk, crepe linen, poplin, ramie fabric, or felt. Nor could they carry weapons, ride in carriages or on horseback. In the eighth moon, officials guilty of undetected offenses were pardoned. In the ninth moon, he returned from Luoyang to the capital, followed by the kings of Huainan,

【原文】

九年冬十月，淮南王、梁王、赵王、楚王朝未央宫，置酒前殿。上奉玉卮为太上皇寿，曰：“始大人常以臣亡赖，不能治产业，不如仲力。今某之业所就孰与仲多？”殿上群臣皆称万岁，大笑为乐。

十一月，徙齐楚大族昭氏、屈氏、景氏、怀氏、田氏五姓关中，与利田宅。十二月，行如雒阳。

贯高等谋逆发觉，逮捕高等，并捕赵王敖下狱。诏敢有随王，罪三族。郎中田叔、孟舒等十人自髡钳为王家奴，从王就狱。王实不知其谋。春正月，废赵王敖为宣平侯。徙代王如意为赵王，王赵国。丙寅，前有罪殊死以下，皆赦之。

二月，行自雒阳至。贤赵臣田叔、孟舒等十人，召见与语，汉廷臣无能出其右者。上说，尽拜为郡守、诸侯相。

夏六月乙未晦，日有食之。

十年冬十月，淮南王、燕王、荆王、梁王、楚王、齐王、长沙王来朝。

【今译】

九年冬十月，淮南王、梁王、赵王、楚王在未央宫朝见皇上，设酒宴于前殿。皇上奉玉杯给太上皇祝寿，说：“当初大人常说臣无赖，不能治产业，不如刘仲勤快。今天我所成就的事业和刘仲相比谁的多？”殿上群臣都高呼万岁，大笑为乐。

十一月，迁徙齐楚大族昭氏、屈氏、景氏、怀氏、田氏五姓到关中，给与很好的田宅。十二月，前往雒阳。

贯高等因谋杀皇上事被发觉，被逮捕，并捕赵王张敖下狱。下诏说：敢有跟随赵王到长安的，罪及三族。郎中田叔、孟舒等十人自髡发钳颈扮成赵王家奴，跟随赵王入狱。赵王实在不知贯高谋刺之事。春正月，废赵王张敖为宣平侯。改迁代王如意为赵王，统治赵国。初三，以前有死罪以下的罪犯，都赦免。

二月，皇上从雒阳回到京师。以赵臣田叔、孟舒等十人为贤德之人，召见并与他们谈话，汉廷臣没有能在他们之上的。皇上喜悦，全拜为郡守、诸侯国相。

夏六月乙未晦日，日食。

十年冬十月，淮南王、燕王、荆王、梁王、楚王、齐王、长沙王来长安朝见皇上。

Liang, Zhao, and Chu.

In the tenth moon of Gaozu's year nine, King of Huainan, King of Liang, King of Zhao, and King of Chu paid homage in Weiyang Palace, and a banquet was given in the front hall. The Emperor toasted the Super-Emperor's birthday with a jade wine cup, saying: "In the beginning, you, Sire, always said I was a rascal, who could not own property, unlike the industrious Liu Zhong. Today, who has accomplished more, I or Liu Zhong?" The courtiers in the hall shouted "Long live the Emperor," laughing in amusement.

In the 11th moon, the five large clans of Zhao, Qu, Jing, Huai, and Tian from Chu and Qi were relocated to Guanzhong, provided with good fields and houses. In the 12th moon, he went to Luoyang.

Guan Gao and others were discovered and arrested for plotting high treason, The King of Zhao Zhang Ao was also imprisoned. An edict was issued, saying: "He who dares follow the King of Zhao to Chang'an will face punishment reaching three clans – those of father, mother and wife." Gentlemen of the interior Tian Shu, Meng Shu, and eight others shaved their hair on top and wore cangues as the King of Zhao's slaves, following their king into prison. The king really had not known about Guan Gao's assassination plot. In the first moon, the King of Zhao Zhang Ao was demoted to Marquis of Xuanping. Ruyi King of Dai was moved as the King of Zhao, to rule the kingdom. On the 28th day, convicted criminals were pardoned, excepting for capital offenses.

In the second moon, the Emperor returned to the capital from Luoyang. Zhao's ministers Tian Shu, Meng Shu and eight others were declared virtuous persons, given an audience and the Emperor talked with them; not a courtier at the Han could surpass them. The Emperor was overjoyed, appointed them all as prefectural governors, and vassal state premiers.

In the sixth moon, on the 29th day, there was a solar eclipse.

In the 10th moon of year 10, the kings of Huainan, Yan, Jing,

【原文】

夏五月，太上皇后崩。秋七月癸卯，太上皇崩，葬万年。赦栎阳囚死罪以下。八月，令诸侯王皆立太上皇庙于国都。

九月，代相国陈豨反。上曰："豨尝为吾使，甚有信。代地吾所急，故封豨为列侯，以相国守代，今乃与王黄等劫掠代地！吏民非有罪也，能去豨、黄来归者，皆赦之。"上自东，至邯郸。上喜曰："豨不南据邯郸而阻漳水，吾知其亡能为矣。"赵相周昌奏常山二十五城亡其二十城，请诛守尉。上曰："守尉反乎？"对曰："不。"上曰："是力不足，亡罪。"上令周昌选赵壮士可令将者，白见四人。上嫚骂曰："竖子能为将乎！"四人惭，皆伏地。上封各千户，以为将。左右谏曰："从入蜀汉，伐楚，赏未遍行，今封此，何功？"上曰："非汝所知。陈豨反，赵代地皆豨有。吾以羽檄征

【今译】

夏五月，太上皇后崩。秋七月初十，太上皇崩，葬在万年县。赦免栎阳死罪以下的囚犯。八月，令诸侯王在国都都立太上皇庙。

九月，代相国陈豨反叛。皇上说："陈豨曾作过我的使臣，很讲信用。代地是我重视之地，因此封陈豨为列侯，以相国身份镇守代，今天竟然与王黄等劫掠代地！官吏百姓没有罪，能离开陈豨、王黄来归者，全部赦免。"皇上亲自率军东征，至邯郸。皇上高兴地说："陈豨不南据邯郸而防御漳水，我知他不能有作为。"赵相周昌上奏说：常山二十五城丢失二十城，请杀郡守、郡尉。皇上说："守、尉反了没有？"回答说："没反。"皇上说："是兵力不足，无罪。"皇上下令周昌选赵壮士可以带兵的人，报告天子而后召见了四人。皇上谩骂说："小子能当将军吗！"四人羞惭，全伏在地上。皇上各封千户，任为将军。左右劝阻说："对从军入蜀汉，伐楚的，封赏还没有完，今天封这四人，他们有什么功？"皇上说："不是你所能知道的。陈豨反，赵代地区都被陈豨占有。我曾以羽檄征天下之兵，没

Liang, Chu, Qi and Changsha came to Chang'an for an audience with the Emperor.

In the fifth moon, the Super-Empress died. On the 14th day of the seventh moon, the Super-Emperor also passed away and was buried in Wannian County. The criminals in Liyang were pardoned, apart from those facing a death penalty. In the eighth moon, it was ordered that a temple to the Super-Emperor be built in the capital of every vassal state.

In the ninth moon, Prime Minister Chen Xi of Dai rebelled. The Emperor said: "Chen used to be my go-between, a very persuasive one. Dai is of great importance to me, so I made him an adjunct marquis to rule Dai in the capacity of prime minister, but today, he has the audacity to steal Dai in cahoots with Wang Huang! The officials and people there are not at fault. Those who leave Chen and Wang and come back are all pardoned." The Emperor personally led his army east to Handan, and said happily: "Chen did not hold Handan in the south to block the River Zhang, so I know he cannot prevail." Zhou Chang the prime minister of Zhao reported that 20 of the 25 Changshan towns had been lost, so he asked to put to death the governor and his commandant. The Emperor asked: "Did they rebel?" He replied: "No." the Emperor said: "The fault was shortage of troops, so they are innocent." The Emperor ordered Zhou Chang to choose Zhao warriors who could be commissioned as generals, and the latter reported four soldiers, whom the Emperor then summoned. The Emperor hurled abuse: "Can such boys become generals!" The four felt ashamed, all lying prostrate on the ground. The Emperor gave them each a fief of 1,000 households, and appointed them generals. His attendants remonstrated: "You have not yet finished rewarding everybody who joined the army in Shu and Han to attack Chu, What are their deeds, those four whom you rewarded today?" The Emperor said: "Nothing that you know about. When Chen Xi rebelled, occupying all of Zhao and Dai, I

【原文】

天下兵，未有至者，今计唯独邯郸中兵耳。吾何爱四千户，不以慰赵子弟！”皆曰：“善。”又求：“乐毅有后乎？”得其孙叔，封之乐乡，号华成君。问豨将，皆故贾人。上曰：“吾知与之矣。”乃多以金购豨将，豨将多降。

十一年冬，上在邯郸。豨将侯敞将万馀人游行，王黄将骑千馀军曲逆，张春将卒万余人度河攻聊城。汉将军郭蒙与齐将击，大破之。太尉周勃道太原入定代地，至马邑，马邑不下，攻残之。豨将赵利守东垣，高祖攻之不下。卒骂，上怒。城降，卒骂者斩之。诸县坚守不降反寇者，复租赋三岁。

春正月，淮阴侯韩信谋反长安，夷三族。将军柴武斩韩王信于参合。

上还雒阳。诏曰：“代地居常山之北，与夷狄边。赵乃从山南有之，远，数有胡寇，难以为国。颇取山南太原之地益属代，代之云中

【今译】

有来的。今天看来，只有靠邯郸中的兵了。我何必舍不得四千户，不用来慰劳赵国子弟！”都说：“很好。”又问：“乐毅有没有后代？”找到了他的孙子乐叔，封在乐乡，号华成君。问陈豨将是何人，都是旧时商人。皇上说：“我知道怎么办了。”于是多用黄金收买陈豨的将属，陈豨的将属多降。

十一年冬，皇上在邯郸。陈豨之将侯敞率万余人游动行军，王黄率千余骑驻扎在曲逆县，张春率卒万余人渡黄河攻聊城。汉将军郭蒙与齐将迎击，大破他们。太尉周勃取道太原进入代地，到马邑，马邑不降，攻破并进行残杀。陈豨之将赵利守东垣，高祖攻击不下。赵利的士兵在城上辱骂，皇上大怒。东垣城降，辱骂的士兵被斩各县坚守不降陈豨者，免除租赋三年。

春正月，淮阴侯韩信谋反于长安，被诛杀三族。将军柴武在参合斩韩王信。

皇上返回雒阳。下诏说：“代地位于常山以北，与夷狄接壤，赵的国境从山的南面开始，距代很远，代常有胡人入寇，难以保全国土。割取山南太原之地增属代国，代的云中以西设云中郡，代受到的

sent feathered letters summoning soldiers from across the land, but nobody came. It seems that we can count only on the soldiers of Handan. Why should I grudge 4,000 households, and not to use it to mollify the boys in Zhao!" Everyone said: "Very well." The Emperor asked again: "Did Yue Yi have no descendants?" They found his grandson Yue Shu, and enfeoffed him at Yue Town, with the title Lord Huacheng. The Emperor asked about Chen Xi's generals, who were all former merchants. The Emperor then said: "I know how to deal with them." So he offered much gold as an incentive to surrender. Most of them did.

In the winter of year 11, the Emperor was in Handan. Hou Chang, Chen Xi's general, marched about with 10,000 troops, Wang Huang stationed in Quni with some 1,000 cavalry, and Zhang Chun crossed the Yellow River at the head of 10,000 men to attack Liaocheng. The Han General Guo Meng and Qi generals engaged and destroyed them. Defender-in-General Zhou Bo entered to subjugate Dai via Taiyuan, and reached Mayi, which would not surrender, so he broke in, and carnage ensued. Chen's general Zhao Li guarded Dongyuan, and the Emperor did not conquer it. Zhao's soldiers on the wall kept abusing the Emperor, to his great fury. When the city finally surrendered, the abusive soldiers were beheaded. Those counties that had held out against the rebels were exempted from rent and taxes for three years.

In the first moon, Marquis of Huaiyin Hann Xin plotted a revolt in Chang'an, and his three clans were exterminated. General Chai Wu killed King of Hann Xin at Canhe. On the Emperor's return to Luoyang, he issued an edict: "Dai area is located north of Changshan, on the border with the barbarians, while Zhao's territory ranges from the south of the mountains, very far away. So Dai is often pillaged by the Huns, making it difficult to preserve the state. We shall augment Dai with some land excised from Taiyuan in the south of the mountains, and establish Yunzhong Prefecture west

【原文】

以西为云中郡，则代受边寇益少矣。王、相国、通侯、吏二千石择可立为代王者。”燕王绾，相国何等三十三人皆曰：“子恒贤知温良，请立以为代王，都晋阳。”大赦天下。

二月，诏曰：“欲省赋甚。今献未有程，吏或多赋以为献，而诸侯王尤多，民疾之。令诸侯王、通侯常以十月朝献，及郡各以其口数率，人岁六十三钱，以给献费。”又曰：“盖闻王者莫高于周文，伯者莫高于齐桓，皆待贤人而成名。今天下贤者智能岂特古之人乎？患在人主不交故也，士奚由进！今吾以天之灵，贤士大夫定有天下，以为一家，欲其长久，世世奉宗庙亡绝也。贤人已与我共平之矣，而不与吾共安利之，可乎？贤士大夫有肯从我游者，吾能尊显之。布告天下，使明知朕意。御史大夫昌下相国，相国酂侯下诸侯王，御史中执法下郡守，其有意称明德者，必身劝，为之驾，遣诣相国府，署行、

【今译】

边寇就减少了。王、相国、通侯、二千石官吏请选择可立为代王的人。”燕王卢绾、相国萧何等三十三人都说：“皇子刘恒贤德、聪明、温和、善良，请立为代王，建都晋阳。”大赦天下。

二月，下诏说：“很想减少赋敛。如今献赋没有章程，官吏有的以多收赋税以为献费，而诸侯王征收更多，百姓十分痛恨这件事。下令诸侯王、通侯都在十月朝见时纳献费，及郡纳献费都要各以人口实际数计算，每人一年六十三钱，用来缴纳献费。”又说：“听说帝王没有高于周文王的，霸主没有高于齐桓公的，都是依靠贤人而成名。今天下贤者智者岂能只有古代有吗？毛病出在人主不去结交的缘故，贤士由何处进见呀！今天我凭藉天的神灵、贤士大夫夺取天下，一统江山，想让它长久传下去，世世代代祭祀宗庙不断绝。贤人已经与我一道平定天下了，而不与我共安定同享受，可以吗？贤士大夫有肯跟随我的，我能够让他位尊名显。布告天下，使人们明知我的心意。御史大夫周昌低于相国，相国酂侯萧何低于诸侯王，御史中执法低于郡守，凡是诚意推举有贤明之德者，郡守必须亲自前往劝勉，为之驾

of Dai's Yunzhong. Thus incursions across Dai's border will be reduced. Kings, prime ministers, marquises and officials with two thousand piculs of salary shall select someone to be established as King of Dai." The King of Yan Lu Wan, Prime Minister Xiao He and others, 33 in all, said: "Your son Liu Heng is virtuous, smart, gentle, and kind, so please establish him as its King, with his capital in Jinyang." There was a nationwide amnesty.

In the second moon, the Emperor issued an edict saying: "I very much want to reduce taxes. Today there is no regulation over offerings, and some officials levy extra taxes in order to make this offerings to us, and the vassal kings levy even more, thus the people suffer deeply. I hereby order the vassal kings and marquises to pay homage at court and make their offerings at every 10th moon, and each prefecture to calculate the amount based on their population. Each year 63 cash per capita shall be the contribution." And "I heard that no monarch is higher than King Wen of Zhou, and no hegemon higher than Duke Huan of Qi; both of them became famous by relying on worthy people. Is it only antiquity that could boast virtuous and wise scholars? The problem is that the monarch does not make friends with them. Where will the scholars come from! Now that I have subjugated and unified the world through the spiritual power of heaven, virtuous scholars and grand masters, I want to make it endure, and continue my ancestral worship from generation to generation. At my side, worthy men have pacified the world with me, and how can they not enjoy its stability with me? I can make honored and illustrious those virtuous literati and grand masters who are willing to follow and befriend me. Notify the world, and let my mind be made plain. Censor-in-Chief Zhou Chang shall refer it down to Prime Minister Xiao He, Marquis of Zan, who shall refer it to the vassal kings, and the aide to the Censor-in-Chief shall refer it to the prefectural governors. The prefects must go in person to all those known to be wise and virtuous, exhorting

【原文】

义、年。有而弗言，觉，免。年老癃病，勿遣。”

三月，梁王彭越谋反，夷三族。诏曰：“择可以为梁王、淮阳王者。”燕王绾、相国何等请立子恢为梁王，子友为淮阳王。罢东郡，颇益梁；罢颍川郡，颇益淮阳。

夏四月，行自雒阳至。令丰人徙关中者皆复终身。

五月，诏曰：“粤人之俗，好相攻击，前时秦徙中县之民南方三郡，使与百粤杂处。会天下诛秦，南海尉它居南方长治之，甚有文理，中县人以故不耗减，粤人相攻击之俗益止，俱赖其力。今立它为南粤王。”使陆贾即授玺绶。它稽首称臣。

六月，令士卒从入蜀、汉、关中者皆复终身。

秋七月，淮南王布反。上问诸将，滕公言故楚令尹薛公有筹策。

【今译】

车，送到相国府，登记品行、事迹、年龄。有贤明之人而不报，一旦发现，即行免职。年老疲病，不要送来。”

三月，梁王彭越谋反，诛灭三族。下诏说：“选择可以立为梁王、淮阳王的人。”燕王卢绾、相国萧何等请立皇子刘恢为梁王，皇子刘友为淮阳王。撤销东郡建置，扩增为梁国封地；撤销颍川郡建置，扩增为淮阳国封地。

夏四月，皇上从雒阳返回京师。下令凡丰邑人迁徙到关中的都终身免赋役。

五月，下诏说：“粤人风俗喜好互相械斗，以前秦朝迁徙中原之民到南方桂林、象郡、南海三郡，使与百粤人杂居。正逢天下反秦，南海尉赵它在南方长期治理当地，很有条理，中原人因此不减少，粤人相械斗的风俗进一步制止，全靠赵它之力。今立赵它为南粤王。”派陆贾前去授与玺绶。赵它叩头称臣。

六月，下令从军入蜀郡、汉中郡、关中的人全都免除终身赋役。

秋七月，淮南王英布反。皇上问诸将怎么办，滕公说原楚令尹薛

them, providing them with carriages, and sending them to the Prime Minister's residence, with their conduct, appearance and age written clearly. If non-reporting of a wise person is detected, that prefect shall be removed from office. Those who are old and senile, do not send them."

In the third moon, the King of Liang Peng Yue rebelled, and was exterminated together with his three clans. An edict was issued saying: "Select persons for the positions of King of Liang, and King of Huaiyang." The King of Yan Lu Wan, Prime Minister Xiao He and others asked him to appoint his own sons Liu Hui King of Liang, and Liu You King of Huaiyang. Dongjun Prefecture was revoked and incorporated into an enlarged Liang; and the former Yingchuan Prefecture was subsumed into an expanded Huaiyang.

In the fourth moon, the Emperor returned from Luoyang to the capital. He decreed that Feng people who immigrated to Guanzhong should be exempted from all taxes and labor service for life.

In the fifth moon, the Emperor declared that: "The habit of Yue (Guangdong) people was to fight each other. Under the Qin Dynasty, people of the Central Plains were resettled to the southern prefectures of Guilin, Xiangjun and Nanhai, to live intermixed with local Yue people. While the whole world was trying to destroy Qin, Commandant Zhao Ta of Nanhai lived in the south and governed it as its chieftain, quite properly. Thanks to the efforts of Zhao, the Central Plains migrants are no fewer, and the local people's fights have been curbed. Hereby we make Zhao King of South Yue." Lu Jia was sent to grant the seal and cord of office and Zhao kowtowed to express allegiance.

In the sixth moon, the Emperor ordered that the army men who had followed into Shu, Hanzhong, and Guanzhong should be exempt from taxes and labor service for life.

In the seventh moon, Tattooed Bu, King of Huainan, rebelled. The Emperor asked the generals for advice, and the Magistrate

【原文】

上(见公)[召见]，薛公言布形势，上善之，封薛公千户。诏王、相国择可立为淮南王者，群臣请立子长为王。上乃发上郡、北地、陇西车骑、巴蜀材官及中尉卒三万人为皇太子卫，军霸上。布果如薛公言，东击杀荆王刘贾，劫其兵，度淮击楚，楚王交走入薛。上赦天下死罪以下，皆令从军；征诸侯兵，上自将以击布。

十二年冬十月，上破布军于会缶，布走，令别将追之。

上还，过沛，留，置酒沛宫，悉召故人父老子弟佐酒。发沛中儿得百二十人，教之歌。酒酣，上击筑，自歌曰："大风起兮云飞扬，威加海内兮归故乡，安得猛士兮守四方！"令儿皆和习之。上乃起舞，慷慨伤怀，泣数行下。谓沛父兄曰："游子悲故乡。吾虽都关中，万岁之后吾魂魄犹思(乐)沛。且朕自沛公以诛暴逆，遂有天下，其以沛

【今译】

公有平叛的计谋。皇上召见，薛公说了英布所处形势，皇上称善，封薛公千户。诏令王、相国选择可以立为淮南王的人。群臣请立皇子刘长为王。皇上征发上郡、北地、陇西骑兵，巴郡、蜀郡步兵及中尉卒三万人为皇太子卫士，驻扎霸上。英布果然像薛公所预言，东进击杀荆王刘贾，胁迫其兵，渡淮击楚，楚王刘交逃入薛城。皇上赦天下死罪以下的罪犯，全让他们从军；征调诸侯兵，皇上亲率军击英布。

十二年冬十月，皇上在会缶击败英布军。英布逃走，皇上命别将追击。

皇上返回，经过沛县，在沛宫留住并设酒宴，全部召来故人父老子弟助酒。征沛中儿童一百二十人，教他们唱歌。酒喝得正酣，皇上击筑，并自己唱起来："大风起兮云飞扬，威加海内兮归故乡，安得猛士兮守四方！"让儿童都一同习唱．皇上于是起舞，慷慨悲伤，泪水一行一行流下来。对沛父兄说："游子悲故乡。我虽然定都关中，死后我的魂魄还是思念故乡沛。况且我自称沛公诛讨暴逆，然后才有

of Teng said that the former Chu premier Mr. Xue had counter-insurgency stratagems. The Emperor duly summoned him, who described Bu's situation, and the Emperor acceded. He granted Mr. Xue a fief of 1,000 households. He ordered the kings, and prime minister to choose a man to be King of Huainan. The courtiers recommended his son Prince Liu Chang. Emperor mobilized chariots and cavalry from Shangjun, Beidi and Longxi, infantry from Ba and Shu Prefectures, plus 30,000 imperial guards as the Crown Prince's guard, to be stationed at Bashang. Just as Mr. Xue had predicted, Bu did attack to the east and killed Liu Jia the King of Jing, commandeered his soldiers, and then attacked Chu across the River Huai, causing Liu Jiao the King of Chu to flee to Xue. The Emperor pardoned all non-capital-offense criminals, so that they joined the army; the troops of the vassal kings were drafted in, and the Emperor personally led the military attack against Bu.

In the tenth moon of year 12, the Emperor defeated Bu's troops at Kuaizhui. Bu ran away, and the Emperor ordered a detached general to pursue him.

The Emperor returned via Pei, where he tarried for a while. He held a banquet in the palace, summoning all the elders and old friends to the feast. One hundred and twenty children of Pei were gathered, and were taught to sing. Mellow with drink, the Emperor fingered the *zhu* lute, accompanying himself with the song: "When a gale rises,/ Clouds scud by./ I return home/ With my power over the world./ Where can I get warriors,/ To guard the four quarters!" The children were required to learn to sing it in concert. The Emperor rose to dance, expressive and full of feeling, his tears streaming with every line. He told the fathers and brothers of Pei: "The wanderer yearns sadly for his home. Although I live in my capital in Guanzhong, when I die my soul will still miss my home Pei. Moreover, it was in the name of Magistrate of Pei that I exterminated the despot, and then conquered the world. This is my

【原文】

为朕汤沐邑，复其民，世世无有所与。”沛父老诸母故人日乐饮极欢，道旧故为笑乐。十馀日，上欲去，沛父兄固请。上曰：“吾人众多，父兄不能给。”乃去。沛中空县皆之邑西献。上留止，张饮三日。沛父兄皆顿首曰：“沛幸得复，丰未得，唯陛下哀矜。”上曰：“丰者，吾所生长，极不忘耳。吾特以其为雍齿故反我为魏。”沛父兄固请之，乃并复丰，比沛。

汉别将击布军洮水南北，皆大破之。追斩布番阳。

周勃定代，斩陈豨于当城。

诏曰：“吴，古之建国也，日者荆王兼有其地，今死亡后。朕欲复立吴王，其议可者。”长沙王臣等言：“沛侯濞重厚，请立为吴王。”已拜，上召谓濞曰：“汝状有反相。”因拊其背，曰：“汉后五十年东南有乱，岂汝邪？然天下同姓一家，汝慎毋反。”濞顿首曰：“不敢。”

【今译】

天下，今以沛为我的汤沐邑，免除沛县百姓的赋役，世世代代都不缴纳租税。”沛父老诸母故人整日畅饮欢乐，以讲旧故往事为乐。十余日后，皇上想离去，沛父兄坚持请留。皇上说：“我手下人众多，父兄管不起饭吃。”便离开了。沛县全县皆空，都去城西面献酒。皇上又停下来，设帐痛饮三日。沛父兄皆叩头说：“沛有幸得到免赋役的恩赐，丰邑未得到，只求陛下哀怜。”皇上说：“丰邑是我生长之地，最不能忘的。我是因他们曾为雍齿的缘故背叛我去降魏。”沛父兄坚持请求，才同时免丰邑赋役，与沛相同。

汉别将击英布军于洮水南北，都大破英布军，在番阳追斩英布。

周勃平定代地，斩陈豨于当城。

皇上下诏说：“吴是古代所建之国。从前荆王兼有其地，今王死无后。我欲再立吴王，应该议一议谁可以为吴王。”长沙王吴臣等说：“沛侯刘濞稳重厚道，请立为吴王。”已拜，皇上召刘濞说：“你的相貌有反相。”随即拊其背，说：“汉以后五十年东南有乱，难道是你吗？然而天下同姓一家，你要谨慎，不要造反。”刘濞叩头说：“不敢。”

fief for sacrificial bathing, the County of Pei. Therefore I say, the people of Pei shall be exempt from taxes and labor service, for all generations." The Pei elders, matrons, and old friends drank all day, happily relating old anecdotes. After a dozen days, the Emperor wanted to leave, against the protestations of the elders. They insisted that he stay. The Emperor said: "My entourage is numerous, and you cannot afford to feed us." Then he left. The entire population of Pei came out to offer wine at the west side of the city. The Emperor stopped, and quaffed in the tent for three days. The Pei fathers and brothers all kowtowed, saying: "Pei is blessed with the gift of freedom from taxation, but Feng town is not. We beg Your Majesty to take pity on them." The Emperor said: "Feng is where I grew up, the hardest place to forget. But I was reluctant because they betrayed me for Yong Chi's sake and surrendered to Wei." They kept on imploring, resulting in Feng being exempted, like Pei.

The Han detached general attacked Bu's forces in the north and south of Tao River, and destroyed his army. He pursued the rebel to Boyang, decapitating him there.

Zhou Bo subjugated Dai, killing Chen Xi in Dangcheng.

The Emperor issued an edict saying: "Wu is a kingdom built by the ancients. It was under the jurisdiction of the King of Jing, who died without issue, but now I wish to re-establish the King of Wu. We should propose someone for the position." The King of Changsha Wu Chen and others said: "Marquis of Pei Liu Bi is steady and kind, please make him King of Wu." Decided, the Emperor summoned Liu Bi and said: "You have the physiognomy of an insurgent." Then he patted him on the back, and said: "Fifty years on there will be turmoil in the southeast, but will it be you? Those of the same surname are one family. You must watch your step and not rebel." Liu Bi kowtowed: "I dare not."

In the 11th moon, the Emperor returned from Huainan to the capital. He stopped in Lu, where he sacrificed an ox, sheep, and pig

【原文】

十一月，行自淮南还。过鲁，以大牢祠孔子。

十二月，诏曰："秦皇帝、楚隐王、魏安釐王、齐愍王、赵悼襄王皆绝亡后。其与秦始皇帝守冢二十家，楚、魏、齐各十家，赵及魏公子亡忌各五家，令视其冢，复亡与它事。"

陈豨降将言豨反时燕王卢绾使人之豨所阴谋。上使辟阳侯审食其迎绾，绾称疾。食其言绾反有端。春二月，使樊哙、周勃将兵击绾。诏曰："燕王绾与吾有故，爱之如子，闻与陈豨有谋，吾以为亡有，故使人迎绾。绾称疾不来，谋反明矣。燕吏民非有罪也，赐其吏六百石以上爵各一级。与绾居，去来归者，赦之，加爵亦一级。"诏诸侯王议可立为燕王者，长沙王臣等请立子建为燕王。

诏曰："南武侯织亦粤之世也，立以为南海王。"

三月，诏曰："吾立为天子，帝有天下，十二年于今矣。与天下之豪士贤大夫共定天下，同安辑之。其有功者上致之王，次为列侯，下乃食邑。而重臣之亲，或为列侯，皆令自置吏，得赋敛。女

【今译】

十一月，皇上从淮南返回京师。经过鲁，用牛、羊、猪祭祀孔子。

十二月，下诏说："秦皇帝、楚隐王陈胜、魏安釐王、齐愍王、赵悼襄王皆断绝后代。今给秦始皇帝守坟二十家，楚、魏、齐各十家，赵及魏公子无忌各五家，令看管其坟，免除赋役，不加其他差事。"

陈豨降将说陈豨反时，燕王卢绾派人去陈豨住所暗中谋议。皇上派辟阳侯审食其迎卢绾，卢绾称有病。食其说卢绾谋反有端倪。春二月，派樊哙、周勃率军击卢绾。下诏说："燕王卢绾与我是老朋友，爱之如子，听说与陈豨有密谋，我以为没有，因此派人迎接他。他托病不来，谋反之心已明。燕国吏民没有罪，官吏在六百石以上级别的赐爵各一级。曾与卢绾居住在一处，离开卢绾来归顺的，赦免，也加爵一级。"下诏诸侯王议可以立为燕王的人，长沙王吴臣等请立皇子刘建为燕王。

下诏说："南武侯织也是粤人之后，立他为南海王。"

三月，下诏说："我立为天子，称帝有天下，至今十二年了。与天下的豪杰之士贤大夫共同平定天下，举国上下安定和睦。功高的封了王，次的封了侯，再下的还有食邑。重臣之亲者，有的封列侯，都

to Confucius.

In the 12th moon, an edict was issued: "The Qin First Emperor, King Yin of Chu Chen Sheng, King Anli of Wei, King Min of Qi, and King Daoxiang of Zhao have no living issue. I grant hereby 20 households to keep watch at the tomb of Emperor Qin Shi Huang, 10 each to Chu, Wei, and Qi, five each to Zhao and Wei Prince Wuji, so that they take care of their graves, exempt from taxation or other labor service."

A surrendered general of Chen Xi said that when Chen rebelled Lu Wan the King of Yan had sent people to plot with Chen's. The Emperor sent Marquis of Piyang Shen Yiji to see Lu Wan, who declined, pleading sickness. Shen reported that there were clues implicating Lu in the rebellion. In the second moon, the Emperor sent Fan Kuai and Zhou Bo's troops to attack Lu. An edict was issued: "Lu Wan the King of Yan and I are old friends, and I loved him as my own child. I heard about a conspiracy with Chen, but not believing this, I sent someone to meet Lu. On the pretext of illness he declined to come, so it is evident that he planned to rebel. The officials and people of Yan are not guilty, and officials with titles above the level of 600 piculs shall all be promoted by one level. Those who live with Lu Wan, if they leave him and pledge allegiance to us, shall be pardoned, and granted a higher level." Asking the vassal kings to propose a new King of Yan, and King of Changsha Wu Chen and others recommended his son Liu Jian as King of Yan.

An edict was issued: "Marquis of Nanwu Zhi is also a descendant of Yue, so we establish him as King of Nanhai."

In the third moon, the Emperor declared: "It has been 12 years since I became the Emperor, as the Son of Heaven. Together with the gallants and virtuous grand masters, I conquered the world, and pacified the whole country. Those with the highest merits have become kings, those with the next highest are adjunct marquises

【原文】

子公主。为列侯食邑者，皆佩之印，赐大第室。吏二千石，徙之长安，受小第室。入蜀汉定三秦者，皆世世复。吾于天下贤士功臣，可谓亡负矣。其有不义背天子擅起兵者，与天下共伐诛之。布告天下，使明知朕意。”

上击布时，为流矢所中，行道疾。疾甚，吕后迎良医。医入见，上问医，曰：“疾可治。”于是上嫚骂之，曰：“吾以布衣提三尺取天下，此非天命乎？命乃在天，虽扁鹊何益？”遂不使治疾，赐黄金五十斤，罢之。吕后问曰：“陛下百岁后，萧相国既死，谁令代之？”上曰：“曹参可。”问其次，曰：“王陵可，然少戇，陈平可以助之。陈平知有馀，然难独任。周勃重厚少文，然安刘氏者必勃也，可令为太尉。”吕后复问其次，上曰：“此后亦非乃所知也。”

卢绾与数千人居塞下候伺，幸上疾愈，自入谢。夏四月甲辰，帝

【今译】

让他们设置官吏，征收赋税，女子称公主。列侯有食邑的，都佩有印，赏赐大宅第。二千石一级的官吏，迁徙到长安，赏赐小宅第。入蜀郡、汉中郡定三秦而有功者，全都世代免除赋役。我对于天下贤士功臣，可以说是无负于他们了。如果有不义背叛天子而擅自起兵者，与天下共讨伐诛杀之。布告天下，使人们明知我的心意。”

皇上击英布时，被流箭射中，行至途中病重。吕后请良医。医生进宫看病，皇上问医生说：“这病还能治吗？”医生说：“可治。”于是皇上大骂起来，说：“我以平民之身手提三尺剑取天下，这不是命吗？性命在天，即使扁鹊在世有什么益处！”于是不让治病疾，赐黄金五十斤，停止治疗。吕后问道：“陛下百年之后，萧相国死了，谁可以代替？”皇上说：“曹参可以。”问其次，说：“王陵可以，然少有憨厚，陈平可以帮助他。陈平智谋有余，然而难以独当一面。周勃稳重忠厚少文雅，然而安定刘氏天下者一定是周勃，可使任太尉。”吕后又问其次，皇上说：“这以后也不是你所能知道的了。”

卢绾与数千人居塞下等待观望，希望皇上疾愈，即亲自入京谢罪。

and below them there are fiefs. Some of the loved ones of the major ministers have become adjunct marquises, and are allowed to appoint officials and collect taxes; their ladies are called princesses. Adjunct marquises with fiefs are granted a seal of authority, and rewarded with large mansions. Officials of 2,000-picul level were rewarded with small mansions if they moved to Chang'an. Those with merit who moved into Shu and Hanzhong to subjugate the three Qin areas were exempted from taxation and services for all generations. We can say I have not let down my virtuous masters and meritorious generals. If there is any unrighteous person who revolts, betraying the Son of Heaven, we will send a punitive expedition with the people under heaven and kill that person. This notice is published across the land to make people aware of my mind."

In the attack on Bu, the Emperor had been hit by a stray arrow, and fell ill en route. When his illness became serious, Empress Lü called a good doctor. The doctor, responding to the Emperor's questioning, said: "It can be cured." But the Emperor cursed him: "I was just a commoner who took the world with a three-foot sword in my hand. Was this not the Mandate of Heaven? Fate is determined by heaven alone, even if the good doctor Bian Que were alive!" So he refused treatment dismissing the physician with 50 catties of gold.

Empress Lü asked: "When Your Majesty is gone, and Prime Minister Xiao is dead, who can replace him?" The Emperor replied: "Cao Can." Asked about the second successor, he said: "Wang Ling will do. He is a little too simple and honest, but Chen Ping can assist him. Chen has more than enough wit, but would find it difficult to work alone. Zhou Bo is steady and honest, but less refined, but the stabilizer of Liu's house must be Bo, so make him Defender-in-Chief." The Empress asked for who should succeed Bo, but the Emperor said: "What happens after, you cannot know."

Lu Wan waited with thousands of people living near the northern wall. They hoped for the Emperor's recovery, so that they

【原文】

崩于长乐宫。卢绾闻之，遂亡入匈奴。

吕后与审食其谋曰："诸将故与帝为编户民，北面为臣，心常鞅鞅，今乃事少主，非尽族是，天下不安。"以故不发丧。人或闻，以语郦商。郦商见审食其曰："闻帝已崩，四日不发丧，欲诛诸将。诚如此，天下危矣。陈平、灌婴将十万守荥阳，樊哙、周勃将二十万定燕代，此闻帝崩，诸将皆诛，必连兵还乡，以攻关中。大臣内畔，诸将外反，亡可蹻足待也。"审食其入言之，乃以丁未发丧，大赦天下。

五月丙寅，葬长陵。已下，皇太子群臣皆反至太上皇庙。群臣曰："帝起细微，拨乱世反之正，平定天下，为汉太祖，功最高。"上尊号曰高皇帝。

初，高祖不修文学，而性明达，好谋，能听，自监门戍卒，见之如旧。初顺民心，作三章之约。天下既定，命萧何次律令，韩信申军

【今译】

夏四月十一日，皇帝在长乐宫驾崩。卢绾听说，便逃往匈奴。

吕后与审食其谋划说："诸将原与皇帝都是平民百姓，后来北面称臣，心里常常不愉快。今天又事奉少主，如果不尽杀这一帮人，天下不安。"因此不发丧。有人听到了消息，告诉郦商。郦商见审食其说："听说皇帝已崩，四日不发丧，想诛杀诸将。真的这样，天下就危险了。陈平、灌婴率十万兵守荥阳，樊哙、周勃率二十万兵定燕代，这些将领听说帝崩，诸将都被杀，必然连兵返回，攻打关中。大臣内叛，诸将外反，不用有翘足的时间就会发生。"审食其入宫劝说吕后，便在十四日发丧，大赦天下。

五月十七日，高祖葬于长陵。下葬以后，皇太子与群臣都返回至太上皇庙。群臣说："皇帝出身卑微，拨乱反正，平定天下，为汉太祖，功最高。"故上尊号叫高皇帝。

当初，高祖不习文学，而性情明达，好计谋，善于听取臣下之言，从看门人到戍卒，见面如老朋友。开始时顺民心，制订约法三

could apologize personally in the capital. On the 25th day of the fourth moon (June 1, 195 BC), the Emperor died in Changle Palace. When Lu Wan heard this, he fled to the Huns.

Empress Lü cooked up a plan with Shen Yiji: "The generals used to be commoners like the Emperor, and then became his subjects, so they are often unhappy. And now they will serve the young lord. If we do not entirely kill their clans the empire will descend into turmoil." Therefore, they did not announce the funeral. But the news did leak out and Li Shang went to see Shen, saying: "I heard the Emperor has passed, and you have not announced it for four days, preparing to kill off the generals. If this is true, the world will be in danger. Chen Ping and Guan Ying are stationed in Xingyang with 100,000 soldiers, while Fan Kuai and Zhou Bo control Yan and Dai with 200,000. If these men hear that the generals were all killed after the Emperor's death, they will of course lead their armies back to attack Guanzhong. In no time you will face betrayal at court by the ministers, and rebellion by the generals outside." Shen then went in to advise the Empress, and the funeral announcement was made on the 14th day, together with a universal amnesty.

On the 17th day, the Emperor was buried in Changling Mausoleum. After the burial, the Crown Prince and the ministers all returned to the Super Emperor's Temple. The ministers said: "The late Emperor was born humble, but he subjugated the world, establishing order out of chaos. With the highest merit, he will be the Taizu, or Highest Father of the Han Dynasty." Since then, his honorific appellation would be Gaodi, or High Emperor.

At first, the Emperor was not good at book knowledge, but he had incisive intelligence, a good strategic mind, and was good at taking advice from his subjects, from the janitor to the frontier soldier, meeting them like old friends. He started by following the

【原文】

法，张苍定章程，叔孙通制礼仪，陆贾造《新语》。又与功臣剖符作誓，丹书铁契，金匮石室，藏之宗庙。虽日不暇给，规摹弘远矣。

赞曰：《春秋》晋史蔡墨有言，陶唐氏既衰，其后有刘累，学扰龙，事孔甲，范氏其后也。而大夫范宣子亦曰："祖自虞以上为陶唐氏，在夏为御龙氏，在商为豕韦氏，在周为唐杜氏，晋主夏盟为范氏。"范氏为晋士师，鲁文公世奔秦。后归于晋，其处者为刘氏。刘向云战国时刘氏自秦获于魏。秦灭魏，迁大梁，都于丰，故周市说雍齿曰"丰，故梁徙也"。是以颂高祖云："汉帝本系，出自唐帝。降及于周，在秦作刘。涉魏而东，遂为丰公。"丰公，盖太上皇父。其迁

【今译】

章。天下已定，命萧何编次律令，韩信申述兵法，张苍制定律历章程，叔孙通制礼仪，陆贾著《新语》。又与功臣剖符作誓，立丹书铁契，存入金匮石室，藏在宗庙。虽然诸事繁多，可以立制垂范传之久远。

赞曰：《春秋》晋国的史官蔡墨有一段话说：陶唐氏衰败之后，他的后代有刘累，学习驯龙，在夏王孔甲治下称臣，食采于范的晋大夫士会，就是他的后裔。而晋大夫范宣子也说："先祖从虞氏以上称为陶唐氏，在夏为御龙氏，在商为豕韦氏，在周为唐杜氏，晋国称霸华夏时称为范氏。"当时的范氏是晋国的正卿，鲁文公时逃到秦国。后来又回归晋国，留在秦国的称为刘氏。刘向说：战国时刘氏随秦军东进在魏国被俘。秦侵魏都安邑，魏迁往大梁，曾定都丰邑，因此周市劝雍齿说："丰邑，是原来梁迁徙后的国都。"所以，颂扬高祖说："汉朝皇帝的本系，出自唐尧帝。到了周朝，在秦国称刘氏。向东入魏，于是成为丰公。"丰公就是刘氏的太上皇父。他们迁徙的日

people's aspirations and pledging a three-point law. Once the empire was conquered, he ordered Xiao He to arrange the precepts of law, Hann Xin to describe the art of war, and Zhang Cang to develop the calendar and measurement, Shusun Tong to formulate the rites, and Lu Jia to write New Language. He also divided tally pledges with the meritorious, established the system of agreements inscribed on iron with vermilion words, to be kept in rooms of gold and stone, stored in the ancestral temple. Despite his busy schedule, he was able to create exemplary systems of enduring application.

Author's comment: In the *Spring and Autumn Annals*, there is a saying from Cai Mo, the official historian of the State of Jin: After the decline of Yao's Taotang, there was Liu Lei among his descendants, learning to train a dragon, under the rule of Kongjia the King of Xia. The grand master Shi Hui of Jin with a fief in Fan was his descendant. The grand master Fan Xuanzi of Jin also said: "My ancestors were called Taotang from Youyu and earlier, became Yulong (Training Dragon) in the Xia Dynasty, Shiwei in the Shang Dynasty, Tangdu in the Zhou Dynasty, and Fan when the State of Jin dominated the Chinese alliance." At the time, Fan was the Chief Judge of Jin, but fled to the State of Qin during the reign of Duke Wen of Lu. They later returned to Jin, with those staying behind in Qin called Liu. Liu Xiang said: in the Warring States Period, the Lius followed the Qin army east into Wei and were captured. When Qin destroyed Wei, the latter moved to Daliang and made its capital at Feng. Accordingly, Zhou Fu persuaded Yong Chi: "Feng is the resettlement area of the original Wei capital Liang." Thus, we extol Gaozu: "The family tree of Han emperors stemmed from the Emperor Tang Yao. Down to the Zhou Dynasty, their clan in Qin was surnamed Liu. Migrating eastward into Wei, they then became Lords of Feng." The Lord of Feng was the Super Emperor of the Liu clan. Because they had not long resettled in Feng, so there were few family tombs there. When Gaozu ascended the throne, he appointed

【原文】

日浅，坟墓在丰鲜焉。及高祖即位，置祠祀官，则有秦、晋、梁、荆之巫，世祠天地，缀之以祀，岂不信哉！由是推之，汉承尧运，德祚已盛，断蛇著符，旗帜上赤，协于火德，自然之应，得天统矣。

——卷一下《高帝纪》第一下

【今译】

子不长，在丰邑的坟墓也很少。到高祖即位，设置祭祀之官，便有秦、晋、梁、荆巫祝，代代祭祀天地，祭礼不绝，岂不是可信的吗！由此推断，汉朝继承尧的世运，帝王的运气已经很盛，斩白蛇显示符瑞，旗帜崇尚赤色，符合火德，自然相应，取得天命正统。

sacrifice officers, so there were shamans from Qin, Jin, Liang and Jing, worshipping heaven and earth generation after generation, in an unbroken system of rituals. Does this seem credible to you! By inference, the Han Dynasty inherited the fortunes of Yao, with strong imperial luck. The severing of the white snake was a lucky sign, and the flag advocating red tallies with the nature of fire, which corresponded naturally to the Mandate of Heaven bestowing legitimacy.

武帝纪

【原文】

孝武皇帝，景帝中子也，母曰王美人。年四岁立为胶东王。七岁为皇太子，母为皇后。十六岁，后三年正月，景帝崩。甲子，太子即皇帝位，尊皇太后窦氏曰太皇太后，皇后曰皇太后。三月，封皇太后同母弟田蚡、胜皆为列侯。

建元元年冬十月，诏丞相、御史、列侯、中二千石、二千石、诸侯相举贤良方正直言极谏之士。丞相绾奏："所举贤良，或治申、商、韩非。苏秦、张仪之言，乱国政，请皆罢。"奏可。

春二月，赦天下，赐民爵一级。年八十复二算，九十复甲卒。行三铢钱。

夏四月己巳，诏曰："古之立教，乡里以齿，朝廷以爵，扶世导

【今译】

孝武皇帝，景帝诸子中排行居中，其母名王美人。四岁时立为胶东王。七岁时立为皇太子，母为皇后。十六岁时，景帝后三年正月，景帝驾崩。甲子日，太子即皇帝位，尊皇太后窦氏为太皇太后，皇后为皇太后。三月，封皇太后的同母弟田蚡、田胜为列侯。

武帝建元元年冬十月，下诏命丞相、御史大夫、列侯、俸禄满二千石及二千石的官吏、诸侯王国之相都要推荐品德好、威望高、敢于直言进谏的人才。丞相卫绾上奏说："已经推荐上来的贤良之士，有的是提倡申不害、商鞅、韩非、苏秦、张仪学说的，扰乱国政，请全都废除。"武帝批准了这一建议。

春季二月，大赦天下罪犯，赐给百姓爵位一级。年满八十岁的老人免除两份人头税，九十岁的老人免除军赋。发行每枚重三铢的铜钱。

夏四月己巳，下诏说："古代确立教育的标准，百姓之中推重年

Chapter 3

Annals of Emperor Wudi

Of the sons of Emperor Jingdi Emperor Wudi ranked in the middle by seniority, his mother being Imperial Concubine Wang. At the age of four, he was made Prince of Jiaodong. At the age of seven, he was established as Crown Prince, and his mother became Empress. When Wudi was 16 years old, Emperor Jingdi died in the first moon of his later third year (January 29, 141 BC). On March 21, the Crown Prince became Emperor, Empress Dowager Dou became the Grand Empress Dowager, and the Empress became the Empress Dowager. In the third moon, Tian Fen and Tian Sheng (half-brothers of the Empress Dowager) were made adjunct marquises. In the tenth moon of first year of Emperor Wudi's Jianyuan reign period (140 BC), it was decreed that the prime minister, censor-in-chief, adjunct marquises, officials with remuneration of full 2,000 piculs or 2,000 piculs, and prime ministers of the princedoms should recommend to the court talented people of good moral character, high prestige, and courage to speak out. Prime Minister Wei Wan submitted a memorial that "Among the virtuous scholars already recommended are those who advocate the ideas of Shen Buhai, Shang Yang, Han Fei, Su Qin and Zhang Yi, disrupting imperial policy. I submit that their recommendations all be repealed." Emperor Wudi approved the recommendation.

In spring, in the second moon, there was a general amnesty of criminals, and one degree of level was given to the people. 80-year-olds were exempt from two rounds of poll tax, and 90-year-olds were excused sending one son to military service. There was an issue of three-*zhu* coins. On the ninth day of the fourth moon, there came

【原文】

民，莫善于德。然则于乡里先耆艾，奉高年，古之道也。今天下孝子顺孙愿自竭尽以承其亲，外迫公事，内乏资财，是以孝心阙焉。朕甚哀之。民年九十以上，已有受鬻法，为复子若孙，令得身帅妻妾遂其供养之事。”

五月，诏曰：“河海润千里，其令祠官修山川之祠，为岁事，曲加礼。”

赦吴楚七国帑输在官者。

秋七月，诏曰：“卫士转置送迎二万人，其省万人。罢苑马，以赐贫民。”

议立明堂。遣使者安车蒲轮，束帛加璧，征鲁申公。

二年冬十月，御史大夫赵绾坐请毋奏事太皇太后，及郎中令王臧

【今译】

龄，朝廷之上设立爵位，扶正社会风气引导百姓行为，最好的办法在于注重道德。然而在乡村尊重老人，侍奉高龄，是古代的道德标准。今天天下的孝子贤孙都愿意尽全力承担奉养亲人，可是，外面迫于公事繁多，家内又缺乏资财，因此孝心也就难以尽到。朕非常哀伤。百姓年龄九十岁以上，已经有了领粥的办法，还要做到免除其子或孙子的徭役，让他们亲自带着妻妾承担供养老人之事务。”

五月，下诏说：“河、海润泽千里，应让祭祀之官修建山川神庙，每年办理，增加祭祀之礼。”

赦免吴、楚七国叛乱者妻子沦为官奴婢的人。

秋七月，下诏说：“常常用二万新的京城卫士更换旧卫士，应减少万人。废除养马苑林不许百姓入内放牧砍柴的禁令，给百姓以恩惠。”

商讨建立明堂事宜。派使者用蒲草裹轮的安车，带上帛和璧玉，迎接鲁国的申培公。

二年冬十月，御史大夫赵绾因请求奏事不必经太皇太后批准而犯

an edict saying: "In the ancient times, when standards of education were established, among the common people age seniority was highly regarded, and at the court the important thing was rank and title, but righting the social ethos so as to guide the people's behavior nothing is better than focusing on ethics. But in the countryside, they follow the ancient ethic of respecting the elderly and serving old age. Today, the empire's filial offspring are willing to make every effort to take care of their loved parents; however, it is difficult for them to practice filial piety, owing to compulsory service outside the home and lack of financial resources at home. This is a very sad state of affairs. There is already the measure to provide official porridge for those over 90 years of age, but we will also exempt their sons or grandsons from labor service, so that they can lead their wives and concubines to support the elderly persons."

In the fifth moon came the edict: "The rivers and seas nourish thousands of *li* of land, so the sacrifice officers should build temples for the mountain and river gods, worshipping them every year, and enhancing the worship rite."

The government pardoned the official slaves who were the widows and children of the rebel officers in the seven states of Wu, Chu, etc.

In the seventh moon, came an edict saying: "The 20,000 new guards to replace the old guards in the capital shall be reduced to 10,000. Nullify the order that bans the common people from grazing their herd or collecting firewood in the Imperial Forest Park preserve for horses as a favor to them."

There were discussions relating to the construction of the Hall of Enlightened Rule. The Emperor sent envoys in a carriage with rushes wrapped round its wheels and silk and jade, to bring Master Shen Pei of Lu.

In the tenth moon of year two of Jianyuan, Censor-in-Chief Zhao Wan offended by requesting in a memorial not to have to

【原文】

皆下狱，自杀。丞相婴、太尉蚡免。

春二月丙戌朔，日有蚀之。夏四月戊申，有如日夜出。

初置茂陵邑。

三年春，河水溢于平原，大饥，人相食。

赐徙茂陵者户钱二十万，田二顷。初作便门桥。

秋七月，有星孛于西北。

济川王明坐杀太傅、中傅废迁防陵。

闽越围东瓯，东瓯告急。遣中大夫严助持节发会稽兵，浮海救之。未至，闽越走，兵还。

九月丙子晦，日有蚀之。

四年夏，有风赤如血。六月，旱。秋九月，有星孛于东北。

五年春，罢三铢钱，行半两钱。

置五经博士。

夏四月，平原君薨。

五月，大蝗。

秋八月，广川王越、清河王乘皆薨。

【今译】

罪，牵涉到郎中令王臧都被关进监狱，二人都自杀。丞相窦婴、太尉田蚡免官。

春二月初一，日食。夏四月戊申日，好像夜间升起了太阳。

开始为武帝建造茂陵。

三年春，黄河水在平原郡决口，出现大饥荒，人吃人。

赏赐迁往茂陵居住的每户二十万钱，田二顷。开始修建跨过渭水通往茂陵的便门桥。

秋七月，有彗星向西北方向飞去。

济川王刘明因杀太傅、中傅犯罪而废除王号迁往防陵。

闽越围击东瓯，东瓯向汉朝廷告急。武帝派中大夫严助持节征调会稽兵士，由海上去救援。未到东瓯，闽越便逃走，朝廷也退兵。

九月丙子月最后一天，日食。

四年夏，刮的风和红色的血液一样。六月，天旱。秋九月，彗星向东北方向而去。

五年春，废除三铢钱，推行半两钱。

设立五经博士。

夏四月，武帝外祖母平原君去世。

五月，发生大的蝗虫灾害。

秋八月，广川王刘越、清河王刘乘都去世。

get the approval of the Grand Empress Dowager. Chamberlain of Imperial Attendants Wang Zang was also implicated. Both were jailed, and committed suicide. Prime Minister Dou Ying and Defender-in-Chief Tian Fen were dismissed from their posts.

On the first day of the second moon that spring, there was a solar eclipse. On the 24th day of the fourth moon that summer, day seemed to turn into night.

The building of Emperor Wudi's Maoling Mausoleum began.

In the spring of year three of Jianyuan, the Yellow River burst its banks at Pingyuan. A major famine and cannibalism ensued.

The court awarded 200,000 cash and two hectares of land to each household who moved to live in Maoling area. It began to build the Gateway Bridge across the Wei River leading to the Mausoleum. In the seventh moon, a comet flew in the direction of the northwest. Liu Ming Prince of Jichuan was guilty of killing his Head Mentor and Palace Mentor, abdicated and was removed to Fangling. Minyue State laid siege to Dong'ou, which appealed to the Han court for emergency help. The Emperor sent Yan Zhu the Grand Master of the Palace with a tally requisitioning Kuaiji soldiers to go to the rescue of Dong'ou from the seaward side, but before they got there, the Minyue troops fled, so the Emperor's forces also withdrew.

On the 30th day of the ninth moon, there was a solar eclipse.

In the summer of year four, there was a windstorm as red as blood, followed by drought in the sixth moon. In the ninth moon, a comet flew northeastwards.

In the spring of year five, three-*zhu* coins were repealed, and half-tael cash were issued.

The system of Erudites of the Five Classics was established.

In the fourth moon, the Emperor's maternal grandmother Princess Pingyuan died.

In the fifth moon, there was a major plague of locusts.

The eighth moon saw the deaths of both Prince of Guangchuan

【原文】

六年春二月乙未，辽东高庙灾。夏四月壬子，高园便殿火。上素服五日。

五月丁亥，太皇太后崩。

秋八月，有星孛于东方，长竟天。

闽越王郢攻南越。遣大行王恢将兵出豫章，大司农韩安国出会稽，击之。未至，越人杀郢降，兵还。

元光元年冬十一月，初令郡国举孝廉各一人。

卫尉李广为骁骑将军屯云中，中尉程不识为车骑将军屯雁门，六月罢。

夏四月，赦天下，赐民长子爵一级。复七国宗室前绝属者。

五月，诏贤良曰："朕闻昔在盛虞，画象而民不犯，日月所烛，

【今译】

六年春二月乙未，辽东郡的高庙发生火灾。夏四月壬子，高祖陵园便殿起火。皇上素服五日。

五月丁亥，窦太皇太后去世。

秋八月，彗星出现在东方，首尾长度达到天空两边。

闽越王郢进攻南越。武帝派大行王恢率兵从豫章出发，大司农韩安国从会稽出发，攻击闽越。没有到达，越人便杀郢降汉，汉朝兵退。

元光元年冬十一月，开始让郡国推举孝悌者和廉吏各一人。

卫尉李广为骁骑将军驻屯云中，中尉程不识为车骑将军驻屯雁门，六月撤回。

夏四月，大赦天下，赏赐百姓长子一级爵位。恢复吴、楚七国宗室中被取消的继承权。

五月，下诏策问贤良说："朕听说过去在尧、舜时，画不同颜色的衣服象征五刑百姓就不犯罪，日月所照之处，没有不尽职听

Liu Yue and Prince of Qinghe Liu Cheng.

On the third day of the second moon of his sixth year, the Temple of Gaodi in Liaodong Prefecture was destroyed by fire, and on the 21st day of the fourth moon, the main palace of Emperor Gaodi's Mausoleum caught fire. The Emperor wore mourning clothes for five days.

On the 26th day of the fifth moon, Grand Empress Dowager Dou died.

In the eighth moon, a comet appeared in the east, its tail crossing the full width of the sky.

Ying the King of Minyue attacked South Yue. The Emperor launched a counter-attack on Minyue, dispatching Chamberlain for Dependencies Wang Hui to lead troops starting from Yuzhang Prefecture, and Chamberlain for Treasury Han Anguo starting from Kuaiji. But before the two armies got there, the Yue people themselves killed Ying and submitted to Han, so the Emperor's troops withdrew.

In the 11th moon of year one of the Yuanguang reign period (134 BC), the court started to order the prefectures and fiefs each to recommend a filial son and upright official.

Chamberlain for the Palace Garrison Li Guang was made General of the Imperial Guard, stationed at Yunzhong. Chamberlain for the Imperial Insignia Cheng Bushi was made Chariot Horse General, garrisoned in Yanmen, to be withdrawn in the sixth moon.

In the fourth moon, in summer, there was a general amnesty, and the eldest sons of common people were granted level one rank. Inheritance rights were restored to those in the seven rebel princedoms whose royal clan qualification had been canceled.

In the fifth moon, an edict was issued to ask the worthy and excellent: "I heard that in the ancient reigns of Yao and Shun, the color designs of clothes symbolized five punishments, so the people did not break the laws, and nobody disobeyed under the shining sun

【原文】

莫不率俾。周之成康，刑错不用，德及鸟兽，教通四海。海外肃昚，北发渠搜，氐羌徕服。星辰不孛，日月不蚀，山陵不崩，川谷不塞；麟凤在郊薮，河洛出图书。呜虖，何施而臻此与！今朕获奉宗庙，夙兴以求，夜寐以思，若涉渊水，未知所济。猗与伟与！何行而可以章先帝之洪业休德，上参尧舜，下配三王！朕之不敏，不能远德，此子大夫之所睹闻也。贤良明于古今王事之体，受策察问，咸以书对，著之于篇，朕亲览焉。”于是董仲舒、公孙弘等出焉。

秋七月癸未，日有蚀之。

二年冬十月，行幸雍，祠五畤。

春，诏问公卿曰：“朕饰子女以配单于，金币文绣赂之甚厚，单

【今译】

从使用的。周朝的成王、康王，刑罚搁置不使用，恩德及于鸟兽，教令到达各地。海外到肃慎族，向北征发至渠搜，氐族、羌族前来臣服。星辰不变色，日月不侵蚀，大山不崩塌，河流山谷不堵塞；麒麟、凤凰停留在郊外草泽之中，黄河中的龙马载河图而出，洛水中的神龟负洛书而现。啊，实施什么办法而达到如此完美的境地呀！如今朕获得了承继皇家基业的地位，早起追求，晚睡思念，犹如渡涉深水，还不知怎样渡过去。美好啊！伟大啊！怎样做才能弘扬先帝宏业美德，向上追溯加入尧、舜行列，往下追寻与禹、汤、文王匹配！朕不够聪敏，不能远施恩德，这是诸位大夫所耳闻目见的。贤良之士深知古今王事之体制，接受写于简策上的问题的考问，都写出来回答，著之于简策之上，朕要亲自阅览。”于是，董仲舒、公孙弘等人便以策问方式步入仕途。

秋七月癸未日，日食。

二年冬十月，武帝驾临雍县，祭祀五帝。

春，下诏询问大臣说：“朕使子女美容修饰之后许配与单于，黄金锦绣彩礼相赠丰厚，单于对朝廷命令更加怠慢，侵扰盗抢事件没有

and moon. In the reigns of King Cheng and King Kang of the Zhou Dynasty, punishments were set aside and disused, their kindness extended even to animals, and their doctrines permeated the country. Beyond our borders, the Sushen tribes came to kowtow, and in the north Qusou accepted being drafted, and even Di and Qiang tribes submitted. The stars did not change color because of comets; there were no solar or lunar eclipses; mountains did not collapse, nor did river valleys get blocked; qilin and phoenixes stayed in their countryside swamps; a fairy horse carried the Map out of the Yellow River, and the divine turtle appeared bearing the Diagram from Luohe River. Now, alas! What must we do to achieve such a perfect state? Now that I am entitled to contribute to the imperial enterprise, I rise early in pursuit of it, and stay up late in pondering, just like standing before a river with little idea of how to cross its deep waters. How beautiful! How majestic! What shall I do to promote the lofty cause and virtues of the late emperor, to join the ranks of Yao and Shun, and emulate King Yu, King Tang, and King Wen? I am not smart enough, cannot spread benevolence far and wide, as you grand masters have seen and heard for yourselves. You, worthy and excellent gentlemen who know the ways of imperial affairs both ancient and modern, accept my questions scribed on these bamboo slips, return your answers also on bamboo slips, and I will read them personally." Thus, through this mode of policy questioning, Dong Zhongshu, Gongsun Hong, and others began their careers as officials.

That autumn, on the 29th day of the seventh moon, there was a solar eclipse.

In the 10th moon of year two of Yuanguang, Emperor Wudi visited Yong County, to worship the Five Heavenly Emperors.

In the spring, an edict was issued asking the ministers: "I sent pretty girls, beautified and adorned, as a match for Chanyu King of the Huns, together with generous gifts of gold and rich embroidery,

【原文】

于待命加嫚，侵盗亡已。边境被害，朕甚闵之。今欲举兵攻之，何如？”大行王恢建议宜击。夏六月，御史大夫韩安国为护军将军，卫尉李广为骁骑将军，太仆公孙贺为轻车将军，大行王恢为将屯将军，(大)[太]中大夫李息为材官将军，将三十万众屯马邑谷中，诱致单于，欲袭击之。单于入塞，觉之，走出。六月，军罢。将军王恢坐首谋不进，下狱死。

秋九月，令民大酺五日。

三年春，河水徙，从顿丘东南流入勃海。

夏五月，封高祖功臣五人后为列侯。

河水决濮阳，泛郡十六。发卒十万救决河。起龙渊宫。

四年冬，魏其侯窦婴有罪，弃市。

春三月乙卯，丞相蚡薨。

夏四月，陨霜杀草。五月，地震。赦天下。

【今译】

停止。边境遭受祸害，朕非常忧虑。现在打算出兵攻击匈奴，怎么样？”大行令王恢建议应该攻击。夏六月，御史大夫韩安国为护军将军，卫尉李广为骁骑将军，太仆公孙贺为轻车将军，大行令王恢为将屯将军，太中大人李息为材官将军，率领三十万大军隐避于马邑山谷中，引诱单于前来，打算进行伏击。单于入塞，发觉有伏兵，跑出塞外。六月，撤回大军。将军王恢犯了首议出兵而临阵不进击匈奴之罪，下狱死。

秋九月，下令让百姓公开聚会饮酒五日。

三年春，黄河水改道，从顿丘东南流入渤海。

夏五月，封高祖功臣五人的后代为列侯。

黄河水在濮阳决口，淹没十六郡。朝廷派兵十万人堵塞黄河决口。建造龙渊宫。

四年冬，魏其侯窦婴有罪，在街头处死。

春三月乙卯，丞相田蚡去世。

夏四月，严霜冻死草木。五月，地震。大赦天下罪人。

but Chanyu became even more disobedient to imperial orders, not putting a stop to his harassment and looting. The harm and pain inflicted on the border region cause me great worry. Now I intend to send troops to attack the Huns. What is your opinion?" Wang Hui replied with the recommendation that they should attack in the sixth moon. Censor-in-Chief Han Anguo was made Protector-General, Chamberlain for the Palace Garrison Li Guang was made General of the Imperial Guard, Chamberlain for the Imperial Stud Gongsun He was made General of Light Chariots, Chamberlain for Dependencies Wang Hui was made Frontier-Garrison General, and Superior Grand Master of the Palace Li Xi was made Construction General; they led the 300,000 troops stationed in the valley of Mayi, luring Chanyu toward their ambushes. Chanyu came inside the frontier pass, found the ambush, and fled back beyond the Great Wall. In the sixth moon, the troops were disbanded. General Wang Hui was imprisoned for hesitating to attack after being the first to propose it. He died in prison.

In the ninth moon, an order came down for the people to have a social gathering and drink for five days.

In the spring of year three, the Yellow River changed its course, emptying into the Bohai Sea southeast of Dunqiu.

In the fifth moon, descendants of Emperor Gaozu's five meritorious ministers were made adjunct marquises.

The Yellow River burst its banks in Puyang, flooding 16 prefectures. The court sent 100,000 troops to fill in the breaches in its banks. Construction of Longyuan Palace was completed.

In the winter of year four, Marquis of Weiqi Dou Ying was found guilty, and was executed in the streets.

On the 17th day of the third moon, Prime Minister Tian Fen died.

In the fourth moon in summer, a severe frost killed vegetation. In the fifth moon, an earthquake struck. A general amnesty was

【原文】

五年春正月，河间王德薨。

夏，发巴蜀治南夷道，又发卒万人治雁门阻险。

秋七月，大风拔木。

乙巳，皇后陈氏废。捕为巫蛊者，皆枭首。

八月，螟。

征吏民有明当时之务、习先圣之术者，县次续食，令与计偕。

六年冬，初算商车。

春，穿漕渠通渭。

匈奴入上谷，杀略吏民。遣车骑将军卫青出上谷，骑将军公孙敖出代，轻车将军公孙贺出云中，骁骑将军李广出雁门。青至龙城，获首虏七百级。广、敖失师而还。诏曰："夷狄无义，所从来久。间者匈奴数寇边境，故遣将抚师。古者治兵振旅。因遭虏之方入，将吏新

【今译】

五年春正月，河间王刘德去世。

夏，征发巴、蜀之民开通南方少数民族地区通路，又派出士兵一万修建雁门险阻屏障。

秋七月，大风拔起树木。

乙巳日，皇后陈氏被废黜。逮捕搞巫蛊术的人，都处死悬首示众。

八月，农田出现钻心虫灾害。

征集官吏、百姓中明白当世时务、熟习圣人治世方法的人，沿途由各县供给饮食，让他们与郡国上计吏同来京师。

六年冬，开始征收商人车船税。

春，挖凿水渠沟通渭河。

匈奴进入上谷，杀害官吏、百姓，抢掠财物。朝廷派车骑将军卫青从上谷出兵，骑将军公孙敖从代郡出兵，轻车将军公孙贺从云中出兵，骁骑将军李广从雁门出兵。卫青到达龙城，斩杀七百匈奴兵。李广、公孙敖损兵而还。皇帝下诏说："夷狄不讲仁义，由来已久。近来匈奴多次侵扰边境，因此派遣将军抚慰军队。古代治理军队严明戒律，今天出兵，因刚刚遭受寇虏为害，将士官兵不久才聚集起来，上

implemented across the nation.

In the first moon of year five, Prince of Hejian Liu De died.

In summer, the people in Ba and Shu were drafted to improve the roads to barbarian areas in the south, and 10,000 soldiers were sent to build Yanmen fortress pass.

In the seventh moon, strong gales uprooted trees.

On the 14th day, Empress Chen was deposed. Sorcerers engaging in witchcraft with venomous worms were arrested and put to death, their heads hung aloft for all to see.

In the eighth moon, there was a plague of snout moths.

The court summoned together officials and private citizens with an understanding of current affairs and familiar with the statecraft of sages old. They were required to come to the capital along with the accounts clerks and were provided food along the way by the successive counties through which they passed.

In the winter of year six, the court began to impose taxes on merchant carts and ships.

In spring, canals were dug to connect to the Weihe River.

The Huns entered Shanggu Prefecture, killing and wounding officials and ordinary people, looting and pillaging. Chariot Horse General Wei Qing was sent from Shanggu, Cavalry General Gongsun Ao from Dai, Light Chariot General Gongsun He from Yunzhong, and General of the Imperial Guard Li Guang from Yanmen. Wei Qing reached Longcheng and beheaded 700 enemy troops, but Li Guang and Gongsun Ao returned with loss of soldiers. The emperor issued an edict: "It has been a long time that the barbarians have not observed righteousness. Recently, the Huns have repeatedly invaded our border area, so I sent generals to express appreciation to the army. In days of old, military discipline was strictly enforced. But today the generals, officials and soldiers of the expeditionary troops have only just joined forces following depletion at the hands of the barbarians due to bad coordination

【原文】

会，上下未辑，代郡将军敖、雁门将军广所任不肖，校尉又背义妄行，弃军而北，少吏犯禁。用兵之法：不勤不教，将率之过也；教令宣明，不能尽力，士卒之罪也。将军已下廷尉，使理正之，而又加法于士卒，二者并行，非仁圣之心。朕闵众庶陷害，欲刷耻改行，复奉正(议)[义]，厥路亡繇。其赦雁门、代郡军士不循法者。”

夏，大旱，蝗。

六月，行幸雍。

秋，匈奴盗边。遣将军韩安国屯渔阳。

元朔元年冬十一月，诏曰：“公卿大夫，所使总方略，壹统类，广教化，美风俗也。夫本仁祖义，褒德禄贤，劝善刑暴，五帝三王所繇昌也。朕夙兴夜寐，嘉与宇内之士臻于斯路。故旅耆老，复孝敬，选豪俊，讲文学，稽参政事，祈进民心，深诏执事，兴廉举孝，庶几

【今译】

下尚未协调一致，代郡将军公孙敖、雁门将军李广不称职，校尉军官们又违背道义不知约束自己行为，抛弃军队而败北，下级官吏触犯禁律。用兵的方法是：不尽心训练教育士兵，是将帅的过错；教令已经宣布明确，不能尽力去照办，是士卒的罪过。将军已经交廷尉，按法律明正其罪，如果再对士兵施加刑罚，二者并行，就不是圣人仁义之心了。朕忧虑众士卒遭到陷害，打算洗刷耻辱改正错误，再度奉行正义，又担心无路可走。因此，应赦免雁门、代郡士兵不遵守军法的人。”

夏，大旱，蝗虫灾。

六月，驾临雍县。

秋，匈奴侵扰边境。派遣将军韩安国驻屯渔阳。

元朔元年冬十一月，武帝下诏说：“公卿大夫，其职责是总握方略，统一众事，广传教化，美善风俗。以仁义为根本，表彰道德、加禄给贤人，奖励善良，禁止暴行，是五帝、三王所倡导的。朕起早睡晚，鼓励天下之士完善这条道路。因此嘉惠老人，优待孝敬老人的人，选拔才能出众者，宣讲文章之学，考究政事，激励民心，严令执事官

between commanders and men. General Gongsun Ao from Dai and General Li Guang from Yanmen were incompetent, and the commandants acted recklessly and treacherously, deserting their army to defeat, resulting in their subordinate officials violating prohibitions. The military regulation is: it is a fault in generals not to give their all in training soldiers; whereas it is a crime on the part of soldiers not to exert themselves when orders have been clearly pronounced. The generals have been put to jail in the hand of the Chamberlain of Law Enforcement, to be punished according to the law, but if a penalty is to be imposed on the soldiers, the resulting parallcl punishment would not accord with the mind of a benevolent sage. I am worried that if the common soldiers are charged, they would have no way out, even if they intended to wash away the shame, correct the error, and revert to the pursuit of justice. Therefore, soldiers in Yanmen and Dai shall be pardoned for not complying with military rules."

In summer, there was drought and locust disaster.

In the sixth moon, the Emperor visited Yong County.

In autumn, the Huns invaded the border. General Han Anguo was sent to deal with them and garrisoned in Yuyang.

In the 11th moon of year one (128 BC) of his Yuanshuo reign period, the Emperor issued an edict: "It is the courtiers' duty to uphold the general strategy and unify implementation, with a view to enlightenment and perfecting customs. This is what the Five Emperors and Three Kings of antiquity advocated: to grant moral recognition to the virtuous and material reward to the wise, and to admonish and prohibit violence, in accordance with the fundamental principles of benevolence and righteousness. I work from early morning till late at night, to encourage all people to perfect themselves on this road. So we keep being charitable to the elderly, favoring the filial by exempting them from levy, selecting the talented, preaching literary learning, studying political affairs,

【原文】

成风，绍休圣绪。夫十室之邑，必有忠信；三人并行，厥有我师。今或至阖郡而不荐一人，是化不下究，而积行之君子雍于上闻也。二千石官长纪纲人伦，将何以佐朕烛幽隐，劝元元，厉蒸庶，崇乡党之训哉？且进贤受上赏，蔽贤蒙显戮，古之道也。其与中二千石、礼官、博士议不举者罪。”有司奏议曰：“古者，诸侯贡士，壹適谓之好德，再適谓之贤贤，三適谓之有功，乃加九锡；不贡士，壹则黜爵，再则黜地，三而黜爵地毕矣。夫附下罔上者死，附上罔下者刑，与闻国政而无益于民者斥，在上位而不能进贤者退，此所以劝善黜

【今译】

员，推荐孝子、廉洁之士，可望成为风气，承继先圣美好伟大的业绩。有十户人家的小镇，必定有忠信诚实的人；三人一路同行，其中就有我的老师。如今有的全郡不推荐一人，是教化不向下贯彻，而有品行的君子不能被君主闻知。二千石一级的长官统管人伦道德，将怎样佐助朕照亮黑暗之处，劝勉百姓，激励大众，推广乡里训令呢？而且推荐贤人受到奖赏，遮蔽贤人匿藏知名人士要处死，是古代通行的办法。应该让朝中二千石一级官员、礼官、博士拿出不举荐贤人而治罪的办法来。”朝中执事官员上奏建议说：“古代，诸侯推荐人才，第一次推举了人才属于品德好，第二次推荐了人才叫做贤人中最好的贤人，第三次推荐了人才就是有功之臣，便要奖赏车马、衣服、乐器、朱户、纳陛、虎贲百人、斧钺、弓矢、秬鬯这九种贵重物品；不推举人才，第一次废除爵位，第二次削除领地，第三次全部削去爵位和领地。迎合部下欺骗上司者处死，迎合上司欺骗部下者处以刑罚，参预国政而不为民谋利者罢斥，在上位而不能推荐贤人者贬退，这就是为了奖励善良废止邪恶。今天诏书显扬先帝传业，下令太守举荐孝

inspiring public opinion, and I have strictly ordered officials in charge to recommend filial and upright people, which we aspire to make the norm, in the hope that we can succeed in the fine cause of the great sages. In a town of ten households there must be one faithful and honest person; among three companions walking side by side, there may be one person to serve as my teacher. But now some of the prefectures do not even recommend one person, which means that enlightenment does not permeate downward, and the monarch does not get to hear of gentlemen of virtue. Officials of the 2,000-piculs level are in charge of legality and morality. How will they help me illuminate the darkness, exhort the people, encourage the public and ensure government orders reach all parts of the empire? Moreover, it was the ancient way to reward those who recommended the worthy gentlemen, and to inflict death on those who covered up and hid the worthy celebrities. The officials of 2,000-piculs level, minister of rites, and the erudites should recommend a rule to impose punishment on those who do not recommend the worthy." The court officials involved memorialized: "In ancient times, when the princes recommended men of talent for the first time, they were praised as 'virtue lovers,' those recommending for a second time were called 'worthy among the worthy,' and those making a third recommendation were regarded as 'meritorious,' and rewarded with nine awards: chariots, clothes, musical instruments, red-painted house gate, heightened thresholds, one hundred warriors, long ax, bow and arrow, millet wine; those who did not recommend talents were first deprived of their titles, a repeat violation resulted in loss of their fiefdom, and a third time meant being deprived of all titles and territory. Those who conspired with their inferiors to cheat the monarch risked the death penalty, and those who assisted their superiors in cheating the subjects were penalized; those who participated in national governance but not to the benefit of the people were dismissed, while those in the upper ranks who could

【原文】

恶也。今诏书昭先帝圣绪，令二千石举孝廉，所以化元元，移风易俗也。不举孝，不奉诏，当以不敬论。不察廉，不胜任也，当免。”奏可。

十二月，江都王非薨。

春三月甲子，立皇后卫氏。诏曰：“朕闻天地不变，不成施化；阴阳不变，物不畅茂。易曰‘通其变，使民不倦’。诗云‘九变复贯，知言之选’。朕嘉唐虞而乐殷周，据旧以鉴新。其赦天下，与民更始。诸逋贷及辞讼在孝景后三年以前，皆勿听治。”

秋，匈奴人辽西，杀太守；入渔阳、雁门，败都尉，杀略三千馀人。遣将军卫青出雁门，将军李息出代，获首虏数千级。

东夷薉君南闾等口二十八万人降，为苍海郡。

【今译】

悌、廉洁之士，是为了开导百姓，移风易俗。不举荐孝悌，不执行诏令，应当以不尊敬罪论处。不能发现廉洁之士，是不称职，应当罢免官职。”上奏建议被批准。

十二月，江都王刘非去世。

春三月甲子，立卫氏为皇后。下诏说：“朕听说天地不变化，不能完成给予万物的变化；阴阳不变化，万物不能畅通繁茂。《易》说‘通达变化，使百姓不知疲倦’。《诗》说‘多次变化的事都是循环往复进行，从中择其善而从之’。朕赞赏唐尧、虞舜的质朴，也喜爱商、周的文采，借鉴旧的事物以立新政。应减免罪人罪行，与百姓除旧布新。景帝后三年以前百姓各种欠赋官之物及诉讼之辞，都不必再去办理。”

秋，匈奴侵入辽西郡，杀死太守；侵入渔阳、雁门，击败都尉，杀掠三千余人。派遣蘙将军卫青出兵雁门，将军李息出兵代郡，斩获数千人。

东夷族薉君南闾等二十八万人降汉，在该地设置了苍海郡。

not recommend the worthy had to resign. All this was done in the interest of rewarding the good and putting an end to evil. This edict is to show the late emperor's tradition. We order those with a salary of 2,000 piculs to recommend filial and upright persons, in order to guide the people, and reform their ways and manners. Therefore, those who do not recommend the filial, who do not act in accordance with this edict, should be punished for the crime of contempt. Those who cannot find incorrupt persons are incompetent and should be dismissed from the posts." The proposal was approved.

In the 12th moon, Prince of Jiangdu Liu Fei died.

On the 13th day of the third moon, Wei was established as Empress. An edict was issued saying: "I heard that if heaven and earth do not change, the changes to all things cannot be completed; if *yin* and *yang* do not change, things cannot thrive and flourish. According to the *Book of Changes*, 'Carry through the changes, so the people will not know exhaustion.' According to the *Book of Odes*, 'Those things that experience multiple changes are constantly renewed and recycled so we choose the good from them.' I appreciate the simplicity of Tang Yao and Yu Shun, and the literary talent of Shang and Zhou times. I want to draw on the old for my new governance. There should be a general amnesty to allow the people to renew themselves. Cases of debt arrears and legal actions predating year three of the last reign period of the late emperor shall be written off, we do not need to hear them."

In autumn, the Huns invaded Liaoxi Prefecture, killing its governor; they went on to invade Yuyang and Yanmen, defeating the Defender, and killing or taking captive 3,000 people. General Wei Qing was sent to Yanmen, and General Li Xi to Dai, taking thousands of enemy heads.

Nan Lü, King of Hui of the eastern barbarians, and others surrendered to Han with 280,000 people, and Canghai Prefecture

【原文】

鲁王馀、长沙王发皆薨。

二年冬，赐淮南王、菑川王几杖，毋朝。

春正月，诏曰："梁王、城阳王亲慈同生，愿以邑分弟，其许之。诸侯王请与子弟邑者，朕将亲览，使有列位焉。"于是藩国始分，而子弟毕侯矣。

匈奴入上谷、渔阳，杀略吏民千馀人。遣将军卫青、李息出云中，至高阙，遂西至符离，获首虏数千级。收河南地，置朔方、五原郡。

三月乙亥晦，日有蚀之。

夏，募民徙朔方十万口。又徙郡国豪杰及訾三百万以上于茂陵。

秋，燕王定国有罪，自杀。

三年春，罢苍海郡。三月，诏曰："夫刑罚所以防奸也，内长文所以见爱也；以百姓之未洽于教化，朕嘉与士大夫日新厥业，祗而不解。其赦天下。"

夏，匈奴入代，杀太守；入雁门。杀略千馀人。

【今译】

鲁王刘馀、长沙王刘发都去世。

二年冬，赐给淮南王刘安、菑川王刘志茶几与拐杖，不必上朝朝见皇帝。

春正月，下诏说："梁王、城阳王是一母亲生兄弟，愿意把封邑分给其弟，应允许。诸侯王请求给与子弟封邑者，朕将亲自过问，使子弟都有列侯位置。"于是藩国开始分而治之，而子弟都受封为侯。

匈奴侵入上谷、渔阳，杀掠吏民千余人。派遣将军卫青、李息出兵云中，到达高阙，接着西至符离，斩获数千人。收复了河套以南的河南地区，设置了朔方、五原郡。

三月乙亥为月末日，发生日食。

夏，招募百姓迁往朔方十万人。又迁徙郡国豪富及资产在三百万钱以上的大富户定居于茂陵。

秋，燕王刘定国有罪，自杀。

三年春，撤苍海郡。三月，下诏说："刑罚是为了防止奸邪的，对内尊崇文德为的是显示亲爱；由于百姓没有受到教育，朕奖励士大夫每日更新职守，恭敬不懈。应减免天下有罪人的罪行。"

夏，匈奴侵入代郡，杀死太守；侵入雁门郡，杀掠千余人。

was set up in the area.

Prince of Lu Liu Yu and Prince of Changsha Liu Fa both died.

In the winter of year two, tea tables and walking sticks were granted to Prince of Huainan Liu An and Prince of Zichuan Liu Zhi, signifying their exemption from audiences with the Emperor.

In the first moon, an edict was issued: "Prince of Liang and Prince of Chengyang are my own brothers, whose wish to share out their fiefs are granted. I will examine in person the princes' request to share their fiefs with their sons and brothers, so that they also have titles." Hence, the princedoms began to divide under different rulers, and the sons and brothers became all marquises.

The Huns invaded Shanggu and Yuyang, killing and seizing more than 1,000 officials and people. General Wei Qing and Li Xi were sent to Yunzhong, proceeding to Gaoque Fortress, then west toward Fuli Fortress, beheading thousands of barbarians. The region south of Hetao, or the Great Bend of the Yellow River, was restored to Han rule and Shuofang and Wuyuan prefectures were set up.

The end of the third moon saw a solar eclipse.

In summer, the government recruited 100,000 people to move to Shuofang, and resettled in the area of Maoling the rich and powerful in the prefectures and fiefs and super-rich households with assets of more than three million cash.

In autumn, Prince of Yan Liu Dingguo was found guilty, and committed suicide.

In the spring of year three, Canghai Prefecture was revoked. In the third moon, an edict was issued: "Penalties are to prevent the treacherous, while the upholding of literary endeavor is to show love. Because people have not been schooled, I award scholars and grand masters who show new commitment to their duties daily and persistent respect. There shall be a general amnesty."

In summer, the Huns invaded Dai, killing its governor;

【原文】

六月庚午，皇太后崩。

秋，罢西南夷，城朔方城。令民大酺五日。

四年冬，行幸甘泉。

夏，匈奴入代、定襄、上郡，杀略数千人。

五年春，大旱。大将军卫青将六将军兵十馀万人出朔方、高阙，获首虏万五千级。

夏六月，诏曰："盖闻导民以礼，风之以乐，今礼坏乐崩，朕甚闵焉。故详延天下方闻之士，咸荐诸朝。其令礼官劝学，讲议洽闻，举遗兴礼，以为天下先。太常其议予博士弟子，崇乡党之化，以厉贤材焉。"丞相弘请为博士置弟子员，学者益广。

秋，匈奴入代，杀都尉。

六年春二月，大将军卫青将六将军兵十馀万骑出定襄，斩首三千馀级。还，休士马于定襄、云中、雁门。赦天下。

【今译】

六月庚午，皇太后去世。

秋，停止开通西南夷道路，建造朔方城。让百姓举行五日酒宴。

四年冬，驾临甘泉宫。

夏，匈奴侵入代郡、定襄郡、上郡，杀掠数千人。

五年春，大旱。大将军卫青率六将、兵卒十余万人从朔方、高阙出发，斩获一万五千人。

夏六月，下诏说："听说用礼指导百姓，用音乐进行劝谕，今天礼乐制度破坏，朕很忧虑。因此要把天下博闻有识之士全部请来，都举荐给朝廷。应让礼官劝进学业，讲论见闻，推举遗逸之民倡兴礼学，作为天下的表率。太常应商讨给予博士弟子，推崇乡里教化，以便培养贤能人才。"丞相公孙弘请求为博士设立弟子，学礼乐者更为增加。

秋，匈奴侵入代郡，杀死都尉。

六年春二月，大将军卫青率领六将军、十万余骑兵从定襄郡出兵，斩首三千余。返回，在定襄、云中、雁门休整士兵、战马。大赦天下。

then they invaded Yanmen, killing and seizing more than 1,000 people.

On the second day of the sixth moon, the Empress Dowager died.

In autumn, the government suspended building the road to the southwestern barbarians and started construction of Shuofang city; the people were given five days feasting.

In the winter of year four, His Majesty visited Ganquan Palace.

In summer, the Huns invaded the prefectures of Dai, Dingxiang, and Shangjun, killing and seizing thousands.

In the spring of year five, there was a great drought. General-in-Chief Wei Qing led expeditions of six generals and more than 100,000 soldiers from garrisons at Shuofang and Gaoque, taking 15,000 heads. In the sixth moon, an edict came down saying: "I have heard about guidance of the people through the rites and bringing them to reason through music, but it grieves me that today the system of ritual and music is damaged. We should, therefore, invite all the upright and insightful gentlemen under Heaven and recommend them to the court. I hereby order the Erudites to encourage learning, to talk of what they know; among the lax people they should champion the lost learning and ritual as the model for the world. The Chamberlain for Ceremonials should recommend that the Erudites be given disciples, and promote local teaching, in order to develop elite talents." Prime Minister Gongsun Hong requested the Erudites to take on disciples, and the numbers of people learning rites and music increased widely.

In autumn, the Huns invaded Dai Prefecture, killing the Defender.

In the second moon of year six, General Wei Qing led six generals and more than 100,000 cavalry troops from Dingxiang County, beheading 3,000 enemy. Back in Dingxiang, Yunzhong and

【原文】

夏四月，卫青复将六将军绝幕，大克获。前将军赵信军败，降匈奴。右将军苏建亡军，独身脱还，赎为庶人。

六月，诏曰："朕闻五帝不相复礼，三代不同法，所繇殊路而建德一也。盖孔子对定公以徕远，哀公以论臣，景公以节用，非期不同，所急异务也。今中国一统而北边未安，朕甚悼之。日者大将军巡朔方，征匈奴，斩首虏万八千级，诸禁锢及有过者，咸蒙厚赏，得免减罪。今大将军仍复克获，斩首虏万九千级，受爵赏而欲移卖者，无所流貤。其议为令。"有司奏请置武功赏官，以宠战士。

元狩元年冬十月，行幸雍，祠五畤。获白麟，作白麟之歌。

十一月，淮南王安、衡山王赐谋反，诛。党与死者数万人。

【今译】

夏四月，卫青又率领六将军横度沙漠，大获全胜。前将军赵信军败，投降匈奴。右将军苏建损失全军，只身逃回，有罪赎为平民。

六月，下诏说："朕听说五帝实行的礼制不相重复，夏、商、周三代的治国之法也各不相同，所走的道路不同而建立的功德伟业是一样的。孔子用招抚边远臣民来回答鲁定公的提问，对鲁哀公的提问用政在选臣来回答，对齐景公的提问用节省开支来回答，不是有不同的对待，所注重的缓急各有区别。今天中原已经一统而北方边境还未安定，朕很伤痛。不久前大将军巡行朔方，征伐匈奴，斩首俘虏一万八千多人，各类受限制不得做官及有过错的人，都蒙受厚赏，得到减免罪过的优待。今大将军频获大捷，斩首俘获一万九千多人，受到奖赏爵位而又想转卖的人，没有转卖的办法。应商议办法写成命令。"朝廷执事官员请求设置武功赏爵，以便奖励爱护战士。

元狩元年冬十月，武帝驾临雍县，祭五帝坛。猎获一只白麒麟，撰写了一首《白麟之歌》。

十一月，淮南王刘安、衡山王刘赐谋反，被杀。同党被处死的有数万人。

Yanmen, they had their soldiers and horses rest. There was a general amnesty.

In the fourth moon, Wei Qing again led six generals across the desert and won a sweeping victory. General of the Front Zhao Xin was defeated and surrendered to the Huns. General of the Right Su Jian lost his entire army and fled back alone. He became a civilian in expiation of his guilt.

In the sixth moon, an edict was issued saying: "I heard that the Five Emperors did not perform identical rites, and that the Xia, Shang and Zhou dynasties had different rules of government, taking diverse paths toward establishing the same meritorious achievements. Confucius responded to Duke Ding of Lu with suggestions to pacify remote subjects, to Duke Ai of Lu with a policy of selecting courtiers, and to Duke Jing of Qi with the policy of frugality. These different suggestions did not imply different expectations, but different priorities. Today, it pains me that while the Middle Kingdom has been unified the northern border is not yet stable. Recently, the General-in-Chief patrolled Shuofang and attacked the Hun, putting to the sword more than 18,000 enemies, and all kinds of people in fault or subject to restrictions enjoyed generous treatment, their faults being excused or punishment mitigated. Now this general has frequent victories, having beheaded and captured 19,000 people, so those who were rewarded with titles have no way to sell them on. You should propose ways of transfer as a written order." The court requested that military titles be established to placate the fighting men.

In the tenth moon of year one of the Yuanshou reign period (122 BC), the Emperor visited Yong County, offering sacrifice to the Five Heavenly Emperors. Having hunted a white qilin unicorn, he wrote "Ode to the White Qilin."

In the 11th moon, Prince of Huainan Liu An and Prince of

【原文】

十二月，大雨雪，民冻死。

夏四月，赦天下。

丁卯，立皇太子。赐中二千石爵右庶长，民为父后者一级。诏曰：“朕闻咎繇对禹，曰在知人，知人则哲，惟帝难之。盖君者心也，民犹支体，支体伤则心憯怛。日者淮南、衡山修文学，流货赂，两国接壤，怵于邪说，而造篡弑，此朕之不德。诗云：‘忧心惨惨，念国之为虐。’已赦天下，涤除与之更始。朕嘉孝弟力田，哀夫老眊孤寡鳏独或匮于衣食，甚怜愍焉。其遣谒者巡行天下，存问致赐。曰‘皇帝使谒者赐县三老、孝者帛，人五匹；乡三老、弟者、力田帛，人三匹；年九十以上及鳏寡孤独帛，人二匹，絮三斤；八十以上米，人三石。有冤失职，使者以闻。县乡即赐，毋赘聚’。”

【今译】

十二月，降大雪，有的百姓冻死。

夏四月，减免天下有罪人的罪行。

丁卯日，立刘据为皇太子。赐中二千石官员右庶长爵位，百姓中继承父业者赐爵一级。下诏说：“朕听说咎繇回答禹的提问时，说是在于了解人，了解了人就会聪明有智，就是帝王也难以办到。君主是心脏，百姓犹如肢体，肢体受到伤害心脏就惨痛。不久前，淮南王、衡山王研修文学，买卖货物，两国相连接，被邪说诱惑，因而酿成篡逆谋反大罪，这是朕没有恩德所造成的。《诗》说：‘忧伤之心戚惨，思念国事最为沉重。’已经大赦天下，洗涤旧俗使百姓开始新的生活。朕奖励孝子、尊敬兄长、致力于耕种的人，同情老年鳏寡孤独者或缺少衣食的人，非常令人怜悯。应派遣谒者巡视天下，慰问赏赐。就说：‘皇帝派谒者赏赐县三老和孝子帛，每人五匹；乡三老、敬兄长者、努力耕种者赐帛，每人三匹；年九十以上及鳏寡孤独者赐帛，每人二匹，丝絮三斤；八十以上赐米，每人三石。有冤而失去职业者，由使者报告皇帝。在县乡就居住地赏赐，不必征召聚众。”

Hengshan Liu Ci rebelled, and were killed. Tens of thousands in their party were put to death.

In the 12th moon, a heavy snow fell, and people froze to death.

In the fourth moon, there was a general amnesty.

On the 21st day, Liu Ju was named Crown Prince. The Emperor granted the title of Right Chief (grandee of the 11th order) to officials with full 2,000 piculs, and one order of rank to people who inherited their father's patriarchy. An edict was issued saying: "I heard that Gao Yao responded to Yu's question stressing the importance of understanding what people are capable of. Indeed it is wise to understand people, but it is difficult for the Emperor to do this. The monarch is the heart, and the people are like limbs, and hurts in the limbs are felt also in the heart. Not long ago, Princes of Huainan and Hengshan cultivated literary learning, and the trading of goods, since the two princedoms are connected. That they were both led by heresy into temptation and hence rebellion happened because of my own lack of virtue. As the *Book of Odes* expressed it: 'The sad heart is miserable, reflecting on the nation's suffering.' I have declared amnesty, to wash away old customs so that people can start a new life. I reward filial sons and dutiful brothers, as well as those committed to farming, comfort the old, those without kin or support, or the needy people, who are worthy of sympathy. Messengers should be sent to tour the empire, to comfort and reward them. Let them say this: 'The emperor has sent a messenger to award five rolls of silk apiece to the three seniors of the county and the filial sons; three rolls of silk apiece to the three seniors of the town and the dutiful brothers as well as those committed to farming; two rolls of silk and three *jin* of silk wadding apiece to folks over 90 years of age and to those without kin or support; three stone of rice to old folks over 80. Those who lost their posts due to injustice shall be reported to me by the messenger. They should be rewarded in their county or town of residence, without calling a formal gathering."

【原文】

五月乙巳晦，日有蚀之。

匈奴入上谷，杀数百人。

二年冬十月，行幸雍，祠五畤。

春三月戊寅，丞相弘薨。

遣骠骑将军霍去病出陇西，至皋兰，斩首八千馀级。

夏，马生余吾水中。南越献驯象、能言鸟。

将军去病、公孙敖出北地二千馀里，过居延，斩首虏三万馀级。

匈奴入雁门，杀略数百人。遣卫尉张骞、郎中令李广皆出右北平。广杀匈奴三千馀人，尽亡其军四千人，独身脱还，及公孙敖、张骞皆后期，当斩，赎为庶人。

江都王建有罪，自杀。胶东王寄薨。

秋，匈奴昆邪王杀休屠王，并将其众合四万馀人来降，置五属国以处之。以其地为武威、酒泉郡。

三年春，有星孛于东方。夏五月，赦天下。立胶东康王少子庆为六安王。封故相国萧何曾孙庆为列侯。

秋，匈奴入右北平、定襄，杀略千馀人。

【今译】

五月乙巳为月末日，发生日食。

匈奴侵入上谷郡，杀数百人。

二年冬十月，驾临雍县，祭祀五帝。

春三月戊寅，丞相公孙弘去世。

派遣骠骑将军霍去病出兵陇西，到达皋兰，杀敌八千余人。

夏，马生在余吾水中。南越进献驯象、鹦鹉。

将军霍去病、公孙敖出北地二千余里，越过居延县，杀敌三万余人。

匈奴侵入雁门，杀掠数百人。派遣卫尉张骞、郎中令李广同时出兵右北平郡。李广杀匈奴三千余人，丧失全军四千人，只身脱险逃回，还有公孙敖、张骞都失约迟到，以法当斩，赎为百姓。

江都王刘建有罪，自杀。胶东王刘寄去世。

秋，匈奴昆邪王杀休屠王，并且率其部众合计四万余人前来投降，安置在原来五个属国境内。把这些地区划分为武威郡、酒泉郡。

三年春，彗星出现于东方。夏五月，赦天下。立胶东康王少子刘庆为六安王。封故相国萧何曾孙萧庆为列侯。

秋，匈奴侵入右北平郡、定襄郡，杀掠千余人。

On the 30th day of the fifth moon, a solar eclipse occurred.

The Huns invaded Shanggu Prefecture, killing hundreds of people.

In the 10th moon of year two, the Emperor visited Yong County, offering sacrifice to the Five Heavenly Emperors.

On the seventh day of the third moon, Prime Minister Gongsun Hong died.

Cavalry General Huo Qubing was sent from Longxi, reaching Gaolan, and beheaded over 8,000 enemy.

In summer, horses were born in the waters of the Yuwu River. South Yue offered tribute of trained elephants and parrots.

General Huo Qubing and Gongsun Ao marched from Beidi 2,000 *li*, through Juyan County, killing over 30,000 enemy.

The Huns invaded Yanmen, killing and taking captive hundreds of people. Zhang Qian, Chamberlain for the Palace Garrison, and Li Guang, Chamberlain for Attendants, were sent from Youbeiping Prefecture. Li killed over 3,000 of the enemy, but at the cost of his 4,000-strong army, he being the only one to escape home. He, Zhang Qian and Gongsun Ao were all later than scheduled, an offense punishable by death, but were instead demoted to commoner rank.

Liu Jian, Prince of Jiangdu committed an offense, and committed suicide. Liu Ji, Prince of Jiaodong died.

In autumn, King Hunye killed King Xiutu, and led their Hun tribes, totaling more than 40,000, to surrender, whom the government placed in the original five vassal states. These areas were divided into Wuwei and Jiuquan prefectures.

In the spring of year three, a comet appeared in the east. In the fifth moon, there was a general amnesty. Prince Kang of Jiaodong's younger son Liu Qing was made Prince of Liu'an. Xiao Qing, the great-grandson of the late Prime Minister Xiao He, became an adjunct marquis.

In autumn, the Huns invaded Youbeiping and Dingxiang

【原文】

遣谒者劝有水灾郡种宿麦。举吏民能假贷贫民者以名闻。

减陇西、北地、上郡戍卒半。

发谪吏穿昆明池。

四年冬，有司言关东贫民徙陇西、北地、西河、上郡、会稽凡七十二万五千口，县官衣食振业，用度不足，请收银锡造白金及皮币以足用。初算缗钱。

春，有星孛于东北。

夏，有长星出于西北。

大将军卫青将四将军出定襄，将军去病出代，各将五万骑。步兵踵军后数十万人。青至幕北围单于，斩首万九千级，至阗颜山乃还。去病与左贤王战，斩获首虏七万馀级，封狼居胥山乃还。两军士(战)死者数万人。前将军广、后将军食其皆后期。广自杀，食其赎死。

五年春三月甲午，丞相李蔡有罪，自杀。

天下马少，平牡马匹二十万。

【今译】

派遣谒者在遭水灾郡县提倡种冬小麦。推举官员、百姓能借贷给贫民钱粮者把名字报上朝廷。

把征调陇西郡、北地郡、上郡的戍边兵卒减少一半。

征调有罪官吏开凿昆明池。

四年冬，朝廷官员报告关东贫民迁徙到陇西、北地、西河、上郡、会稽的共七十二万五千口，国家供应衣食扶持产业，用费不足，请求收集银、锡铸造白金及皮币以便满足使用。开始征收商业税、手工业资产税。

春，彗星出现于东北。

夏，彗星出现于西北。

大将军卫青率四将军出兵定襄，将军霍去病出兵代郡，各率五万骑兵。步兵跟在后面的有数十万人。卫青到达沙漠以北包围单于，杀敌一万九千人，到阗颜山返回。霍去病与左贤王交战，杀敌七万余人，在狼居胥山祭天后返回。卫、霍两军死亡士卒数万人。前将军李广、后将军赵食其都失约迟到。李广自杀，食其赎免死罪。

五年春三月甲午，丞相李蔡有罪，自杀。

天下马匹缺少，平抑雄马每匹价格为二十万钱。

prefectures, killing and capturing over 1,000 people.

Envoys were sent to flooded prefectures to urge the planting of winter wheat species. Those officials and people who could lend money and grain to the poor had their names reported to the court.

The number of frontier soldiers sent to Longxi, Beidi and Shangjun prefectures was reduced by half.

Officials guilty of offenses were drafted to dig Kunming Pool in Xi'an.

In the winter of year four, court officials reported that poor households totaling 725,000 people had migrated from Guandong to Longxi, Beidi, Xihe, Shangjun and Kuaiji, but the magistrates supplying them with food and clothing and supporting their production were short of funds, so they requested to collect silver and tin for casting silver coins and deer hide coins in order to meet the expense. The government began to levy string-cash taxes on business and handicrafts industry.

In spring, a comet appeared in the northeast.

In summer, a comet appeared in the northwest.

General-in-Chief Wei Qing led four generals from Dingxiang and General Huo Qubing started from Dai Prefecture, each with 50,000 cavalry. The infantry followed, hundreds of thousands strong. General Wei surrounded Chanyu at the north of the desert, beheading 19,000 enemies, only turning back when they reached Tianyan Mountains. Huo engaged King Zuoxian in battle, beheading more than 70,000 people, and returned after holding a sacrificial ceremony in Langjuxu Mountains before turning back. Tens of thousands of Wei's and Huo's troops were killed. General of the Front Li Guang and General of the Rear Zhao Yiji were late to arrive. Li committed suicide, and Zhao escaped the death penalty by redemption.

On the 11th day of the third moon of year five, Prime Minister Li Cai was found guilty, and committed suicide.

There was a shortage of horses, so that an average stallion cost

【原文】

罢半两钱，行五铢钱。

徙天下奸猾吏民于边。

六年冬十月，赐丞相以下至吏二千石金，千石以下至乘从者帛，蛮夷锦各有差。

雨水亡冰。

夏四月乙巳，庙立皇子闳为齐王，旦为燕王，胥为广陵王。初作诰。

六月，诏曰：“日者有司以币轻多奸，农伤而末众，又禁(以)[兼]并之涂，故改币以约之。稽诸往古，制宜于今。废期有月，而山泽之民未谕。夫仁行而从善，义立则俗易，意奉宪者所以导之未明与？将百姓所安殊路，而挢虔吏因乘势以侵蒸庶邪？何纷然其扰也！今遣博士大等六人分循行天下，存问鳏寡废疾，无以自振业者贷与之。谕三老孝弟以为民师，举独行之君子，征诣行在所。朕嘉贤者，乐知其人。

【今译】

废除半两钱，发行五铢钱。

迁徙天下奸猾官、民到边地。

六年冬十月，赏赐丞相以下至太守一级官员黄金，县级以下官员至随从人员帛，少数民族锦各不相等。

下雨水不结冰。

夏四月乙巳，在祖庙中册立皇子刘闳为齐王，刘旦为燕王，刘胥为广陵王。开始作封王策文。

六月，下诏说：“不久前朝廷官员由于钱币重量轻又多伪造，伤害了农业，而从事商业和手工业的人增多起来，又要堵塞大家富户兼并弱小贫民的道路，因此更换钱币以便加以限制。考查古代，制订适合今天的办法。废除旧币已有一年零一个月的时间了，而山泽之民还没有晓得告示之意。实行仁爱政策人们就可以从事善良之事，确立了正义就可以改变社会风俗，究竟是奉旨执行命令的人宣示引导不明呢？还是安置百姓有不同办法，而妄托上命乘机侵夺民众的官吏造成的？怎么这样杂乱烦扰！今派遣博士褚大等六人分别巡察天下，慰问鳏寡残疾人，没有力量兴办产业者由官方借贷给予支持。晓谕天下命三老、孝悌为民师，推举有特殊才能和品德的人，请来到朕所在之处。

200,000 cash.

The half-tael coin was abolished and the five-*zhu* coin issued.

The government implemented forced removal of deceitful officials and people in the empire to the frontier regions.

In the tenth moon of year six, gold was awarded from the prime minister down to officials of 2,000-piculs grade, silk to the officials of 1,000-piculs and below, down to the entourage, while diverse quantities of brocade were awarded to barbarian officials. It rained but did not freeze.

On the 29th day of the fourth moon, in the Ancestral Temple, Prince Liu Hong was formally established as Princc of Qi, Liu Dan as Prince of Yan and Liu Xu as Prince of Guangling. The first ever Imperial Mandate was prepared. In the sixth moon, an edict was issued saying: "Not long since, the court office replaced the coin system because of the light-weight coins and counterfeit money in circulation, that was harming agriculture, also to curb the growth of sideline occupations such as trade and manual industry, and to block the acquisition by the affluent of the land of weak or poor households. After examining the ancient records, we developed what is appropriate for today. It is more than a year since we repealed the old coinage, but the rural people have not got the notice. When benevolent policy is implemented, the people can engage in good things; when the righteous state is established, society's customs can be changed. Does this mean that the people who carried the decree did not declare our intentions clearly? Or did the lack of uniform arrangements allow treacherous and extorting officials to take the opportunity to violate the people? Such chaos and vexation! I hereby assign six people led by Erudite Chu Da, to make separate inspections of the empire, bringing consolation to the widowers and widows, the disabled and sick, and lending to those without the wherewithal to start business. Inform the three seniors in the empire, filial sons and dutiful brothers to serve as teachers of the populace,

【原文】

广宣厥道，士有特招，使者之任也。详问隐处亡位，及冤失职，奸猾为害，野荒治苛者，举奏。郡国有所以为便者，上丞相、御史以闻。”

秋九月，大司马骠骑将军去病薨。

元鼎元年夏五月，赦天下，大酺五日。

得鼎汾水上。

济东王彭离有罪，废徙上庸。

二年冬十一月，御史大夫张汤有罪，自杀。十二月，丞相青翟下狱死。

春，起柏梁台。

三月，大雨雪。夏，大水，关东饿死者以千数。

秋九月，诏曰：“仁不异远，义不辞难。今京师虽未为丰年，山林池泽之饶与民共之。今水潦移于江南，迫隆冬至，朕惧其饥寒不

【今译】

朕嘉奖贤人，高兴见到和认识这些人。广泛宣扬他们的品德，才德兼备之士受特殊招请，责任在于使者鉴别与推举。详细询问隐身之处、不被任用，以及蒙冤失去正常职业等情况，奸邪狡猾为害百姓的人，农田没有开垦为政又苛薄的官吏，一律揭发上奏。郡国能妥善处理事务的人，都要上报丞相、御史大夫，呈给皇帝。”

秋九月，大司马骠骑将军霍去病去世。

元鼎元年夏五月，大赦天下，允许百姓宴饮五日。

在汾水岸边得到古鼎。

济东王刘彭离有罪，废除王号迁徙至上庸旧邑。

二年冬十一月，御史大夫张汤有罪，自杀。十二月，丞相庄青翟被关进监狱而死。

春，建造柏梁台。

三月，下大雪。夏，大水灾，函谷关以东地区饿死的人以千计算。

秋九月，下诏说：“仁爱不分远近，正义不怕艰难。今天京师虽然没有获得丰收，山林池泽的财富与百姓共享。现在水灾移到江南，寒冬就要迫近，朕害怕百姓饥寒交加无法存活下去。江南地区，烧草

recommend those of special ability and moral quality to the imperial residence. I appreciate the wise, and am glad to know these people. It is the responsibility of the envoys to widely promote their character, and let it be known that those combining talent and virtue shall come in a special recruitment. Detailed investigations and reports shall be made about those passed over and not appointed, of those wronged who lost their normal occupation, of the treacherous and cunning who harm people, and of the tyrannical officials who leave the fields to wasteland. Those in the prefectures and fiefs who can ameliorate the situation shall report to the prime minister and censor-in-chief, and to the Emperor."

In the ninth moon, Command-in-Chief General Huo Qubing died.

In the fifth moon of year one of the Yuanding reign period (116 BC), there was a general amnesty, and a five-day feast ordained.

On the shore of Fenshui River, an ancient tripod vessel was found.

Prince of Jidong Liu Pengli committed an offense, and as a result was stripped of his princely title , and removed to Shangyong County.

In the 11th moon of year two, Censor-in-Chief Zhang Tang was guilty of an offense, and committed suicide. In the 12th moon, Prime Minister Zhuang Qingzhai was put in jail, where he died.

In spring, Cedar Beams Terrace was constructed.

In the third moon, there was heavy snow. Summer saw floods, and thousands of people starved to death east of Hangu Pass.

In the ninth moon, an edict was issued saying: "Love spreads regardless of distance, and justice shuns no difficulty. Although there is no bumper harvest in the capital, the wealth of the forests and lakes shall be shared with the people. Now flooding has moved to South China, and winter is approaching, I fear the people may not survive the cold and hunger. In Jiangnan region south of the

【原文】

活。江南之地，火耕水耨，方下巴蜀之粟致之江陵，遣博士中等分循行，谕告所抵，无令重困。吏民有振救饥民免其厄者，具举以闻。”

三年冬，徙函谷关于新安。以故关为弘农县。

十一月，令民告缗者以其半与之。

正月戊子，阳陵园火。夏四月，雨雹，关东郡国十馀饥，人相食。

常山王舜薨。子教嗣立，有罪，废徙房陵。

四年冬十月，行幸雍，祠五畤。赐民爵一级，女子百户牛酒。行自夏阳，东幸汾阴。十一月甲子，立后土祠于汾阴脽上。礼毕，行幸荥阳。还至洛阳，诏曰：“祭地冀州，瞻望河洛，巡省豫州，观于

【今译】

灌水种田，刚刚从巴、蜀运出粟米到江陵，派遣博士中等人分路前往巡视，晓谕所到之处，不许加重百姓负担使之困苦。官吏和百姓有能救济饥民使其摆脱饥饿困境者，全都上报朝廷。”

三年冬，迁徙函谷关到新安县，在旧关设立弘农县。

十一月，下令让百姓告发隐瞒产业逃避资产税的人，给予隐瞒财产的一半以奖励。

正月戊子，景帝的阳陵园失火。夏四月，下冰雹，关东地区十几个郡国发生饥荒，出现人吃人现象。

常山王刘舜去世。其子刘教继王位，因有罪，废王号迁徙到房陵。

四年冬十月，驾临雍县，祭祀五帝庙。赏赐百姓爵位一级，受爵者之妻计一百户宰食牛一头、赏酒若干斗。从夏阳出行，向东驾临汾阴。十一月甲子日，在汾阴高丘上建后土祠。礼仪完毕后，驾临荥阳。返回到了洛阳，下诏说：“在冀州祭祀土地神，瞻望黄河、洛水，巡视豫州，观览周王室旧址，一切都成过去而没有人祭扫。询问

Yangtze River, they grow rice by burning the grass and irrigating to drown weeds. We have just shipped millet from Ba and Shu down to Jiangling, and dispatched Erudite Zhong and others to conduct individual inspections, making it known wherever they go that it is prohibited to heap more burdens on the people and put them in further hardship. Those officials and people able to relieve hungry people and rescue them from the plight of hunger shall all be reported to the court."

In the winter of year three, Hangu Pass was moved to Xin'an County, and Hongnong County was set up in its place.

In the 11th moon, it was decreed that people exposing those cheating on business tax by concealing strings of cash would be rewarded with half the assets of the tax dodgers.

On the 28th day of the first moon, the Yang Mausoleum of Emperor Jingdi caught fire.

In the fourth moon, it hailed and poured, causing famine in a dozen prefectures and fiefs in Guandong region. Some cannibalism occurred.

King of Changshan Liu Shun died. His son Liu Bo succeeded to the throne, but abdicated due to his crime, being removed to Fangling.

In the 10th moon of year four, the Emperor visited Yong County, offering sacrifice to the Five Heavenly Emperors. He granted the ordinary man one level of rank, and one woman per one hundred households with a buffalo and wine. He traveled eastward from Xiayang to Fenyin. On the eighth day of the 11th moon, he officiated at the Temple of the Spirit of Earth, newly built on a hill in Fenyin County. After the ceremony, he visited Xingyang. Back in Luoyang, he issued an edict saying: "In Jizhou, I worshipped Earth, looked ahead to the Yellow River and Luoshui River, and inspected Yuzhou. Then I found the former Zhou royal clan, long gone and with no one to serve the altar. After enquiries to the elderly, and

【原文】

周室，邈而无祀。询问耆老，乃得孽子嘉。其封嘉为周子南君，以奉周祀。”

春二月，中山王胜薨。

夏，封方士栾大为乐通侯，位上将军。

六月，得宝鼎后土祠旁。秋，马生渥洼水中。作宝鼎、天马之歌。

立常山宪王子商为泗水王。

五年冬十月，行幸雍，祠五畤。遂逾陇，登空同，西临祖厉河而还。

十一月辛巳朔旦，冬至。立泰畤于甘泉。天子亲郊见，朝日夕月。诏曰：“朕以眇身托于王侯之上，德未能绥民，民或饥寒，故巡祭后土以祈丰年。冀州脽壤乃显文鼎，获(祭)[荐]于庙。渥洼水出马，朕其御焉。战战兢兢，惧不克任，思昭天地，内惟自新。诗云：‘四牡翼翼，以征不服。’亲省边垂，用事所极。望见泰一，修天文襢。

【今译】

老人，才得到旁支后代姬嘉。就封姬嘉为周子南君，以侍奉周朝香火。”

春二月，中山靖王刘胜去世。

夏，封方士乐大为乐通侯，职位相当于上将军。

六月，在后土祠旁挖得宝鼎一个。秋，在渥洼水中出现神马。作《宝鼎》、《天马之歌》。

封立常山宪王刘舜之子刘商为泗水王。

五年冬十月，驾临雍县，祭祀五畤。于是越过陇山，登上空同山，西到祖厉河岸而返回。

十一月初一黎明，冬至。在甘泉宫建造太一神庙。天子亲自祭祀，早晨向东拜揖太阳，夜晚向西南拜揖月亮。下诏说：“朕以微小之身寄托于王侯之上，恩德未能安抚百姓，百姓有的忍受饥寒，因此巡行祭祀土神以祈求丰收之年。冀州高丘于是显示镂有铭文之宝鼎，得以供献宗庙。渥洼水出神马，朕可以驾驭。终日谨慎小心，畏惧不能胜任国政，思念向天地表明心志，只有内省自新。《诗》云‘四匹雄马驾驭战车飞奔，去征伐没有服从的人’。亲自巡视边防，用兵极

found Ji Jia, a collateral offspring of Zhou. I hereby make Ji Jia the monarch Zinan of Zhou, to serve the Zhou ancestral sacrifice."

In the second moon, Liu Sheng Prince of Zhongshan died.

In summer, alchemist Yue Da was made Marquis of Yuetong, a position equivalent to generalissimo.

In the sixth moon, a tripod vessel was dug from the soil behind the Temple of the Spirit of Earth. In autumn, a fairy horse appeared in Wowa River. The Emperor composed odes to the "Treasure Tripod", and "Heavenly Horse."

Prince Xian of Changshan Liu Shun's son Liu Shang was made Prince of Sishui.

In the 10th moon of year five, the Emperor visited Yong County, offering sacrifice to the Five Heavenly Emperors. He crossed over Longshan Mountain, climbed Kongtong Mountain, and went west to Zuli River before returning.

At dawn of the winter solstice, the first day of the 11th moon, the Temple of Taiyi (Supreme God) was built in Ganquan Palace. The Emperor himself officiated there, bowing eastward to the sun in the morning, and southwest to the moon at night. He issued an edict saying: "I, tiny person that I am, am positioned above the nobility of the empire, but my benevolence has failed to satisfy the people's needs, and some people suffer hunger and cold, so I went out to worship the Spirit of Earth, to pray for a good harvest year. Then, at Jizhou Hill there appeared an inscribed tripod vessel, for offering to the ancestral temple, and a fairy horse emerged from Wowa water, allowing me to harness it. Trembling with awe, I fear I am inadequate for the task of government; so I must continue to examine and renew myself because I want to show the natural principle of heaven and earth.

According to the *Book of Odes*: 'Four chariots and steeds in battle array went flying, to conquer those who did not obey.' I personally inspected the border defenses and strengthened our

【原文】

辛卯夜，若景光十有二明。易曰：‘先甲三日，后甲三日。’朕甚念年岁未咸登，饬躬斋戒，丁酉，拜况于郊。”

夏四月，南越王相吕嘉反，杀汉使者及其王、王太后。赦天下。

丁丑晦，日有蚀之。

秋，蛙、蝦蟆斗。

遣伏波将军路博德出桂阳，下湟水；楼船将军杨僕出豫章，下浈水；归义越侯严为戈船将军，出零陵，下离水；甲为下濑将军，下苍梧。皆将罪人，江淮以南楼船十万人。越驰义侯遗别将巴蜀罪人，发夜郎兵，下牂柯江，咸会番禺。

九月，列侯坐献黄金酎祭宗庙不如法夺爵者百六人，丞相赵周下狱死。乐通侯栾大坐诬罔要斩。

西羌众十万人反，与匈奴通使，攻故安，围枹罕。匈奴入五原，杀太守。

【今译】

盛。见到了太一天神之庙，修撰祭天之文辞。辛卯日夜晚，其巨大光芒有十二次明亮起来。《易》说：‘初一日的前三天是辛日，后三天是丁日。’朕非常挂念年景没有全部获得丰收，整饬身体以备斋戒，初四，在祭祀天神处行拜赐之礼。”

夏四月，南越王丞相吕嘉叛汉朝，杀汉使者及南越王、王太后。大赦天下。

四月的最后一天，发生日食。

秋，蛙与虾蟆群斗。

派遣伏波将军路博德出兵桂阳，顺湟水而下；楼船将军杨仆出豫章，顺浈水而下；归义越侯严任戈船将军，出零陵，顺离水而下；甲为下濑将军，从苍梧出发。诸将均率罪人，江淮以南楼船水兵十万人。越人驰义侯遗另外统率巴、蜀罪人，征发夜郎兵，顺牂柯江而下，各路大军在番禺会齐。

九月，列侯为宗庙祭祀时所献酎金成色分量不合规定而犯法被削爵位的有一百零六人，丞相赵周入狱而死。乐通侯乐大因谎言欺骗皇帝被腰斩。

西羌族十万之众反汉朝，与匈奴联络，攻击故安，包围枹罕县。匈奴侵入五原，杀死太守。

military might as best I could. To see the Supreme God Taiyi, I prepared his temple for Heaven's worship. On the evening of the 11th day, it lit up like the sun 12 times. According to the *Book of Changes*, 'Three days before the jia day is xin, which means fasting to renew oneself, while three days after jia is ding, meaning urging repeatedly.' I am very worried about losing an all-round good harvest this year, so I cleansed my body in preparation for fasting. On the fourth (ding) day, I bowed to the god in the temple ceremony."

In the fourth moon, the King of Nanyue's prime minister Lü Jia rebelled, killing the Han envoys, the King and the Queen Mother. General amnesty was pronounced.

On the last day of the fourth moon, there was a solar eclipse.

In autumn, groups of frogs and toads battled each other.

Harnessing-Waves General Lu Bode was dispatched to the region from Guiyang, down along Huangshui River; Towered Warship General Yang Pu was sent from Yuzhang, down Zhenshui River; allied Yue Marquis of Guiyi Yan as Weapon Warship General came from Lingling, down Lishui River; Navy General Jia came from Cangwu. They all commanded criminals, with 100,000 sailors in the warships from south of the Yangtze and Huaihe Rivers. Allied Yue Marquis of Chiyi Yi also commanded criminals from Ba and Shu and mobilized Yelang soldiers in his progress along Zangke River. They all assembled at Panyu.

In the ninth moon, 106 adjunct marquises were found guilty of giving short weight in their tribute gold for imperial ancestral sacrifice. They were stripped of their titles. Prime Minister Zhao Zhou was imprisoned and committed suicide. Marquis of Yuetong Yue Da was cut in two at the waist for deceiving the emperor.

Ten thousand Western Qiang people rebelled and liaised with the Huns. They attacked Gu'an and surrounded Baohan. They invaded Wuyuan, killing its governor.

【原文】

六年冬十月，发陇西、天水、安定骑士及中尉，河南、河内卒十万人，遣将军李息、郎中令(一)[徐]自为征西羌，平之。

行东，将幸缑氏，至左邑桐乡，闻南越破，以为闻喜县。春，至汲新中乡，得吕嘉首，以为获嘉县。驰义侯遗兵未及下，上便令征西南夷，平之。遂定越地，以为南海、苍梧、郁林、合浦、交阯、九真、日南、珠厓、儋耳郡。定西南夷，以为武都、牂柯、越嶲、沈黎、文山郡。

秋，东越王馀善反，攻杀汉将吏。遣横海将军韩说、中尉王温舒出会稽，楼船将军杨僕出豫章，击之。又遣浮沮将军公孙贺出九原，匈河将军赵破奴出令居，皆二千馀里，不见虏而还。乃分武威、酒泉地置张掖、敦煌郡，徙民以实之。

元封元年冬十月，诏曰："南越、东瓯咸伏其辜，西蛮北夷颇未辑睦，朕将巡边垂，择兵振旅，躬秉武节，置十二部将军，亲帅师

【今译】

六年冬十月，征发陇西、天水、安定各郡县骑兵及中尉，河南、河内兵卒十万人，派遣将军李息、郎中令徐自为征讨西羌反叛，反叛被平息。

巡行东方，将要驾临缑氏县，到左邑桐乡时，听说南越兵败，改左邑县为闻喜县。春，到汲新中乡时，斩获吕嘉人头，改汲县为获嘉县。驰义侯遗所率军未及出发，武帝便命令去征讨西南夷，平息骚乱。于是平定南越，设置南海、苍梧、郁林、合浦、交阯、九真、日南、珠厓、儋耳九郡。平定西南夷，设置武都、牂柯、越嶲、沈黎、文山五郡。

秋，东越王馀善反叛，攻杀汉朝军将和官吏。汉朝派遣横海将军韩说、中尉王温舒出兵会稽，楼船将军杨仆出兵豫章，攻击东越。又派浮沮将军公孙贺出兵九原，匈河将军赵破奴出兵令居，距离都长达二千余里，没有遇见匈奴兵而返回。于是分出武威、酒泉二郡地另置张掖、敦煌郡，迁徙百姓前去充实边防。

元封元年冬十月，下诏说："南越、东瓯都辜负了汉朝，西部、北部各民族尚未和睦，朕将要巡行边防，整编军队振奋士气，亲自掌

In the 10th moon of year six, cavalry and fief guards from Longxi, Tianshui and Anding and 100,000 infantry from Henan and Henei were mobilized and General Li Xi and Chamberlain for Attendants Xu Ziwei were sent against the Qiang rebels, who were suppressed.

The Emperor inspected the East, and was going to Goushi County. While at Tongxiang of Zuoyi County, he heard that Nanyue was defeated, so he renamed the county Wenxi (Happy News). In spring, he was at Xinzhong Town of Jixian County when Lü Jia's head was taken, so he changed the name of Jixian to Huojia (Taking Jia). The Marquis of Chiyi Yi's army had not yet started out, so the Emperor ordered him to attack the Southwestern barbarians, and quell their rebellious behavior. With Nanyue area settled, nine prefectures were established in its stead, namely, Nanhai, Cangwu, Yulin, Hepu, Jiaozhi, Jiuzhen, Rinan, Zhuya, Daner. The Southwestern barbarians were settled and divided into Wudu, Zangke, Yuexi, Shenli, and Wenshan prefectures.

In autumn, the King of East Yue Yu Shan rebelled, attacking and killing the Han generals and officials. The court dispatched Transverse Sea General Han Shuo and local officer Wang Wenshu from Kuaiji, and Towered Warship General Yang Pu from Yuzhang to attack Yu Shan. Also, Fuju General Gongsun He was sent from Jiuyuan, and Xionghe General Zhao Ponu from Lingju, both marching more than 2,000 *li* to Fuju Well and Xionghe River, but they returned without engaging enemy soldiers. Thus the Prefectures of Zhangye and Dunhuang were separated from Wuwei and Jiuquan. Immigrants were moved there to enrich the border areas.

In the 10th moon of the first year of the Yuanfeng reign period (110 BC), an edict was issued: "Both southern Nanyue and eastern Dong'ou have submitted, but the western and northern barbarians are not quite harmonious yet, so I will be inspecting the borders, to encourage the armed forces and boost their morale. As military

【原文】

焉。”行自云阳，北历上郡、西河、五原，出长城，北登单于台，至朔方，临北河。勒兵十八万骑，旌旗径千馀里，威震匈奴。遣使者告单于曰：“南越王头已县于汉北阙矣。单于能战，天子自将待边；不能，亟来臣服。何但亡匿幕北寒苦之地为！”匈奴詟焉。还，祠黄帝于桥山，乃归甘泉。

东越杀王馀善降。诏曰：“东越险阻反覆，为后世患，迁其民于江淮间。”遂虚其地。

春正月，行幸缑氏。诏曰：“朕用事华山，至于中岳，获驳麃，见夏后启母石。翌日亲登嵩高，御史乘属、在庙旁吏卒咸闻呼万岁者三。登礼罔不答。其令祠官加增太室祠，禁无伐其草木。以山下户三百为之奉邑，名曰崇高，独给祠，复亡所与。”行，遂东巡海上。

【今译】

握统军号令，设立十二方面将军，亲临前线统率军队。”巡行从云阳开始，北经上郡、西河、五原，出长城，北面登上单于台，到朔方和北河岸边。检阅骑兵十八万骑，旌旗长达千余里，威震匈奴。派遣使者告诉单于说：“南越王人头已经挂在汉朝北门。单于敢应战，天子亲自率军在边界等待；不能应战，速来臣服汉朝。为什么只是躲藏在漠北寒苦之地呢！”匈奴畏惧起来。武帝返回，在桥山祭祀黄帝，然后回到甘泉。

东越人杀其王馀善降汉。下诏说：“东越地形险阻而其王反复无常，成为后世祸患，应迁徙其民至江淮地区。”于是东越地区便无人居住。

春正月，驾临缑氏。下诏说：“朕祭祀华山，又到中岳，猎驳麃，见到夏启母之化身石。次日亲身登上嵩高山，护车随从的御史，在庙旁官吏、兵卒都听到三声呼喊万岁的声音。登山祭祀的礼仪没有不回答的。应让祭祀官修缮加固太室祠，禁止砍伐山上草木。用山下三百户的赋税作为祭祀费用，命名为崇高邑，专供祭祀，免除其徭役及其他杂务。”起驾后，便向东巡行海上。

chief on the front-line I will command the military ranks in person with the establishment of 12 generals." He started from Yunyang, going north via Shangjun, Xihe, and Wuyuan, beyond the Wall, as north as the Chanyu Terrace, to Shuofang and the bank of the North River. He commanded 180,000 cavalry, whose flags extended more than a thousand *li*, to awe the Huns and make them tremble. He sent envoys to tell Chanyu: "The King of Nanyue's head hangs on the north gate of the Han Palace. If Chanyu dares to wage battle, I, the Son of Heaven, will personally lead my army that awaits him on the border; if you will not fight, make speed to surrender. Why skulk in hiding in the cold and desolate land north of thc desert!" The Huns were deterred. The Emperor returned to Ganquan Palace, going via Qiaoshan to worship the Yellow Emperor.

The East Yue people killed their King Yu Shan and yielded to Han. An edict was issued: "East Yue will become a scourge for later generations because of its difficult terrain and obstacles and its capricious king, so its people shall move to the area between the Yangtze and Huaihe Rivers." Hence the eastern Yue region became uninhabited.

In the first moon, the Emperor visited Goushi, issuing an edict: "I worshipped at Huashan Mountain, went to Songshan, hunted a qilin in the form of a roebuck and saw Xia Qi's mother transformed as rock. I climbed Songshan Mountain in person the next day, and the retinue of censors, officials and soldiers near the temple all hcard the cry of "Long live" shouted three times. The divination rituals of those who made the ascent were answered without exception. The sacrifice officials were ordered to expand Taishi Temple and to prohibit the cutting of mountain vegetation. The tax revenue from 300 households at the foot of the mountain shall be made sacrificial revenue, and it shall be called Chonggao Town, exclusively for worship, exempt from corvee labor and other duties." Resuming his inspection, he went east to the coast.

【原文】

夏四月癸卯，上还，登封泰山，降坐明堂。诏曰："朕以眇身承至尊，兢兢焉惟德菲薄，不明于礼乐，故用事八神。遭天地况施，著见景象，屑然如有闻。震于怪物，欲止不敢，遂登封泰山，至于梁父，然后升禮肃然。自新，嘉与士大夫更始，其以十月为元封元年。行所巡至，博、奉高、蛇丘，历城、梁父，民田租逋赋贷，已除。加年七十以上孤寡帛，人二匹。四县无出今年算。赐天下民爵一级，女子百户牛酒。"

行自泰山，复东巡海上，至碣石。自辽西历北边九原，归于甘泉。

秋，有星孛于东井，又孛于三台。

齐王闳薨。

二年冬十月，行幸雍，祠五畤。春，幸缑氏，遂至东莱。夏四

【今译】

夏四月癸卯，武帝返回，上山祭祀泰山，下山坐于明堂朝见大臣。下诏说："朕以微小身躯承担尊贵的帝位，每日都担心的是恩德浅薄，对礼乐制度不够明了，因此祭祀天地恭请八方之神。遇到了天地神灵的恩赐，显现出神灵景象，倏然听到呼喊万岁之声。被怪物震慑，欲制止又不敢轻动，于是登上泰山祭祀天神，下至梁父山祭祀地神，然后又上肃然山祭祀。从此有了新的起点，鼓励士大夫也去旧更新，应以十月为元封元年。巡行所到之处，博县、奉高县、蛇丘县、历城县、梁父县，百姓的田租、借贷之官物、赋税，都已免除。增加赏赐年七十岁以上的孤寡者帛，每人二匹。四个县不交今年的人口税。赐天下百姓爵位一级，受爵者之妻以百户计算赏给牛和酒。"

巡行从泰山出发，又向东巡行海上，到碣石。从辽西经历北边九原，回到甘泉宫。

秋，彗星出现在东井星，又出现在三台星。

齐王刘闳去世。

二年冬十月，驾临雍县，祭祀五畤。春，驾临缑氏县，又到东莱。夏四月，返回祭祀泰山。到瓠子堤，正遇黄河决口，命令随从大

On the seventh day of the fourth moon, the Emperor returned, and climbed Mount Tai to worship it, descended and sat down in the Hall of Enlightened Rule in audience with his court. He issued an edict: "I, as a tiny being, nevertheless hold the supreme position. Trembling with awe, I fear I am weak in grace and ignorant of the ritual system and music; I therefore worshipped the Gods of heaven and earth of all directions. I was lucky enough to meet the grace of heaven and earth, and saw signs, and heard something roaring "Long Live." I was made afraid by these strange phenomena but dared not stop the worshipping. Then I climbed Mount Tai to worship the gods, down to Liangfu, and up Suran Mountain to establish the altar. As a new starting point, and also to encourage the scholars to renew themselves, I pronounce the 10th moon as the beginning of the first year of my Yuanfeng reign. Wherever I went on this tour, in Bo, Fenggao, Yiqiu, Licheng and Liangfu counties, the people are exempted from farm rents, overdue official loans and property tax. I increased grants of silk for widows and lone seniors over 70 years of age to two rolls apiece. Four counties need not pay toll tax this year. I hereby reward the private man with one level of rank, and one woman per one hundred households with a buffalo and wine."

Leaving Mount Tai, he went eastward toward the coast, to Jieshi Mountain. From Liaoxi, he went via Jiuyuan in the North Border back to Ganquan Palace.

In autumn, a comet appeared at Dongjing star in the Gemini constellation, and again in three stars in Ursa Major.

The King of Qi Liu Hong died.

In the 10th moon of year two, the Emperor visited Yong County, offering sacrifice to the Five Heavenly Emperors.

In spring, he visited Goushi County, then to Donglai. In summer, in the fourth moon, he returned to worship Mount Tai. It so happened that when he reached Huzi Dike, the Yellow River

【原文】

月，还祠泰山。至瓠子，临决河，命从臣将军以下皆负薪塞河堤，作《瓠子之歌》。赦所过徒，赐孤独高年米，人四石。还，作甘泉通天台、长安飞廉馆。

朝鲜王攻杀辽东都尉，乃募天下死罪击朝鲜。

六月，诏曰："甘泉宫内中产芝，九茎连叶。上帝博临，不异下房，赐朕弘休。其赦天下，赐云阳都百户牛酒。"作《芝房之歌》。

秋，作明堂于泰山下。

遣楼船将军杨仆、左将军荀彘将应募罪人击朝鲜。又遣将军郭昌、中郎将卫广发巴蜀兵平西南夷未服者，以为益州郡。

三年春，作角抵戏，三百里内皆(来)观。

夏，朝鲜斩其王右渠降，以其地为乐浪、临屯、玄菟、真番郡。

楼船将军杨仆坐失亡多免为庶民，左将军荀彘坐争功弃市。

【今译】

臣将军以下都背柴填塞河堤，作《瓠子之歌》。赦免经过地之罪犯，赐孤独年高者米，每人四石。返回后，建造甘泉宫的通天台、长安的飞廉馆。

朝鲜王攻杀辽东都尉，于是招募天下死刑罪犯去攻打朝鲜。

六月，下诏说："甘泉宫内室生长出灵芝，九茎叶与叶相连。上方天帝博施恩德，连下房内室也降临恩泽，赐朕宏大美好之物。今赦天下，赏赐云阳都每百户牛和酒。"作《芝房之歌》。

秋，建造明堂于泰山之下。

派遣楼船将军杨仆、左将军荀彘率领应募罪人攻打朝鲜。又派遣将军郭昌、中郎将卫广征发巴、蜀兵平定西南夷骚乱的人，设置益州郡。

三年春，表演角抵戏，三百里内的人都来观看。

夏，朝鲜人杀其王右渠降汉，在其地设立乐浪、临屯、玄菟、真番郡。

楼船将军杨仆因作战伤亡太重而触犯军法，被免职沦为平民，左将军荀彘因争功犯罪在街头处死。

burst through, so he commanded those in his entourage below the rank of generals and ministers to carry firewood to shore up the embankment. He created the "Song of Gourd (Huzi)." He pardoned criminals wherever he went through and gave four piculs of rice to each orphan, issueless widower and senior. On his return, he ordered the construction of Tongtian Tower in Ganquan Palace and Feilian Hall in Chang'an.

A Korean king assaulted and killed the defender of Liaodong, so the court drafted all those awaiting the death penalty in the empire to attack Korea. In the sixth moon, an edict was issued: "In a room in Ganquan Palace grows a magic fungus, with leaves connected on nine stems. The God of Heaven illuminates the world, reaching even into this secluded room, and blessing me with limitless grace. There shall be a general amnesty. I grant every 100 households in the city of Yunyang a buffalo and wine." He composed the "Song of Fungus Room."

In autumn, the Hall of Enlightened Rule was constructed at the foot of Mount Tai.

Towered Warship General Yang Pu and Left General Xun Zhi were sent, leading drafted criminals to attack Korea. As well as this, General Guo Chang and the General of Court Gentlemen Wei Guang were sent to mobilize the army in Ba and Shu to put down riots among the southwestern barbarians and set up Yiye Prefecture.

In the spring of year three, people from 300 *li* around came to watch a performance of wrestling drama.

In summer, the Koreans killed their king Youqu and surrendered to Han. It was replaced by new prefectures of Lelang, Lintun, Xuantu and Zhenfan.

Towered Warship General Yang Pu was charged under military law for excessively heavy combat casualties, and was dismissed from his post to become a civilian, while Left General Xun Zhi was

【原文】

秋七月，胶西王端薨。

武都氐人反，分徙酒泉郡。

四年冬十月，行幸雍，祠五畤。通回中道，遂北出萧关，历独鹿、鸣泽，自代而还，幸河东。春三月，祠后土。诏曰："朕躬祭后土地祇，见光集于灵坛，一夜三烛。幸中都宫，殿上见光。其赦汾阴、夏阳、中都死罪以下，赐三县及杨氏皆无出今年租赋。"

夏，大旱，民多暍死。

秋，以匈奴弱，可遂臣服，乃遣使说之。单于使来，死京师。匈奴寇边，遣拔胡将军郭昌屯朔方。

五年冬，行南巡狩，至于盛唐，望祀虞舜于九嶷。登灊天柱山，自寻阳浮江，亲射蛟江中，获之。舳舻千里，薄枞阳而出，作《盛唐枞阳之歌》。遂北至琅邪，并海，所过礼祠其名山大川。春三月，还至泰

【今译】

秋七月，胶西王刘端去世。

武都氐人反汉，把这些人分批迁徙到酒泉郡。

四年冬十月，驾临雍县，祭祀五帝。经过回中通道，于是从萧关北面出发，经独鹿、鸣泽，从代郡返回，驾临河东。春三月，祭土地神。下诏说："朕亲自祭后土地神，看见灵光出现在灵坛，一夜三照。驾临中都宫，殿上出现光。应赦汾阴、夏阳、中都等县的死罪及以下罪犯，赐三县及杨氏县都免交今年租赋。"

夏，大旱，很多百姓中暑而死。

秋，由于匈奴势力削弱，应及时使其臣服汉朝，于是便派使臣前去说降。单于派使臣来京，死于京师。匈奴偷袭边地，派拔胡将军郭昌驻屯朔方。

五年冬，向南方巡视游猎，到达南郡盛唐地区，遥祭葬于九嶷山的虞舜。登上灊县的天柱山，从寻阳县上船游长江，武帝亲射江中之蛟，捕获。船只前后接连千里，在枞阳停船登岸，作《盛唐枞阳之歌》。于是北到琅邪，傍依大海而行，沿途拜祭名山大川。春三月，

executed in public for claiming the credit that was not his.

In the seventh moon, the Prince of Jiaoxi Liu Duan died. The Di people in Wudu rebelled, and groups of them were removed to Jiuquan Prefecture.

In the tenth moon of year four, the Emperor visited Yong County, offering sacrifice to the Five Heavenly Emperors. The Huizhong Channel was completed, so he proceeded north from Xiao Pass over the Dulu Mountain and Ming Marshes, and returning from Dai, he visited Hedong. In the third moon, he made offerings to the Spirit of Earth. He issued an edict: "I personally offered sacrifice to the Spirit of Earth, saw light focused on the spirit altar, revealing itself three times in a night. I visited Zhongdu Palace, and saw light on the throne. I pardoned criminals in Fenyin, Xiayang and Zhongdu counties, except for capital offenses, and exempted these three counties and Yangshi County from rents and taxes this year. "

In summer, there was severe drought, and many people died of heat stroke.

In autumn, as the Hun forces weakened, making it feasible to force them into rapid submission, the Han court sent envoys to induce them to capitulate. Chanyu sent down an envoy, who died in the capital. The Huns invaded our frontier, and the government sent Hun Taking General Guo Chang to the garrison in Shuofang.

In the winter of year five, the Emperor went on an inspection tour to the south. On reaching Shengtang Hill, he worshipped from afar Yu and Shun who were buried in Jiuyi Mountain. He climbed Tianzhu Mountain in Qianxian County, and sailed along the Yangtze River from Xunyang County. The Emperor shot at a flood dragon in the river and captured it. The Emperor's boat retinue stretched a thousand *li*. He stopped at Zongyang and came ashore. He wrote the "Song of Shengtang and Zongyang." Then he went north to Langya,

【原文】

山，增封。甲子，柯高祖于明堂，以配上帝，因朝诸侯王列侯，受郡国计。夏四月，诏曰："朕巡荆扬，辑江淮物，会大海气，以合泰山。上天见象，增修封禅。其赦天下。所幸县毋出今年租赋，赐鳏寡孤独帛，贫穷者粟。"还幸甘泉，郊泰畤。

大司马大将军青薨。

初置刺史部十三州。名臣文武欲尽，诏曰："盖有非常之功，必待非常之人，故马或奔踶而致千里，士或有负俗之累而立功名。夫泛驾之马，跅弛之士，亦在御之而已。其令州郡察吏民有茂材异等可为将相及使绝国者。"

六年冬，行幸回中。春，作首山宫。

【今译】

回到泰山，加高山上祭坛。甲子日，在明堂祭祀高祖，牌位配于天帝之旁，随之朝见诸侯王及列侯，让郡国上报地方钱粮、户口、治安等情况。夏四月，下诏说："朕巡游荆州、扬州，邀集江淮之神，汇聚大海之气，聚合致于泰山。上天显示景象，增修了祭坛。应大赦天下。驾临所过之县免去今年租赋，赏赐鳏寡孤独者帛，贫穷人家赐粟。"返回后驾临甘泉宫，郊祀太一神。

大司马大将军卫青去世。

初次设置十三州部刺史。知名的文武大臣大都快没有了，下诏说："建立丰功伟业，必须依赖特殊人才，因此有的马狂奔踢踢而能一日跑完千里，士人有的被世俗讥议反而能建立功业。翻车之马、放纵不羁之士，也都在于主人驾驭罢了。应令州郡访察官吏、百姓中有超群出类拔萃可以胜任将相及出使遥远的国家的人才。"

六年冬，驾临回中宫。春，建造首山宫。

near the coast, worshipping the gods at the famous mountains and rivers along the way. In the third moon, he returned to Mount Tai, where he increased the height of the altar on the mountain. On the 21st day, the Emperor worshipped his great grandfather emperor Gaozu in the Hall of Enlightened Rule and had Gaozu's memorial tablet alongside the Heavenly God. He then received reports on local statistics (land tax, accounts, law and order) from the princes and adjunct marquises. In the fourth moon, he issued an edict saying: "I inspected Jingzhou and Yangzhou, invited deities from Yangtze and Huaihe Rivers, and gathered the vital energy of the sea, to be combined at Mount Tai. Heaven showed signs and I upgraded the worship altars. There shall be a general amnesty. The counties I visited on the road shall be exempted from rents and taxes this year and I award silk to those without kin and family support and millet to impoverished households." Returned, he visited Ganquan Palace, and worshipped the Supreme God Taiyi.

General-in-Chief serving as Commander-in-Chief Wei Qing died.

Regional governors were established initially in thirteen regions. But the number of civil and military personnel of renown was almost zero. An edict was issued saying: "We must have men of special talent in order to achieve outstanding feats, so some horses can gallop a thousand *li* a day even if they bolt and kick, while some literati can work to a meritorious cause despite the burden of worldly criticism. But, horses that overturn chariots and unbiddable scholars are out there for the master to control. The regions and prefectures are ordered to find officials and people with superior talent and outstanding quality who are capable of becoming generals and prime ministers or envoys to distant countries."

In the winter of year six, he visited Huizhong. In spring, the construction of Shoushan Palace was completed.

【原文】

三月，行幸河东，祠后土。诏曰："朕礼首山，昆田出珍物，化或为黄金。祭后土，神光三烛。其赦汾阴殊死以下，赐天下贫民布帛，人一匹。"

益州、昆明反，赦京师亡命令从军，遣拔胡将军郭昌将以击之。

夏，京师民观角抵于上林平乐馆。

秋，大旱，蝗。

太初元年冬十月，行幸泰山。

十一月甲子朔旦，冬至，祀上帝于明堂。

乙酉，柏梁台灾。

十二月，禷高里，祠后土。东临勃海，望祠蓬莱。春还，受计于甘泉。

二月，起建章宫。

夏五月，正历，以正月为岁首。色上黄，数用五，定官名，协音律。

遣因杅将军公孙敖筑塞外受降城。

秋八月，行幸安定。遣贰师将军李广利发天下谪民西征大宛。

【今译】

三月，驾临河东郡，祭祀后土神庙。下诏说："朕祭祀首山，山下田地里挖出珍宝，有的化为黄金。祭祀后土，神光三照。应赦汾阴县死罪以下罪犯，赐天下贫民布帛，每人一匹。"

益州、昆明人反汉，赦免京师死囚令其从军，派遣拔胡将军郭昌率领这些士兵前往袭击。

夏，京师百姓在上林平乐馆观看杂技戏。

秋，大旱，蝗虫灾。

太初元年冬十月，驾临泰山。

十一月初一晨，冬至，在明堂祭祀上帝。

乙酉，柏梁台失火。

十二月，在高里山下祭祀后土。东行至渤海岸，遥祭蓬莱。春天返回，在甘泉宫召见郡国计簿使。

二月，建造建章宫。

夏五月，确定新历法，以正月为一年之开始。祭祀时的服装以黄色为上，计数以五为贵，确定官名，协调音律。

派遣因杅将军公孙敖建造塞外受降城。

秋八月，驾临安定。派遣贰师将军李广利征调天下有罪百姓西征大宛。

In the third moon, he visited Hedong Prefecture, worshipping the Spirit of Earth. He issued an edict saying: "I worshipped Shoushan Mountain, and in the fields below, treasures were dug up, and some turned into gold. I worshipped the Spirit of Earth, and heavenly light appeared three times. I hereby pardon the criminals in Fenyin County except for capital offenses, and reward the poor under Heaven cloth and silk, one roll for each."

When Yizhou and Kunming rebelled, he pardoned people on death row in the capital and ordered them to join the army, to be led by Hun Taking General Guo Chang to attack them.

In summer, the people in the capital watched acrobatics at Peaceful Amusement Hall of Imperial Forest Park.

In autumn, there was a severe drought, and then a plague of locusts. In the 10th moon of the first year (104 BC) of Taichu reign period, the emperor visited Mount Tai.

On the first day of the 11th moon, the winter solstice, he worshipped the Supreme God in the Hall of Enlightened Rule.

On the 22nd day, Cedar Beams Terrace caught fire.

In the 12th moon, the Emperor worshipped under Gaoli Mountain the Spirit of Earth. Then he went east to the Bohai Sea coast, and worshipped distant Penglai. He returned in spring, receiving the accounts clerks at Ganquan Palace.

In the second moon, construction of Jianzhang Palace began.

In the fifth moon, the new calendar was formulated, taking the first moon of the year as the start. Yellow ritual clothing were the best when making sacrificial offerings and the digit five was of the highest rank, as titles of office were determined and the music coordinated.

Yinyu General Gongsun Ao was sent to build a city beyond the Wall for settling those who surrendered.

In the eighth moon, the Emperor visited Anding. Ershi General

【原文】

蝗从东方飞至敦煌。

二年春正月戊申，丞相庆薨。

三月，行幸河东，祠后土。令天下大酺五日，媵五日，祠门户，比腊。

夏四月，诏曰：“朕用事介山，祭后土，皆有光应。其赦汾阴、安邑殊死以下。”

五月，籍吏民马，补车骑马。

秋，蝗。遣浚稽将军赵破奴二万骑出朔方击匈奴，不还。

冬十二月，御史大夫兒宽卒。

三年春正月，行东巡海上。夏四月，还，修封泰山，禋石闾。

遣光禄勋徐自为筑五原塞外列城，西北至卢朐，游击将军韩说将兵屯之。强弩都尉路博德筑居延。

秋，匈奴入定襄、云中，杀略数千人，行坏光禄诸亭障；又入张掖、酒泉，杀都尉。

【今译】

蝗虫从东方飞到敦煌。

二年春正月戊申，丞相石庆去世。

三月，驾临河东郡，祭祀后土。让天下百姓大饮五日，祭饮五日，祭祀宗族，以及腊祭百神。

夏四月，下诏说：“朕祭祀介山，祭祀后土，皆有神光反应。今赦汾阴、安邑死罪以下的犯人。”

五月，登记官吏、百姓养马数量，从中征调一批补充驾车马、战马。

秋，蝗灾。派遣浚稽将军赵破奴率二万骑兵从朔方出击匈奴，没有返回。

冬十二月，御史大夫兒宽死。

三年春正月，东行巡游海上。夏四月，返回，修理增高泰山祭坛，祭祀石闾山。

派遣光禄勋徐自为建造五原塞外防御城塞，西北到卢朐山，游击将军韩说率兵屯驻此地。强弩都尉路博德建造居延城。

秋，匈奴侵入定襄郡、云中郡，杀掠数千人，袭击破坏了光禄勋所筑边塞堡垒；又侵入张掖、酒泉，杀死都尉。

Li Guangli was sent to mobilize the empire's convicts to march against Dayuan.

Swarms of locusts flew from the east to Dunhuang.

On the 23rd day of first moon of year two, Prime Minister Shi Qing died.

In the third moon, the Emperor visited Hedong Prefecture, worshipping the Spirit of Earth. Throughout the empire the people were given five days of revelry. Then they worshipped their kins and a hundred gods for five days. In the fourth moon, an edict was issued saying: "I worshipped on Jieshan Mountain, worshipping the Spirit of Earth, and was answered with sacred light. I hereby pardon prisoners in Fenyin and Anyi, except for capital offenses."

In the fifth moon, there was a count of the number of horses kept by officials and people, for requisitioning of chariot horses and war horses.

In autumn, there was a plague of locusts. Junji General Zhao Ponu was sent with 20,000 cavalry from Shuofang to attack the Huns, but did not return.

In the 12th moon, Censor-in-Chief Ni Kuan died.

In the first moon of year three, the Emperor went east to inspect his maritime areas by boat. In the fourth moon, on returning, he repaired and heightened the altar at Mount Tai, and worshipped Shilü Mountain.

He sent Chamberlain for Attendants Xu Ziwei to construct the Wuyuan defense citadel beyond the Wall, which reached Mount Luqu in the northwest. Guerrilla General Han Shuo garrisoned his forces here. Archery Commander Lu Bode constructed Juyan Town.

In autumn, the Huns invaded Dingxiang and Yunzhong Prefectures, killing and capturing thousands of people, and destroyed the citadels built by the Chamberlain for Attendants; then they

【原文】

四年春，贰师将军广利斩大宛王首，获汗血马来。作《西极天马之歌》。

秋，起明光宫。

冬，行幸回中。

徙弘农都尉治武关，税出入者以给关吏卒食。

天汉元年春正月，行幸甘泉，郊泰畤。三月，行幸河东，祠后土。

匈奴归汉使者，使使来献。

夏五月，赦天下。

秋，闭城门大搜。发谪戍屯五原。

二年春，行幸东海。还幸回中。

夏五月，贰师将军三万骑出酒泉，与右贤王战于天山，斩首虏万馀级。又遣因杅将军出西河，骑都尉李陵将步兵五千人出居延北，与单于战，斩首虏万馀级。陵兵败，降匈奴。

秋，止禁巫祠道中者。大搜。

【今译】

四年春，贰师将军李广利斩大宛王头，获得汗血马返回。作《西极天马之歌》。

秋，建造明光宫。

冬，驾临回中宫。

调弘农县都尉治理武关，收取出入者的关税供给关口官兵食用。

天汉元年春正月，驾临甘泉宫，祭太一天神。三月，驾临河东，祭后土神。

匈奴放回汉朝使者，派使者前来献礼。

夏五月，赦天下罪人。

秋，关闭城门搜索违法奢侈者。征发罪人屯戍五原。

二年春，驾临东海郡。返回时驾临回中。

夏五月，贰师将军率骑兵三万从酒泉郡出发，与匈奴右贤王大战于天山，斩获万余人。又派遣因杅将军从西河郡出兵，骑都尉李陵率兵五千人从居延城北出发，与单于交战，斩匈奴万余人。李陵兵败，投降匈奴。

秋，下令禁止使用巫术在道路上祭祀。在京师大搜奸人。

invaded Zhangye and Jiuquan, killing the commanders.

In the spring of year four, Ershi General Li Guangli decapitated the King of Dayuan, seizing and bringing back a Ferghana horse. The Emperor composed the "Song of the West Heavenly Horse."

In autumn, the construction of Mingguang Palace was completed.

In winter, the Emperor visited Huizhong Palace.

Hongnong County Commander was transferred to Wuguan Pass to control the customs and he charged travelers to supply food to the officers and soldiers at the Pass.

In the first moon of the first year (100 BC) of Tianhan reign, the Emperor visited Ganquan Palace to worship the Supreme God. In the third moon, he visited Hedong Prefecture, worshipping the Spirit of Earth.

The Huns released the Han imperial envoys back to the country, sending envoys to present gifts.

In the fifth moon, there was a general amnesty.

In autumn, the gates were closed to search for illegal spendthrifts. Criminals were drafted to be stationed in Wuyuan.

In the spring of year two, the Emperor visited Donghai Prefecture. On his return, he visited Huizhong.

In the fifth moon, Ershi General led 30,000 cavalry from Jiuquan to fight King Youxian of the Huns in the Tianshan Mountains killing or capturing over 10,000 enemy. And Yinyu General Gongsun Ao was sent from Xihe and Commandant of Cavalry Li Ling with 5,000 infantry from north of Juyan. They joined battle with Chanyu and killed 10,000 or more Huns. Li Ling was defeated, and surrendered to the Huns.

In autumn, an order came down prohibiting roadside sorcery rituals. There was a witch hunt in the capital.

Six western countries like Quli sent envoys to present gifts.

【原文】

渠黎六国使使来献。

泰山、琅邪群盗徐敦等阻山攻城，道路不通。遣直指使者暴胜之等衣绣衣杖斧分部逐捕。刺史郡守以下皆伏诛。

冬十一月，诏关都尉曰："今豪杰多远交，依东方群盗。其谨察出入者。"

三年春二月，御史大夫王卿有罪，自杀。

初榷酒酤。

三月，行幸泰山，修封，祀明堂，因受计。还幸北地，祠常山，瘗玄玉。夏四月，赦天下。行所过毋出田租。

秋，匈奴入雁门，太守坐畏愞弃市。

四年春正月，朝诸侯王于甘泉宫。发天下七科谪及勇敢士，遣贰师将军李广利将六万骑、步兵七万人出朔方，因杅将军公孙敖万骑、步兵三万人出雁门，游击将军韩说步兵三万人出五原，强弩都尉路博

【今译】

渠黎等西域六国派使者前来献礼。

泰山、琅邪百姓徐敦等占据山险攻打当地县城，道路不通。朝廷派遣直指绣衣使者暴胜之等穿绣衣、持杖斧分别前往各州追捕。刺史郡守以下官员都处死。

冬十一月，下诏通告都尉说："如今仗势横行的强人多去远方交结同党，依靠东方反叛的百姓。应谨慎察验出入关的人。"

三年春二月，御史大夫王卿有罪，自杀。

初次实行酒类专卖。

三月，驾临泰山，修理祭坛祭天，在明堂祭祖，随之召见郡国上计簿使。返回时驾临北地，祭祀常山地神，埋黑玉于地下。夏四月，赦天下罪人。驾临所过之地不要交当年田租。

秋，匈奴侵入雁门郡，太守因畏懦获罪被处死在街头。

四年春正月，在甘泉宫朝见诸侯王。征发天下有罪官吏、逃亡者、赘婿、商人、原来是商人户籍的人、父母是商人户籍、祖父母是商人户籍的这七种人及勇敢之士，派遣贰师将军李广利率六万骑兵、七万步兵从朔方出兵，因杅将军公孙敖率万骑、步兵三万从雁门郡出兵，游击将军韩说率步兵三万人从五原出发，强弩都尉路博德率步兵

Xu Bo and other bandits in Taishan and Langya occupied mountain areas as a base to attack the local towns, and making roads impassable. Straight-pointer envoys like Bao Shengzhi were sent wearing embroidered robes and carrying battle axes, and hunted down the bandits. The regional governor, prefects and lower officials were executed. In the 11th moon, the Emperor decreed to commanders of passes: "The rampant strongmen mostly have like-thinking contacts in distant places, relying on the Eastern rebels. You shall carefully examine people coming and going at the passes."

In the second moon of year three, Censor-in-Chief Wang Qing was guilty of crime, and committed suicide.

Government monopoly of trade in liquors was initiated.

In the third moon, the Emperor visited Mount Tai, increasing the height of the altar for heaven. He worshipped the ancestors in the Hall of Enlightened Rule, and then received reports on local statistics. On his return journey he visited Beidi, worshipped at Changshan, and buried dark jade in the ground. In the fourth moon, there was a general amnesty. The lands he passed through had their land rent waived.

In autumn, the Huns invaded Yanmen, whose prefect was convicted and executed in the streets for being daunted.

In the first moon of year four, the Emperor received the princes in audience at Ganquan Palace. Mobilizing seven kinds of banished people (demoted officials, fugitives, uxorilocal husbands, merchants, ex-merchants, men with merchant parents or grandparents) and the brave people under Heaven, the court sent Ershi General Li Guangli with 60,000 cavalry and 70,000 infantry troops from Shuofang, Yinyu General Gongsun Ao with 10,000 cavalry and 30,000 infantry troops from Yanmen, Guerrilla General Han Shuo with 30,000 infantry from Wuyuan, and Archery Commander Lu Bode with more than 10,000 infantry to join Ershi General. Li Guangli fought

【原文】

德步兵万馀人与贰师会。广利与单于战余吾水上连日，敖与左贤王战不利，皆引还。

夏四月，立皇子髆为昌邑王。

秋九月，令死罪(人)[入]赎钱五十万减死一等。

太始元年春正月，因杅将军敖有罪，要斩。

徙郡国吏民豪桀于茂陵、云陵。

夏六月，赦天下。

二年春正月，行幸回中。

三月，诏曰："有司议曰，往者朕郊见上帝，西登陇首，获白麟以馈宗庙，渥洼水出天马，泰山见黄金，宜改故名。今更黄金为麟趾褭蹄以协瑞焉。"因以班赐诸侯王。

秋，旱。九月，募死罪(人)[入]赎钱五十万减死一等。

御史大夫杜周卒。

三年春正月，行幸甘泉宫，飨外国客。

二月，令天下大酺五日。行幸东海，获赤雁，作《朱雁之歌》。

【今译】

一万多人与贰师将军会合。李广利与单于在余吾水连日交战，公孙敖与左贤王交战失利，都带兵返回。

夏四月，立皇子刘髆为昌邑王。

秋九月，让死刑罪犯交五十万钱赎减死罪一级。

太始元年春正月，因杅将军公孙敖有罪，处以腰斩死刑。

迁徙郡国豪杰、官吏中仗势不守法者到茂陵、云陵居住。

夏六月，赦天下罪人。

二年春正月，驾临回中宫。

三月，下诏说："朝中官员议论说，不久前朕祭天时见到天帝，西方登上陇首山，猎获白麟以祭祀宗庙，渥洼水出现天马，泰山显出黄金，宜改旧的钱币名称。今改黄金为麟足马蹄形以便适应祥瑞。"用此黄金赏赐诸侯王。

秋，旱灾。九月，招犯死罪者交出钱五十万减死罪一级。

御史大夫杜周死。

三年春正月，驾临甘泉宫，宴请外国宾客。

二月，让天下百姓饮酒五日。驾临东海郡，猎获赤雁，作《朱雁

Chanyu on Yuwu River for days, but Gongsun Ao lost the war against King Zuoxian of the Huns. They both returned with their troops.

In the fourth moon, the Emperor's son Liu Bo was made Prince of Changyi.

In the ninth moon, criminals facing a death penalty were allowed to reduce their capital offense by one level by paying atonement money of 500,000 cash.

In the first moon of year one (96 BC) of Taishi reign period, Yinyu General Gongsun Ao was convicted and sentenced to be sliced in half at the waist.

Non-law-abiding officials and rampant bullies in local prefectures and fiefs were removed to Maoling and Yunling.

In the sixth moon, there was a general amnesty.

In the first moon of year two, the Emperor visited Huizhong

In the third moon, the imperial edict declared: "When I worshipped the Emperor of Heaven, I climbed Longshou Mountain in the west, and obtained a white qilin unicorn for the ancestral temple, a fairy horse came out of Wowa River, and gold appeared in Mount Tai. For these reasons, my court officials suggest I should change the name of the old coins. I hereby change gold to unicorn hoof shape, as appropriate for such good fortune." Thus the princes were rewarded with such gold according to their ranks.

Autumn saw drought. In the ninth moon, those who committed a capital offense were mobilized to hand over 500,000 cash to reduce their offense by one level.

Du Zhou the Censor-in-Chief died.

In the first moon of year three, the Emperor visited Ganquan Palace, and entertained foreign guests.

In the second moon, five days of drinking was decreed. The Emperor visited Donghai Prefecture and hunted a red goose,

【原文】

幸琅邪，礼日成山。登之罘，浮大海。山称万岁。冬，赐行所过户五千钱，鳏寡孤独帛人一匹。

四年春三月，行幸泰山。壬午，祀高祖于明堂，以配上帝，因受计。癸未，祀孝景皇帝于明堂。甲申，修封。丙戌，禅石闾。夏四月，幸不其，祠神人于交门宫，若有乡坐拜者。作《交门之歌》。夏五月，还幸建章宫，大置酒，赦天下。

秋七月，赵有蛇从郭外入邑，与邑中蛇群斗孝文庙下，邑中蛇死。

冬十月甲寅晦，日有蚀之。

十二月，行幸雍，祠五畤，西至安定、北地。

征和元年春正月，还，行幸建章宫。

三月，赵王彭祖薨。

冬十一月，发三辅骑士大搜上林，闭长安城门索，十一日乃解。巫蛊起。

【今译】

之歌》。驾临琅邪郡，在成山上拜日。登上之罘山，乘船于大海上。山中有呼万岁声。冬，赏赐驾临所过之地每户五千钱，鳏寡孤独者帛每人一匹。

四年春三月，驾临泰山。壬午，在明堂拜祭高祖，以其牌位配于天帝之侧，遂召见郡国上计簿使。癸未日，在明堂拜祭孝景帝。甲申，修理祭坛以祭天神。丙戌，在石闾山祭天。夏四月，驾临不其县，在交门宫拜祭神人，像是对座位上的神拜祭一样。作《交门之歌》。夏五月，返回驾临建章宫，大设酒宴，赦天下罪人。

秋七月，赵国有蛇从城外进入，与城中蛇群斗于孝文帝庙下，城中蛇死。

冬十月甲寅为当月最后一天，日食。

十二月，驾临雍县，拜祭五帝，西到安定、北地。

征和元年春正月，返回，驾临建章宫。

三月，赵王刘彭祖去世。

冬十一月，征派三辅骑士大搜上林苑，关闭长安城门搜查行巫术者，十一日才放行。巫术诅咒、埋木偶害人事件发生了。

thus composing "Song of Red Goose." He then went to Langya Prefecture, worshipping the sun on Chengshan Hill. He climbed Zhifu Mountain and sailed on the open sea. Cheering could be heard from the mountains. In winter, he rewarded the residents in the lands he visited, 5,000 cash for each household and a roll of silk each for those without kin and unable to support themselves.

In the third moon of year four, the Emperor visited Mount Tai. On the 25th day, he worshipped Emperor Gaozu in the Hall of Enlightened Rule and put Gaozu's memorial tablet on the side of Supreme God, and received local accounts clerks. On the 26th day, he worshipped Emperor Jingdi in the Hall of Enlightened Rule. On the 27th, he repaired the altar to worship Heavenly God. On the 29th, he worshipped Heaven at Shilü Hill. In the fourth moon, he visited Buqi County, worshipping the immortals at Jiaomen Palace, as if to the gods on the facing mountains. He composed the "Song of Jiaomen." In the fifth moon, he returned to visit Jianzhang Palace, arranging a large banquet, and announcing a general amnesty.

In the seventh moon, snakes from Zhao came into the city from outside, engaging the city snakes in a mass fight under Emperor Wendi's temple. The city snakes perished.

On the last day of the 10th moon, there was a solar eclipse.

In the 12th moon, the Emperor visited Yong County, offering sacrifice to the Five Heavenly Emperors. Then he proceeded west to Anding and Beidi.

In the first moon of the first year (92 BC) of Zhenghe reign period, he returned and visited Jianzhang Palace.

In the third moon, Liu Pengzu, Prince of Zhao, died. That winter, in the 11th moon, the cavalry in the capital was sent on a large-scale search of the Imperial Forest Park, and Chang'an's gates were shut for 11 days as witches were hunted down. There had been incidents of toxic curses and injury through buried puppet voodoo.

【原文】

二年春正月，丞相贺下狱死。

夏四月，大风发屋折木。

闰月，诸邑公主、阳石公主皆坐巫蛊死。

夏，行幸甘泉。

秋七月，(桉)[按]道侯韩说、使者江充等掘蛊太子宫。壬午，太子与皇后谋斩充，以节发兵与丞相刘屈氂大战长安，死者数万人。庚寅，太子亡，皇后自杀。初置城门屯兵。更节加黄旄。御史大夫暴胜之、司直田仁坐失纵，胜之自杀，仁要斩。八月辛亥，太子自杀于湖。

癸亥，地震。

九月，立赵敬肃王子偃为平[干]王。

匈奴入上谷、五原，杀略吏民。

三年春正月，行幸雍，至安定、北地。匈奴入五原、酒泉，杀两都尉。三月，遣贰师将军广利将七万人出五原，御史大夫商丘成二万人出西河，重合侯马通四万骑出酒泉。成至浚稽山与虏战，多斩首。

【今译】

二年春正月，丞相公孙贺下狱而死。

夏四月，大风吹坏房屋折断树木。

闰四月，诸邑公主、阳石公主都因用巫术犯罪被处死。

夏，驾临甘泉。

秋七月，按道侯韩说、使者江充等人在太子住处掘出木偶人。壬午日，太子与皇后合谋杀江充，拿兵符调军队与丞相刘屈氂大战于长安城，死者数万人。庚寅日，太子逃出，皇后自杀。开始设城门屯兵。更换节加上黄色牦牛尾。御史大夫暴胜之、司直田仁因失于放纵而犯罪，胜之自杀，田仁处以腰斩死刑。八月辛亥日，太子自杀于湖县。

癸亥日，地震。

九月，立赵敬肃王刘彭祖之子刘偃为平干王。

匈奴侵入上谷、五原，杀掠官民。

三年春正月，驾临雍县，然后到达安定、北地。匈奴侵入五原、酒泉，杀死两地都尉。三月，派遣贰师将军李广利率七万人出五原，御史大夫商丘成率二万人出西河，重合侯马通率四万骑出酒泉。丘成

In the first moon of year two, Prime Minister Gongsun He died behind bars.

In the fourth moon, a gale destroyed housing and snapped trees.

In the leap fourth moon, the princesses Zhuyi and Yangshi were executed for the crime of witchcraft.

In summer, the Emperor visited Ganquan Palace.

In the seventh moon, Marquis of Andao Han Shuo, envoy Jiang Chong, etc. dug for poisonous puppets in the Palace of the Crown Prince. On the ninth day, the Crown Prince and Empress conspired to kill Jiang Chong, dispatching armed forces with his military tally to fight a huge battle with Prime Minister Liu Qumao in Chang'an City, and leaving tens of thousands dead. On the 17th day, the Prince escaped, and the Empress committed suicide. Garrisons began to be stationed at the city gates. Yellow yak tails were added to the tally. Censor-in-Chief Bao Shengzhi and Rectifier Tian Ren were guilty of indulgence; Bao committed suicide, and Tian was executed by being cut in half.

On the eighth day of the eighth moon, the Crown Prince committed suicide in Huxian County.

On the 20th day of the eighth moon, there was an earthquake.

In the ninth moon, Liu Yan, son of Liu Pengzu, the Prince Jingsu of Zhao, was made Prince Pinggan.

The Huns invaded Shanggu and Wuyuan, killing and capturing officials and people.

In the first moon of year three, the Emperor visited Yong County, and then went to Anding and Beidi. The Huns invaded Wuyuan and Jiuquan, killing the two commanders. In the third moon, Ershi General Li Guangli was sent from Wuyuan with 70,000 men under him, Censor-in-Chief Shang Qiucheng came with 20,000 soldiers from Xihe, and Marquis of Chonghe Ma Tong came with 40,000 cavalry from Jiuquan. Qiucheng engaged the Huns at

【原文】

通至天山，虏引去，因降车师。皆引兵还。广利败，降匈奴。

夏五月，赦天下。

六月，丞相屈氂下狱要斩，妻(子)枭首。

秋，蝗。

九月，反者公孙勇、胡倩发觉，皆伏辜。

四年春正月，行幸东莱，临大海。

二月丁酉，陨石于雍，二，声闻四百里。

三月，上耕于钜定。还幸泰山，修封。庚寅，祀于明堂。癸巳，禧石闾。夏六月，还幸甘泉。

秋八月辛酉晦，日有蚀之。

后元元年春正月，行幸甘泉，郊泰畤，遂幸安定。

昌邑王髆薨。

二月，诏曰："朕郊见上帝，巡于北边，见群鹤留止，以不罗罔，靡所获献。荐于泰畤，光景并见。其赦天下。"

【今译】

到达浚稽山与匈奴交战，杀敌甚众。马通到达天山，匈奴退去，于是降车师国。丘成、马通都率部返回。李广利兵败，投降匈奴。

夏五月，赦天下罪人。

六月，丞相刘屈氂下狱用腰斩罪罚处死。其妻悬首示众。

秋，蝗灾。

九月，谋反人公孙勇、胡倩被发现，都伏法。

四年春正月，驾临东莱，到达大海岸边。

二月丁酉日，陨石落在雍县，有两块，声响传至四百里。

三月，武帝在钜定耕田。返回后驾临泰山，修理坛台祭祀天神。庚寅日，在明堂拜祭。癸巳日，祭石闾山。夏六月，返回后驾临甘泉。

秋八月辛酉为当月最后一天，发生日食。

后元元年春正月，驾临甘泉，祭祀太一神庙，然后驾临安定。

昌邑王刘髆去世。

二月，下诏说："朕祭祀天神时见到上帝，在北边巡游时，见到群鹤停留。由于未用网捕，所以没有献上猎物。进献太一神庙，神光、景象同时出现。今赦天下罪人。"

Junji Mountain, beheading many enemy soldiers. Ma reached the Tianshan Mountains, but the Huns retreated, and then conquered Jushi. The two led their troops back. Li Guangli was defeated, surrendering to the Huns.

In the fifth moon, there was a general amnesty.

In the sixth moon, Prime Minister Liu Qumao was imprisoned and executed by being cut in half. His wife's head was hung in public display.

In autumn, there was a plague of locusts.

In the ninth moon, rebels Gongsun Yong and Hu Qian were found and executed.

In the first moon of year four, the Emperor visited Donglai, reaching the sea shore.

On the third day of the second moon, two meteorites fell in Yong County. The noise of them could be heard 400 *li* away. In the third moon, the Emperor tilled the fields in Juding County. Returning, he visited Mount Tai, repaired the altar and worshipped Heaven. On the 26th day, he worshipped in the Hall of Enlightened Rule. On the 29th day, he worshipped at Shilü Hill. In the sixth moon, he returned and visited Ganquan Palace.

On the last day of the eighth moon, a solar eclipse was seen.

In the first moon of the first year (88 BC) of Houyuan reign period, the Emperor visited Ganquan Palace, worshipped at Temple of the Supreme God, and then visited Anding.

Liu Bo, Prince of Changyi, died.

In the second moon, an edict came down saying: "I worshipped the God of Heaven, and inspected in the northern border, and saw auspicious cranes settle. I did not use nets, so there was no catch to offer up. When I worshipped Heaven at the Temple of the Supreme God, the divine light and signs appeared simultaneously. I hereby announce a general amnesty."

【原文】

夏六月，御史大夫商丘成有罪自杀。侍中仆射莽何罗与弟重合侯通谋反，侍中驸马都尉金日磾、奉车都尉霍光、骑都尉上官桀讨之。

秋七月，地震，往往涌泉出。

二年春正月，朝诸侯王于甘泉宫，赐宗室。

二月，行幸盩厔五柞宫。乙丑，立皇子弗陵为皇太子。丁卯，帝崩于五柞宫，入殡于未央宫前殿。三月甲申，葬茂陵。

赞曰：汉承百王之弊，高祖拨乱反正，文景务在养民，至于稽古礼文之事，犹多阙焉。孝武初立，卓然罢黜百家，表章《六经》。遂畴咨海内，举其俊茂，与之立功。兴太学，修郊祀，改正朔，定历数，协音律，作诗乐，建封禫，礼百神，绍周后，号令文章，焕焉可述。后嗣得遵洪业，而有三代之风。如武帝之雄材大略，不改文景之恭俭以

【今译】

夏六月，御史大夫商丘成有罪自杀。侍中仆射莽何罗与弟重合侯马通谋反，侍中驸马都尉金日磾、奉车都尉霍光、骑都尉上官桀讨平反叛。

秋七月，地震，常常涌出泉水。

二年春正月，在甘泉宫朝见诸侯王，赏赐宗室。

二月，驾临盩厔县五柞宫。乙丑，立皇子弗陵为皇太子。丁卯，武帝驾崩于五柞宫，在未央宫前殿入殓。三月甲申，葬在茂陵。

赞曰：汉承接了历代弊端，高祖拨乱反正，文帝、景帝注重养民，对于考究古代礼乐制度之事，还很缺乏。孝武帝刚刚继位，卓有远见地罢黜百家，突出《六经》的地位。于是谁能为天下谋事，推举为优秀人才，让他建功立业。兴办太学，修建祭祀庙祠，改正月为一年的第一个月，确定历法，协调音律，作诗赋乐曲，建造祭天禅台，祭祀百神，继续周朝传统，号令制度，光彩值得称述。后继者得以继承宏大事业，而具备夏、商、周三代的风气。像汉武帝这样的雄才大

In the sixth moon, the guilty Censor-in-Chief Shang Qiucheng committed suicide. Supervisor of Palace Attendants Mang Heluo and his younger brother Marquis of Chonghe Ma Tong rebelled, and were put down by Commandant Escort Jin Midi, Commandant-in-Chief of Chariot Huo Guang, and Commandant of Cavalry Shangguan Jie. In the seventh moon, there were earthquakes, with frequent gushing springs.

In the first moon of year two, the Emperor had an audience with the princes at Ganquan Palace, rewarding the royal clan.

In the second moon, he visited Wuzha Palace in Zhouzhi County. On the 12th day, he made his son Liu Fuling Crown Prince. On the 14th day, Emperor Wudi died in Wuzha Palace, and was encoffined in the front hall of Weiyang Palace. On the second day of the third moon, he was buried in Maoling Mausoleum.

Author's comment: the Han Dynasty inherited the political abuses of ancient Chinese kings. Emperor Gaozu brought order out of chaos, Emperors Wendi and Jingdi focused on recuperation of the population but the elegant ritual system of ancient traditions was still lacking. When Emperor Wudi came to the throne, he farsightedly prescribed hundreds of academic schools, focusing on the "Six Classics." So he looked for whoever could do the job within the Empire, selected the talents, having them make their contribution. He set up the Imperial College, constructed temples for worshipping, corrected the first moon of the year to determine the calendar, coordinated music, made poetry and music, established heaven and earth worship, paying homage to all kinds of gods, restored the illustrious and pride-inspiring Zhou tradition with its orders and ritual system. His successors inherited his great cause, inspired by the ethos of the Xia, Shang and Zhou. Such ingenious capability and lofty plans as Wudi's, had he not changed the policy of courteous restraint of emperors Wendi and Jingdi to

【原文】

济斯民，虽诗书所称何有加焉！

——卷六《武帝纪》第六

【今译】

略，不改变文、景时恭俭以救助百姓的政策，虽是《诗》、《书》上所赞美的制度又能超过多少呢！

rescue the people, would not have surpassed them very much even though the system would be praised in the *Book of Odes* and the *Collection of Ancient Texts*!

食货志（上）

【原文】

《洪范》八政，一曰食，二曰货。食谓农殖嘉谷可食之物，货谓布帛可衣，及金刀龟贝，所以分财布利通有无者也。二者，生民之本，兴自神农之世。“斲木为耜，煣木为耒，耒(耜)[耨]之利以教天下”，而食足；“日中为市，致天下之民，聚天下之货，交易而退，各得其所”，而货通。食足货通，然后国实民富，而教化成。黄帝以下，“通其变，使民不倦”。尧命四子以“敬授民时”，舜命后稷以“黎民祖饥”，是为政首。禹平洪水，定九州，制土田，各因所生远近，赋入贡棐，楙迁有无，万国作乂。殷周之盛，《诗》《书》

【今译】

《洪范》的八种政务官员中，一是管民食的官，二是管财货的官。食是指农民生产的可以吃的好谷，货是指可穿的布帛，以及金刀龟贝，用来分配财产扩散利益以通有无。这两者，是人民生活的根本，从神农的时代就开始兴起。“砍下木头作为耜，弄弯木头作为耒，把耒耨的好处传给天下”，这样食物就充足了；“到中午时就形成了集市，招来天下的人民，聚积天下的货物，交换后就走开，使他们各自得到自己想要的东西”，这样财物就流通了。食物充足，货物流通，然后国家充实，人民富足，这样政教风化就形成了。黄帝以下“为百姓变通，使他们不感到厌倦”。尧帝命令羲仲、羲叔、和仲、和叔四人“把天时节令告诉给人民”，舜帝在“百姓开始饥饿”时任命后稷，把这作为政治的首位。大禹平定了洪水，安定了九州，规范了田地，各自根据所出生的远近，把田赋交到盛贡物的椭圆竹器中，劝勉天下交换有无，万国就得到治理。商、周的强盛，《诗》

Chapter 4

The Treatise on Food and Commodities, Part I

Hong Fan (*The Great Norms*) elaborated on eight political affairs, of which one was food and another was commodities. Food refers to the good crops grown by farmers and which can be eaten. Commodities is defined as cloth and silk that can be worn as well as metals and cash distributed via those who buy and sell.

These two arose in the era of Shen Nong the Divine Farmer and are the source of life for the people. "He fashioned wood to form the plow-share, and bent wood to make the handle. The advantages of plowing and weeding were then taught to all under Heaven." Thus food became sufficient. "He caused markets to be held at midday, thus bringing together all the people, and assembling in one place all their wares. They made their exchanges and withdrew, every one having got what he wanted." In this way commodities are distributed. After there was enough food and commodities in general circulation the kingdom was prosperous, the people were wealthy, and moral education became established.

The Yellow Emperor and others "carried through the (necessarily occurring) changes, so that the people did (what was required of them) without being wearied." Yao appointed the Four Scholars to "respectfully give time to the people and allocate the seasons," and Shun appointed Hou Ji as Minister of Agriculture to focus on the political priorities as starvation began among the people. Yu harnessed the flood, demarcated the nine prefectures, and rated cultivatable fields, each of which was taxed in baskets of tribute according to its location. Encouraged to exchange what they had and what they needed, the ten-thousand states were brought under good

【原文】

所述，要在安民，富而教之。故《易》称“天地之大德曰生，圣人之大宝曰位；何以守位曰仁，何以聚人曰财”。财者，帝王所以聚人守位，养成群生，奉顺天德，治国安民之本也。故曰：“不患寡而患不均，不患贫而患不安；盖均亡贫，和亡寡，安亡倾。”是以圣王域民，筑城郭以居之，制庐井以均之，开市肆以通之，设庠序以教之；士农工商，四民有业。学以居位曰士，辟土殖谷曰农，作巧成器曰工，通财鬻货曰商。圣王量能授事，四民陈力受职，故朝亡废官，邑亡敖民，地亡旷土。

理民之道，地著为本。故必建步立晦，正其经界。六尺为步，步

【今译】

和《书》上有所记述，主要在于安定百姓，使他们富足后再来加以教育。所以《易》上称“天地的大德是生命，圣人最宝贵的事物是帝位；怎么守住帝位叫仁，怎么聚积人叫财。”财物，是帝王用来聚积人员保守帝位、抚养群众、顺从上天的恩德、治理国家安定人民的根本。所以说：“不担心少而担心不平均，不担心贫苦而担心不安定；因为平均了就没有贫苦，协调了就没有多寡，安定了就不会倾覆。”因此英明的君王界定百姓，就建筑城邑让他们居住，在井田中建屋庐使他们平均，开设市场让他们进行财物流通，设立学校来教育他们；士、农、工、商，四种人有自己的事业。学习后来做官叫士，开辟土地生产谷物叫农，利用技术制成器物叫工，流通财物买卖货物叫商。英明的君王根据才能授予官职，四种人根据自己的力量承受职责，所以朝廷没有荒废的官员，城邑没有闲游的人，地上没有荒芜的田地。

治理人民的方法，使他们定居一地是根本。所以一定要建立步来

rule. At the time when Shang and Zhou prospered, as is recorded in the *Book of Odes* and the *Book of Documents*, the main point was pacifying the people, making them rich and then educating them. Therefore, the *Book of Changes* states "The great virtue of heaven and earth is the giving and maintaining of life. What is most precious for the sage is to get the (highest) place. What will guard this position for him? Benevolence. How shall he collect a large population round him? By the power of his wealth." Wealth is what the monarchs have all relied on to assemble the people and guard their position, to raise and feed the people, to respectfully go along with the virtue of Heaven; this is the foundation for administering the kingdom and pacifying the people. Therefore, it is said: "not troubled that they have little wealth, but troubled that things are not distributed equally; not troubled by fears of poverty, but by want of contentment. For when there is equality, there will be no poverty; when harmony prevails, there will be no scarcity of people; and when there is contentment, there will be no rebellious overturning." So it was that the sage kings designated territories for the people and built walled cities for them to live in. A system of nine squares and huts was established to distribute them equally, markets were set up with shops for exchange, and schools were built to educate the people. Scholarship, agriculture, craftsmanship, and business were the four occupations. Studying to hold a position of status was called scholarship. Developing the soil and propagating grains was called agriculture. Using skill to make things was called craftsmanship. Circulating wealth and selling commodities was called business. The sage kings measured ability and conferred duties; those of the four people who displayed capability received positions and there were no neglected offices at court; no people wandering without attachment, and no uncultivated fields in the land.

Fundamental to the proper managing of people is to settle them on the land, so it is essential to establish the *bu* for the measurement

【原文】

百为亩，亩百为夫，夫三为屋，屋三为井，井方一里，是为九夫。八家共之，各受私田百亩，公田十亩，是为八百八十亩，馀二十亩以为庐舍。出入相友，守望相助，疾病(则)[相]救，民是以和睦，而教化齐同，力役生产可得而平也。

民受田，上田夫百亩，中田夫二百亩，下田夫三百亩。岁耕种者为不易上田；休一岁者为一易中田；休二岁者为再易下田；三岁更耕之，自爰其处。农民户人已受田，其家众男为馀夫，亦以口受田如比。士工商家受田，五口乃当农夫一人。此谓平土可以为法者也。若山林薮泽原陵淳卤之地，各以肥硗多少为差。有赋有税。税谓公田什一及工商衡虞之入也。赋共车马甲兵士徒之役，充实府库赐予之用。

【今译】

设置田亩，纠正土地的分界。六尺作为一步，百步是一亩，百亩是一夫，三夫是一屋，三屋是一井，井的方圆是一里，这就是九夫。八家共同拥有它，各自接受百亩私田，十亩公田，这是八百八十亩，剩下二十亩作为屋舍。进出互相是朋友，守卫和了望互相帮助，有疾病就互相救护，人民因此和睦，而且政教风化统一，劳役生产可以得到且平均。

百姓接受田地，好田是一百亩，中田就是二百亩，差田就是三百亩。每年耕种的人不交换好田；休耕一年的交换一次中田；休耕两年的交换两次差田；三年就交换耕种，自行改变位置。农民户主自己接受田亩，他家中的其他男子是余夫，也按比例依照人口分田。士、工、商家里分田，五个人才相当于农夫一人。这是说在平原上可以作为法则的。如果是山地、林地、大湖、丘陵、盐碱浸渍之地，就各按肥沃贫瘠的程度作为等级。有赋有税。税是公田的十分之一以及工、商、衡、虞的收入。赋是供给车马铠甲兵器士兵的劳役，充实官府储存财物兵甲的仓库以及赏赐之用。税用来供给郊祭宗庙百神，天子供

of land in order to adjust the boundaries of nine squares. One *bu* is six *chi* and 100 *bu* are one *mu*, and 100 *mu* a *fu*, three *fu* make a *wu*, and three *wu* make a *jing* (nine squares). The *jing* is one *li* square, or nine *fu*. Of eight families that share a *jing*, each receives 100 *mu* of private farmland, and also 10 *mu* of public farmland. This makes 880 *mu*, the remaining 20 *mu* are for hut dwellings. Going in and coming out together with friendship, they help each other with their watchful guard. In case of illness, they aid each other. The people then live with harmony and friendliness, and they all the same receive moral education. Labor service and products are also available evenly.

Of the fields given to the people, each man was given 100 *mu* of the best kind of field, 200 *mu* of the average kind, or 300 *mu* of the worst. Those fields that could be plowed and planted every year were called the never changing; these were best fields. Those that lay fallow every other year were called the once changing; these were the average fields. Those which lay fallow for two years were called the twice changing; these were the worst fields. After three years there was rotation in cultivation, and each would therefore change his place. Of the men of the farming families who had already received land, the other men of their family were called extra men and they would also receive land in proportion to their number. The families of scholars, craftsman, and merchants received land, and five of them would be considered one farmer. This was the standard when referring to flat land. As to mountains, forests, lakes, hills, barren soil and brackish land, they were graded according to their fertility. There were taxes on land and taxes on products. Taxes on products were one tenth of the public farmland, and taxes were paid by craftsman, merchants, and those who made a living out of the specialties of forests or rivers. Normal taxes were used for chariots, horses, armor and weapons as well as for military service and they filled the imperial coffers to be used as official rewards. Taxes on products were given to the ancestral temples or the open

【原文】

税给郊社宗庙百神之祀，天子奉养百官禄食庶事之费。民年二十受田，六十归田。七十以上，上所养也；十岁以下，上所长也；十一以上，上所强也。种谷必杂五种，以备灾害。田中不得有树，用妨五谷。力耕数耘，收获如寇盗之至。还庐树桑，菜茹有畦，瓜瓠果蓏殖于疆易。鸡豚狗彘毋失其时，女修蚕织，则五十可以衣帛，七十可以食肉。

在野曰庐，在邑曰里。五家为邻，五邻为里，四里为族，五族为党，五党为州，五州为乡。乡，万二千五百户也。邻长位下士，自此以上，稍登一级，至乡而为卿也。于[是]里有序而乡有庠。序以明教，庠则行礼而视化焉。春令民毕出在野，冬则毕入于邑。其《诗》曰："四之日举止，同我妇子，馌彼南亩。"又曰："十月蟋蟀，入

【今译】

养百官薪俸食物以及众事的费用。百姓年龄满二十就分田，六十就归还田亩。七十岁以上，是皇上所来奉养的；十岁以下，是皇上所要抚养的；十一岁以上，是皇上所要使他们强壮的。种谷一定要夹杂五谷，以防备灾害。田中不能有树，以免妨碍五谷。勤奋耕耘，收获时就像盗贼要来了。围绕庐舍种植桑树，菜地有田垄，瓜果类作物种植在田边，养殖鸡、猪、狗、彘不要误时，女子进行蚕织，那么五十岁就可以穿帛布，七十岁可以吃肉。

屋在田野中叫庐，在人们聚居的地方叫里。五家成为一邻，五邻成为一里，四里成为一族，五族形成一党，五党形成一州，五州形成一乡。一乡，有一万二千五百户。一邻的首长官位是下士，从这往上，官位稍加一级，到乡一级的官位就是卿了。这样里有序，乡有庠。序是用来彰明教化，庠则是用来演习礼仪以示范教化。春天命令百姓全都到田野里去，冬天全到邑中去。《诗》这样说："四月的时候动腿，带上妇人孩子，把饭送给南面田里的人吃。"又说："十月

spaces where the hundred spirits were sacrificed to; they helped the Son of Heaven support the hundred officials with blessings of food, and for various duties performed. At 20 years of age a man would receive fields and at the age of 60 he would return them. All those over 70 would be taken care of by the empire and all those under 10 would be raised by the empire; all of those 11 or older would be strengthened. The grain sown should vary between the five types, so as to guard against calamity and disaster. In the fields it was not good to have trees, for they would interfere with the cereal crops. With energetic plowing and frequent weeding, the harvest would be done as if thieves and robbers were arriving. Circling the huts were mulberry trees, and there were spaces planted with vegetables as well as cucumber, bottle gourd, fruit and melon which all were grown on the field edges. Chickens, pigs, dogs, and swine were not neglected. Women were engaged in sericulture so that people over 50 could be clothed in silk and those over 70 were able to eat meat.

Dwellings out in the wild were called huts, while those in the settlements were called villages. Five families would make a neighborhood, and five neighborhoods would make a village. Four villages would make a clan, and five clans would make a faction. Five factions would make a borough, and five boroughs would make a township. A township was made up of 12,500 households. The head of a neighborhood was a junior serviceman, the larger the unit the higher the rank, and the official in charge of a township was a minister. In each village there was a lower school, and in each township there was a higher school. In the village school, the teachings were clarified. In the higher school, transformative ritual propriety was practiced to demonstrate moral education. With spring came the order for all the people to go out into the countryside and in the winter to enter the towns. The *Book of Odes* says: "In the fourth moon, taking to my feet, with my woman and children, I carry food to those in the south fields." It also says: "In the tenth moon

【原文】

我床下，嗟我妇子，聿为改岁，入此室处。”所以顺阴阳，备寇贼，习礼文也。春，(秋)[将]出民，里胥平旦坐于右塾，邻长坐于(右)[左]塾，毕出然后归，夕亦如之。入者必持薪樵，轻重相分，班白不提挈。冬，民既入，妇人同巷，相从夜绩，女工一月得四十五日。必相从者，所以省费燎火，同巧拙而合习俗也。男女有不得其所者，因相与歌咏，各言其伤。

是月，馀子亦在于序室。八岁入小学，学六甲五方书计之事，始知室家长幼之节。十五入大学，学先圣礼乐，而知朝廷君臣之礼。其有秀异者，移乡学于庠序；庠序之异者，移国学于少学。诸侯岁贡少学之异者于天子，学于大学，命曰造士。行同能偶，则别之以射，然后爵命焉。

【今译】

的时候，蟋蟀躲到我的床底下，把妇人孩子唤来，告诉他们一年快完了，可以走进屋子里了。”这是用来顺应阴阳，防备贼寇，学习礼节仪式。春天，人们将出去，里胥清晨坐在右边的房屋，一邻之长坐在左边的房屋，等人们全走了然后回来，晚上也是这样。回来的人一定要拿着柴火，按照轻重分开，头发斑白的人不提柴禾。冬天，人们已经回来了，妇人们同在一个屋子里，一起在夜晚织布，女工一个月早晚共有四十五个工作日。一定要在一块，是为了节省火炬的费用，使技术高明和笨拙的一样，使习俗相合。男女中有没有完成他所应完成的，就互相唱歌，进行讽刺。

这个月，不去劳役的男子也在学堂里。八岁进入小学，学习用天干地支相配计算时日以及各方的文字与筹算，开始知道家中长幼的礼节。十五岁进入大学，学习前代圣人的礼乐，就知道了朝廷中君臣的礼仪。其中有杰出的学生，就从乡学转移到庠序；庠序中杰出的，就从国学转移到少学。诸侯每年把少学中杰出的学生推荐给天子，在大学里学习，叫做造士。在同辈中有才能的，就另外用射来考试，然后任命爵位。

are crickets that enter under my bed. I call my woman and children, now with the ending of the year they will move into the rooms." In this way following *yin* and *yang*, they prepared against bandits and thieves as well as practicing ritual propriety. In the spring, the people would go out and the village officers would sit at dawn in the hall on the right of the gate, as the heads of the neighborhoods sat in the hall on the left of the gate. After everyone had left they returned and it was the same every evening. As they returned they were required to bring kindling and firewood, a light or heavy load according to the division made among themselves. Those with graying hair would not carry wood. In the winter, the people having come back indoors and the women living in the same room, would weave together by night. Female labor worked 45 shifts day and night every month. They were required to work in groups in order not to waste light and heat, with the skilled working with the clumsy to absorb the techniques. Men and women who had not completed what they should have would sing to each other and be mocked. During these months, all the non-laboring boys were in classrooms. At eight they began their basic studies, studying the six heavenly stems for the calendar and the five directions for geography, written language, math and so on; and they began to know the relations between the old and the young in the family. At 15 they began their advanced studies, studying the ritual and music of the former sages; and they would know of the protocols of ruler and ministers at court. As for the especially talented, they would be promoted from the township school to the community school; those who excelled there would be transferred to the state junior school. Annually, feudal lords presented extraordinarily good students of the realm to junior schools before the Son of Heaven and they studied at the higher school as accomplished scholars. Those equal in conduct and ability were then classified through archery, and titles were given to them accordingly.

【原文】

孟春之月，群居者将散，行人振木铎徇于路，以采诗，献之大师，比其音律，以闻于天子。故曰王者不窥牖户而知天下。

此先王制土处民富而教之之大略也。故孔子曰："道千乘之国，敬事而信，节用而爱人，使民以时。"故民皆劝功乐业，先公而后私。其《诗》曰："有渰凄凄，兴云祁祁，雨我公田，遂及我私。"民三年耕，则馀一年之畜。衣食足而知荣辱，廉让生而争讼息，故三载考绩。孔子曰"苟有用我者，期月而已可也，三年有成"，成此功也。三考黜陟，馀三年食，进业曰登；再登曰平，馀六年食；三登曰泰平，二十七岁，遗九年食。然后(⾂)[至]德流洽，礼乐成焉。故曰

【今译】

孟春的时候，居住在一起的人们将要分散，有人摇着大铃巡走于路上，来采集民间歌谣，献给掌管音律的大师，把音律排列在一起，告诉天子。所以说做君王的人不用察看千家万户就能知道天下的事情。

这就是先代帝王按土地的优劣分等级安置人民使他们富裕后再来教育的大方针。所以孔子说："治理有一千辆车的国家，谨慎办事，讲求信用，节约开支，爱护人民，在合适的时候役使人民。"因此百姓都努力立功，乐于本业，先公而后私。《诗》上这么说："阴云慢慢升起，雨慢慢落下，先落到公田里，再顺便落到我的私田。"百姓耕种三年，就留一年蓄养。衣服和食物充足了，才知道光荣和耻辱，廉洁、谦让产生，争斗、官司就停止了，所以三年考察一次功绩。孔子说："如果有用我的人，一年便差不多了，三年便会取得成功"，就是成就这样的功业。三年考核一次，决定降免或提升，遗留三年的食物，把生产东西上交叫登；登两次叫平，留下六年食物；登三次叫泰平，二十七年，留下九年食物。然后至高无上的道德流行，礼乐行

During the first month in spring, when those living in communities were about to disperse, traveling commissioners, ringing their bells with wooden clappers, journeyed along the roads in order to collect odes. They were sent up to the Grand Musician at court, who arranged the tunes which would be presented before the Son of Heaven to hear. For this reason it is said that kings knew everything under Heaven without prying at windows and doors.

This is the general picture of the land institutionalized by the former kings, keeping the people in place and giving them wealth and instruction. For this reason Confucius said: "To rule a country of 1,000 chariots, there must be reverent attention to undertakings, faithfulness, economy in expenditure, love for men, and employment of people according to the seasons." It was for this reason that the people were all encouraged in service and took pleasure in their occupations. They put the common good before their own. Of this the *Book of Odes* says: "The mist rolls in dense masses,/ Clouds slowly form overhead;/ May it rain first on state fields,/ then come to our private ones." From three years of growing, the people could put a year's yield into storage. When food and clothes were made sufficient there was glory and disgrace; with fairness and honesty, and the courteous yielding of priority, then contention and litigation ceased. For these reasons every three years there was an examination of merits and achievements. Confucius said: "If there was one who would employ me, in the course of a year I would have done something considerable. In three years there would be success." He was referring to the creation of such government. After the triennial examination when some were downgraded and some were advanced, there was a surplus of food for a three year period, so this success in production was called a "climb." Two successive "climbs" was called a "peace," when there was a surplus of food for six years. Three consecutive "climbs" was called "great peace," when there would be a surplus of food for nine years which had accumulated

【原文】

“如有王者，必世而后仁”，繇此道也。

周室既衰，暴君污吏慢其经界，繇役横作，政令不信，上下相诈，公田不治。故鲁宣公“初税亩”，《春秋》讥焉。于是上贪民怨，灾害生而祸乱作。

陵夷至于战国，贵诈力而贱仁谊，先富有而后礼让。是时，李悝为魏文侯作尽地力之教，以为地方百里，提封九万顷，除山泽邑居参分去一，为田六百万亩，治田勤谨则亩益三升，不勤则损亦如之。地方百里之增减，辄为粟百八十万石矣。又曰籴甚贵伤民，甚贱伤农；民伤则离散，农伤则国贫。故甚贵与甚贱，其伤一也。善为国者，使

【今译】

成。所以说“如有称王的人，一定要经过三十年后，仁政才形成”，就是根据这个道理。

周室衰落后，暴君污吏忽视他们的国界，徭役泛滥，政令没有信用，上下的人相互欺诈，公田没有人去耕作。所以鲁宣公的“初税亩”，遭到《春秋》的讥刺。于是在上位的人贪婪，百姓产生怨恨，灾害一发生，祸乱就起来了。

周室衰落到了战国时代，推崇诈伪和暴力而轻视仁义，以物质充足为先，以礼貌谦让为后。这个时候，李悝为魏文侯制定了充分利用土地生产能力的教令，认为土地方圆百里，总共有九万顷，除去山地大湖村居所占的三分之一，还有田亩六百万亩，耕耘田地勤奋小心则每亩加收三斗，不勤奋那么也减去三斗。方圆百里土地上的粮食增减一下，就是一百八十万石粟。又说买进谷物太贵会伤害士、工、商，太便宜又会伤害农民；士、工、商受到伤害，就会出现离散，农民受到伤害就会出现国家贫困。因此太贵和太便宜，一定要伤害一方。善于治理国家的，使士、工、商不受到伤害而使农民更加勤勉。现在一

during the 27 years. Thereafter, kingly virtue spread and permeated to the people, and this established ritual propriety and music among them. So it was said: "If a truly royal ruler were to arise, it would still require a generation before virtue would prevail." The saying is based on this principle.

As the house of Zhou was already in decline, oppressive rulers and corrupt officials neglected the defining of the boundaries, and labor services were unreasonably required. The administrative orders could not be trusted, and authorities and underlings deceived each other. The public fields were not managed. For this reason Duke Xuan of Lu introduced the "first tax by the *mu*," a practice criticized in the *Spring and Autumn Annals*. Then, rulers grew greedy, and the people complained. Disaster was born, unleashing misfortune and chaos. The situation deteriorated up to the Warring States Period, when intrigues and force were esteemed whereas humanity and righteousness were despised; riches came first, as protocol and courteous yielding to others were left behind. At this time, Li Kui worked out, for the Marquis Wen of Wei, a doctrine for the fullest exploitation of the bearing capacity of the land. He reckoned that a territory of 100 square *li* held totally 90,000 hectares. Subtracting one-third for mountains and lakes, settlements and field huts, that left six million *mu* for cultivation. If the land was diligently and carefully managed, then each *mu* could yield an extra three liters. If it was not diligently cultivated, then a decrease of similar magnitude would ensue. On 100 square *li* of land the average margin of increase or decrease was 1,800,000 piculs of millet. He also said that if grain was very expensive it would injure non-farmers, while if it were very cheap it would injure the farmers. If the non-farmers were injured then there would be population dispersal, and if the farmers were injured the kingdom would become poor. For this reason however expensive or cheap, one group would be harmed. For those versed in matters of state, they should ensure that non-farmers were not

【原文】

民毋伤而农益劝。今一夫挟五口，治田百亩，岁收亩一石半，为粟百五十石，除十一之税十五石，馀百三十五石。食，人月一石半，五人终岁为粟九十石，馀有四十五石。石三十，为钱千三百五十，除社闾尝新春秋之祠，用钱三百，馀千五十。衣，人率用钱三百，五人终岁用千五百，不足四百五十。不幸疾病死丧之费，及上赋敛，又未与此。此农夫所以常困，有不劝耕之心，而令粜至于甚贵者也。是故善平粜者，必谨观岁有上中下孰。上孰其收自四，馀四百石；中孰自三，馀三百石；下孰自倍，馀百石。小饥则收百石，中饥七十石，大饥三十石。故大孰则上籴三而舍一，中孰则籴二，下孰则籴一，使民适足，贾平则止。小饥则发小孰之所敛，中饥则发中孰之所敛，大饥则发大孰之所敛，而粜之。故虽遇饥馑水旱，籴不贵而民不散，取有

【今译】

个带着五口人的户主，种地百亩，一年的收成是一亩一石半，打成粟是一百五十石，除去十分之一的税十五石，还剩下一百三十五石。食用，一个人一月要一石半，五个人一年要九十石粟，还剩四十五石。卖去三十石，得到一千三百五十钱，除去社闾尝食新收获的五谷以及春秋的祭祀，用去三百钱，还剩一千零五十钱。穿衣，一个人大致用钱三百，五个人全年用钱一千五百，差四百五十钱。不幸有疾病死丧的费用，及上交赋税，还没算在这里面。这就是农民所以经常贫困的原因，没有勤勉耕种的心思，而使谷物买进太贵的原因。因此善于按平价购粮储存的人，一定小心观察每年有上、中、下三种成熟收成。上熟能收到原来的四倍，最后剩四百石；中熟收获是原来的三倍，最后还剩三百石；下熟是原来的一倍，最后还剩一百石。小饥荒能收一百石，中饥荒能收到七十石，大饥荒能收到三十石。所以丰收之年则用上熟年的政策买入一般年景三倍的粮食而留一份给百姓，中熟之年则买入二倍，下熟之年则买入一倍，使百姓合适满足，粮价平均饥荒的现象就中止了。小饥荒时就发放小熟时所征的赋税，中饥荒就发放中熟时所征的赋税，大饥荒时就发放大熟时所征的赋税，去卖掉

injured, and that those who farmed were encouraged the more. If a man of a family of five were to cultivate 100 *mu* of land, harvesting one picul and a half, from each *mu* each year he would produce 150 piculs of millet in total. With one-tenth or 15 piculs taken for taxes, he would be left with 135 piculs. Reckoning consumption at one and a half piculs per person per month, for five persons, it would be 90 piculs per year. That would leave 45 piculs to sell, which at 30 cash per picul would amount to 1,350 cash. Allowing for new offerings to the local shrines, and for spring and autumn sacrifices at the village altars, costing 300 cash, there would remain 1,050. Clothing usually required 300 cash per person, and five persons through the whole year would use 1,500, producing a deficit of 450. Expenses at the time of afflictions, illnesses both slight and grave, deaths, burials, as well as taxes and other state levies, were not included, but the farmers were often frustrated with these and had not the heart to cultivate, thus making the price of grain excessively dear. For these reasons, those versed in leveling the price of grain must keep careful watch every year: there were three kinds of good harvest; bumper, average, and good. In a bumper harvest there would be four times as much normal, with a surplus of 400 piculs. In an average harvest there would be three times as much, with a surplus of 300 piculs. In a good harvest there would be twice as much, with a surplus of 100 piculs. A first degree crop failure would only produce 100 piculs; a second degree failure 70 piculs, and a great failure 30 piculs. Therefore, of the best harvests the state then purchased three parts, leaving one part to the people. In an average harvest it bought two-thirds, and in a good harvest, one. This caused people to have just a sufficiency for all needs; and when the price returned to its ordinary level things would be stopped. In a first degree failure, what had been bought after a good harvest would be put on sale; in a second degree failure, grain bought after an average harvest would be put on sale. In a great failure, grain bought after a bumper harvest would be

【原文】

馀以补不足也。行之魏国，国以富强。

及秦孝公用商君，坏井田，开仟伯，急耕战之赏，虽非古道，犹以务本之故，倾邻国而雄诸侯。然王制遂灭，僭差亡度。庶人之富者累巨万，而贫者食糟糠；有国强者兼州域，而弱者丧社稷。至于始皇，遂并天下，内兴功作，外攘夷狄，收泰半之赋，发闾左之戍。男子力耕不足粮饟，女子纺绩不足衣服。竭天下之资财以奉其政，犹未足以澹其欲也。海内愁怨，遂用溃畔。

汉兴，接秦之敝，诸侯并起，民失作业，而大饥馑。凡米石五千，人相食，死者过半。高祖乃令民得卖子，就食蜀汉。天下既

【今译】

它们。所以，即使遇到荒年和水旱灾害，所买进的不贵就不会造成士、工、商离散，用有余的去补充不足的。它在魏国实行，国家得以富强。

等到秦孝公任用商鞅，破坏井田，开辟田间的通道，以耕田和作战的赏赐作为急迫的事情，即使不是古代的方法，但仍以致力于根本的缘故，倾轧邻近国家而雄霸诸侯。但王朝的制度便不复存在，超越等级没有了节制。百姓中富有的人积累了大量的财富，而贫苦的人却以糟糠为食；强大的国家兼吞州县，弱小的丧失了社稷。到了秦始皇的时候，便吞并天下，内部大兴土木，外面排斥夷狄，收取过半的赋税，征发居里门左侧的平民去防守边疆。男子用力耕种不足以自给，女子纺织不足以供穿着。竭尽天下的资金财产来奉行他的政策，还不足以满足他的欲望。海内的人悲愤，于是开始逃离叛乱。

汉朝建立后，承接了秦朝的弊端，诸侯共同起事，百姓失掉了所从事的工作，出现大荒年。大凡米一石要五千钱，人吃人，死的人过半数。高祖乃命百姓卖掉孩子，到蜀、汉去生活。天下平定后，百姓

put on sale. Therefore, though there occurred famines from failures of grain crops and dearth of vegetables, or floods, or drought, the price of grain was not high and the people did not leave their land, thanks to the collecting of surpluses to make up for deficiencies. When this policy was practiced in Wei, Wei became rich and strong.

When the Duke Xiao of Qin employed Lord Shang Yang, the latter abolished the nine-square field land division system, established roads running south-north and east-west and prioritized rewards for the cultivation of land and for exploits in war. This was a departure from the old ways. Nevertheless by prioritizing the basics, he crushed the neighboring states and dominated the feudal lords. But it caused the kingly institutions to perish, and there was unseemly leapfrogging of social grades. The rich among the commoners accumulated prodigious wealth, whereas the poor ate only mash and husks of grain. The strong among the feudatories annexed prefectures while the weak lost their fiefs. The First Emperor of Qin unified all under Heaven. Within the empire he started construction on a heroic scale and on its borders he drove back the Yi and the Di barbarians. He took over half the harvest in taxes and mobilized those on the left of the villages away to guard the frontiers. Though the men used their strength to cultivate, there was not enough to feed themselves. The women wove fabric, but not enough to clothe themselves. Although the wealth of the whole empire was exhausted to support his regime, it was still not enough to satisfy his desires. The consequence of domestic anxiety and resentment was absconding and revolt.

The Han Dynasty was built on and inherited the wreckage of the Qin. Rulers of vassal states arose side by side, the people lost their livelihoods, and famine raged. Generally, husked grain cost 5,000 cash a picul. Man ate man and more than half the people died. Emperor Gaozu therefore ordered that the people be allowed to sell their children, and to find food in Shu and Han. Even when stability

【原文】

定，民亡盖臧，自天子不能具醇驷，而将相或乘牛车。上于是约法省禁，轻田租，什五而税一，量吏禄，度官用，以赋于民。而山川园池市肆租税之入，自天子以至封君汤沐邑，皆各为私奉养，不领于天子之经费。漕转关东粟以给中都官，岁不过数十万石。孝惠、高后之间，衣食滋殖。文帝即位，躬修俭节，思安百姓。时民近战国，皆背本趋末，贾谊说上曰：

筦子曰："仓廪实而知礼节。"民不足而可治者，自古及今，未之尝闻。古之人曰："一夫不耕，或受之饥；一女不织，或受之寒。"生之有时，而用之亡度，则物力必屈。古之治天下，至孅至悉也，故其畜积足恃。今背本而趋末，食者甚众，是

【今译】

没有东西可以储藏，从天子不能具备纯色的四匹马，到将相有的只能乘坐牛车。皇上于是颁布法令约束节俭，减轻田租，收取十五分之一的税，根据官薪和政府的开支，向百姓收取赋税。但山川园池市场租税的收入，从天子到受封邑者的私邑，都各自自己供给，不向天子领取平常的费用。用水道运输关东的粟到京师给各官府，一年不超过几十万石。孝惠帝、高后的时代，衣物和食物逐渐增多。文帝即位后，亲自实行节俭，为百姓安定操劳。当时人民都离战国时不远，都背弃根本，趋向末端，贾谊劝谏皇上说：

管仲说"仓库充足后才知道礼节"。百姓物资不充足而可治理的，从古代到现在，还没曾听说过。古代的人说："一个男子不耕种，就有人受到饥饿；一个妇女不纺织，就有人要受到寒冷。"生产物资有季节，而使用却没有节制，那么物资一定会穷尽。古代治理天下，相当细致和全面，所以他们的积蓄足以放心。现在背弃根本，趋向末端，吃闲饭的人相当多，这是天下最

returned the people lacked things to put in reserve. From the Son of Heaven, who was unable to get a team of four horses of the same color, so down to army generals and first ministers at the time, who had to ride on ox carts. The throne therefore relaxed the laws, abated restrictions, and lightened the tax on fields to one-fifteenth of the produce. Emoluments of state officials were measured and expenses of the officers calculated, before taxes were levied upon the people. However, taxes on income from mountains, streams, orchards and ponds, and from booths and markets, all were deemed to be for personal upkeep, from the Emperor down to the enfeoffed lords and ladies who had been granted such territory, and were not entered in the national budget. Millet, transported by boat or cart from the land east of the pass to the imperial capital for the support of the state offices, amounted to less than a few hundred thousand piculs annually. Under Emperor Huidi and the Empress-Consort of Gaozu, clothes and food grew plentiful.

When Emperor Wendi ascended the throne, he himself practiced frugality and economy, striving to bring contentment to his subjects. At that time, the people, so close to the times of the Warring States, had turned their backs against the fundamental to pursue the secondary. Jia Yi advised the Emperor saying: Master Guan said: "Only when granaries and stores are full will rites and duties be respected." From ancient times to the present day there has never yet been a case of people without enough being kept under control. Men of old said: "If a farmer does not cultivate, some will go hungry; and if a woman does not weave, some will suffer cold." Since production is ruled by the seasons, if the use thereof is irregular, then the produce will inevitably be exhausted. In ancient times everything under Heaven was administered and ordered to the broadest extent and in the smallest detail. Therefore, grain in storage was dependably sufficient. Nowadays, the people have turned against the fundamental, rushing to the secondary, and

【原文】

天下之大残也；淫侈之俗，日日以长，是天下之大贼也。残贼公行，莫之或止；大命将泛，莫之振救。生之者甚少而靡之者甚多，天下财产何得不蹶！汉之为汉几四十年矣，公私之积犹可哀痛。失时不雨，民且狼顾；岁恶不入，请卖爵、子。既闻耳矣，安有为天下阽危者若是而上不惊者！

世之有饥穰，天之行也，禹、汤被之矣。即不幸有方二三千里之旱，国胡以相恤？卒然边境有急，数十百万之众，国胡以馈之?兵旱相乘，天下大屈，有勇力者聚徒而衡击，罢夫羸老易子而咬其骨。政治未毕通也，远方之能疑者并举而争起矣，乃骇而图之，岂将有及乎?

夫积贮者，天下之大命也。苟粟多而财有馀，何为而不成?以攻则取，以守则固，以战则胜。怀敌附远，何招而不至？今殴

【今译】

大的伤害；过分奢侈的风俗，一天一天地增长，这是天下最大的害处。残忍暴虐的行为公开进行，没有人来制止；国家大命将倾覆，没有人来拯救。生产的人更加减少而浪费的人更多，天下的财产怎么能不竭尽呢？汉朝建立近四十年了，公家和私人的积累尤其值得哀痛。该下雨的时候不下雨，百姓就要感到畏惧；年成很坏没有收入，就要卖官位和孩子。听说了这些，哪里有治理天下面临危险像这样但皇上仍不震惊的呢！

世上有荒年，这是上天的安排，大禹、商汤已遭受到了。假使不幸有方圆二、三千里的旱灾，国家用什么去救济？突然边境上有急事，几十万上百万的军队，国家拿什么作为粮饷？战争和旱灾同时发生，天下就会相当穷困，有勇力的人聚众闹事，疲惫的男子衰弱的老人交换孩子而咬他们的骨头。政治不一定行得通，远方的和君主相比拟的人一同争着起事，于是惊骇着去图划这件事，难道还来得及吗？

积累贮藏，是天下的大命。如果粟多而且财物有余，干什么事不成功呢？进攻就能夺取，防守就会坚固，进行战争就取得胜利。使敌人归顺，使远方的人归附，招集什么而不到来呢？现在

idlers are many; this all spells harm to the empire. These extravagant customs are spreading by the day; this is the empire's biggest peril. These extravagances and outrages are practiced openly, and no one puts a stop to it. The great mandate is about to capsize, and who is there to rescue it? If producers decline in number, while wastrels become more numerous, how can this not exhaust the wealth and property of the empire! The Han Dynasty has ruled for more than 40 years, but state and private stores are still lamentably depleted. Since the rains do not fall in the proper season, the more the people feel anxious. Since the year is lean and nothing harvested, they beg to sell their offices and their children. Apprised of such tidings, how can it be possible that while all under Heaven face such grave peril, the Emperor is not alarmed?

That there is starvation and abundance in the world is Heaven's doing. Even Yu and Tang were affected by this. Suppose there was a drought in an area of 2,000 or 3,000 square *li*, what could the state draw on to give relief? If on the frontiers a suddenly emergency arose, how would the government feed an army of up to a million? If war and drought were to coincide then the empire would come to peril! Those of boldness and physical power would gather followers, and violently attack others. Weary men and weak seniors would trade children and chew on their bones. State control has not yet reached every part of the land. If in remote areas there were simultaneous risings of those who would emulate my Lord, how - panic-stricken and unprepared - would you be able to form plans to crush them? To keep supplies in reserve is the great mandate under Heaven. If there is an abundance of millet and a surplus of wealth, whatsoever is undertaken, will it not be accomplished? Every attack would result in seizure; defenses would stand firm; every battle would result in victory. Enemies would pledge allegiance, and those far away would submit. Whosoever is called on to muster, would he not come? Now let people be driven to return to farming,

【原文】

民而归之农，皆著于本，使天下各食其力，末技游食之民转而缘南亩，则畜积足而人乐其所矣。可以为富安天下，而直为此廪廪也，窃为陛下惜之！

于是上感谊言，始开籍田，躬耕以劝百姓。晁错复说上曰：

圣王在上而民不冻饥者，非能耕而食之，织而衣之也，为开其资财之道也。故尧、禹有九年之水，汤有七年之旱，而国亡捐瘠者，以畜积多而备先具也。今海内为一，土地人民之众不避汤、禹，加以亡天灾数年之水旱，而畜积未及者，何也？地有遗利，民有馀力，生谷之土未尽垦，山泽之利未尽出也，游食之民未尽归农也。民贫，则奸邪生，贫生于不足，不足生于不农，不农则不地著，不地著则离乡轻家，民如鸟兽，虽有高城深池，严法重刑，犹不能禁也。

夫寒之于衣，不待轻暖；饥之于食，不待甘旨；饥寒至身，

【今译】

驱逐百姓回归到农业，都附着于根本，使天下的人各自依靠自己的力量获得食物，工商业不务农而食的人转向农作，那么积蓄充足，人人高兴自己所从事的事。可以使天下富强安定，却形成这样一种危险局面，臣私下为陛下惋惜！

于是皇上为贾谊的话所感动，就开始设置籍田，亲自耕种来勉励百姓。晁错又劝说皇上道：

英明君王在上位而百姓不感到寒冷饥饿，不是耕种而使他们有吃的，纺织而使他们有穿的，而是为他们开辟积累财物的道路。所以尧帝、禹帝有九年的水灾，商汤有七年的旱灾，但国家没有因饥饿而死的人，这是因为积蓄多而防备已先具有了。现在国家统一，土地和人口的数量不比商汤、大禹时候少，加上没有天灾和几年的水旱灾害，但积蓄却不充足，这是什么道理?土地上有剩余的利润，百姓有剩余的力气，生产谷物的土地没有得到全面开垦，山地大湖的资源没有完全开发出来，不务农而食的人没有完全回到农业上去。人民贫苦，那么邪恶就出现。贫苦产生于不充足，不充足产生于不务农，不务农就不依附土地，不依附土地就会离开家乡轻视家庭，百姓就像鸟兽，即使有高墙深池，严刑峻法，仍不能加以禁止。

寒冷的时候，对于衣服不要求华丽；饥饿时，对于食物不求

so that all will settle themselves in the fundamental; and we may cause all under Heaven to live by his own labor, turning those in the secondary trades back into farming. Then the stores of supplies will be sufficient, and the people will be happy in their occupations. It is possible to make all under Heaven wealthy and peaceable; but it grieves your servant to report to Your Majesty that such a perilous situation has come about!"

Moved by Jia Yi's counsel, the Emperor opened for the first time the Sacred Fields set aside for the Imperial Court, himself guiding the plow in order to encourage the common people. Chao Cuo also admonished the emperor: "Under the sage kings, the people did not freeze or starve; this was not because by growing they could feed themselves, or by weaving clothe themselves, but because the way to wealth had been opened. Therefore, despite Yao and Yu having nine years of flood, and Tang seven years of drought, yet in the kingdom none were left to starve. And this was because precautions had been taken and reserves were plentiful. Today all within the seas are united. The amount of land and the number of inhabitants, being great, are not inferior to those of Tang and Yu. In addition, there have been no calamities from Heaven, nor years-long floods or droughts. So why are our reserves inadequate? The land has neglected benefits; the people have unused physical strength; cultivable land has not been opened up to grow grains; the produce of mountains and lakes has not been best exploited, and non-farmers have not wholly returned to farming for their livelihood. When the people are poor, crime and depravity are born. Poverty is born of insufficiency; insufficiency is born of lack of farming; lack of farming means that the land is not settled; that the land is not settled means detachment from homelands and families. People are like birds and beasts; despite high walls and deep moats, strict laws and severe punishments, they cannot be restrained by prohibitions.

When cold, one does not demand the lightest and warmest of

【原文】

不顾廉耻。人情，一日不再食则饥，终岁不制衣则寒。夫腹饥不得食，肤寒不得衣，虽慈母不能保其子，君安能以有其民哉！明主知其然也，故务民于农桑，薄赋敛，广畜积，以实仓廪，备水旱，故民可得而有也。

民者，在上所以牧之，趋利如水走下，四方亡择也。夫珠玉金银，饥不可食，寒不可衣，然而众贵之者，以上用之故也。其为物轻微易臧，在于把握，可以周海内而亡饥寒之患。此令臣轻背其主，而民易去其乡，盗贼有所劝，亡逃者得轻资也。粟米布帛生于地，长于时，聚于力，非可一日成也；数石之重，中人弗胜，不为奸邪所利，一日弗得而饥寒至。是故明君贵五谷而贱金玉。

今农夫五口之家，其服役者不下二人，其能耕者不过百亩，百亩之收不过百石。春耕夏耘，秋获冬臧，伐薪樵，治官府，给

【今译】

甘美；饥饿寒冷到来了，就不顾廉耻。人的本性是一天不吃两餐就饿，整年不制作衣服就寒冷。腹内饥饿得不到食物，皮肤寒冷得不到衣服，即使是慈母也不能保护她的孩子，君主怎么能拥有他的人民！英明的君主知道这回事，所以要求人民致力于农业和桑业，减轻赋税，增加积蓄，来充实仓库，防备水旱灾害，所以就可以得到并拥有百姓了。

人民，在上位的之所以要控制他们，是因为他们追逐利益就像水往下流，四方没有选择。珠玉金银，饿了不能吃，冷了不能穿，但众人都以它们为贵，是因为在上位的人使用了它们的缘故。它们作为货币又轻又小，容易收藏，可以拿在手里，周游海内而没有饥饿寒冷的忧患。这使大臣轻易背弃他的主上，百姓容易离开他们的家乡，盗贼受到鼓励，逃亡的人有了便于携带的财物。粟米布帛生长于土地，按季节生长，在市场上聚合，不是可以在一天之内能成的；几石的重量，一般的人不能负担，不被邪恶的人所利用，一天得不到，饥寒就要到了。因此英明的君主重视五谷而轻视金玉。

现在一个有五口人的农民家庭，他们中服役的人不少于二人，能耕种的超不过百亩，百亩田的收获超不过百石。春天耕种

clothing, nor demand sweet delicacies to quell hunger. When one's body is hungry and cold, one has no regard for integrity, and no sense of shame towards misconduct. According to man's nature, if he does not eat twice in one day he hungers; if through the whole year one does not cut himself garments, then he is cold. When hunger gnaws at the stomach and no food can be got, when cold bites the skin and no clothes can be got, and the most loving mother cannot protect her child, how can a ruler be able to hold his people? An enlightened ruler knows the truth of this. He, therefore, strives to keep his people at agriculture and sericulture, lightens the poll tax and other government levies, and increases the reserves to fill the granaries and prepare against floods and droughts, so that his people may be held.

The people depend on the methods by which the emperor shepherds them, for they hasten after benefits just as water runs downhill in any direction. Pearls, jade, gold, and silver cannot be eaten when food is lacking, nor used as clothing when one is cold. Nevertheless they are precious to the many simply because they are used by the ruler. They are light and small, easy to conceal. With such things on one's person, one can travel all around the land without fear of hunger or cold. These cause those in state positions to turn their backs upon their lord. People lightly leave their native townships; thieves and robbers have incentive to steal; and fugitives can carry lightweight wealth. Grains, unprocessed and processed, and textiles, fibrous and silken, are produced from the land, grown according to the seasons and labor-intensive, and it is not something that can be accomplished in one day. Several piculs are too heavy for an ordinary man to carry, and hence unprofitable for criminals. A single day without them is one of hunger and cold. For this reason an enlightened ruler esteems the "five grains" and despises gold and jade. Now in a five-member farming family two men at least are required to perform corvee labor, and those who are able to cultivate

【原文】

繇役；春不得避风尘，夏不得避暑热，秋不得避阴雨，冬不得避寒冻，四时之间，亡日休息；又私自送往迎来，吊死问疾，养孤长幼在其中。勤苦如此，尚复被水旱之灾，急政暴(虐)[赋]，赋敛不时，朝令而暮改。当具有者半贾而卖，亡者取倍称之息，于是有卖田宅鬻子孙以偿责者矣。而商贾大者积贮倍息，小者坐列贩卖，操其奇赢，日游都市，乘上之急，所卖必倍。故其男不耕耘，女不蚕织，衣必文采，食必(梁)[粱]肉；亡农夫之苦，有仟伯之得。因其富厚，交通王侯，力过吏势，以利相倾；千里游敖，冠盖相望，乘坚策肥，履丝曳缟。此商人所以兼并农人，农人所以流亡者也。

【今译】

夏天除草，秋天收获冬天储藏，砍伐薪柴，修理官府，服徭役；春天不能躲避风尘，夏天不能避开暑热，秋天不能避开阴雨，冬天不能躲避寒冻，四季之间没有时间休息；还有私人的送往迎来，吊问死者，探问疾病，抚养孤独、老人、孩子都在其中。勤劳辛苦如此，倘使又遭受到水旱灾害，严峻的政治和残暴的赋税，赋敛不按时间，早晨的命令晚上就更改了。在收租税时只好半价而卖，没有的就要收取两倍的利息等情况，于是就有卖田宅和子孙用来偿还债务的人。但商贾中大的就积累贮藏获得双倍利息，小的就坐在市场上叫卖，带着他们积累的财产聚藏的货物，天天在都市中游荡，乘着皇上的所急，就加一倍的价卖出他们的东西。所以他们的男子不耕耘，女子不养蚕织布，所穿的一定华丽，吃的一定是美食佳肴；没有农夫的辛苦，却有千百钱的收入。凭着他们的富有，勾结王侯，势力超过官吏，因为利益而相互倾轧；千里游逛，一路上前后不绝，乘着好车驾着好马，穿着丝绸拉着白缯。这就是商人兼并农民，农民流亡的原因。

have less than 100 *mu*, which yield less than 100 piculs. In spring they plant; in summer they weed; in autumn they reap; and in winter they store; and they cut undergrowth and wood for fuel; repair state buildings; and perform labor services. In spring they cannot escape wind and dust; in summer they cannot avoid sultry heat; in autumn they are unable to flee from dampness and rain; and in winter they cannot shun cold and ice. During the four seasons, not for a day can they stop and rest. Furthermore, in the midst of these is their private life; accompanying and welcoming visitors, mourning the dead, inquiring after the sick, caring for the orphaned, the elderly and the young. No matter how diligently they work or how bitterly they suffer, time and again they are hit by floods and droughts. Insistent, the state is tyrannical and oppressive; capricious in poll taxes and other government levies. Orders are issued in the morning only to be changed by evening. When tax-paying comes, they are obliged to sell at half price, and those with nothing, have to borrow at 100 percent interest. Thereupon, in many cases fields and dwellings are sold, and children and grandchildren are sold in order to pay debts. On the other hand, large traveling traders and resident merchants hoard stock at 100 percent profit; small ones sit in the market shouting their wares. Those who have cornered great quantities of things in short supply wander about daily in cities and markets, taking advantage of the ruler's intransigence to sell at double their value. Therefore, their sons do not tend the fields, nor do their daughters raise silkworms or weave. But they must wear the finest embroidered clothes and eat nothing but top quality grain and meat. They do not suffer the hardships of the farmer, yet they receive the profits of farming. Taking advantage of their great riches they may associate with vassal kings and marquises. Their power exceeds the authority of officers, and vying for financial clout, they try to do each other down. They roam at large for 1,000 *li*, the roads full of their fine carriages and fat horses, dressed in silks and trailing white silk.

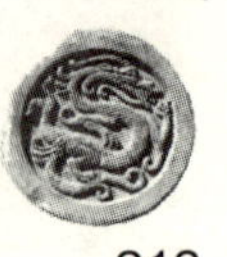

【原文】

今法律贱商人，商人已富贵矣；尊农夫，农夫已贫贱矣。故俗之所贵，主之所贱也；吏之所卑，法之所尊也。上下相反，好恶乖迕，而欲国富法立，不可得也。方今之务，莫若使民务农而已矣。欲民务农，在于贵粟；贵粟之道，在于使民以粟为赏罚。今募天下入粟县官，得以拜爵，得以除罪。如此，富人有爵，农民有钱，粟有所渫。夫能入粟以受爵，皆有馀者也；取于有馀，以供上用，则贫民之赋可损，所谓损有馀补不足，令出而民利者也。顺于民心，所补者三：一曰主用足，二曰民赋少，三曰劝农功。今令民有车骑马一匹者，复卒三人。车骑者，天下武备也，故为复卒。神农之教曰："有石城十仞，汤池百步，带甲百万，而亡粟，弗能守也。"以是观之，粟者，王者大用，政之本务。

【今译】

现在的法律轻视商人，商人却已富贵了；尊崇农夫，农夫却已贫贱了。所以世俗所尊贵的，是君主所轻视的；官吏所贬低的，是法律所尊重的。上下的人思想相反，好恶不同，而想国家富强，法制建立，是行不通的。现在的事情，不如使人民致力于农业。想要人民去致力于农业，在于以粟为贵；以粟为贵的方法是使人们用粟作为赏罚。征求天下把粟交给官府，可以授给爵官，免除罪过。这样的话，富人就有爵位，农民有钱，粟有所分散。能交粟被授予爵位的，都是有富余的；从有富余的人那里取得，以供给皇上使用，那么贫苦人民的赋税就可减少，这就是所说的减少有富余的来补充不足，命令一颁布百姓就得利。顺应民心，用来补充不足的地方有三：一是君主的花费充足，二是百姓的赋税减少，三是勉励农事。现在法令规定百姓有战马一匹的，可以免除三人的兵役或免纳三人算赋。战马，是天下的武装装备，所以要免服兵役或免纳算赋。神农氏的教导说："有石头砌成的城墙宽十仞，有宽百步的城池，披着蹬甲的士卒百万，但没

That is why traders annex land from the farmers and farmers are cut adrift.

"Under our present laws the merchant is held in low esteem, but even so the merchant is rich and honored. They respect the farmer, but he is poor and despised notwithstanding. Thus, what usage honors is what the ruler holds light; what officials belittle is what law dignifies. Since the ideas of the state and the people are contradictory, and their likes and dislikes are opposed, it is impossible to desire both that the state be rich and the law be upheld. At the moment nothing is more urgent than to make the people devote themselves to farming. If one desires to make the people devote themselves to farming, it is necessary to enhance the value of grain. The way to do so lies in causing the people to use grain for rewards and penalties. Let there now be a general call to all under Heaven that whosoever sends grain to the government shall be bestowed with honorary titles, and pardon for crimes; in this way wealthy individuals will have honorary rank, farmers will have money, and grain can be distributed. Those able to present grain in order to receive rank are those with more than enough. Should these surpluses be taken away for the use of the Emperor, then the taxes on the poor could be reduced. This is called 'reducing surpluses to supply deficiencies,' which as soon as ordered will immediately benefit the people. To meet the people's wishes, three things would be supplied: the ruler would have a sufficiency for expenses; the people would pay a lower poll tax; and service in agriculture would be encouraged. At this time, it is ordered that those of the people in possession of a battle horse may, in return for that horse, get exemption from military service for three men of draft age. Battle horses are part of the empire's military preparedness, and therefore, donors are deserving of exemption. According to the teaching of the Divine Farmer: "A city may have stone walls of 10 *ren*, a moat of boiling water measuring 100 paces, a million armored men, but

【原文】

令民入粟受爵至五大夫以上，乃复一人耳，此其与骑马之功相去远矣。爵者，上之所擅，出于口而亡穷；粟者，民之所种。生于地而不乏。夫得高爵与免罪，人之所甚欲也。使天下[人]入粟于边，以受爵免罪，不过三岁，塞下之粟必多矣。

于是文帝从错之言，令民入粟边，六百石爵上造，稍增至四千石为五大夫，万二千石为大庶长，各以多少级数为差。错复奏言："陛下幸使天下入粟塞下以拜爵，甚大惠也。窃恐塞卒之食不足用，大渫天下粟。边食足以支五岁，可令入粟郡县矣；足支一岁以上，可时赦，勿收农民租。如此，德泽加于万民，民俞勤农。时有军役，若遭水旱，民不困乏，天下安宁；岁孰且美，则民大富乐矣。"上复从其言，乃下诏赐民十二年租税之半。明年，遂除民田之租税。

【今译】

有粟，城不能守住。"从这看来，粟，是称王的人最大的需要，政治的根本。让百姓纳粟得到爵位至五大夫以上，才免除一人的徭役，这跟军马的功劳相差很远了。爵位，是皇上所专有的，从口中说出是没有穷尽的；粟，是百姓所种植的，从地上生长不会绝。得到高爵位和免除罪罚，是人非常向往的。使天下人把粟纳给边境军队，用来得到爵位和免除罪罚，不超过三年，边境地区的粟一定很多了。

于是文帝就听从了晁错的话，叫百姓纳粟给边境，纳六百石爵位是第二等，稍稍增到四千石，爵位是第九等，一万二千石爵位是第十八等，各以纳粟多少和爵位等级作为差别。晁错又上奏道："陛下有幸使天下人纳粟给边境来授爵，恩惠很大。我私下怕守边士卒的食物不足以使天下粟充分分散。边境上的粮食足以支付五年，可命令向郡县纳粟了；足以支持一年以上，可以到时赦免，不收农民田租。这样，恩泽加给万民，人民更加勤勉务农。碰巧有军役，或者遭受水旱灾害，百姓不贫困，天下安宁；每年五谷成熟而且质量很好，那么人民就很富足安乐了。"皇上又听从了他的话，就下诏赏赐人民十二年一半的租税。第二年，就免除了百姓田地的租税。

without grain it cannot be defended." Seen in this light, grain is the most useful thing for the ruler, and is a fundamental to the state. The people are allowed to offer grain for titles up to and above the rank of *wudafu*, to win exemption from military service for one male member of their family. The merit won from such action is way below that of furnishing battle horses. Bestowal of rank is the sole prerogative of the Emperor, and there is no end to them when he speaks; grain is something which the people grow; it is produced on the land, and there is no shortage of it. Now, high rank and pardon for crime are what men most desire. If people all over the empire are allowed to present grain at the frontiers in order to receive rank or to have offenses pardoned, in less than three years there would be plentiful reserves of grain at the border.

Thereupon, Emperor Wendi followed Chao Cuo's advice, and ordered the people to send up grain for the frontiers. For 600 piculs they got a second-degree title, rising according to the amount presented up to 4,000 piculs for a ninth-degree title. For 12,000 piculs, the donor was granted 18th rank. The rank distinctions all reflected the amounts donated. Chao Cuo again presented a memorial saying: "The throne has fortunately allowed all under Heaven to send grain for the border region for the granting of rank: this is indeed a great grace. It was my secret worry that food supplies for the frontier guards would not be enough to sufficiently disperse grains all over the empire. Now that frontier food supplies are enough for five years, let it be ordered that grain be sent to the prefectures and counties. Where one year's supply or more is secured, let there be amnesty, and exemption of farmer's field taxes. By doing so, virtue and mercy will fall upon the multitudes; and the people will be more motivated to farm. If, in time, military or labor service is required, or should there be flood or drought, then the people will not be destitute and the empire will remain stable. If the year's harvest ripens and is of prime quality, then the people are abundantly rich and very content."

【原文】

后十三岁，孝景二年，令民半出田租，三十而税一也。其后，上郡以西旱，复修卖爵令，而裁其贾以招民；及徒复作，得输粟于县官以除罪。始造苑马以广用，宫室列馆车马益增修矣。然娄敕有司以农为务，民遂乐业。至武帝之初，七十年间，国家亡事，非遇水旱，则民人给家足，都鄙廪庾尽满，而府库馀财。京师之钱累百巨万，贯朽而不可校。太仓之粟陈陈相因，充溢露积于外，腐败不可食。众庶街巷有马，仟伯之间成群，乘牸牝者摈而不得会聚。守闾阎者食粱肉；为吏者长子孙；居官者以为姓号。人人自爱而重犯法，先行谊而黜愧

【今译】

过十三年后，到了孝景帝二年，叫百姓出一半的田租，收取三十分之一的税。这之后，上郡以西的地方有旱灾，又重新整治卖爵的法令，减少价格来招揽百姓；至于按刑律服劳役的妇女，可以向县官纳粟以免除罪罚。开始建造苑囿养马以扩大备用，宫室各馆车马加以增建和修理。但屡次命令有关官员以农业作为本业，百姓才渐渐安于本业。到武帝初年的七十年间，国家没有事变，不遭受水旱灾害的话，百姓就可以人人自给家庭自足，京都和封邑的粮仓都全满了，而且官府仓库有了剩余的财物。京师里的钱积累了上百万，穿钱的绳索腐朽后钱没法计数。京师积累谷物的仓库里的粟，逐年增积，满仓后就堆积于仓外，腐坏不能食用。百姓街头巷口有马，田间小道上马匹成群，乘母牛的人被排斥不得与众人在一起。看守里门的人食精美的饭食；当官的生长子孙；居官位的以之作为官号。人人自爱而难以犯

The emperor again took his advice, and issued a decree granting the people one half of the produce tax for the 12th year (167 BC) of his reign. The next year he abolished the people's tax on the produce of their fields.

Thirteen years on, in the second year of the reign of Emperor Jingdi (155 BC), it was ordered that the people pay half of their field tax, that is, one-thirtieth of its output. When, some time afterwards, drought occurred in Shang Prefecture and to the west, the ordinance for sale of rank was reissued, but at lower cost in order to attract more people; men sentenced to forced labor were allowed to transport grain to the empire in expiation of their crimes. For the first time there was established a park for raising horses to expand military readiness; equipages for horses in palaces or high residences on imperial estates were increased and improved. However, officials were repeatedly commanded to pay particular attention to farming; and the people gradually settled back into this occupation. For 70 years, up to the early years of Emperor Wudi, the nation lived without disturbance, and except when flood or drought came, the people were able to provide adequately for their families. The grain stores, in cities and fiefs alike, were completely full; the government treasury and storehouses, moreover, had surpluses of every kind of wealth. In the capital cash had accumulated in millions, but the number could not be checked because the strings had rotted. In the central granary, one year's grain had been piled on top of the previous, time after time so that it filled and overflowed, piled up outside, exposed to the elements to get stale, spoiled and inedible. The great masses of the common people had horses, congregating on the paths between the fields. Anyone riding a mare, however, was ejected, not being allowed to join in. Even those that guarded gates in the villages and lanes ate fine grain and meat. Official servants remained in employment while their sons and grandsons grew to manhood. Officials took their surnames from their positions.

【原文】

辱焉。于是罔疏而民富，役财骄溢，或至并兼，豪党之徒以武断于乡曲。宗室有土，公卿大夫以下争于奢侈，室庐车服僭上亡限。物盛而衰，固其变也。

是后，外事四夷，内兴功利，役费并兴，而民去本。董仲舒说上曰：“《春秋》它谷不书，至于麦禾不成则书之，以此见圣人于五谷最重麦与禾也。今关中俗不好种麦，是岁失《春秋》之所重，而损生民之具也。愿陛下幸诏大司农，使关中民益种宿麦，令毋后时。”又言：“古者税民不过什一，其求易共；使民不过三日，其力易足。民财内足以养老尽孝，外足以事上共税，下足以畜妻子极爱，故民说从

【今译】

法，尊崇品行道义而摒弃丑恶的行为。于是法网疏阔而百姓富足，依靠他们的富有而骄傲自满，有的到了兼并土地的地步，豪族之辈凭藉威势在乡里主观妄断曲直。宗室有封邑，公卿大夫以下都争相奢侈，房子车骑服饰犯上没有限度。事物由极盛而转为衰败，本来就是变化的规律。

这之后，在外对付四夷，在内讲求功名利欲，劳役和费用一同兴起，而百姓放弃本业。董仲舒劝说皇上道：“《春秋》不记载其他谷物，而麦和稻子没有成熟就加以记载，以此可见圣人对于五谷最重视麦与稻子。现在关中民俗不喜欢种麦子，这一年中失去《春秋》所重视的，而损害了使百姓生活所需具备的物质。愿陛下诏令大司农，使关中的百姓增加隔年熟的麦子的种植，让他们不要误了季节。”又说：“古代官府征收人民的税不过十分之一，他们的要求容易供给；役使人民不过三天，他们需求的劳力容易满足。人民的财力内足以奉养老人，尽到孝心，外足以事奉皇上供给税赋，下足以尽心爱护妻子

Everyone had self-respect, loath to break the laws of the land. They valued righteousness above all, condemning shameful and disgraceful behavior. Thereupon, the net of justice was slackened, and the people became affluent. But reliance on their wealth made them arrogant and complacent; some even annexed land or organized mobs of ruffians to settle matters by force in smaller places within townships. Fief-holding members of the imperial clan, great nobles of the realm, chief ministers of state, high officials and their underlings – all vied in excess and extravagance. In mansions and dwellings, in carriages and costumes, higher ranks were arrogated without any restriction. Things that flourish must in turn decay; this is, of course, the principle of change.

As time passed, in the border territories there were expeditions against the barbarians, while within the heartlands there was growing appetite for rewards and material gains. Both labor services and state expenses mounted and the people abandoned their primary work. Dong Zhongshu addressing the throne said: "In the *Spring and Autumn Annals* no mention is made of other grains apart from records of wheat and millet not ripening. From this it may be seen that the sages placed the greatest importance upon wheat and millet among the five grains. At the present time in Guanzhong (district inside the Pass), the sowing of wheat is not popular. This signifies that what was important in the *Annals* is neglected year after year, and that the means for maintenance of the people is diminished. I wish the favor of a decree that the Chamberlain for the National Treasury will cause the people in Guanzhong to increase the sowing of winter wheat; and to see that they do not miss the seasonal time." He also said: "The ancients taxed the people not more than a tithe, and requisitions were easy to meet. The corvee was not more than three days, and laborers were plentiful. The wealth of the people was sufficient to take care of the old, and fulfill all the duties of filial piety; it was enough to serve the Emperor and to contribute taxes

【原文】

上。至秦则不然，用商鞅之法，改帝王之制，除井田，民得卖买，富者田连仟伯，贫者亡立锥之地。又颛川泽之利，管山林之饶，荒淫越制，逾侈以相高；邑有人君之尊，里有公侯之富，小民安得不困？又加月为更卒，已复为正，一岁屯戍，一岁力役，三十倍于古；田租口赋，盐铁之利，二十倍于古。或耕豪民之田，见税什五。故贫民常衣牛马之衣，而食犬彘之食。重以贪暴之吏，刑戮妄加，民愁亡聊，亡逃山林，转为盗贼，赭衣半道，断狱岁以千万数。汉兴，循而未改。古井田法虽难卒行，宜少近古，限民名田，以澹不足，塞并兼之路。

【今译】

儿女，所以人们高兴地服从皇上。到了秦朝就不是这样，实行商鞅的法制，改变帝王的制度，废除井田，百姓能够进行贸易，富有的人田地纵横交错，贫困的人没有放下锥子的地方。又独占河流大湖的利益，占有山地森林的富饶，放纵越制，以奢侈相贵；邑中也有人君的尊贵，里中也有公侯的富有，弱小的百姓怎么能不穷困呢？又连月轮番服兵役，完了后，又为中都官服役一年，驻守边境一年，所服的劳役是古代的三十倍；田租人口赋，盐铁的利润，是古代的二十倍。有的人耕种豪民的田地，交纳十分之五的税。所以贫困的人常穿牛马的衣服，食猪狗的食物。又加上贪婪暴虐的官吏，妄自加重刑戮，百姓担忧没有寄托，就逃亡山林，转变为盗贼，囚犯塞满了道路的一半，审判案件一年以千万计数。汉朝建立后，因循不加以改变。古代的井田制虽然难以猝然实行，应尽量接近古制，限制百姓以私人名义占有土地，用来补充不足，并堵住兼并的道路。使盐铁的利润都回到百姓

and to support wives and children to the highest degree of love. Consequently the people were delighted to follow the ruler. Under Qin, it was not so. The methods of Shang Yang were adopted, and the institutions of the kings were changed. The nine-square land system was abolished, and the people were allowed to sell and buy land. The rich had their fields connected along both north-south and east-west roads, while the poor had not even land into which to stick an awl. Furthermore, they alone had possession of the profits of streams and marshes, and controlled the abundant resources of mountains and forests. Profligate and dissipated, they overrode state institutions, and overstepped extravagances to outdo one another. In the cities their awesome dignity matched the monarch's; in the villages they had riches to rival great nobles and feudal lords. How could the lowly people but be distressed? Moreover, there was compulsory local military service of one month by turn, regular military service of one year on the frontier and one year of corvee labor. This was 30 times more than in ancient times, and taxes on fields, poll taxes and profits from salt and iron were 20 times more. Some worked land belonging to knights, and they had to give half of the output in rent. Consequently, poor people would wear cattle and horse covers, and ate food meant for dogs and swine. Things were aggravated by covetous and cruel officers who imposed penalties and capital punishments without due authority. The people, with no means of livelihood, escaped to mountains and forests where they became thieves and robbers.

Half of the roads were blocked by prisoners in red ocher. Those brought to judgment and imprisoned each year numbered in the thousands and tens of thousands. When Han came to power, it followed the same path without change. Although it would be difficult to precipitately revert to the ancient land system, it is proper to make things somewhat nearer to it. Let individual ownership of land be limited, so as to supplement at times of shortage, and to

【原文】

盐铁皆归于民。去奴婢，除专杀之威。薄赋敛，省徭役，以宽民力。然后可善治也。”仲舒死后，功费愈甚，天下虚耗，人复相食。

武帝末年，悔征伐之事，乃封丞相为富民侯。下诏曰：“方今之务，在于力农。”以赵过为搜粟都尉。过能为代田，一亩三圳。岁代处，故曰代田，古法也。后稷始圳田，以二耜为耦，广尺深尺曰圳，长终亩。一亩三圳，一夫三百圳，而播种于圳中。苗生叶以上，稍耨陇草，因隤其土以附(根苗)[苗根]。故其《诗》曰：“或芸或芓，黍稷儗儗”。芸，除草也。(耔)[芓]，附根也。言苗稍壮，每耨辄附根，比盛暑，陇尽而根深，能风与旱，故儗儗而盛也。其耕耘下种田器，皆有便巧。率十二夫为田一井一屋，故亩五顷，用耦犁，

【今译】

手中。释放奴婢，废除擅自杀人的权威。减轻赋税，减省徭役，来宽松百姓的负担。然后可以很好地加以治理。”董仲舒死后，事情的花费更加多，天下损耗空虚，人又开始相食。

武帝末年，对征伐之事感到后悔，就封丞相为富民侯。下令说：“目前的要务，在于致力于农业。”任赵过为搜粟都尉。赵过懂得种代田，一亩田开三条垄沟。每年更换垄沟的位置，所以叫代田，是一种古代的方法。后稷时开始在田间开垄沟，用两耜并在一起两人并耕，宽深各一尺叫甽，延长到亩的终端。一亩有三甽，一个劳力有三百甽，把种子就播洒在甽中。禾苗生长出叶子后，就稍稍除掉垄上的草，顺便把土培附在苗的根上。所以《诗》上就说：“有的拔草，有的培土，黍米和稷米，已是茂盛得很。”芸，是除草。芓，是培土。是说禾苗稍微壮了一点，就常常除草培土，到了盛暑，垄就没有了而根也深了，能经得住风灾和旱灾，所以就很茂盛了。代田耕耘播种的器械，都方便灵巧。大概十二个劳力有田一井一屋，所以一亩有

block the road to annexations. The profit from salt and iron should go to the people where it belongs. Liberate serfs, and eliminate the prerogative of killing on one's own authority. Reduce poll taxes and other government levies, and lessen corvee labor, so as to lighten the burden on the people. Then they can be well governed." After the death of Zhongshu, expenditure got even more out of control. All under Heaven became utterly wasted, and once again man ate man.

In the last years of his reign, Wudi repented of his punitive military expeditions, and accordingly created for his prime minister the honorary title "Marquis for Enriching the People." He issued an edict saying: "At the present moment the priority lies in strengthening agricultural production." For this purpose, Zhao Guo was appointed Defender in charge of searching for millet. Guo understood the art of "field-changing," in which one *mu* had three channels, the locations of which were changed each year. It was an ancient method, one initiated by Hou Ji, Shun's minister of agriculture. By plowing two parallel furrows, one *chi* wide and deep respectively, one made a ridge called a *quan*. They were the full length of one *mu*, and each *mu* had three *quan*. In these trenches, three hundred to a *fu*, the seeds were scattered and once the shoots that came forth had sprouted leaves, the raised earth between the trenches was weeded, causing the soil to slide down to support the roots of the young plants. As is put in the *Book of Odes*, "Some weed; some gather earth around the roots;/ Each millet plant spurts and burgeons." Now "to weed" means to take out the grass; and "to gather earth around the roots" means to support the roots. This is to say, as the shoots gradually grew sturdier, at each weeding the roots got more support. When the height of summer came, the earth ridges were completely removed, and the roots buried deep in the soil to endure wind and drought. And so they flourished luxuriantly. Plowing, weeding, and sowing seeds, their agricultural implements were convenient and ingenious. It is reckoned that 12 laborers

【原文】

二牛三人，一岁之收常过缦田亩一斛以上，善者倍之。过使教田太常、三辅，大农置工巧奴与从事，为作田器。二千石遣令长、三老、力田及里父老善田者受田器，学耕种养苗状。民或苦少牛，亡以趋泽，故平都令光教过以人挽犁。过奏光以为丞，教民相与庸挽犁。率多人者田日三十亩，少者十三亩，以故田多垦辟。过试以离宫卒田其宫壖地，课得谷皆多其旁田亩一斛以上。令命家田三辅公田，又教边郡及居延城。是后边城、河东、弘农、三辅、太常民皆便代田，用力少而得谷多。

至昭帝时，流民稍还，田野益辟，颇有畜积。宣帝即位，用吏多

【今译】

五顷，用两人并耕，二牛三人，一年的收获经常超过不作垄沟耕作的田地每亩达一斛以上，会耕种的甚至达到两倍。赵过就派人教太常、三辅，大司农设立善于制作田器的奴仆来进行工作，制作种田的器械。二千石派遣令长、三老、力田以及里父老中善于种田的人接收种田的器械，学习耕种和培养禾苗的方法。百姓有的苦于没有牛，失去雨后土润及时耕种的农时，所以平都令光教赵过用人拉犁的方法。赵过上奏要求任光为丞相，教民相互雇佣来拉犁。人多的大概一天能耕三十亩，少的能耕十三亩，因此田地大多被开垦。赵过用离宫中士卒耕种宫殿内外墙之间的土地作为试验，打的谷都比别的田每亩多一斛以上。教家田和三辅公田，又教边郡以及居延城。这之后，边境上的城市、河东、弘农、三辅、太常的百姓都认为代田便利，用力少却得到的谷多。

到昭帝的时候，流亡的百姓渐渐回乡。田野的开辟增多，很有一

cultivate a *jing* of land. So the acreage is five hectares. A double plow was used, three men to two oxen. By means of this system, the annual yield from one *mu* of land was generally one bushel higher than from an untrenched field. Those who were experienced could double the margin. Zhao Guo had people educate the Chamberlain of Ceremony and the three Guardians of the Capital in the art of cultivation. The Chamberlain of National Treasury established artisan serfs to do this and to produce farming implements. Officials of 2,000 piculs grade sent forth the county magistrates, the Three Seniors, the farming-invigorators, as well as village fathers who were experienced farmers, to receive the implements and to study how to plow and sow, and how to nurture young shoots. Some of the people suffered lack of oxen, or could not catch the wet season, so, Guang the Magistrate of Pingdu taught Zhao Guo how to plow using manpower only. Guo recommended to the Emperor to appoint Guang as his assistant, to teach the people to cooperate in pulling the plow. It is reckoned that those employing many laborers could work 30 *mu* in one day, whereas those with few laborers could work only 13. Thus, it came to pass that much uncultivated land was opened up for arable use. Guo launched an experiment using guards at palaces of the imperial household outside the city, having them cultivate idle untilled lands lying between enclosing walls. In the trials, grain yields far exceeded those produced by neighboring fields by a margin of at least one bushel per *mu*. At the Emperor's behest he instructed families of rank in tilling government lands in the metropolitan area of the capital. He also taught the frontier prefectures as well as the city of Juyan. The people of the border cities, Hedong, Hongnong, the capital area and imperial mausoleums all found the "field-changing" system much better, because it produced more grain for less physical effort.

In the time of Emperor Zhaodi, drifters gradually made their way back to the fields, and wastelands were more than ever

【原文】

选贤良，百姓安土，岁数丰穰，谷至石五钱，农人少利。时大司农中丞耿寿昌以善为算能商功利得幸于上，五凤中奏言：“故事，岁漕关东谷四百万斛以给京师，用卒六万人。宜籴三辅、弘农、河东、上党、太原郡谷足供京师，可以省关东漕卒过半。”又白增海租三倍，天子皆从其计。御史大夫萧望之奏言：“故御史属徐宫家在东莱，言往年加海租，鱼不出。长老皆言武帝时县官尝自渔，海鱼不出，后复予民，鱼乃出。夫阴阳之感，物类相应，万事尽然。今寿昌欲近籴漕关内之谷，筑仓治船，费直二万万馀，有动众之功。恐生旱气，民被其灾。寿昌习于商功分铢之事，其深计远虑，诚未足任，宜且如

【今译】

些积蓄。宣帝即位后，任用官吏多半选用有德行的人，百姓安于本土，每年的收入丰盛，谷价到每石五钱，农民利益很少。当时大司农中丞耿寿昌善于计算和测量，能计算工程用工多少，受到皇上的宠幸，五凤年间上奏道：“按旧例，每年水运关东的谷四百万斛来供给京师，用士卒六万人。应买入三辅、弘农、河东、上党、太原郡的谷足以供应京师，可以节省关东水运的士卒一半多。”又请示增加海租三倍，天子都依从他的建议。御史大夫萧望之上奏说道：“原先御史大夫的部属徐宫家在东莱，说往年增加海租，鱼就不出来。长老都说武帝时县官曾亲自捕鱼，海鱼不出来，后来又还给百姓，鱼才出来。阴阳相感，事物同类相应，万物都是这样。现在耿寿昌打算就近购买水运关内的谷物，建筑仓库打造船只，花费值二亿多，有劳动大众的工程，怕产生旱灾的气象，百姓遭受它的灾害。耿寿昌习于测算一分一铢的事情，他的深远的计算和思考，实在不足胜任，应和原先一样

cultivated. There was a considerable accumulation of stores. When Emperor Xuandi came to the throne, he employed government officials selected for the most part on the basis of worthy and excellent character. The common people were content on the land; years were repeatedly abundant and luxuriant. Grain could sell for only five cash a picul, bringing farmers little profit. At that time, the second in rank in the Ministry of National Treasury, Geng Shouchang, was a favorite of the Emperor for his skill in calculation and estimating for projects. During the Wufeng reign period (57-54 BC), he memorialized the throne, saying: "In the past, four million bushels of grain a year was transported by water from east of the Pass to provision the capital, a task that employed 60,000 men. It is fitting that grain, sufficient to supply the capital, should be bought within the metropolitan area prefectures of Hongnong, Hedong, Shangdang, and Taiyuan. This would save more than half of the manpower used in shipments that come by water from east of the Pass." Also he suggested a tripling of sea taxes. The Son of Heaven agreed all of his plans. In opposition, the Censor-in-Chief, Xiao Wangzhi, memorialized the throne, saying: "Xu Gong, former clerk attached to this office, whose home was in Donglai, stated that whenever in former years sea duty had been increased, the fish did not come out. Village elders all said that during the time of Emperor Wudi the government officials themselves tried to fish, but the fish of the sea did not come out. Later, when the tax was returned to the people, the fish returned too. Now under the influence of *yin* and *yang*, like creatures of the natural world interact. This is a universal truth. Now Shouchang wants grain to be bought and transported by water from nearby within the Pass. Expenses for building granaries and constructing boats would cost more than 200 million. This means a highly labor-intensive enterprise. My fear is that it will give the impression of drought, and that the people will suffer calamities so caused. Shouchang is experienced in the matter of calculating

【原文】

故。”上不听。漕事果便，寿昌遂白令边郡皆筑仓，以谷贱时增其贾而籴，以利农，谷贵时减贾而粜，名曰常平仓。民便之。上乃下诏，赐寿昌爵关内侯。而蔡癸以好农使劝郡国，至大官。

元帝即位，天下大水，关东郡十一尤甚。二年，齐地饥，谷石三百馀，民多饿死，琅邪郡人相食。在位诸儒多言盐铁官及北假田官、常平仓可罢，毋与民争利。上从其议，皆罢之。又罢建章、甘泉宫卫，角抵，齐三服官，省禁苑以予贫民，减诸侯王庙卫卒半。又减关中卒五百人，转谷振贷穷乏。其后用度不足，独复盐铁官。

【今译】

为好。”皇上没有听从。水运的事情果然便利，耿寿昌就请示命令边郡都建筑仓库，在谷价低时增价买入，以对农民有利，谷贵时就减价出卖，称做常平仓。百姓感到便利。皇上就下诏，赐给耿寿昌关内侯的爵位。蔡癸因为喜好农业而作为使者去劝勉郡国，当上了大官。

元帝即帝位，天下发大水，关东十一郡尤其厉害。元帝二年，齐地发生饥荒，谷一石三百余钱，百姓有很多被饿死，琅邪郡人吃人。在官位的各位儒生大多说盐铁官及北假田官、常平仓可以罢免，不要同百姓争夺利益。皇上听从了他们的议论，把盐铁官及北假田官、常平仓都罢免了。又罢免了建章、甘泉的宫卫，角抵，齐三服官，减少禁苑来给予贫民，裁减诸侯王庙的卫士一半。又裁减关中的士卒五百人，转运谷物来救济穷困的人。这之后，费用不足，只恢复了盐铁官。

small coins, but his deep schemes and far-reaching plans are not to be trusted. It is better to do as hitherto." The Emperor rejected the appeal, and the matter of transport by water was actually found advantageous. Shouchang then suggested that frontier prefectures be ordered to build granaries so that at times when grain was cheap it might be bought at a higher price in order to benefit farmers, and that at times when grain was expensive it might be sold at a lower price. These were given the name "ever normal granaries" and were popular with the people. So then the Emperor issued an edict elevating Shouchang to Marquis of Guannei. Because Cai Gui was enthusiastic about farming, he, moreover, was appointed commissioner to encourage it in the prefectures and the fiefs, and thus he rose to high office.

When Emperor Yuandi came to the throne, there was a great flood which was especially calamitous in 11 prefectures east of the Pass. In the following year, crops in the territory of Qi failed. Grain was more than 300 cash a picul and a great many people starved to death. In the prefecture of Langya the people started eating each other. Most of the scholars in substantial government posts stated that the salt and iron government offices, as well as the Beijia agricultural offices, and "ever-normal granaries," should all be abolished, and that they ought not to be those striving with the people for profits. The Emperor followed their proposal, and abolished them all. Furthermore, guards at the palaces at Jianzhang and Ganquan were discontinued, wrestling shows, the Qi's Office for Imperial Costumes of the Three Seasons, and imperial parks were disestablished in order to give to the poor. The guards at the ancestral temples of the vassal kings were halved, and the number of conscript soldiers within the Pass was reduced by 500 men. Grain was carted in and distributed to the poverty-stricken and destitute. Later, there not being sufficient to cover expenditure, just the salt and iron offices were reinstituted.

【原文】

成帝时，天下亡兵革之事，号为安乐，然俗奢侈，不以畜聚为意。永始二年，梁国、平原郡比年伤水灾，人相食，刺史守相坐免。

哀帝即位，师丹辅政，建言："古之圣王莫不设井田，然后治乃可平。孝文皇帝承亡周乱秦兵革之后，天下空虚，故务劝农桑，帅以节俭。民始充实，未有并兼之害，故不为民田及奴婢为限。今累世承平，豪富吏民訾数巨万，而贫弱俞困。盖君子为政，贵因循而重改作，然所以有改者，将以救急也。亦未可详，宜略为限。"天子下其议。丞相孔光、大司空何武奏请："诸侯王、列侯皆得名田国中。列

【今译】

成帝的时候，天下没有战争，称得上安乐，但是民俗奢侈，不考虑积蓄聚藏。永始二年，梁国、平原郡连年遭受水灾，发生人吃人的现象，刺史、郡守都因犯罪免官。

哀帝即帝位，师丹辅佐政事，他建议说："古代英明的君王没有不设立井田，然后治理才可太平。孝文皇帝承接在灭亡的周朝和暴乱的秦朝战事之后，天下空虚，所以致力于鼓励人民进行农桑业，用节俭作为天下表率。百姓才开始充实，没有兼并的灾害，所以不为民田和奴婢作出限制。现在几代太平相承，大富豪和官吏的财产极多，但贫苦弱小的人更加穷困。君子从事政治，以守旧法不加以改变为贵而很难有改动创造，然而之所以还是有改革的，是因为要用来救急。但也没有全改，宜大略加以限制。"天子把他的建议下达给臣下。丞相孔光、大司空何武上奏请求："诸侯王、列侯都得到国家中的以私人名义占有的土地。列侯在长安，公主在各县以私人名义占有的土地，

In the time of Emperor Chengdi, the empire was free of military actions, offensive or defensive, and tranquility and happiness reigned. But the habit of excess and extravagance was deep-rooted, and little attention was paid to gathering and storing. In the second year of the Yongshi reign period (15 BC), in the Princedom of Liang and in Pingyuan Prefecture, inhabitants ate each other, driven to this by consecutive years of floods and concomitant calamities. The inspector for the locality, the prefect, and the first minister for the fief were considered responsible and were dismissed from their posts.

When Emperor Aidi came to the throne, Shi Dan, who advised on policy, made the following proposal: "Of the sage kings of ancient times, there was none who did not establish the nine-square system, and thanks to this their government was able to keep the peace. During the time of Emperor Wendi the empire was bare and desolate – a legacy of the ruined Zhou, and the disruption of military operations against Qin. Consequently, he turned his attention to encouraging agriculture and sericulture, and he took the lead in the practice of economy and frugality. Thus the people began to have plenty, and there were no unscrupulous land grabs. No restrictions, therefore, were made against the people owning land and serfs. Now we have had several successive generations of peace in which the fortunes of despotic plutocrats and officials have waxed, but the poor and weak face an even harder plight. Now the gentleman ruler honors traditional methods, and does not lightly make changes, but the reason why some changes are made is in order to save in times of crisis. However, even though it has not yet been possible to go into details, it is proper to introduce general restrictions." When the Son of Heaven handed this down for discussion, Prime Minister Kong Guang and Grand Minister of Works He Wu memorialized the throne, with a petition: "Let the princes and the adjunct marquises, we beg, own fields within their own fiefs, and let the lands in

【原文】

侯在长安，公主名田县道，及关内侯、吏民名田皆毋过三十顷。诸侯王奴婢二百人，列侯、公主百人，关内侯、吏民三十人。期尽三年，犯者没入官。”时田宅奴婢贾为减贱，丁、傅用事，董贤隆贵，皆不便也。诏书且须后，遂寝不行。宫室苑囿府库之臧已侈，百姓訾富虽不及文景，然天下户口最盛矣。

平帝崩，王莽居摄，遂篡位。王莽因汉承平之业，匈奴称藩，百蛮宾服，舟车所通，尽为臣妾，府库百官之富，天下晏然。莽一朝有之，其心意未满，狭小汉家制度，以为疏阔。宣帝始赐单于印玺，与天子同，而西南夷钩町称王。莽乃遣使易单于印，贬钩町王为侯。二

【今译】

以及关内侯、官吏以私人名义占有的土地都不要超过三十顷。诸侯王的奴婢是二百人，列侯、公主的奴婢是一百人，关内侯、官吏的奴婢是三十人。以三年为期限，违反的没收入官府。”当时田宅奴婢的价格减少降低，丁、傅当权，董贤显贵，对他们都不利。皇帝下令暂且拖后，后来便停止没有实行。宫室苑囿府库的收藏已很多了，百姓的资财富有虽比不上文帝、景帝的时候，但天下的人口是最多的了。

平帝崩后，王莽摄政，他便篡夺帝位。王莽因袭汉朝治平相承的业绩，匈奴称臣，百蛮顺服，舟车所通的地方，都是臣民，府库百官的富有，使天下安逸。王莽有一天占有了它，但他的心意却没有得到满足，鄙视汉家制度，认为它不精密。宣帝时开始赐给单于印玺，和天子相同，而西南夷钩町则称王。王莽就派遣使者更换单于的印玺，贬钩町王为侯。这两方开始心怀怨恨，侵犯边境。王莽便发动军队，

counties and circuits owned by the adjunct marquises who live in Changan and the princesses of the realm, as well as the lands owned by marquises of Guannei, government officers, and the people, in no case exceed 30 hectares. Let princes have 200 slaves, male and female; let the adjunct marquises and imperial princesses have 100; and let marquises of Guannei, government officers, and the people own 30. At the end of three years, let those who disobey forfeit to the government." At the time, the prices of fields, houses and slaves, became cheaper. But Ding and Fu were in power in the government, and Dong Xian was affluent and honored. All stood to lose by this and soon there came an edict postponing implementation. Later it was stopped and never put into effect. The contents of imperial palaces and government storehouses were already profuse and luxurious, and though the wealth of the common people was less than they had enjoyed under Wendi and Jingdi, nevertheless the population of the empire was most numerous.

When Emperor Pingdi died, his regent Wang Mang assumed the authority of a sovereign and then usurped the throne. The legacy of the peace created by Han all redounded to him: the Huns proclaimed themselves subjects; all the barbarians came to pay homage and acknowledge submission; wherever boats and carts could travel, subservience was absolute. With treasuries and storehouses full, all the officials now were rich, all under Heaven was serene. Overnight Wang Mang obtained this; yet his heart's desire was not fulfilled. He despised the institutions of the House of Han, regarding them as lax and inefficient. Emperor Xuandi for the first time had bestowed upon Chanyu an official seal of government authority, like that of the Son of Heaven; and to Gou Ding, a tribal chief in the southwest, he had given the title of vassal king. Now Wang Mang sent a mission to change the seal of Chanyu, and he demoted Gou Ding from king to marquis. The two peoples became embittered against him, and they harried and harassed the frontier regions.

【原文】

方始怨，侵犯边境。莽遂兴师，发三十万众，欲同时十道并出，一举灭匈奴；募发天下囚徒丁男甲卒转委输兵器，自负海江淮而至北边，使者驰传督趣。海内扰矣。又动欲慕古，不度时宜，分裂州郡，改职作官，下令曰："汉氏减轻田租，三十而税一，常有更赋，罢癃咸出，而豪民侵陵，分田劫假，厥名三十，实什税五也。富者骄而为邪，贫者穷而为奸，俱陷于辜，刑用不错。今更名天下田曰王田，奴婢曰私属，皆不得卖买。其男口不满八，而田过一井者，分馀田与九族乡党。"犯令，法至死，制度又不定，吏缘为奸，天下謷謷然，陷刑者众。

后三年，莽知民愁，下诏诸食王田及私属皆得卖买，勿拘以法。

【今译】

派遣三十万的军队，打算同时分十路一同出发，一举消灭匈奴；征发天下囚徒、成年男子、兵士转运军用物资和兵器，从背靠大海的江、淮而到北边，使者驾着车督促，海内被扰乱了。又动辄仿照古代，不考虑时宜，分裂州郡，改动官员的职能，设立官位，下令说："汉代减轻田租，收取三十分之一的税，常有出钱以代服兵役的赋税，残废疾病的人都要交纳，而且豪民侵犯，分田夺取税收。名义上是三十收一，实际上是收十分之五的税。富有的人骄横邪恶，贫困的人走投无路而走上邪路，都陷于无辜，刑具没有闲置的。现在把天下田改名为王田，奴婢叫私属，都不允许买卖。有家庭男子人数不满八个，而田超过一井的，把多余的田分给九族乡亲。"违反法令的，法令上要判处死刑，制度上又没有确定，官吏以此为奸，天下怨声鼎沸，陷入刑罚的人相当多。

三年后，王莽知道百姓凄惨，下诏令各王田以及私属都可买卖，

Thereupon, Wang Mang mobilized the army, sending out 300,000 men, desiring to dispatch ten columns simultaneously to exterminate the Huns at a single decisive blow. Everywhere in the empire he conscripted and sent out prisoners, youthful and adult males, as well as armored soldiers to transport military supplies and weapons. From the coastal Yangtze and Huai up to the northern borders of the realm, imperial commissioners rode by post chaise to supervise and urge. Disorder was universal. Furthermore, in every act he liked to imitate the ancients, oblivious to the need of the times. He partitioned and reapportioned regions and prefectures; he altered governmental duties and created new government offices. He sent down an order in which he said: "Han lightened taxes on fields to one-thirtieth of the produce. However, there were always charges to commute forced military service, which aged and ill persons all paid. In addition there were encroachments by adventurers, who allotted fields but stole the tax revenue. Hence, nominally it was one-thirtieth; but in reality it was half. These rich, being haughty, perpetrated depravity; the poor, being distressed, perpetrated crimes. Both have sunk into malfeasance; no punishments were not used. Now let the term be altered and the land throughout the empire be designated 'sovereign fields,' and serfs, male and female, be called 'private adherents.' Neither is to be sold or bought. Those families with fewer than eight adult males and having more than a *jing* of arable land shall divide the surplus lands among their nine generations of direct kin and their fellow-townspeople." Violators of the order were punishable by death under the law. Institutions and rulings, furthermore, were never determined. Taking advantage of this, government officers perpetrated crimes. There was much moaning and lamentation among the people, and many were those who met punishment.

Three years on, Wang Mang, aware of the piteous condition of the common man, issued an edict permitting the sale and

【原文】

然刑罚深刻，它政悖乱。边兵二十馀万人仰县官衣食，用度不足，数横赋敛，民俞贫困。常苦枯旱，亡有平岁，谷贾翔贵。

末年，盗贼群起，发军击之，将吏放纵于外。北边及青徐地人相食，雒阳以东米石二千。莽遣三公将军开东方诸仓振贷穷乏，又分遣大夫谒者教民煮木为酪；酪不可食，重为烦扰。流民入关者数十万人，置养澹官以禀之，吏盗其禀，饥死者什七八。莽耻为政所致，乃下诏曰："予遭阳九之厄，百六之会，枯旱霜蝗，饥馑荐臻，蛮夷猾夏，寇贼奸轨，百姓流离。予甚悼之，害气将究矣。"岁为此言，以至于亡。

——卷二十四上《食货志》第四上

【今译】

不要以法律拘捕。但刑罚峻刻，政治混乱。边境上的士兵二十多万人仰仗天子的衣食，费用不足，几次残暴征税，百姓更加贫困。常苦于旱灾，没有平安的年份，谷价飞涨。

王莽末年，盗贼群起，派军队去攻打他们，将吏又在外放任士兵。北边及青、徐地区出现人吃人的现象，雒阳以东米一石二千钱。王莽派遣三公将军打开东方的各粮仓救济贫困百姓，又分头派遣大夫、谒者教百姓煮草木为酪；酪不能吃，又增添了烦扰。流民进入关中的数十万人，设置养赡官来供给他们，官吏又盗取了他们的供给物，饥饿而死的人十有七八。王莽对自己的政治感到可耻，就下诏说："我遭受阳九的困厄，百六的会合，旱灾、霜灾、蝗灾，荒年重现，蛮夷扰乱华夏，寇贼为非作歹，百姓流离失所。我很哀痛，恐怕气数要完了。"每年都这样说，一直到他消亡。

purchase, without legal restrictions, of all the "sovereign fields" and "private adherents." However, punishments were extremely severe, and government affairs were in disarray. Over 200,000 frontiers soldiers looked to the central government for clothing and food. Governmental expenses could not be met; time and again unreasonable poll taxes and other government levies were imposed. The people became all the more impoverished and straitened. With frequent droughts, and no one year of peace, the price of grain soared. Towards the end of his regime, thieves and robber bands sprang up, and troops were sent out to suppress them. Military leaders and officials in outlying regions ignored their military responsibilities. On the northern borders as well as in Qingzhou and Xuzhou there was cannibalism. East of Luoyang, husked millet cost 2,000 cash a picul. Wang Mang dispatched the three highest ministers with military commanders to open the several government granaries in the eastern part of the empire, to provide emergency aid to the needy. He also sent into different parts the grand masters and imperial receptionists to show the people how to boil vegetation to make gruel. The gruel was inedible, which served to aggravate the disturbances. Refuge drifters entering Guanzhong numbered several hundred thousand. A relief office was set up to provide them with food at government expense, but officials embezzled the supplies, and of every ten of these people seven or eight starved to death. Wang Mang was ashamed of these results of his maladministration, and issued an edict, saying: "I have suffered 'yang nine' disasters and the calamities of 'hundred and six.' Severe drought, hoarfrosts, locusts, crop failures have come time and again. Barbarians ravage the empire; robbers and despots are here to reign. The common people have scattered and drift from place to place. This causes me great grief. I fear I near the end." Every year he made this same statement until he was overthrown.

食货志（下）

【原文】

凡货，金钱布帛之用，夏殷以前其详靡记云。太公为周立九府圜法：黄金方寸，而重一斤；钱圜函方，轻重以铢；布帛广二尺二寸为幅，长四丈为匹。故货宝于金，利于刀，流于泉，布于布，束于帛。

太公退，又行之于齐。至管仲相桓公，通轻重之权，曰："岁有凶穰，故谷有贵贱；令有缓急，故物有轻重。人君不理，则畜贾游于市，乘民之不给，百倍其本矣。故万乘之国必有万金之贾，千乘之国必有千金之贾者，利有所并也。计本量委则足矣，然而民有饥饿者，谷有所臧也。民有馀则轻之，故人君敛之以轻；民不足则重之，故人

【今译】

凡是财物，金钱布帛的用途，夏、殷以前它们的详细情况没有记载。姜太公为周朝建立了九府流通财币的办法：黄金一寸见方，就重一斤；钱圆而内孔方，以铢为轻重；布帛宽二尺二寸是一幅，长四丈是一匹。所以货币比金宝贵，比刀锐利，比泉水更流畅，比布更能分散，比帛更能束聚。

姜太公退到封国后，又在齐地加以实行。到管仲辅佐齐桓公，通行了轻重的衡量标准，他说："年岁有荒年和丰收之年，所以谷有贵有贱；命令有慢有急，所以货物有轻有重。皇上不治理，那么囤积居奇的商贾就在市场游荡，乘百姓不能自给时，就把价格提高到是它成本的一百倍。所以有一万辆车的国家一定有万金的商贾，千辆车的国家一定有千金的商贾，是因为利润有所隐藏。按照所生产的去进行消费，那么费用就能自足，然而百姓中有饥饿的人，那是谷有所隐藏的原因。百姓有余就轻视谷物，所以君主征收的价也低；百姓不足就重视谷物，所以君主以高价散发。凡是低价、高价以及征收、散发都按

Chapter 5

The Treatise on Food and Commodities, Part II

We have no documented details of the use, prior to the Xia and Yin, of assets such as gold, coins, silks, and textiles of woven vegetable fibers. Taigong established for the Zhou the Nine Fiscal Agencies to regulate the methods of circulation. Gold units, one inch square, weighed one catty; coins were round with a square hole, and their weight went by the *zhu*. The width of silks and textiles was two feet two inches; and the length of the roll was four *zhang*. Therefore, currency is as precious as gold, as keen as a knife, as mobile as a stream, as widespread as textiles, and as compressible as silk.

When Taigong returned to his fief, this practice was followed in Qi. When Guan Zhong became the first minister for Duke Huan of Qi, he practiced the balancing priorities in regulating commodities. He said: "As a year is disastrous or prosperous, so grain is accordingly expensive or cheap. As levy orders are slow or urgent, so articles accordingly become neglected or important. If the ruler fails to take heed, then hoarding traders wander the markets, taking advantage of want among the people to demand prices 100 times more than the original cost. It was because profits were concealed that in a state of 10,000 chariots there were sure to be merchants of 10,000 catties of gold, and in states of 1,000 chariots there were sure to be merchants with 1,000 catties of gold. By calculating the produce and measuring the storage there should be a sufficiency. That the people, nevertheless, are starving for lack of food is because of grain hoarding. When the people have a surplus, they neglect it, so the ruler should take it at a low price. When the people do not have enough of something, then they value it, and for this

【原文】

君散之以重。凡轻重敛散之以时，则准平。[守准平]，使万室之邑必有万钟之臧，臧繦千万；千室之邑必有千钟之臧，臧繦百万。春以奉耕，夏以奉耘，耒耜器械，种饟粮食，必取澹焉。故大贾畜家不得豪夺吾民矣。”桓公遂用区区之齐合诸侯，显伯名。

其后百馀年，周景王时患钱轻，将更铸大钱，单穆公曰：“不可。古者天降灾戾，于是乎量资币，权轻重，以救民。民患轻，则为之作重币以行之，于是有母权子而行，民皆得焉。若不堪重，则多作轻而行之，亦不废重，于是乎有子权母而行，小大利之。今王废轻而作重，民失其资，能无匮乎？民若匮，王用将有所乏；乏将厚取于民；民不给，将有远志，是离民也。且绝民用以实王府，犹塞川原为

【今译】

一定时机，那么调节供求，物价就稳定了。遵守调节供求，稳定物价的措施，使有万户人口的邑一定有万钟的收藏，用绳穿着的钱有千万串；千户人口的邑一定要有千钟的收藏，用绳穿的钱有百万串。春天进行耕作，夏天进行除草，耒耜器械，种子粮食一定要富足。因此大商人和囤积居奇的商人就不能仗势强夺百姓了。”齐桓公便用小小的齐国联合诸侯，显扬了霸主的名声。

一百多年后，到周景王的时候他担忧钱太轻，准备改为铸造大钱，单穆公说：“这样不行。古代天降灾害，于是乎就要衡量财产和货币，权衡轻重，来拯救百姓。百姓嫌钱轻，就为他们制造重钱来使用，这样大钱小钱并行以重钱为主，百姓都能得到便利。如果不能使用重钱，就多造轻钱来使用，也不废除重钱，于是乎重钱不足的就用轻钱补充，钱小钱大都有利。现在大王废除轻钱而造重钱，百姓失去了他们的资财，能够不匮乏吗？百姓如果匮乏了，大王的开支也要有困难了；有困难就要从百姓那里多收取；百姓不能供给，就将逃亡，这是使百姓离散的做法。况且竭尽百姓财物来充实王府，就像堵塞水

reason the ruler should distribute it dearly. In general, there will be equalization by gathering at times when demand is less than supply, and distributing at times when the converse is true. For adjustment of prices for equalization, a town of 10,000 households must have in its storehouses 10,000 *zhong* of grains, and in its treasuries 10 million strings of coins; while a town of 1,000 households must have in its storehouses 1,000 *zhong* of grains, and in its treasuries a million strings of coins. In order that they may obediently do their plowing in the spring, and in the summer their weeding, plow handles and shares, utensils and implements, seeds and food for family meals must be provided in full. As a result, the great merchants and the hoarders have no way to rob our people." Then the Duke Huan, by allying the very small Qi with other feudal lords, enhanced his name as an ascendant leader among the feudal rulers.

Over a century later, King Jing of Zhou, distressed at the debasement of coins, was about to have larger coins cast, but Duke Mu of Shan told him: "It would not be good to do so. In ancient times when Heaven sent down calamities and tribulations, they measured their wealth and currencies, and weighed priorities in order to relieve the people. Whenever the people suffered from light cash, there was made a heavier currency, and it was put into circulation. So there were the mother coins for circulation as equivalents of child coins. This was more convenient for the people. If they could not bear the heavy coins any longer, then greater quantities of light coins were made and put into circulation. Yet the heavy coins were not withdrawn. Thus, there was the child coin in circulation as a partial equivalent of the mother coin. Now the king is to abolish the light and introduce the heavy. Thus the people will lose their wealth. Can this be done without creating bankruptcy? If the people are bankrupt, the king's revenue will suffer, and making up such deficiency would involve taking heavily from the people. Not having enough, the people start thinking of distant places. This is 'to scatter the people.'

【原文】

潢洿也，竭亡日矣。王其图之。”弗听，卒铸大钱，文曰“宝货”，肉好皆有周郭。以劝农澹不足，百姓蒙利焉。

秦兼天下，币为二等：黄金以溢为名，上币；铜钱质如周钱，文曰“半两”，重如其文。而珠玉龟贝银锡之属为器饰宝臧，不为币，然各随时而轻重无常。

汉兴，以为秦钱重难用，更令民铸荚钱。黄金一斤。而不轨逐利之民畜积馀赢以稽市物，痛腾跃，米至石万钱，马至匹百金。天下已平，高祖乃令贾人不得衣丝乘车，重税租以困辱之。孝惠、高后时，为天下初定，复弛商贾之律，然市井子孙亦不得(宦为吏)[为官吏]。孝

【今译】

源而使水停流，水枯竭是不用几天的。请大王定夺。”景王没有听从他的话，终于造了大钱，上面刻着“宝货”，钱的圆形边和孔都有轮廓，用来劝勉农民补充不足，百姓得到了好处。

秦国兼并天下，货币分为二等：黄金以镒为单位，是上等货币；铜钱的形质像周朝的钱，其正面文字为“半两”，重半两。而珠玉龟贝银锡之类就作为器物装饰和宝藏，不作为货币，但各自随时改变，轻重没有常规。

汉朝兴起后，认为秦朝钱币重而难以应用，改命百姓铸造荚钱。黄金的单位恢复周制为斤。而不守法追逐利益的人以自己的盈余蓄积货物使市场上的货物积聚在自己手里，让物价飞涨，米价达到一石一万钱，马匹一匹值一百金。天下平定后，高祖就下令商贾不得穿丝乘车，加重税租来使他们受挫。孝惠帝、高后的时候，考虑天下刚刚安定，重新放松对商人的法律，但市井之人的子孙同样不能成为官吏。孝文帝五年，由于钱更加多而且轻，就改为铸造四铢钱，其正

Furthermore, to deprive people of the basics for the sake of filling the sovereign's treasury is like damming a stream in order to make a pool of stagnant water. It will not be many days before it dries. The king may think on this." He did not listen. He went ahead and had the large coins cast. Their inscription read: "precious ware." In shape they were round with a hole in the center, and a raised rim. He used them to encourage agriculture and to provide in times of insufficiency. The common people benefitted from this action.

When Qin united all under Heaven, two grades of currency were issued. Gold was issued in units of *yi* and was the upper currency. Their copper coins were the same as those of the Zhou on the reverse, and bore the inscription "half-a-tael," which is what they weighed. Pearls, tortoiseshells, cowries, silver, and tin, though used in or as vessels or ornaments, valuables or treasures, did not constitute money. However, their value tended to fluctuate according to market conditions.

With the rise of Han, Qin money was thought too heavy and impractical, so the order went out that the people should cast *jia*, pod-shaped money. Gold units reverted to one catty. However, people pursuing profit by illegal means accumulated and hoarded surpluses, and were thus able to leverage the market. As a result, prices soared. Husked millet reached 10,000 cash a picul, and a horse could fetch 100 gold catties. When all under Heaven had become pacified, Emperor Gaozu ordered that trades people should not wear garments of silk, nor ride in chariots; and he increased taxes in order to hamper and humiliate them. During the reigns of Emperor Huidi and the Empress Dowager, because the empire was still at an early stage of settlement, there was a relaxation of the regulations applying to hawkers and merchants. Nevertheless, the sons and grandsons of such people were not permitted to be officials. By the fifth year of Emperor Wendi (175 BC), because money in circulation had become lighter and more plentiful, accordingly, a new four-*zhu*

【原文】

文五年，为钱益多而轻，乃更铸四铢钱，其文为“半两”。除盗铸钱令，使民放铸。贾谊谏曰：

法使天下公得顾租铸铜锡为钱，敢杂以铅铁为它巧者，其罪黥。然铸钱之情，非淆杂为巧，则不可得赢；而淆之甚微，为利甚厚。夫事有召祸而法有起奸，今令细民人操造币之势，各隐屏而铸作，因欲禁其厚利微奸，虽黥罪日报，其势不止。乃者，民人抵罪，多者一县百数，及吏之所疑，榜笞奔走者甚众。夫县法以诱民，使入陷阱，孰积于此！曩禁铸钱，死罪积下；今公铸钱，黥罪积下。法若此，上何赖焉？

又民用钱，郡县不同：或用轻钱，百加若干；或用重钱，平称不受。法钱不立，吏急而壹之乎，则大为烦苛，而力不能胜；

【今译】

面为“半两”二字。废除盗铸钱的法令，让百姓任意铸造。贾谊上谏说道：

法律使天下都得以公开花钱雇人用铜锡铸造钱币，敢用铅铁掺杂而为奸巧的人，他的罪罚是黥。但铸钱的情况是，没有掺杂弄巧，就不能得到利益；而掺杂的越精妙，得到的利益就越丰厚。事情能招来祸害，法律能引起邪恶，如今令小民都能铸造货币，各自躲藏着进行铸造，打算禁止他们的厚利和奸巧，即使每天判处黥罪，这样的形势也不能停止。近来，百姓抵偿其应负的罪责，多的一县有一百，至于官吏所怀疑的，被鞭笞拷打因此逃亡的人甚多。制定法律来诱导百姓，使他们落入陷阱，没有比这更多的！以前禁止铸造钱币，死罪积累到下面；现在公开铸钱，黥罪积累到下面。制定这样的法律，皇上将依赖什么呢？

另外，百姓使用钱币，各郡县有所不同：有的用轻钱，一百再加若干；有的用重钱，即使所称重量相同也不能被接受。依法制定的钱币没有立足之地，官吏着急就统一吧，又太烦琐，而且

coin was cast bearing the words "half-a-tael." The decree prohibiting the clandestine casting of coins was revoked, to allow the people to duplicate money. In admonition to the throne, Jia Yi said:

"The law allows the empire equal privilege to hire people and, when tax is paid, to cast copper and tin to make coins. Those who dare, by sleight of hand, to debase the compound with lead and iron face the penalty of having their faces tattooed with black pigment for this crime. Nevertheless the circumstances of casting coins are such that unless the alloy is very skillfully done, one cannot obtain a material profit; but when the mixture is debased to the slightest degree, it makes a very substantial profit. Now there are things men do that may invite calamities, and there are laws that themselves encourage crime. It has now been ordered that civilians have the authority to fashion money, each carrying on his casting in concealed private quarters, and, therefore, in spite of the will to prohibit fat profits and fraud, there will be no stopping the trend even if face-tattooing sentences are handed down daily. Recently those punished for this offense numbered 100 in a single county, while those whom officials suspected and caned have run away in droves. What could be worse than this, to set up a law that lures the people to sink into such a trap! In the past, when the casting of coins was prohibited, the capital cases accumulated waiting for a verdict. At this time when casting is now open to everyone, cases facing the face-tattooing penalty pile up waiting for a verdict. In formulating a law like this one, of what benefit is it to the Emperor?

What is more, the coins in use vary from prefecture to prefecture, and from county to county. In some places they are so light that to every 100 must be added a certain number. In other places they are so heavy that it is impossible to accept even if their weight is correct. Legal-standard coins have not been upheld. Should officers in charge act in haste to fix a standard, then it will be too complicated and demanding to work properly. Should they adopt

【原文】

纵而弗呵乎，则市肆异用，钱文大乱。苟非其术，何鄉而可哉！

今农事弃捐而采铜者日蕃，释其耒耨，冶熔炊炭，奸钱日多，五谷不为多。善人怵而为奸邪，愿民陷而之刑戮，刑戮将甚不详，奈何而忽！国知患此，吏议必曰禁之。禁之不得其术，其伤必大。令禁铸钱，则钱必重；重则其利深，盗铸如云而起，弃市之罪又不足以禁矣。奸数不胜而法禁数溃，铜使之然也。故铜布于天下，其为祸博矣。

今博祸可除，而七福可致也。何谓七福？上收铜勿令布，则民不铸钱，黥罪不积，一矣。伪钱不蕃，民不相疑，二矣。采铜铸作者反于耕田，三矣。铜毕归于上，上挟铜积以御轻重，钱轻则以术敛之，重则以术散之，货物必平，四矣。以作兵器，以假

【今译】

力量不够；放任自流不加以责罚吧，那么市场上使用不同，钱币就会极其混乱。如果得不到治理这种状况的方法，百姓就不知往哪里走才可以！

现在放弃农事而去开采铜的人日益增多，放下他们的农具，用炉炭冶炼钱模，不正当的钱一天天增多，五谷却不见增多。善良的人心动而走上邪路，小心谨慎的百姓陷入刑戮，刑戮就会很不公平，这如何能忽略呢！国家知道忧患是这样，官吏的议论一定说要禁止铸钱。禁止铸钱不得其法，伤害一定很大。命令禁止铸钱币，那么钱币一定贵重；贵重的话那么利就大，偷着铸钱就像云一样兴起，弃市的罪刑又不足以禁止了。邪恶几次没有穷尽而法令禁止几次崩溃，是铜所造成的。铜散布天下，所以它所造成的祸害大矣。

现在大祸可以免除，而七种福可以得到。什么是七种福呢？皇上把铜收集起来不让它散布，那么百姓就不会铸钱，黥罪就不会增多，这是一种。假钱不多，百姓不互相怀疑，这是第二种。开采铜矿进行铸钱的人回到种田上，这是第三种。铜全归集于皇上，皇上就凭藉积累很多的铜来驾驭轻重，钱币轻就设法收集，钱币重就设法散发，钱和物一定会平衡，这是第四。用来制作兵

a laissez-faire approach, different coins will be used in the market booths and monetary chaos will reign. If things are not done by the proper means, where shall one turn for a solution!

At his time agricultural pursuits are abandoned, but copper miners multiply daily. Plows and hoes have been abandoned in favor of smelters, coin-molds, and bellows. Counterfeit coins increase daily, but the 'five grains' do not increase. The good among the people are enticed into crime and depravity. Honest citizens are ensnared into penalties and capital punishment. Should penalties become very excessive, it would be inequitable. How can this be disregarded? When the gravity of the situation is realized in the state, the government authorities in their discussions will surely say, 'Prevent it!' But if the prohibition is not carried out with skill, the injury done will be very great. Once private casting of coins becomes illegal, then coins will surely be more valuable. When valuable, there will be big profits to be made. Thieving counterfeiters will then arise like clouds, and even execution in the market-place will not be a sufficient deterrent. The counterfeiters are too numerous to be counted, and legal prohibition has oftentimes failed. Copper is the underlying cause of all this. When copper is widely available across the empire, it makes the calamity extensive.

Now the extensive calamity can be eradicated and the seven blessings attained. What are these seven blessings? If the monarch collects copper, prohibiting its dissemination, then the people will no longer cast coins, and face-tattooing penalties will not accumulate. This is the first blessing. False coins will not multiply, and the people will no more suspect one another. This is the second blessing. Those mining and casting copper will return to farming. This is the third blessing. If all the copper reverts to the monarch, the monarch will rely on the copper reserve to control the weights. When coins are light, then by an appropriate method they will be collected; when they are heavy, then likewise by an appropriate method they will be

【原文】

贵臣，多少有制，用别贵贱，五矣。以临万货，以调盈虚，以收奇羡，则官富实而末民困，六矣。制吾弃财，以与匈奴逐争其民，收敌必怀，七矣。故善为天下者，因祸而为福，转败而为功。今久退七福而行博祸，臣诚伤之。

上不听。是时，吴以诸侯即山铸钱，富埒天子，后卒叛逆。邓通，大夫也，以铸钱财过王者。故吴、邓钱布天下。

武帝因文、景之畜，忿胡、粤之害，即位数年，严助、朱买臣等招徕东瓯，事两粤，江淮之间萧然烦费矣。唐蒙、司马相如始开西南夷，凿山通道千馀里，以广巴蜀，巴蜀之民罢焉。彭吴穿秽貊、朝

【今译】

器，用来赐予贵臣，多少有限制，使用能分别贵贱，这是第五。用来监视市场，用来调节盈亏，用来收取盈余，那么官府富足而工商业者贫乏，这是第六种。控制住了我们多余的钱财，来和匈奴竞争它的人民，那么敌人一定会归顺，这是第七种。所以善于统治天下的，可以藉着灾祸而转化为幸福，把失败转化为成功。现在长期屏退七种福而为大祸放行，臣下实在为此感到哀痛。

皇上没有听从他的话。这时，吴国凭藉自己是诸侯就在山里铸造钱币，富比天子，后来终于成为叛逆。邓通，是大夫，因为铸钱币，财产超过君王。因此吴国、邓通的钱流行于天下。

武帝凭藉文帝、景帝的积蓄，忿恨胡、粤的危害，登上帝位几年后，严助、朱买臣等人收复东瓯，对付两粤，江淮间骚动不安，花费巨大。唐蒙、司马相如开始开通西南夷，凿山开通了千余里的道路，来扩充巴蜀，巴蜀的百姓疲乏了。彭吴穿越秽貊、朝鲜，设立了沧海

distributed. Thus money and commodities will surely be balanced. This is the fourth blessing. The copper can be used to make military equipment, and bestowed upon distinguished ministers within strict gradations to distinguish the honorable from the lowly. This is the fifth blessing. Thus, all moneys will be supervised, overweight and underweight adjusted, and all of the surplus gathered. As a result the government coffers will be full, while people in secondary occupations will be straitened. This is the sixth blessing. Getting control over our lost wealth will enable us to vie with the Huns and wrest their subjects from them. Then will our enemies surely come to heel. This is the seventh blessing. Therefore he who governs well the empire may transform evils into blessings and defeat into success. Now for a long time, the seven blessings have been shunned, while the evils have been given free rein. Your minister is in all sincerity distressed by this."

The Emperor did not listen. At that time Wu Guo, a vassal lord, was casting money in the mountains and his wealth rivaled that of the Son of Heaven, and eventually he rebelled. Grand Master Deng Tong was richer than a vassal king thanks to casting coins on his own account. Consequently the coins of Wu and Deng spread all over the empire.

The Emperor Wudi made use of the reserve supplies inherited from the emperors Wendi and Jingdi, and he was angered at the depredations of the northern Huns and southern Yue. A few years after Wudi's accession, Yan Zhu, Zhu Maichen, and others enlisted Dong'ou, via an amnesty, to settle the two Yue states. The regions of the Yangtze and the Huai were in turmoil, and costing great expenditures, and Tang Meng and Sima Xiangru, for the first time, opened contacts to the southwestern tribes. They cut through mountains, and constructed a great highway more than a thousand *li* in length in order to expand Ba and Shu, driving the population of Ba and Shu to exhaustion. Peng Wu penetrated Hui, Mo and

【原文】

鲜，置沧海郡，则燕齐之间靡然发动。及王恢谋马邑，匈奴绝和亲，侵扰北边，兵连而不解，天下共其劳。干戈日滋。行者赍，居者送，中外骚扰相奉，百姓抏敝以巧法，财赂衰耗而不澹。入物者补官，出货者除罪，选举陵夷，廉耻相冒，武力进用，法严令具。兴利之臣自此而始。

其后，卫青岁以数万骑出击匈奴，遂取河南地，筑朔方。时又通西南夷道，作者数万人，千里负担餽饷，率十馀钟致一石，散币于邛僰以辑之。数岁而道不通，蛮夷因以数攻（吏），吏发兵诛之。悉巴蜀租赋不足以更之，乃募豪民田南夷，人粟县官，而内受钱于都

【今译】

郡，这样燕国和齐国相继发动变难。等到王恢在马邑设谋，匈奴断绝和亲，侵扰北部边境，战事连年不止，天下都为此而劳苦。战事一天天多起来，远行的人随身带着行李，不走的人就去相送，内外骚扰而相连接，百姓凋敝，只好巧诈躲避刑法，财货损耗而造成不足。交纳财物的可补任官职，出钱的可免除罪罚，选举衰落，不顾廉耻，武力被利用，法令严密。追逐利益的大臣从此而开始。

这以后，卫青每年以数万骑兵出击匈奴，便攻取了河套以南地区，建筑朔方城。当时又开通了西南夷的通道，劳作的人数万，千里挑送军队的供给，大概花费十多钟才能送去一石，散发钱币于邛、僰两地来征集人员。几年后，道路仍然不通，蛮夷因此而几次攻击，官吏派兵诛杀了他们。用尽了巴、蜀的租赋却不足以抵偿所花的费用，就征求豪民到南夷种田，把粟交给地方政府，从都内接受粟钱。

Chaoxian, establishing Canghai Prefecture. Then the regions of Yan and Qi were mobilized throughout. When Wang Hui set up an ambush at Mayi, the Huns responded by breaking the alliance for peace and amity, invading and marauding the northern borders of the empire. Warfare ensued without cease, and all the empire shared the wearisome burden. Shields and spears multiplied daily. Those who went forth had to carry their own bundles; those who remained at home went to see them off. Both in the capital and in the far-flung corners of the empire, trouble was succeeded by disturbance. In their distressed state, the common people resorted to crooked schemes. Their assets wasted away, resulting in insufficiency. Those who presented gifts were appointed to office, and money would buy pardon for crimes. Official appointment by recommendation fell into disuse, and integrity counted for nothing. Force was exploited, laws were harsh, and orders minutely detailed. This was the start of ministers pursuing private profit.

After this, Wei Qing, at the head of tens of thousands of cavalry, would set out every year to take the fight to the Huns. He seized the land south of the Great Bend of the Yellow River and built the city of Shuofang there. It was at this time too that the highway was being made through to the southwestern barbarians. Those laboring on the road numbered several tens of thousands, rations for whom had to be physically carried for a thousand *li*. Of the supplies sent, on an average, one picul by weight out of a dozen *zhong* (or 70 piculs in capacity) reached the final destination. Money was distributed in Qiong and Bo in order to recruit people. For several years, however, the roads were not open all the way, and because of this the barbarians made frequent attacks, and so officers sent out soldiers to kill them. All of the land taxes and poll taxes in Ba and Shu could not pay for this level of activity. Thereupon, bold people were called on to cultivate the southern Yi lands, submit the grain produced to the local government, and receive payment from the

【原文】

内。东置沧海郡，人徒之费疑于南夷。又兴十馀万人筑卫朔方，转漕甚远，自山东咸被其劳，费数十百巨万。府库并虚。乃募民能入奴婢得以终身复，为郎增秩，及入羊为郎，始于此。

此后四年，卫青比岁十馀万众击胡，斩捕首虏之士受赐黄金二十馀万斤，而汉军士马死者十馀万，兵甲转漕之费不与焉。于是大司农陈臧钱经用，赋税既竭，不足以奉战士。有司请令民得买爵及赎禁锢免(臧)罪；请置赏官，名曰武功爵。级十七万，凡直三十馀万金。诸买武功爵官首者试补吏，先除，千夫如五大夫；其有罪又减二等，爵得

【今译】

在东面设置沧海郡，人员的花费同南夷相比拟。又发动十多万人筑城守卫朔方，水上转运相当远，从山东开始百姓都要遭受劳累，花费几十万至百亿，府库更加空虚。皇上就号召百姓能够提供奴婢的可以终身免除赋税或劳役，是郎的可以增加俸禄。纳羊做郎官，开始于这时候。

这以后四年，卫青每年率十多万人攻击匈奴，斩杀捕捉敌人的兵士受到的赏赐有黄金二十多万斤，但汉朝的兵士和马匹死的有十多万，兵器和铠甲以及运粮的费用还不包括在内。于是大司农上奏说常用的钱以及赋税已用完，不足以支付战士的费用。有关官员请示令百姓可以买爵位以及用钱来换取免除或减除不准工商业者为官的罪罚；请求设置受赏的官职，叫做武功爵，每级十七万，共值三十多万金。各买武功爵官位的人先试着授官；千夫武功爵与五大夫相同；有罪再

Imperial Treasury. When Canghai Prefecture was established in the east, expenditure on corvee labor was as much as in the southern Yi areas. Furthermore, over 100,000 men were mobilized to build and guard Shuofang. Grain had to be brought a great distance by water. From Shandong onwards, all the land suffered the burden of this, as tens of billions were spent. The imperial treasury and government storehouses emptied. The ruler called on those people able to do so to present serfs. In return they would get lifetime exemption from military service; for gentlemen of the court, their salary would be raised. It was in these years that the practice of presenting a sheep in exchange for gentleman status began.

In the following four years, Wei Qing went out to attack the Huns with a force of 100,000 men. Those officers and soldiers who cut off the heads of barbarians, or captured them, received gifts, totaling more than 200,000 catties of gold. Of Han forces, the dead cavalry and horses exceeded 100,000. There was the additional expense of weapons and armor, as well as that transportation of supplies. Therefore, the chamberlain for the national treasury reported that the financial reserves were exhausted, and budgetary taxes very close to that state; there was not enough to support the troops in the field. Officials in charge begged for an imperial order that would permit the people to purchase titular rank, buy back the privilege of government positions, and secure cancellation or mitigation of penalties. They proposed the creation of a rank of award, to be called the order of military merit. Each level would cost 170,000 cash, altogether being more than 300,000 gold pieces. Among the purchasers those of the fifth grade, *guanshou*, or officials on probation, would have preference in appointment. Those of the seventh grade, *qianfu*, would be equal to *wudafu*, the ninth grade of the established rank. Those who were under sentence for crime would, however, have their grades lowered by two; and they would be unable to purchase any grade higher than eighth, *leqing*. In this

【原文】

至乐卿，以显军功。军功多用超等，大者封侯卿大夫，小者郎。吏道杂而多端，则官职秏废。

自[公]孙弘以《春秋》之义绳臣下取汉相，张汤以峻文决理为廷尉，于是见知之法生，而废格沮诽穷治之狱用矣。其明年，淮南、衡山、江都王谋反迹见，而公卿寻端治之，竟其党与，坐而死者数万人，吏益惨急而法令察。当是时，招尊方正贤良文学之士，或至公卿大夫。公孙弘以宰相，布被，食不重味，为下先，然而无益于俗，稍务于功利矣。

其明年，票骑仍再出击胡，大克获。浑邪王率数万众来降，于是

【今译】

减二等；买爵可以到乐卿武功爵，以突出军功。军功多数使用超等封赏，功大的封侯和卿大夫，小的封郎。官途杂而且头绪多，这样官职就乱了。

从公孙弘用《春秋》的道义约束臣下取得汉朝丞相，张汤以苛酷严细的法条来判决官司而当上廷尉后，于是官吏知道他人犯罪而不举报，与犯人同罪的法律出现，而搁置诏令，行动不力以及诋毁、彻底处理的刑罚也开始实行了。过了一年，淮南王、衡山王、江都王阴谋造反的迹象被发现，公卿就寻找线索来审理案情，追究他们的党羽，定死罪的人有几万，官吏更加用法刻毒而法令更加苛细了。在这个时候，招揽尊敬方正、贤良、文学的士人，有的当上了公卿大夫。公孙弘以宰相的地位，盖布制的被子，不吃多种菜肴，作为天下的表率，但对民俗没有益处，只是稍微有益于功利罢了。

又过了一年，骠骑将军依然再次出兵攻打匈奴，大获全胜。浑邪王率领几万人来投降，于是汉朝派出三万辆车去迎接他们。到来后，

way, military merit was distinguished. Military merit was so widely rewarded that all proportion was lost. Great merit made one a marquis, or grand master; lesser merit brought gentleman status. As the avenues to government appointment multiplied and tangled, then official posts and duties were thrown into chaos.

After Gongsun Hong became First Minister of Han by restraining ministers and subordinates through righteousness (as set forth in the *Spring and Autumn Annals*), and after Zhang Tang was made Chamberlain of Law Enforcement because of his strict legal judgments and clear-cut codes of law, the law was instituted that if officials had personal knowledge of a crime being committed but did not report it, they themselves would face the same penalty for that crime; the court practice also began inflicting maximum penalties upon those who nullified, frustrated, or vilified the imperial edicts. The following year, indications were discovered of a conspiracy for rebellion instigated by the princes of Huainan and of Hengshan, and of Jiangdu. After an inquiry to determine the origins, the great nobles of the realm, and the chief ministers of state at court punished the princes, and extirpated their faction. Those found guilty and put to death were several tens of thousands. The government authorities grew ever more cruel and exacting; laws and ordinances became minutely detailed. At this time, the straightforward and upright, worthy and excellent, and those versed in the classics were summoned from all parts of land and were honored. Some were elevated to noble rank or chief ministers. Gongsun Hong, as the first minister to the throne, slept on rough bedding, and ate very simply, thus setting an example for all under Heaven. But this had no impact on customs; the people grew more and more fixated on fame and wealth.

The following year, the General-in-Chief of Cavalry went out again to fight against the Huns. He won a great victory, and King Hunye, leading a multitude of tens of thousands, came to surrender.

【原文】

汉发车三万两迎之。既至，受赏赐及有功之士。是岁费凡百馀巨万。

先是十馀岁，河决，灌梁、楚地，固已数困，而缘河之郡堤塞河，辄坏决，费不可胜计。其后番係欲省底柱之漕，穿汾、河渠以为溉田；郑当时为渭漕回远，凿漕直渠自长安至华阴；而朔方亦穿溉渠。作者各数万人，历二三期而功未就，费亦各以巨万十数。

天子为伐胡故，盛养马，马之往来食长安者数万匹，卒掌者关中不足，乃调旁近郡。而胡降者数万人皆得厚赏，衣食仰给县官。县官不给，天子乃损膳，解乘舆驷，出御府禁臧以澹之。

其明年，山东被水灾，民多饥乏，于是天子遣使虚郡国仓廪以振贫。犹不足，又募豪富人相假贷。尚不能相救，乃徙贫民于关以西，

【今译】

授给他们赏赐，赏赐包括有功的人。这一年耗费共一百多亿。

在这之前十多年，黄河决口，淹没了梁国、楚国地区，本来已几次陷入困境，又依着黄河旁边的郡县筑堤堵塞黄河决口，很快又崩溃，耗费不计其数。这以后，番系打算节省底柱的水运，沟通汾水、黄河的水渠用来灌溉田地；郑当时认为渭水的漕运曲折路远，就开凿漕运的笔直水渠从长安一直到华阴；而且朔方也在开通灌溉水渠。劳作的人各有几万人，费时两三年而仍未成功，花费也各以十亿计。

天子因为攻打匈奴的缘故，就大养马匹，马匹往来长安取用饲料的有几万匹，牧马的人看到关中不足，就调用长安边靠近的郡县。而匈奴投降的几万人都得到很厚的赏赐，衣食都依靠政府供给，政府供给不足，天子就减少饭食，解下座车的马匹，拿出御府收藏的财物来供给他们。

又过了一年，山东遭受水灾，百姓很多都饥饿困乏，于是天子派使者用尽郡国仓库的粮食来救济贫民。仍不够，就召集富人来借贷。

Thereupon, Han sent forth 30,000 carriages to receive them. When they arrived, rewards were bestowed, including to officers who had performed feats of merit. That year expenditure exceeded 10 billion.

A dozen years prior to these events, the Yellow River had breached its banks, inundating lands in Liang and Chu that had already been hit with hardship several times. In prefectures with lands bordering the river, moreover, the dikes raised to confine the river had frequently broken and collapsed. This had cost an incalculable amount. Subsequently Po Xi, in order to save on waterborne grain transportation by way of Dizhu Hill, dug canals from the Fen and Yellow rivers in order to irrigate fields. Zheng Dangshi considered the transport of grain on the Wei circuitous and long, so he cut a canal direct from Chang'an to Huayin. Irrigation canals were dug in Shuofang too. These several projects used tens of thousands of laborers for two or three years, without being completed, each one swallowing sums of ten times a hundred million.

For use in campaigns against the Huns, the Son of Heaven had a tremendous number of horses raised. Several tens of thousands of them were brought to be foddered at Changan. Locally, there were not enough herders to care for them, so others were selected from neighboring prefectures. At that time several tens of thousands of surrendered Huns had received liberal rewards, and looked to the government for clothes and food. As government funds were insufficient, the Son of Heaven limited imperial food; he left off use of the state carriage, and took from his own treasury, in order to provide for them.

The following year, the lands lying east of the mountain suffered floods and calamities, plunging many into destitution and starvation. Thereupon, the Son of Heaven sent commissioners to empty the government granaries in the prefectures and fiefs for relief of the poor. Still there was not enough. He called upon the very

【原文】

及充朔方以南新秦中，七十馀万口，衣食皆仰给于县官。数岁，贷与产业，使者分部护，冠盖相望，费以亿计，县官大空。而富商贾或墆财役贫，转毂百数，废居居邑，封君皆氐首仰给焉。冶铸煮盐，财或累万金，而不佐公家之急，黎民重困。

于是天子与公卿议，更造钱币以澹用，而摧浮淫并兼之徒。是时禁苑有白鹿而少府多银锡。自孝文更造四铢钱，至是岁四十馀年，从建元以来，用少，县官往往即多铜山而铸钱，民亦盗铸，不可胜数。钱益多而轻，物益少而贵。有司言曰："古者皮币，诸侯以聘享。金有三等，黄金为上，白金为中，赤金为下。今半两钱法重四铢，而奸

【今译】

这些仍不能相拯救，就迁徙贫民到关以西的地方，以及补充到朔方以南的新秦中，有七十多万人，衣食都要依靠政府供给。好几年，贷钱给生产和作业，使者分批护送，前后车相连，花费以亿计，政府大空虚。而富有的商人有的积贮财货，役使贫民，运输的车子有好几百辆，有的住在邑中囤积居奇，贱买贵卖，封国的君主都低头仰仗他们供给。冶炼铜铁，铸造器物以及煮盐，财产有的积累达万金，但不支援政府的困难，百姓更加困苦。

于是天子和公卿商议，改造钱币来补充费用，以打击那些骄奢淫逸侵占他人财产的人。这时帝王苑囿有白鹿而少府多银锡。从孝文帝改造四铢钱起，到这一年已四十多年，从建元以来，流通的很少，官府往往到多铜的山去铸造钱币，百姓也有的偷着铸钱，不可计算。钱越多越轻，物质越少但贵。有关官员说道："以前是皮币，诸侯用来互相问好和向天子献纳。金有三种等级，黄金是上等，白银是中等，铜是下等。现在半两钱法定重四铢，而邪恶的人有的就偷偷地磨擦钱

rich to make loans. But even with this help, it was unable to effect a rescue; accordingly, 700,000 or more of the poor were made to migrate west of the Pass to fill New Qinzhong south of Shuofang. All had to be fed and clothed by the government. For years on end, money was loaned on produce and trades. District commissioners were sent out in droves, virtually clogging the roads. Expenses were reckoned in hundreds of millions, and the government coffers were bare. On the other hand, some rich traders forced the poor to transport their stored-up assets on hundreds of carts; or those living in the settlements hoarded and profiteered. Enfeoffed lords, humbled, looked to these people for their needs. By smelting and casting, and the making of salt, some had amassed fortunes of 10,000 gold pieces. Even so they did not help the government in its hour of need. The people's suffering became even more acute.

Thereupon, the Son of Heaven, having consulted with his high nobles and ministers, changed the issue of money. This had a dual intent: to help meet government expenditures, and to curb extravagant and unscrupulous monopolists. At the time there were white deer in the imperial parks, while the Chamberlain for Palace Revenues had much silver and tin. Forty years had passed since Emperor Wendi had changed to four-*zhu* coins, but since the reign of Wudi they had been little used. The local governments had from time to time gone to copper-rich mountains, and cast coins. The people, too, had made coins on the quiet, in quantities impossible to estimate. Coins were multiplying and getting lighter, while goods were going down in quality and up in price. An official said: "In ancient times deerskin currency was presented by feudal lords on the occasion of formal visits. We use three types of metal currency: gold is the highest grade; next comes silver, and then copper. According to the law of the land a half-tael piece should weigh four *zhu*. However, some criminal persons secretly grind the reverse side of the coins, and in this way obtain filings. The result is that

【原文】

或盗摩钱质而取鋊，钱益轻薄而物贵，则远方用币烦费不省。”乃以白鹿皮方尺，缘以缋，为皮币，直四十万。王侯宗室朝觐聘享，必以皮币荐璧，然后得行。

又造银锡白金。以为天用莫如龙，地用莫如马，人用莫如龟，故白金三品：其一曰重八两，圜之，其文龙，名“白撰”，直三千；二曰以重差小，方之，其文马，直五百；三曰复小，椭之，其文龟，直三百。令县官销半两钱，更铸三铢钱，重如其文。盗铸诸金钱罪皆死，而吏民之犯者不可胜数。

于是以东郭咸阳、孔仅为大农丞，领盐铁事，而桑弘羊贵幸。咸阳，齐之大鬻盐，孔仅，南阳大冶，皆致产累千金，故郑当时进言

【今译】

取得铜屑，钱更加轻薄而物质更加贵重，远方的人使用钱币的耗费没有减少。”就用白鹿的皮一尺见方，边缘绘上五彩，成为皮币，价值四十万。王侯宗室朝见天子互相问好以及向皇上献纳，一定要用皮币表示效忠，然后才能通行。

又铸造银锡合金的货币称之为白金。认为天用没有比龙更好的，地用没有比马更好的，人用没有比龟更好的，所以白金有三个品级：一种是重八两，圆形，其正面的图案为龙，叫“白撰”，价值三千；一种是重量稍轻，方形，其正面的图案为马，价值五百；一种更小，椭圆形，其正面的图案为龟，价值三百。命令官府销毁半两钱，改铸三铢钱，使重量和所刻的一样。偷着铸造各种金钱的，按罪都要处死，而官民犯法的数不胜数。

于是任命东郭咸阳、孔仅为大农丞，掌管盐铁事情，而桑弘羊受到宠幸。东郭咸阳，是齐国的煮盐大户，孔仅，是南阳的大冶炼匠，

the coins have rapidly become lighter and thinner, while goods are rising in price; and there has been no abating in the use of money for expenditure in the distant regions." Accordingly, they made a currency out of one-foot squares of white deerskin, with borders in variegated colors. Each unit was valued at 400,000 cash Thereafter, princes and marquises of the realm and members of the imperial clan, whenever they came to court to render homage in spring and in autumn, and to present gifts to the throne, would be required to present their jade insignia lying on the skin currency. Only then would they be allowed to proceed.

As well as this, they made an alloy of silver and tin, calling the result "white metal." Considering that for Heaven there is nothing more appropriate than a dragon, for earth nothing more appropriate than a horse, and for man nothing more appropriate than a tortoise, they issued three denominations. The highest value coin, weighing eight taels, was round in shape and bore a dragon design. It was called "white composition" and its value was 3,000 cash. The next coin, weighing somewhat less and worth 500 cash, was square in shape and bore a horse design. Last came the lightest coin, oval in shape and bearing a tortoise design; it was worth 300 cash. By imperial order the government melted down the half-tael coins, and once again cast three-*zhu* cash, their actual weight corresponding to their inscription. Counterfeiting of the several metal coins and cash was punishable by death. Even so innumerable people in government and among the common folk flouted this law.

At this time, Dongguo Xianyang and Kong Jin were assistants to the Chamberlain of the National Treasury, with concurrent responsibility for government control of salt and iron; Sang Hongyang enjoyed the special favor of the Emperor. Dongguo Xianyang was a great salt magnate in Qi, and Kong Jin a great iron smelter in Nanyang. Both had accumulated fortunes of a thousand gold. For this reason Zheng Dangshi recommended them to the

【原文】

之。弘羊，洛阳贾人之子，以心计，年十三，侍中。故三人言利事析秋豪矣。

法既益严，吏多废免。兵革数动，民多买复及五大夫、千夫，征发之士益鲜。于是除千夫、五大夫为吏，不欲者出马。故吏皆适令伐棘上林，作昆明池。

其明年，大将军、票骑大出击胡，赏赐五十万金，军马死者十馀万匹，转漕车甲之费不与焉。是时财匮，战士颇不得禄矣。

有司言三铢钱轻，轻钱易作奸诈，乃更请郡国铸五铢钱，周郭其质，令不可得摩取(铅)[鋊]。

大农上盐铁丞孔仅、咸阳言：“山海，天地之臧，宜属少府，陛下弗私，以属大农佐赋。愿募民自给费，因官器作鬻盐，官与牢盆。

【今译】

都治理产业累积达千金，所以郑当时就推荐了他们。桑弘羊，是洛阳商人的儿子，因为能心算，年仅十三岁就任侍中。所以三人陈述利益能分辨得很细微。

法令既然更加严密，官吏就大部分被罢免。几次发动战争，百姓大都用钱来使自己免除兵役，至于五大夫、千夫，被征服兵役的人更加少。于是就让千夫、五大夫为官吏，不愿为官的人就要贡献马匹；所以官吏都被罚到上林去砍伐荆棘，建造昆明池。

过了一年，大将军、骠骑将军大举出击匈奴，受到五十万金的赏赐，死的军马有十多万匹，还不包括运粮以及运输武器的费用。这时候国库财力空乏，战士很难得到功禄。

有关官员说三铢钱轻，轻钱容易作假，就改让郡国铸造五铢钱，把钱的边缘做成凸起的轮廓，使人们不能磨擦而取得铜屑。

大司农上书给盐铁丞孔仅、东郭咸阳说：“山和海，是天地的宝藏，应归少府管理，陛下没有私心，就让大农丞帮助收取赋税。希望招集百姓自给费用，用官府的器械来煮盐，官府供给煮盐的工具。不

throne. Sang Hongyang, son of a Luoyang merchant, had been made a palace attendant at the age of 13 on the basis of his gift for mental calculations. The three men discussed matters of government revenue in the minutest detail.

As laws became stricter and stricter, a great many officials were dismissed from their posts; the armed forces were frequently sent into action, but the people for the most part bought their way out of military service as much as the *wudafu* and *qianfu*. Those who were impressed and mobilized for military service became all the rarer. Thereupon, men of the grades of *qianfu* and *wudafu* were appointed officials, and those unwilling to serve had to supply a horse. Former officials all were penalized to cut underbrush in the Imperial Forest Park and construct the Kunming Pool.

The next year, the General-in-Chief and the General of Cavalry went out with a great army to attack the barbarians of the north. Rewards bestowed were amounted to half a million gold pieces. Over 100,000 army horses were killed, and there were further expenses for logistics, as well as for chariots and armor. With monetary resources depleted, combat troops barely received any pay.

Officials-in-charge said that three-*zhu* coins were light-weight and hence easy to counterfeit. So they proposed that prefectures and fiefs cast five-*zhu* coins instead, the reverse of which should by ordinance have a raised rim around the edge, so as to make it impossible to grind them off for the filings.

The Chamberlain of the National Treasury presented proposals from the assistants for government control of salt and iron, Kong Jin and Xianyang. They said: "The mountains and the seas are storehouses of Heaven and Earth. They ought properly to belong to the office of the palace revenues; Your Majesty, being selfless, should entrust their control to the Chamberlain of the National Treasury to supplement taxes. We propose to lease to those people who would furnish their own capital and undertake salt evaporation,

【原文】

浮食奇民欲擅斡山海之货，以致富羡，役利细民。其沮事之议，不可胜听。敢私铸铁器煮盐者，钛左趾，没入其器物。郡不出铁者，置小铁官，使属在所县。”使仅、咸阳乘传举行天下盐铁，作官府，除故盐铁家富者为吏。吏益多贾人矣。

商贾以币之变，多积货逐利。于是公卿言：“郡国颇被灾害，贫民无产业者，募徙广饶之地。陛下损膳省用，出禁钱以振元元，宽贷，而民不齐出南亩，商贾滋众。贫者畜积无有，皆仰县官。异时算轺车贾人之缗钱皆有差，请算如故。诸贾人末作贳贷卖买，居邑贮积诸物，及商以取利者，虽无市籍，各以其物自占，率缗钱二千而算一。

【今译】

劳而食的诸侯想擅自掌管山和海的货物，以达到富有，从平民中获取利润。阻止这些事情的议论，听到的不能再多了。敢私自铸造铁器煮盐的人，钳他的左脚趾，没收他的器物。郡县不产铁的，设置小铁官，由他来管辖所在县的铁器。”让孔仅、东郭咸阳驰驿通知天下兴作盐铁，设置盐铁官府，让以前富有的盐铁人家做官。官吏中商人更多了。

商人根据货币的变化，多囤积货物以追逐赢利。于是公卿说：“郡国所遭受的灾害相当大，没有产业的贫民，被广泛征集迁徙到广阔富饶的地方。陛下减少饭食节省费用，拿出官钱来救济平民，放宽贷款，但百姓不都到农田去耕作，商贾更加增多。贫困的人没有积蓄，都依靠官府。以前征收小车税和商人的所得税都有等差，请依旧时征税一样。各商人放取高利贷和贱买贵卖，囤积居奇，以及所有靠经营取得赢利的人，即使没有商人的户籍，各自申报自己的财物，一

giving them use of tools belonging to the state. To them the state shall furnish robust evaporating pans on a rental basis. The parasitic nobles desire to control the resources of mountain and sea without any authority in order to gain riches, enslaving humble folk and profiteering from them. Too often now has it been discussed how to put a stop to this situation. Those who should dare clandestinely to cast iron pans to produce salt by evaporation should be fettered and their instruments and articles confiscated. In prefectures which do not produce iron there should be established government sub-offices to control iron, these commissioners to be subordinate to their respective counties." Jin and Xianyang were then commissioned to travel by post chaise of the third category throughout the whole empire to put into operation the salt and iron, establishing administrative offices. They appointed men already enriched through salt and iron industries as officials, and so officials in ever greater measure were traders.

Traders, taking advantage of changes in currency, accumulated great quantities of goods on which to pursue profit. Therefore, the high nobles and ministers said: "The prefectures and the fiefs have suffered great calamities and perils; those among the poor without possessions or livelihood have been mustered for removal into broad, fertile lands. Your Majesty has cut down on imperial meals to save expenses, disbursed imperial funds to relieve the common people, and liberally provided loans. But the people as a whole do not go out to farm. Merchants proliferate even more, whereas the poor, having nothing put by, rely on government aid. Some time ago there used to be a graduated tax on small carts, and on the income of traders, and we propose that this be reinstated. The divers tradesmen and others engaged in secondary occupations, those who give out loans for high interest, profiteers, hoarders and speculators, those who corner the market and control supply for profit, even if they are not officially registered as traders should each declare his assets.

【原文】

诸作有租及铸，率缗钱四千算一。非吏比者，三老、北边骑士，轺车一算；商贾人轺车二算；船五丈以上一算。匿不自占，占不悉，戍边一岁，没入缗钱。有能告者，以其半畀之。贾人有市籍，及家属，皆无得名田，以便农。敢犯令，没入田货。”

是时，豪富皆争匿财，唯卜式数求入财以助县官。天子乃超拜式为中郎，赐爵左庶长，田十顷，布告天下，以风百姓。初，式不愿为官，上强拜之，稍迁至齐相。语自在其传。孔仅使天下铸作器，三年中至大司农，列于九卿。而桑弘羊为大司农中丞，管诸会计事，稍稍置均输以通货物。始令吏得入谷补官，郎至六百石。

【今译】

律二千贯钱收取一算的税。各种手工业及冶铁和煮盐都有租税，一律四千贯钱收取一算的租税。不是吏比、三老、北部边境的骑士，有小车的都要交一算的税；商贾的小车要交二算；船五丈以上交一算。隐匿不申报，申报有所隐瞒，罚防守边境一年，没收财产。如果有人能举报的，就以举报的一半奖给他。商人有户籍，以及家属，都不得以私名占有田地，以便利农民。有敢违反法令的，没收田和财物。”

这时候，富豪都争相隐匿财产，只有卜式几次请求纳献财产来帮助政府。天子就破格提升卜式为中郎，赐给左庶长的爵位，赏十顷田，向天下宣告，来规劝百姓。开始，卜式不愿做官，皇上强行授予他，才逐渐升迁为齐国相。在他的传里有记载。孔仅使天下铸作铁器，三年内官至大司农，列于九卿之列。而桑弘羊任大司农中丞，管理各种财物及其出纳等事，慢慢设置均输官来流通货物。开始让官员可以交纳谷物补升官职，郎官交纳谷物增加到六百石。

Each string of 2,000 cash should be taxed at one *suan*. For those in manual industry, as well as metal founders and salt makers, the tax rate should be one *suan* per 4,000. Apart from government officers, the three elders, and northern frontier cavalry officers, all shall pay one *suan* on each small cart. Merchants are to pay two *suan* on each small cart, and one *suan* on each boat over 50 feet in length. Anyone failing to make a complete estimate should be sent out to serve on a frontier post for one year, and his strings of cash should be confiscated. Anyone informing of such a violation should receive one half of the amount. In order to give advantage to farmers, registered resident merchants and their family members should be ineligible to obtain ownership of fields. Those who dare infringe this ordinance should have their fields, and their money confiscated

At that time, the exceptionally rich were all desperate to conceal their wealth, the only exception being Bu Shi, who begged several times to be allowed to present money and property in order to assist the government. The Son of Heaven honored Bu Shi by appointing him as a gentleman of the court. He bestowed upon him the title of Left Militia General, the tenth grade of honorary rank, giving him ten hectares of arable land. His example was proclaimed throughout the realm as inspiration to the people. At first Bu Shi was reluctant, but the Emperor compelled him to accept an official office. By gradual stages he was moved to first minister in Qi. A full account of these events is given in the *Biography of Bu Shi*. Some three years after he had been sent throughout the whole empire for casting iron vessels, Kong Jin was appointed Chamberlain of the National Treasury, and became one of the nine chief ministers. Sang Hongyang was assistant to Kong Jin, and had charge of the audits and calculations. Little by little they established offices of tax substitutes, in order to bring about equilibrium between money and merchandise. For the first time, officials had the privilege of career promotions in exchange for presentation of grain, and a court gentleman should

【原文】

自造白金五铢钱后五岁，而赦吏民之坐盗铸金钱死者数十万人。其不发觉相杀者，不可胜计。赦自出者百馀万人，然不能半自出，天下大氐无虑皆铸金钱矣。犯法者众。吏不能尽诛，于是遣博士褚大、徐偃等分行郡国，举并兼之徒守相为利者。而御史大夫张汤方贵用事，减宣、杜周等为中丞，义纵、尹齐、王温舒等用急刻为九卿，直指夏兰之属始出。而大农颜异诛矣。初，异为济南亭长，以廉直稍迁至九卿。上与汤既造白鹿皮币，问异。异曰："今王侯朝贺以仓璧，直数千，而其皮荐反四十万，本末不相称。"天子不说。汤又与异有隙，及人有告异以它议，事下汤治。异与客语，客语初令下有不便者，

【今译】

从铸造白金五铢钱后五年，赦免官民犯非法铸钱当死的人几十万人。而没有被发现有罪而被杀的人，数不胜数。赦免自首的人达一百多万。但自首的人不及半数，天下人大概都在铸钱。犯法的人多，官吏诛杀不完，于是派遣博士褚大、徐偃等人分别巡行各郡国，举告侵占他人财产的人及郡守和诸侯相谋私利的人。而御史大夫张汤正被宠幸掌权，减宣、杜周等人为中丞，义纵、尹齐、王温舒等人因为严峻苛刻官任九卿，直指官夏兰之辈开始出现。而大农颜异被诛杀。起初，颜异任济南亭长，凭藉廉洁正直逐渐升为九卿。皇上和张汤已经制造了白鹿皮钱币，来询问颜异。颜异说："现在王侯用青色玉璧来朝贺，价值几千，而皮币反而要四十万，本末不相称。"天子不高兴。张汤又与颜异有裂痕，等到有人举告颜异有不同的言论，事情被交付张汤审理。颜异和客人交谈，客人说诏令刚下达有不便利的地方，

submit 600 piculs.

During the five years following the issue of white metal coins and five-*zhu* cash, several hundred thousand officials and civilians under sentence of death for counterfeiting were pardoned. Those not found out but killed by others were of an incalculable number. There were pardons for more than a million persons who turned themselves in, but not one-half of the actual number of offenders gave themselves up – casting metal cash had become a virtually universal crime. Offenders were so numerous that the authorities could not inflict capital punishment on all of them. For these reasons, erudites such as Zhu Da and Xu Yan were sent on individual inspections, into the prefectures and fiefs, in order to report on appropriation of property, and on the prefects and first ministers in the fiefs colluding for their own profit. Now the Censor-in-Chief Zhang Tang enjoyed the Emperor's favor and exercised power. Jian Xuan and Du Zhou, both were made Vice Censors; and Yi Zong, Yin Qi, Wang Wenshu and others, because they were exacting and severe, became chamberlains. Outspoken censors such as Xia Lan appeared for the first time. The Chamberlain of the National Treasury Yan Yi was executed. In the beginning Yan Yi had been made secretary of a neighborhood in Jinan. Because of his incorruptibility and straightforwardness he had gradually rose to the position of chamberlain. When the Emperor and Zhang Tang made white deerskin a currency, Yan Yi was asked for his opinion. Yan replied: "Now, when the vassal kings and marquises in formal audience with Your Majesty, present insignia of green jade worth several thousand resting upon a piece of deer skin valued at 400,000, this is surely quite topsy-turvy." The Son of Heaven was not pleased and Zhang Tang never forgave Yan Yi. When he was later accused of dissent, the matter was referred to Zhang Tang for adjudication. Yan had a conversation with a visitor, who voiced his opinion that the ordinance had some disadvantages. Yan did not reply, but his

【原文】

异不应，微反唇。汤奏当异九卿见令不便，不入言而腹非，论死。自是后有腹非之法比，而公卿大夫多谄谀取容。

天(下)[子]既下缗钱令而尊卜式，百姓终莫分财佐县官，于是告缗钱纵矣。

郡国铸钱，民多奸铸，钱多轻，而公卿请令京师铸官赤仄，一当五，赋官用非赤仄不得行。白金稍贱，民弗宝用，县官以令禁之，无益，岁馀终废不行。是岁，汤死而民不思。其后二岁，赤仄钱贱，民巧法用之，不便，又废。于是悉禁郡国毋铸钱，专令上林三官铸。钱既多，而令天下非三官钱不得行，诸郡国前所铸钱皆废销之，输入其

【今译】

颜异没有应对，只是稍微翻唇表示鄙视。张汤上奏判处颜异官为九卿，见诏令有不便利的，不进言而心中认为不对，为死罪。从此以后有腹诽的法律条例，公卿大夫大多用奉承来取悦于人。

天子已经下达关于税收的法令而且尊宠卜式，百姓最终没有拿出财产来帮助政府，于是奖励告发富户隐匿财产逃避税款就风行起来了。

郡国铸造钱币，百姓多数取巧铸造，钱币大多较轻，公卿就请求让京师的铸官铸造赤仄币，用一当五，交赋税以及供给官府用不是赤仄的钱币就不行。白金渐渐跌价，百姓不把它当作宝物来使用，政府下令进行禁止，没有益处，一年多后终于被废除，不再流行。这一年，张汤死了，但百姓没有哀思。这之后二年，赤仄钱又跌价，百姓用巧法来使用它，不便利，又被废除。于是统一禁止郡国不准铸钱，专门命令上林三官来铸造。钱币既然很多，就下令天下不是三官钱不

wry smile and curl of the lip showed his contempt. Zhang Tang memorialized the throne that Yan, as one of the nine chamberlains, having seen the demerits of the ordinance, and disapproving of it, had nevertheless failed to speak against it. His sentence was death. This established a legal regulation regarding unspoken criticism, and great nobles of the realm, chief ministers of the state at court, and high officials in government service for the most part had become profuse in flattery so as to curry favor.

When the Son of Heaven issued the order relating to "strings of cash," and honored Bu Shi, among the common people there was no one willing to dig deep into his own money to help the government. This encouraged accusations against wealthy families concealing wealth to avoid taxes to really soar.

In prefectures and fiefs, where coins were cast, people were generally adulterating them. Cash pieces were generally underweight. Then the great nobles and chief ministers begged for an ordinance by which monetary authorities in the imperial capital should cast *Chice* coins with a red rim, each coin being valued at five cash. These would be the only acceptable medium for paying poll taxes and government expenses. White metal had gradually declined in value; the people did not treasure it. The central government issued an ordinance asking people to treasure white metal, but this was to no avail. After something over a year they were completely abolished and withdrawn from circulation. That year, Zhang Tang died, unmourned. Two years later the red-rimmed coins had dropped in value, the people's guile having won over the law. Their use was of no advantage, and so they were abolished. After this, a general interdiction on the casting of money by the prefectures and the fiefs was issued. A government monopoly for coinage was put in the charge of the Three Officers of the Imperial Forest. Since the number of coins was already huge, no coins were allowed to circulate apart from those cast by the Three Officers. All coins cast in the various

【原文】

铜三官。而民之铸钱益少，计其费不能相当，唯真工大奸乃盗为之。

杨可告缗遍天下，中家以上大氐皆遇告。杜周治之，狱少反者。乃分遣御史廷尉正监分曹往，(往)即治郡国缗钱，得民财物以亿计，奴婢以千万数，田大县数百顷，小县百馀顷，宅亦如之。于是商贾中家以上大氐破，民偷甘食好衣，不事畜臧之业，而县官以盐铁缗钱之故，用少饶矣。益广(幵)[关]，置左右辅。

初，大农(斡)[斡]盐铁官布多，置水衡，欲以主盐铁；及杨可告缗，上林财物众，乃令水衡主上林。上林既充满，益广。是时粤欲与

【今译】

得流行，各个郡国以前所铸造的钱币都废除销毁，把铜输给三官。这样百姓铸造的钱币更加减少，他们计算所花费用和利润不能相等，只有巧妙的工匠和豪民才偷着铸钱。

杨可要求举告隐匿财产、逃避租税的活动遍及天下，中等家庭以上大抵都被告发。杜周来审理案情，官司很少有人能翻案。于是就分别派遣御史、廷尉、正监按不同使命出使诸国，处理郡国隐匿财产的案子，得到百姓的财物数以亿计，奴婢上千万，田地大县数百顷，小县一百多顷，房产也是这个数字。于是商人中等以上的大抵破产，百姓就苟且于美食好衣，不再进行蓄藏的事业，而政府因为有盐铁缗钱的事，费用渐渐宽裕了。扩大关中地域，设置了左右辅。

起初，大农管理的盐铁官布很多，就设置水衡都尉，想让他主管盐铁事；等到杨可鼓励告发隐匿财产的事兴起后，上林的财物就多了起来，就命水衡都尉主管上林。上林既然财物充足了，就要加以扩

prefectures and fiefs were demonetized and melted down, and their copper transported to the Three Officers. Thus fewer and fewer coins were cast by the people, figuring that the benefits of doing so were not in line with the costs. After that, only expert artisans and bold people manufactured them illicitly.

Soon the movement launched by Yang Ke to denounce those with secret stockpiles in avoidance of tax spread across the land, and charges were made against practically every moderately affluent family and those with larger fortunes. Du Zhou adjudicated, and of those brought to trial few were found not guilty. Then they sent out in diverse directions censors and supervisors of law enforcement, who crisscrossed the prefectures and fiefs to give judgment on cases of concealed assets. In this way they got their hands on people's assets counted in hundreds of millions, on tens of thousands of their serfs, on several hundreds of hectares of fields in large counties, and on more than a hundred in small counties; their dwellings were confiscated on a similar scale. As a consequence, traders, whose fortunes made them middle-class and above, were bankrupted for the most part, and the people indulged in the best of food and dress, not giving themselves to the accumulation and storing up of property. Through salt and iron, and "strings of cash," government finances gradually became ample. The area within the Pass was considerably extended, and the posts of left and right deputy prefects were established.

Initially, the salt and iron offices came under the Chamberlain of the National Treasury, but there were too many, so the position of Commandant of Imperial Gardens was established with the intention that he supervise the salt and iron. When, however, Yang Ke hounded out hidden fortunes, and the wealth and resources of the Imperial Forest became exceedingly large, then the Emperor ordered the Commandant to be put in charge of that. About the time the Imperial Forest became too full, and was about to be enlarged,

【原文】

汉用船战逐，乃大修昆明池，列馆环之。治楼船，高十馀丈，旗织加其上，甚壮。于是天子感之，乃作柏梁台，高数十丈。宫室之修，繇此日丽。

乃分缗钱诸官，而水衡、少府、太仆、大农各置农官，往往即郡县比没入田田之。其没入奴婢，分诸苑养狗马禽兽，及与诸官。官益杂置多，徒奴婢众，而下河漕度四百万石，及官自籴乃足。

所忠言："世家子弟富人或斗鸡走狗马，弋猎博戏，乱齐民。"乃征诸犯令，相引数千人，名曰"株送徒"。入财者得补郎，郎选衰矣。

是时山东被河灾，及岁不登数年，人或相食，方二三千里。天子

【今译】

大。这时粤国打算同汉朝用船开战，于是大规模修建昆明池，池周筑观宇环绕。建造楼船，高十多丈，上面插上旗帜，很是壮观。于是天子受这气派的感染，就建造了柏梁台，高达数十丈。宫室的修建，从此日趋于富丽。

于是把缗钱分给各官府，而水衡、少府、太仆、大农各自设置农官，往往就地在各郡县整治没收来的土地，加以耕种。没收来的奴婢，就分给各苑囿去喂养狗马禽兽，以及分给各官府。官职设置的更复杂更多，罪徒奴婢众多，因而由黄河漕运至京的粮食大约有四百万石，并且还要官府自己买一部分谷物才能足用。

所忠说："世家子弟和富人有的斗鸡赛狗赛马，有的射猎赌博游戏，扰乱平民百姓的生活。"于是惩罚诸罪犯，相牵连的有几千人，名叫"株送徒"。纳献财物的得以补为郎官，郎官的选拔从此就衰退了。

当时山东遭黄河水灾，加上连年歉收，有人吃人的现象发生，方圆达二三千里。天子心中怜悯，诏令饥民可以流亡到江淮间谋生，打

Yue was preparing to use boats to fight Han. So the Kunming Pool was extensively remade, with imperial leisure lodges surrounding it. Boats with upper decks were built a hundred feet high; with flags and standards surmounting them, they presented a magnificent sight. Infected by their grandeur the Emperor had built the Tower of Cedar Beams erected even taller than the boats. From this point on, new imperial palace buildings became more splendid by the day.

The revenue obtained by the foregoing measures was split between the several offices, and offices of agriculture were established in the offices of the Imperial Gardens, the Palace Revenues, the Imperial Stud and the National Treasury. Each traveled frequently through the prefectures and counties to have confiscated fields cultivated. Confiscated serfs were sent to the various parks to look after dogs, horses, birds, and beasts, and to diverse government offices also. Government posts were set up in great numbers and complexity; their convict laborers and serfs were numerous too. So the grain transported to the capital by river, estimated at four million piculs, had to be supplemented with supplies bought by the official bureaus themselves.

Suo Zhong stated: "Among the spoiled youth of well-known families and among the rich, there are those who fight cocks, race dogs and horses, hunt or gamble money, disrupting the lives of ordinary people." Summons were issued for such offenders, and several thousands of them were dragged in one after the other; they were called "implicated convicts." Those who presented wealth won positions as gentlemen at court; the system of recommendation of men of worth fell into decay.

At this time the lands east of the mountains suffered from flooding of the Yellow River; this came on top of successive years of failed harvests and in an area of two or three thousand square *li*, cannibalism did occur. The Son of Heaven pitied them and ordered that the famine-stricken people were permitted to leave the area,

【原文】

怜之，令饥民得流就食江淮间，欲留，留处。使者冠盖相属于道护之，下巴蜀粟以振焉。

明年，天子始出巡郡国。东度河，河东守不意行至，不辩，自杀。行西逾陇，卒，从官不得食，陇西守自杀。于是上北出萧关，从数万骑行猎新秦中，以勒边兵而归。新秦中或千里无亭徼，于是诛北地太守以下，而令民得畜边县，官假马母，三岁而归，及息什一，以除告缗，用充入新秦中。

既得宝鼎，立后土、泰一祠，公卿白议封禅事，而郡国皆豫治道，修缮故宫，及当驰道县，县治宫储，设共具，而望幸。

明年，南粤反，西羌侵边。天子为山东不澹，赦天下囚，因南

【今译】

算留在那里的，可在那里定居。使者络绎不绝地在路上往来护送饥民，从巴蜀运来粮食赈济灾民。

第二年，天子开始巡察郡国。东渡黄河，河东太守没有想到天子的车驾会到这里，供具不周到，自杀。西行穿过陇山，很仓促，天子的随从官员连饭都吃不上，陇西太守自杀。于是天子北出萧关，随从数万骑在新秦中打猎，以此治理边防军后回到京城。新秦中有的地方千里之间没有边地哨所，于是诛杀北地太守以下官员，诏令百姓可以到边境各县放牧牲畜，官府贷给母马，三年后归还，利息是十分之一，废除举告隐匿缗钱的法令，用利息来补给新秦中。

得到宝鼎以后，建立了后土祠、泰一祠，公卿讨论有关封禅的事情，而郡国都预先修筑道路，整理旧宫，那些临近驰道的县城，预备供皇帝享用的物品，摆设盛放酒食的器具，等待天子车驾的幸临。

过了一年，南粤反叛，西羌侵犯边境。天子看到山东供给不足，

migrating south to find food in the Yangtze and Huai regions. Those who desired to remain could settle there. So many were the supervising commissioners, they formed a continuous line along the highways. Grain from Ba and Shu was sent as humanitarian aid.

The following year, the Son of Heaven made his first tour of inspection through prefectures and fiefs, crossing the river eastward. This took the Governor of Hedong by surprise and, totally unprepared for the imperial visitation, he committed suicide. The Emperor traveled west, crossing Longshan Mountain, but the accompanying officials could not find food enough. The Governor of Longxi committed suicide. Then the Emperor turned north through the Xiao Pass, accompanied by tens of thousands of light horse. He hunted inside New Qinzhong in order to inspect the frontier defense forces, before returning to the capital. In New Qinzhong, there were stretches of 1,000 *li* without a single sentry post. Therefore the Governor of Beidi and his subordinates were executed, and an edict was issued allowing people to move into the frontier countries to raise livestock. The authorities provided mares on a three-year loan basis, at 10 percent interest. The law to denounce the hiding of accumulated assets was abolished, and the interest on the revenue was used to help populate New Qinzhong.

After the treasure tripod had been discovered Wudi erected the Temple of the Spirit of Earth and the Temple to the Supreme Unity, and the great nobles of the realm and chief ministers of state at court were to come to Mount Tai to deliberate on matters relating to worship of Heaven and Earth there. Meanwhile, in preparation, all the prefectures and fiefs put their roads in good order, and repaired the old palaces. In every county along the imperial route, the authorities made ready palaces and provisions, and set out ceremonial ware for Emperor and his retinue.

The next year, the southern Yue rebelled, and the western Qiang raided the frontiers. Because of privations east of the mountains there

【原文】

方楼船士二十馀万人击粤，发三河以西骑击羌，又数万人度河筑令居。初置张掖、酒泉郡，而上郡、朔方、西河、河西开田官，斥塞卒六十万人戍田之。中国缮道馈粮，远者三千，近者千馀里，皆仰给大农。边兵不足，乃发武库工官兵器以澹之。车骑马乏，县官钱少，买马难得，乃著令，令封君以下至三百石吏以上差出(牡)[牝]马天下亭，亭有畜字马，岁课息。

齐相卜式上书，愿父子死南粤。天子下诏褒扬，赐爵关内侯，黄金四十斤，田十顷。布告天下，天下莫应。列侯以百数，皆莫求从军。至饮酎，少府省金，而列侯坐酎金失侯者百馀人。乃拜卜式为御

【今译】

就赦免天下囚犯，凭藉南方的战船士卒二十多万人攻打粤兵，发动三河以西的骑兵攻打羌人，又派几万人渡过黄河修筑令居城。开始设置张掖、酒泉郡，在上郡、朔方、西河、河西设置田官，扩充防守边境的士卒六十万人一边戍守，一边耕种。中原内地则整治道路以馈运粮食，路远的达三千里，近的也有一千多里，都依靠大司农。边防的兵器不足，就调拨武库和工官的兵器来满足那里的需要。兵车和战马不够，政府钱少，很难买到马匹，就制定命令，令封君以下至年俸三百石以上的官吏，按等级不同缴纳不同数目的母马给天下各亭，亭中有母马的，每年责成交配繁殖。

齐国相卜式上书，表示父子愿意为南粤而死。天子就下诏进行褒奖表扬，赐给他关内侯的爵位，以及黄金四十斤，田十顷。通告天下，天下人没有响应。诸侯有上百名，没有一人要求参加军队。到了饮酎的时候，少府检查酎金，列侯由于酎金份量不足而被削夺侯位的

was an imperial amnesty for prisoners of the realm. Then he sent the storied warships of the south and more than 200,000 men to attack Yue; meanwhile, from areas to the west of the three He prefectures light horse cavalry was sent to attack the Qiang. Additionally, tens of thousands of men crossed the Yellow River to build fortifications at Lingju. The prefectures of Zhangye and Jiuquan [Dunhuang] were established and offices in charge of cultivation and frontier affairs were set up in the prefectures of Shangjun, Shuofang, Xihe, and the area west of the river, where they were to garrison 600,000 soldiers and cultivate the land. Highways in the Central Plains were repaired for the transportation of grains; roads as long as 3,000 *li*, and little as 1,000 *li*, all depended on the Ministry of Treasury. When weapons on the frontiers were not enough, arms and other military equipment were sent from the capital armory and the arsenals in prefectures and fiefs. Chariots and war horses were lacking and the central government was underfunded, making it difficult to secure horses. So an edict was issued by the terms of which all enfeoffed lords and officials earning in excess of 300 piculs should furnish mares to stations throughout the empire, the precise number increasing according to their grades and ranks. At each station mares bred, and colts were submitted yearly as interest.

The First Minister of Qi, Bu Shi, addressed a petition to the throne in which he vowed that he, the father and his sons, were willing to die for him in southern Yue. The Emperor issued an edict to publicize and praise this, elevating him to Marquis of Guannei, and awarding him forty catties of gold and ten hectares of field. This circulated throughout the empire, but failed to elicit a response: of the hundreds of adjunct marquises, not one asked to join the imperial forces. When it came the time of sipping the ritual wine at the Imperial Ancestral Temple, the Chamberlain of the Palace Revenues examined the gold contributed; more than a hundred marquises were stripped of their status for the offense of giving underweight gold.

【原文】

史大夫。式既在位，见郡国多不便县官作盐铁，器苦恶，贾贵，或强令民买之。而船有算，商者少，物贵，乃因孔仅言船算事。上不说。

汉连出兵三岁，诛羌，灭两粤，番禺以西至蜀南者置初郡十七，且以其故俗治，无赋税。南阳、汉中以往，各以地比给初郡吏卒奉食币物，传车马被具。而初郡又时时小反，杀吏，汉发南方吏卒往诛之，间岁万馀人，费皆仰大农。大农以均输调盐铁助赋，故能澹之。然兵所过县，县以为訾给毋乏而已，不敢言轻赋法矣。

其明年，元封元年，卜式贬为太子太傅。而桑弘羊为治粟都尉，领大农，尽代仅斡天下盐铁。弘羊以诸官各自市相争，物以故腾跃，

【今译】

有一百多人。于是就授卜式为御史大夫。卜式当上御史大夫后，看到郡国大多反映政府不便作盐铁，铁器质量差，价格贵，有的强迫百姓购买。而船又有算赋，以船运货的商人少，商品昂贵，就通过孔仅反映船只征收算赋的事。天子由此对卜式不满意。

汉朝接连打了三年仗，杀掉了羌军，灭掉了南北粤，番禺以西直到蜀南地区初次设置了十七郡，暂且按照他们旧有的习俗治理，没有赋税。南阳、汉中一带，各自按照地域的比例供给初设各郡吏卒的薪俸、食物、钱财，以及驿传所用的车马被服等用具。而初设置的各郡又时常有小规模的反叛，杀死官吏，汉朝就派遣南方官兵前往镇压，每隔一年需要一万多人，费用都依靠大司农。大司农就用均输法调拨各地盐铁来补助赋税，所以能应付得了。但军队所经过的县，各县认为只要供给无缺就行了，不敢说要减轻赋税法令了。

第二年，是元封元年，卜式被贬为太子太傅。而桑弘羊任治粟都尉，兼任大农令，完全代替孔仅管理天下盐铁。桑弘羊以为各官各自做买卖相竞争，物价因此而飞涨，而天下所缴纳的赋税有的还不足以

Then Bu Shi was appointed Censor-in-Chief. While in that post, Bu Shi found that the central monopoly of salt and iron was burdensome in the prefectures and the fiefs, the quality of the tools was inferior but the price high, and that sometime they were coerced to buy them. Moreover, the fact that boats were being taxed, and traders were few was driving up the price of goods. Then he petitioned the court via Kong Jin on the matter of boat taxation. The Emperor was not pleased with him.

Han forces were in continuous action for three years: they subdued the Qiang; they annihilated South Yue and East Yue. From Panyu westward to the southern part of Shu, there were, for the first time, established 17 prefectures, which were governed according to their native customs, and no taxes were levied. The prefectures of Nanyang, Hanzhong, and those farther on, each having lands bordering the new prefectures, contributed proportionally towards them, providing for the officials' pay and rations, as well as carts for travel, horses, equipment and bedding. However, in the new prefectures there were from time to time minor uprisings in which officials were murdered. Han would send troops based in the south to quell them. The expenses for over 10,000 men were all shouldered by the Ministry of Treasury. The Ministry was able to meet the bill by supplementing the taxes via the various offices of salt and iron. Nevertheless, whichever counties the soldiers passed through, none dared raise the issue of lightening the tax law, considering the best policy was to pay the full amount.

The following year, the first year of the Yuanfeng reign period, Bu Shi was demoted to position of Grand Mentor to the Heir Apparent, and Sang Hongyang became concurrently Defender in Charge of Searching for Millet and in charge of the Ministry of Treasury, in all matters substituting for Kong Jin in control of salt and iron throughout the empire. Sang Hongyang considered that government offices competing with each other to trade drove

【原文】

而天下赋输或不偿其僦费，乃请置大农部丞数十人，分部主郡国，各往往置均输盐铁官，令远方各以其物如异时商贾所转(贬)[贩]者为赋，而相灌输。置平准于京师，都受天下委输。召工官治车诸器，皆仰给大农。大农诸官尽笼天下之货物，贵则卖之，贱则买之。如此，富商大贾亡所牟大利，则反本，而万物不得腾跃。故抑天下之物，名曰“平准”。天子以为然而许之。于是天子北至朔方，东封泰山，巡海上，旁北边以归。所过赏赐，用帛百馀万匹，钱金以巨万计，皆取足大农。

弘羊又请令民得入粟补吏，及罪以赎。令民入粟甘泉各有差，以复终身，不复告缗。它郡各输急处，而诸农各致粟，山东漕益岁

【今译】

偿还转运所花的费用，就请求设置大农部丞几十人，分别掌管各郡国中的大农事务，各大农部丞又往往设置均输官和盐铁官，令边远地区各自以他们跟以前商人所贩卖的物价为赋税，而互相转输。在京城设置平准机构，总受天下输纳来的物品。召雇工匠制造车辆等器物，都由大农令供给费用。大农所属各机构全部垄断了天下的货物，物价贵时就卖出，贱时就买进来。这样，富商大贾就无法牟取大利，就会返本为农，而所有商品就不会出现大涨大落的现象。所以抑制天下的物价，就叫做“平准”。天子认为有道理，就答应了他的请求。于是天子向北到达朔方，向东封禅泰山，巡行海上，到达北部边境后，就回到京城。所到之处的赏赐，用去帛一百多万匹，金钱数以亿计，都取自大农。

桑弘羊又请求让百姓可以纳献粮食来做官，犯罪时可以纳粮赎罪。命百姓各自按一定等级向甘泉宫纳粮，得以免除终身劳役，不再告发隐匿缗钱的事。其他郡县各自向急需处交纳，每一个农民都要纳粮，

prices sky high, and that the value of the taxes paid did not always cover what it cost to transport them. Then he proposed establishing several tens of assistant positions in the Ministry of Treasury, each responsible for respective sections in prefectures and fiefs, where from time to time would be set up offices of tax substitution, and offices of salt and of iron. Orders would be given that in far distant places, in lieu of taxes they should pay with local products, those previously shipped out of the locality for sale by traders. In the imperial capital would be established a standardization office to receive transported goods from all over the empire. Craftsmen would be commissioned to make the necessary carts and ancillary equipment, all to be paid by the Ministry of Treasury. The several offices of the Ministry would have monopoly control of the empire's money and merchandise. When prices were high, they would sell; when prices were low, they would buy. In this manner, rich traders and great merchants would have no means to make obscene profits, they would return to the fundamental occupation of agriculture, and the extreme rises and falls in the prices of goods would be a thing of the past. The prices of all goods in the empire would be controlled by this process, a process called "price smoothing." The Emperor approved the petition. Thereafter, he went north as far as Shuofang. He went east to offer sacrifice on Mt. Tai. Then after a sea trip, and journeying by the northern frontiers of the empire, he returned to the capital. Wherever he passed, he bestowed rewards, using more than a million rolls of silk, and coins and gold by the hundreds of millions. Payment for all this came from the Ministry of Treasury.

Sang Hongyang again proposed that the people be allowed to present millet in expectation of government posts, and to win pardon for crimes; and that by decree those who presented millet in various amounts at the granary of Ganquan would be exempt from military service for life, and forever free from denunciation of concealed fortunes. Wherever there was urgent need of grain, the provincial

【原文】

六百万石。一岁之中，太仓、甘泉仓满。边馀谷，诸均输帛五百万匹。民不益赋而天下用饶。于是弘羊赐爵左庶长，黄金者再百焉。

是岁小旱，上令百官求雨。卜式言曰：“县官当食租衣税而已，今弘羊令吏坐市列，贩物求利。亨弘羊，天乃雨。”久之，武帝疾病，拜弘羊为御史大夫。

昭帝即位六年，诏郡国举贤良文学之士，问以民所疾苦，教化之要。皆对愿罢盐铁酒(榷)[榷]均输官，毋与天下争利，视以俭节，然后教化可兴。弘羊难，以为此国家大业，所以制四夷，安边足用之本，不可废也。乃与丞相千秋共奏罢酒酤。弘羊自以为国兴大利，伐其

【今译】

山东漕运到京的粮食每年增加到六百万石。一年之中，太仓、甘泉宫的仓满。边境上剩余的谷物，按均输法折算为五百万匹帛。百姓不增加税赋，而天下的费用充足。于是桑弘羊被赐给左庶长的爵位，黄金二百斤。

这一年有轻微的旱灾，天子命令百官求雨。卜式就说：“官府应以租税为衣食，如今桑弘羊使官吏坐于列肆中买卖货物，求取利润。只有将桑弘羊下锅煮了，天才会下雨。”过了一段时间，武帝生病了，就拜桑弘羊为御史大夫。

昭帝在位六年后，就诏令郡国推荐贤良、文学之士，向他们询问民间的疾苦，政教风化的要领。他们都以希望罢免盐铁、酒榷、均输官来答对，不同天下争夺利益，用节俭来昭示天下，然后教化可以兴起。桑弘羊进行诘难，认为这些都是国家的大业，是用来制服四夷，安定边境，满足消费的根本所在，不能废除。于是就同丞相千秋一同上奏要求废除酒税。桑弘羊自以为为国家兴了大利，居功自傲，想为

authorities directly transported to that place; likewise individual farmers all had to present millet. The result was an additional six million piculs a year of grain transported by water to the capital from east of the mountain. Within a year, the Imperial Granary and the granary at Ganquan were filled; the frontiers had a surplus of grains, which was equal to five million rolls of silk in tax substitution. There was ample resource to meet the empire's costs, without adding to the people's tax burden. Thereupon Sang Hongyang was bestowed the title of *Zuoshuzhang* (tenth order) with a money award of 200 catties of gold.

That year saw a small drought. Thc Emperor ordered government officials to pray for rain. Bu Shi remarked: "The central government ought to be fed and clothed with taxes on farming output, and nothing else. Now Sang Hongyang orders that officials sit on market stalls to trade for profit. Boil Sang Hongyang alive and Heaven will then send rain!" Later, Emperor Wudi fell ill and appointed Sang Hongyang as Censor-in-Chief.

When Emperor Zhaodi was in the sixth year of his reign, he sent out an edict calling on the prefectures and fiefs to recommend worthy, excellent and learned people. He questioned them about the people's sufferings, and the important need for civic morality among them. All replied that they wished to see abolished the officials of salt and iron, of the liquor monopoly and of tax substitution too, so there would be no competition with the people for profit; instead there would be an exhibition of frugality and economy. Only then could moral education be advanced. Sang Hongyang refuted this idea, saying they represented the chief mission of the empire, the fundamental way to contain the barbarians on four frontiers, to pacify the borders and meet expenses. They could not be abolished. Together with Prime Minister Tian Qianqiu, he memorialized to abolish tax on alcohol. Sang Hongyang, thinking himself champion of what would profit the empire, bragged about his merits to earn

【原文】

功，欲为子弟得官，怨望大将军霍光，遂与上官桀等谋反，诛灭。

宣、元、成、哀、平五世，亡所变改。元帝时尝罢盐铁官，三年而复之。贡禹言："铸钱采铜，一岁十万人不耕，民坐盗铸陷刑者多。富人臧钱满室，犹无厌足。民心动摇，弃本逐末，耕者不能半，奸邪不可禁，原起于钱。疾其末者绝其本，宜罢采珠玉金银铸钱之官，毋复以为币，除其贩卖租铢之律，租税禄赐皆以布帛及谷，使百姓一意农桑。"议者以为交易待钱，布帛不可尺寸分裂。禹议亦寝。

自孝武元狩五年三官初铸五铢钱，至平帝元始中，成钱二百八十亿万馀云。

王莽居摄，变汉制，以周钱有子母相权，于是更造大钱，径寸二

【今译】

子弟谋取官位，憎恨大将军霍光，便与上官桀等人谋反，被诛灭。

宣帝、元帝、成帝、哀帝、平帝五代，没有什么变化。元帝时曾罢免盐铁官，三年后又恢复了。贡禹说："铸钱要采铜，一年就有十万人不去耕种，百姓犯法偷着铸钱而受到处罚的人很多。富人蓄藏的钱充满屋子，还不知满足。民心动摇，放弃农业的根本而去追逐商业的利益，耕种的人没有一半，奸邪不能加以禁止，是因为钱的缘故。急切从事商业的就会使农业断绝，应罢免开采珠玉金银铸钱的官员，不要再铸造钱币，除去贩卖以及以钱代实物纳税的法令，租税、薪俸、赏赐都用布帛和谷物，使百姓一心一意致力于农桑。"议论的人认为交易需要钱，布帛不能以尺寸分割。贡禹的建议也就没有得到采用。

从孝武帝元狩五年三官开始铸造五铢钱，到平帝元始年间，有钱二百八十亿万多。

王莽摄政之时，改变汉朝制度，因为周朝的钱有子母相平衡，于是改造大钱，直径一寸二分，重十二铢，其正面的文字为"大钱

official posts for his children. Bearing a grudge against General-in-Chief Huo Guang, he conspired to rebel with Shangguan Jie and others; for this he was put to death.

During the reigns of emperors Xuandi, Yuandi, Chengdi, Aidi, and Pingdi, no changes were made. In the reign of Yuandi, the salt and iron offices were abolished for a time, being reinstated after three years. Gong Yu said: "Those who cast coins go to mine copper, so that 100,000 men each year are away from plowing. Counterfeiters are punished in great number. The rich hoard housefuls of coins, and yet they are never satisfied. The hearts of the people are twitchy. They have abandoned the fundamental of farming in pursuit of mercantile profits. Those who work the land account for scarcely a half; crime and depravity cannot be prevented. The reason for this is money. Those who are anxious about the secondary are cut off from the fundamental. It is advised that we abolish the offices in charge of gathering pearls and jade, gold and silver, and of casting coins. Let these no more be regarded as money, repeal the orders for tax on trade and on sales in *zhu*, have taxes levied on earnings from use of land, and let official emoluments and bestowments all be paid in cloth, silk as well as in grain, so that the common people will devote themselves wholeheartedly to agriculture and sericulture." Those in conference considered that for the purpose of mutual exchange it was necessary to use coins. Textiles of either vegetable fibers or silk could not be cut into short lengths to the foot or inch. Yu's proposal was never adopted.

From the fifth year of the Yuanshou reign of Emperor Wudi, when the Sanguan first cast five-*zhu* coins, until the middle of the Yuanshi reign of Emperor Pingdi, coins cast are said to have been more than 28 billion cash. During the Wang Mang regency he changed the Han system, because coins under the Zhou had been large (mother) and small (ones) of related standard weights. Therefore he turned to make large coins, a little over an inch in diameter, 12 *zhu*

【原文】

分，重十二铢，文曰“大钱五十”。又造契刀、错刀。契刀，其环如大钱，身形如刀，长二寸，文曰“契刀五百”。错刀，以黄金错其文，曰“一刀直五千”。与五铢钱凡四品，并行。

莽即真，以为书“劉”字有金刀，乃罢错刀、契刀及五铢钱，而更作金、银、龟、贝、钱、布之品，名曰“宝货”。

小钱径六分，重一铢，文曰“小钱直一”。次七分，三铢，曰“幺钱一十”。次八分，五铢，曰“幼钱二十”。次九分，七铢。曰“中钱三十”。次一寸，九铢，曰“壮钱四十”。因前“大钱五十”，是为钱货六品，直各如其文。

黄金重一斤，直钱万。朱提银重八两为一流，直一千五百八十。它银一流直千。是为银货二品。

元龟岠冉长尺二寸，直二千一百六十，为大贝十朋。公龟九寸，直五百，为壮贝十朋。侯龟七寸以上，直三百，为幺贝十朋。子龟五寸以上，直百，为小贝十朋。是为龟宝四品。

【今译】

五十”。又制造契刀币、错刀币。契刀，它的边缘周围同大钱一样，形状像刀，长二寸，其正面的文字为“契刀五百”。错刀，用黄金镶嵌它的纹刻，上面写着“一刀值五千”。和五铢钱共有四类，一并流通。

王莽正式即皇帝位，认为写“刘”字有金有刀，就废除错刀、契刀以及五铢钱，而改做金、银、龟、贝、钱、布各类钱币，称为“宝货”。

小钱直径六分，重一铢，其正面的文字为“小钱值一”。另外一种小钱直径为七分，重三铢，其正面的文字为“幺钱一十”。另外一种直径八分，重五铢，叫“幼钱二十”。另外一种直径九分，重七铢，叫“中钱三十”。还有一种直径一寸，重九铢，叫“壮钱四十”。根据前面的“大钱五十”，这就是六类钱币，价值各自同它上面的文字一样。

黄金重一斤，值钱一万。朱提银重八两是一流，值一千五百八十钱。其他银一流值钱一千。这是两类银币。

大龟币两边相距一尺二寸，值二千一百六十钱，相当于十朋大贝。公龟有九寸，值五百钱，相当于十朋壮贝。侯龟七寸以上，值三百钱，相当于十朋幺贝。子龟五寸以上，值一百钱，相当于十朋小贝。这是四类龟宝。

in weight, and bearing the words "big cash 50." He also initiated *qidao* knife-shaped money. The lowest denomination of these had a circular head like the big cash but having a two-inch long body in the shape of a knife, and bearing the words "*qidao* knife 500." The highest denomination *cuodao* was inscribed "one *dao* worth 5000" in actual gold inlay. Including the five-*zhu*, there were four types of coinage in circulation at the same time.

When, however, Wang Mang came to the throne as emperor proper, he reflected that in the character for the surname Liu [the clan name of the Han ruling house] there occurred the elements *jin* (gold) and *dao* (knife). Thus he abolished this knife-shaped money as well as the five-*zhu* coins, replacing them with gold, silver, tortoiseshell, cowries, cash, and spade *bu*, to which he gave the name "precious ware." The small cash were six-tenths of an inch in diameter, one *zhu* in weight and bore an inscription reading "small cash worth one." Next came three *zhu*, seven-tenths of an inch across, named "baby cash ten"; next came five *zhu*, eight-tenths of an inch across, named "youth cash 20"; then the seven *zhu*, nine-tenths of an inch across, named "middle cash 30"; then nine *zhu*, one inch across, named "adult cash 40." "Large cash" units were 50. Thus, there were six denominations of coin, each with its value inscribed.

One catty of gold was worth 10,000 cash, and premium silver from the Zhuti Mountains was eight taels per *liu*, valued at 1,580 cash. Other kinds of silver were valued at 1,000 per *liu*. So there were two types of silver currency.

A large tortoiseshell unit was one foot and two inches measured from top to bottom; worth 2,160 cash, it was equivalent to 10 pairs of large cowries. A nine-inch duke shell was valued at 500, and equivalent to 10 pairs of adult cowries; a marquis shell was seven inches and more, valued at 300, and equivalent to 10 pairs of baby cowries; a viscount shell was five inches and more, valued at 100, equivalent to 10 pairs of tiny cowries. These were the four

【原文】

大贝四寸八分以上，二枚为一朋，直二百一十六。壮贝三寸六分以上，二枚为一朋，直五十。幺贝二寸四分以上，二枚为一朋，直三十。小贝寸二分以上，二枚为一朋，直十。不盈寸二分，漏度不得为朋，率枚直钱三。是为贝货五品。

大布、次布、弟布、壮布、中布、差布、厚布、幼布、幺布、小布。小布长寸五分，重十五铢，文曰“小布一百”。自小布以上，各相长一分，相重一铢，文各为其布名，直各加一百。上至大布，长二寸四分，重一两，而直千钱矣。是为布货十品。

凡宝货五物，六名，二十八品。

铸作钱布皆用铜，淆以连锡，文质周郭放汉五铢钱云。其金银与它物杂，色不纯好，龟不盈五寸，贝不盈六分，皆不得为宝货。元龟为蔡，非四民所得居，有者，入大卜受直。

百姓愦乱，其货不行。民私以五铢钱市买。莽患之，下诏：“敢非井田挟五铢钱者为惑众，投诸四裔以御魑魅。”于是农商失业，食

【今译】

大贝有四寸八分以上，二枚为一朋，值二百一十六钱。壮贝三寸六分以上，二枚为一朋，值五十钱。幺贝二寸四分以上，二枚为一朋，值三十钱。小贝一寸二分以上，二枚为一朋，值十钱。不满一寸二分，不合制度，不得为朋，大概一枚值三钱。这就是五类贝货。

大布、次布、弟布、壮布、中布、差布、厚布、幼布、幺布、小布。小布长一寸五分，重十五铢，其正面的文字为“小布一百”。从小布往上，长各加一分，重各加一铢，其正面的文字就是其布的名字，价值各加一百。往上至大布，长二寸四分，重一两，而值一千钱了。这就是十品布货。

宝货共有五种物质，六个名称，二十八类。

铸造钱币都用铜，杂以铅和锡，形状轮廓都仿照五铢钱。其中金银和其他物质相杂，颜色不纯正，龟不满五寸，贝不满六分，都不得成为宝货。大龟就是蔡，不是一般百姓所能畜养的，有大龟的，交给大卜接受报酬。

百姓烦乱，这些货币都行不通。百姓私自用五铢钱到市场上购买货物。王莽对此感到忧患，就下诏说：“敢非议井田挟带五铢钱的就

denominations of tortoiseshell money.

Of the large cowries, above four and eight-tenths inches, two constituted a pair worth 216 cash; a pair of adult cowries above three and six-tenths was worth 50; a pair of baby cowries above two and four-tenths was worth 30; a pair of cowries above one and two-tenths was worth 10. Those under the minimum size of one and two-tenths fell outside of the system, and could not be reckoned in pairs; on average, as individual pieces, they were each worth three cash. This was five denominations of cowry money.

Spade *bu* cash, large, next, younger brother, adult, medial, ranking, graded, adolescent, baby, small, were names for the *bu* money group. Small spade *bu* was one and a half inch, weighing 15 *zhu*, inscribed with "small *bu* 100." From this small spade *bu* up, each denomination was one-tenth inch longer, one *zhu* heavier and worth 100 more than the previous. Each carried its respective *bu* classification – e.g. adult, baby. The top denomination was two and four-tenths long, weighed one tael and was worth 1,000 cash. This was the spade *bu* money in ten denominations.

So there were five kinds of "precious wares" money, six names, and 28 denominations. For casting to make cash and spade *bu* money, copper was used, mixing with it lead and tin. The inscribed obverse and the reverse of the cash had a raised rim, modeled, it is said, after the Han five-*zhu* coin. Gold and silver mixed with other goods, of impure color, tortoiseshells under five inches, and cowries under six-tenths could not be used as "precious wares." A large tortoiseshell was known as *cai* and commoners were not permitted to keep them for themselves. Every *cai* had to be presented to the Grand Diviner, in exchange for its monetary value.

The common people became confused in mind and action. These currencies did not circulate. Privately the people used five-*zhu* coins to buy in the market. Wang Mang, worried, issued an edict: "Those who oppose the nine-square farming system and those who

【原文】

货俱废，民涕泣于市道。坐卖买田宅奴婢铸钱抵罪者，自公卿大夫至庶人，不可称数。莽知民愁，乃但行小钱直一，与大钱五十，二品并行，龟贝布属且寝。

莽性躁扰，不能无为，每有所兴造，必欲依古得经文。国师公刘歆言周有泉府之官，收不雠，与欲得，即《易》所谓“理财正辞，禁民为非”者也。莽乃下诏曰：“夫《周礼》有赊贷，《乐语》有五均，传记各有斡焉。今开赊贷，张五均，设诸斡者，所以齐众庶，抑并兼也。”遂于长安及五都立五均官，更名长安东西市令及洛阳、

【今译】

是惑众，把他们流放到四方边远地区去防御魑魅。”于是农民、商人都失掉本业，粮食、货物都没有了，百姓在市场的道路上哭泣。犯下买卖田宅、奴婢、铸钱的罪行受到处罚的人，自公卿大夫到平民，数不胜数。王莽知道百姓怨恨，就只流行值一钱的小钱和值五十钱的大钱，二类一同使用，龟、贝、布等类暂且停止使用。

王莽性情急躁好动，不能清静无为，每次有所兴作创造，一定要仿造古代取得经上的文字。国师公刘歆说周朝有泉府官，收购市上滞销的货物，给予人们想得到的，即《周易》所说的“用正确的辞令来治理财货，禁止百姓为非作歹”。王莽就下诏说：“《周礼》有赊贷，《乐语》有五均，传记上各自有斡官。现在开放赊贷，实行五均，设立各斡官，是用来统一百姓，抑制兼并。”于是在长安以及五都设立五均官，改长安东西市令以及洛阳、邯郸、临甾、宛、成都的

hold on to five-*zhu* coins are misleading the people. Banish them to the distant four borders so that they may struggle against the demons and goblins of mountains and forests." Farmers and traders lost their livelihoods; neither food nor goods were to be had. The people wept and wailed on the road to market. It is impossible to number the persons who were punished for illicitly buying fields, houses and serfs, and casting money on their own account – the number included every part of society, from the highest down to the lowest in the land. Wang Mang, becoming aware that the common people were very resentful, accordingly circulated only small and large coins worth one and 50 cash respectively. The two denominations were circulated at the same time, while tortoiseshells, cowries, and *bu* money were shelved for the time being.

Wang Mang was by nature impetuous and hyperactive, incapable of leaving well alone. Every time there was anything to be undertaken, he insisted that it must conform to what was written in the classics. Imperial Mentor Liu Xin told him that under the Zhou there was a treasurer for market taxes, whose office received that which was unsold, and gave it to those who desired to obtain. According to Liu, this was in accordance with the *Book of Changes*: "Administer aright the wealth of the land with correct instruction, to prohibit the people from wrongdoing." Wang Mang then sent down an edict saying: "Now, the Ritual of Zhou describes giving credit for purchase of certain things, and lending money with interest in the case of other things; in Music Language there are five cases of price smoothing. The earlier records have each an account of the controls. Now let there be set up a system of making credits and loans; popularize the five cases for equalizing prices; and provide for the several controls. Thereby the masses of the population will be given equality and monopolies will be suppressed." Subsequently, at Changan and at five other metropolitan centers, Five-case Equalization Offices were set up. The titles of Superintendents of

【原文】

邯郸、临甾、宛、成都市长皆为五均司市(称)师。东市称京，西市称畿，洛阳称中，馀四都各用东西南北为称，皆置交易丞五人，钱府丞一人。工商能采金银铜连锡登龟取贝者，皆自占司市钱府，顺时气而取之。

又以《周官》税民：凡田不耕为不殖，出三夫之税；城郭中宅不树艺者为不毛，出三夫之布；民浮游无事，出夫布一匹。其不能出布者，冗作，县官衣食之。诸取众物鸟兽鱼鳖百虫于山林水泽及畜牧者，嫔妇桑蚕织纴纺绩补缝，工匠医巫卜祝及它方技商贩贾人坐肆列里区谒舍，皆各自占所为于其在所之县官，除其本，计其利，十一分

【今译】

市长各为五均司市师。东市称作京，西市称作畿，洛阳称为中，其余四都各用东、西、南、北来称呼，都设置交易丞五人，钱府丞一人。工匠、商人能开采金、银、铜、铅、锡并进献龟贝的，都自己向司市钱府申报，按照一定时机来开采。

又根据《周官》上收取百姓的税法：凡田不耕种为不生产，要交三个劳力的税；城郭中住宅周围不栽树木果实及菜蔬的为不种植，要交三个劳力的布帛；百姓游荡不从事生产的，交劳力役使的费用一匹。其中不能交布的人，做散工，由政府来供给衣食。所有猎取各种物质，包括鸟兽、鱼鳖、百虫于山林、水泽以进行畜养牲畜的人，喂养桑蚕织丝缕和纺织缝补的妇女，工匠、医生、巫师、卜祝以及方技、商贩、商人坐列在市场和客舍的人，在各自向自己所在地的政府申报自己的所作所为，除掉他的本钱，计算他的利润，收取十分之一

the East and West markets at Changan as well as those chiefs of Luoyang, Handan, Linzi, Wan, or Chengdu, were all changed to Masters for Equalizing Markets in Five Cases. The East Market was designated "Capital Master" and the West Market designated "Imperial Domain Master." Luoyang was designated the Middle Master and the other four marts were given the designations East, West, South, and North masters. A system of five exchange deputies and one tax and credit officer was set up in all the seven markets. Craftsmen and traders who were able to gather gold, silver, copper, lead, tin, and to present tortoiseshells and collect cowries were all to make a declaration of their own at the tax and credit offices and to collect such materials and items at fixed times.

Furthermore, in accordance with the *Ritual of Zhou* there were taxes on people. For fields left uncultivated and unproductive, the tax was set at three workmen. For walled estates not planted with trees and vegetables and left as wilderness, there was payable in cloth the equivalent of three workmen. Wanderers without steady employment paid one roll of cloth tax, the equivalent of one workman. Those unable to afford the cloth were assigned for service without fixed duties under the government which clothed and fed them. Under the taxation system came all the following: any person who gathered articles of any kind, birds and beasts, fish and turtles, the hundred insects and reptiles, from mountains and woods, streams and lakes, as well as those who reared and pastured; ladies who worked with mulberry trees, cared for silkworms, wove, laid the warp, drew out fibers, spun threads, mended and sewed; craftsman and mechanics, physicians, sorcerers, diviners, and invokers; as well as practitioners of the alchemical arts, and traders and merchants, traveling or residential, who sat in booths and stalls, and stayed in village inns. All of these were required to make a declaration about their occupations before the local government in their place of residence. In each case they subtracted capital, calculated profits and

【原文】

之，而以其一为贡。敢不自占，自占不以实者，尽没入所采取，而作县官一岁。

诸司市常以四时中月实定所掌，为物上中下之贾，各自用为其市平，毋拘它所。众民卖买五谷布帛丝绵之物，周于民用而不雠者，均官有以考检厥实，用其本贾取之，毋令折钱。万物卬贵，过平一钱，则以平贾卖与民。其贾氐贱减平者，听民自相与市，以防贵庾者。民欲祭祀丧纪而无用者，钱府以所入工商之贡但赊之，祭祀无过旬日，丧纪毋过三月。民或乏绝，欲贷以治产业者，均授之，除其费，计所得受息，毋过岁什一。

羲和鲁匡言："名山大泽，盐铁钱布帛，五均赊贷，斡在县官，唯酒酤独未斡。酒者，天之美禄，帝王所以颐养天下，享祀祈福，扶

【今译】

的税，再以其中之一作为贡，有胆敢不自己申报的，自报不合实际的，全部没收他所收获的，再为政府劳作一年。

各司市经常在四季中间的一月按实际情况确定所掌管的事情，制定货物上、中、下三等的价格，各自适用自己市场稳定即可，不必拘泥于其他地方。所有人买卖五谷、布帛、丝绵等物，只要是百姓所需要的而又滞销的，均官考查检验确实，就用他本来的价格收购，不要使他折本。所有货物涨价，超过平衡价一钱，就以平价卖给百姓。价格跌落至平价以下的，听任百姓自行参与买卖，以防止囤积居奇的人。百姓想祭祀和办丧事却没有费用的，钱府就用所收入的工匠、商人交的贡不计息赊给他们，祭祀不要超过十天，丧事不要超过三个月。百姓有的穷困，打算贷款来治理产业的，要多少贷给多少，除掉他的费用，计算他的所得收取利息，不超过一年的十分之一。

羲和官鲁匡说："有名的大山和大湖，盐铁、钱、布帛，五均、赊贷，都由政府掌管，只有卖酒还没有人主管。酒，是上天的美好赏

divided the income into ten parts, one part of which was payable as tax. He who dared refuse to make a declaration, or was untruthful in his computations was liable to total confiscation of assets, and to work for the government for one full year.

In the middle month of each of the four seasons, the several masters of the markets would settle all affairs in their remit, and would fix price for articles into high, medium and low. Each made use of them to keep their local market stable, without being restrained by other places. In the buying and selling of the "five grains," cloth, and silk, for which there was general demand but remained unsold, the equalization office would examine them closely to determine their condition, and buy them up at cost price without incurring loss. Where the price of a commodity exceeded the equitable value by one cash, the commodity would be sold at the equitable price. If the price dropped below that, the people were permitted to put it on the market themselves in order to guard against speculative hoarding. When the people desired to worship and sacrifice, or to observe mourning rites, but were without means, the tax and credit officer would make them interest-free loans out of the tax revenues from craftsmen and traders. Worship and sacrifice loans were repayable within 10 days, whilst mourning loans were on a three-month term. When the people were destitute and exhausted and applied to borrow money on interest in order to establish a business, they were never refused a loan. Subtracting their expenses and calculating upon the balance, the interest rate was not more than 10 percent a year.

The Minister of Treasury Lu Kuang said: "As for the celebrated mountains and great lakes, salt and iron, coinage and textiles of vegetable fibers and of silk; and the five equalization markets including loans made by both with and without interest, control has been placed in the hands of government. Only in the wine trade alone is there no control. Wine is a beautiful blessing of Heaven, and

【原文】

衰养疾。百礼之会，非酒不行。故《诗》曰‘无酒酤我’，而《论语》曰‘酤酒不食’，二者非相反也。夫《诗》据承平之世，酒酤在官，和旨便人，可以相御也。《论语》孔子当周衰乱，酒酤在民，薄恶不诚，是以疑而弗食。今绝天下之酒，则无以行礼相养；放而亡限，则费财伤民。请法古，令官作酒，以二千五百石为一均，率开一卢以卖，雠五十酿为准。一酿用粗米二斛，曲一斛，得成酒六斛六斗。各以其市月朔米曲三斛，并计其贾而参分之，以其一为酒一斛之平。除米曲本贾，计其利而什分之，以其七入官，其三及醩截灰炭给工器薪樵之费。”

羲和置命士督五均六斡，郡有数人，皆用富贾。洛阳薛子仲、张

【今译】

赐，帝王用来保养天下，祭祀鬼神祈求福赐，抚养衰弱和有疾病的人。百礼的举行，没有酒不行。所以《诗》上说‘没有酒我来买’而《论语》说‘买的酒我不喝’，这两种说法并不相反。《诗》上所说的是根据太平的时代，酒税在官府，和美方便，可以互相进用。《论语》上所说的是孔子正当周朝昏乱，酒税在百姓，轻薄邪恶不诚实，因此怀疑而不喝。如今断绝天下的酒，就没有可用来行使礼仪和进行抚养的东西了；没有限度地放开，就会浪费财物和伤害百姓。请效法古代，命官府造酒，以二千五百石为一均，先开放一个肆来卖酒，以售出五十酿为基准。一酿用糙米二斛。曲一斛，可得到现成的酒六斛六斗。各自用他们自己购买的每月三斛的米曲，并计算他们的价格把他们分成三份，用其中之一作为一斛酒的平价。除去米曲的成本价格，计算利润分成十份，把七份交纳给官府，其余三份以及酒浆灰炭供给工匠器械柴火的费用。”

羲和设立命士监督五均六斡，每郡命士有数人，都用富商。洛阳

is that which the rulers use to foster and nourish all under Heaven in offerings, sacrifices, and invocations for happiness, as well as building up the feeble and nourishing the sick. At every gathering and every rite, it would not do to be without wine. For these reasons, the *Book of Odes* says: 'If without wine for guests, I go to buy!' On the other hand, the *Analects* say 'of bought wine Confucius did not partake.' But the two are not contradictory. The *Book of Odes* shows evidence of a peaceful era, when liquor was sold under official control. Mild and excellent, convenient for all, one could set it before another. The *Analects* have it that Confucius lived just at the period of decadence and disorder of the Zhou, a time when wine was sold under private enterprise. Poor and unclean, it was adulterated, and therefore not to be trusted, so the Sage did not drink it. Now if all the wine under Heaven should be cut off, then there would be nothing with which to conduct the rites and nourish the needy; not to impose government control and restriction is to waste the wealth of the land, and to harm the people. I beg that the model of the ancients be followed, and that we appoint an office for the making of wine. Consider 2,500 piculs as one jun. On average we open one wineshop to sell in 50 fermentations as a benchmark. One fermentation requires two bushels of coarse millet and one bushel of yeast, in order to produce six bushels and six pecks of liquor. For each we take the new-moon market price of three bushels of husked grain and yeast, divide the cost by three, and take one part as the equitable price for one bushel of wine. From the price we take the cost of the raw materials to calculate the profit, and divide that by 10. The government takes seven-tenths; the remaining three-tenths, together with the wine dregs, ashes and charcoal go to the makers as cover for the costs of production. "

The Minister of Treasury set up a system of officials to supervise the Masters for Equalizing Markets in Five Cases and the Six Controls. There were to be several per prefecture, all of them

【原文】

长叔、临菑姓伟等，乘传求利，交错天下。因与郡县通奸，多张空簿，府臧不实，百姓俞病。莽知民苦之，复下诏曰：“夫盐，食肴之将；酒，百药之长，嘉会之好；铁，(曰)[田]农之本；名山大泽，饶衍之臧；五均赊贷，百姓所取平，卬以给澹；铁布铜冶，通行有无，备民用也。此六者，非编户齐民所能家作，必卬于市，虽贵数倍，不得不买。豪民富贾，即要贫弱，先圣知其然也，故斡之。每一斡为设科条防禁，犯者罪至死。”奸吏猾民并侵，众庶各不安生。

后五岁，天凤元年，复申下金银龟贝之货，颇增减其贾直。而罢大小钱，改作货布，长二寸五分，广一寸，首长八分有奇，广八分，其圜好径二分半，足枝长八分，间广二分，其文右曰“货”，左曰“布”，重二十五铢，直货泉二十五。货泉径一寸，重五铢，文右曰

【今译】

薛子仲、张长叔、临菑姓伟等人，坐着驿站的车去追求利润，在全国到处往来。顺便与郡县相勾结，造了很多假账，官府收藏不充实，百姓更加担心。王莽知道人民为这些事所困苦，重新下诏说：“盐，是饭菜的主帅；酒，是百药的领袖，举行宴会的美物；铁，是进行农作的本钱；名山大湖，是富饶的物质所隐藏的地方；五均赊贷，是百姓用来平价取得物质和供给的依靠；熔铸钱币，是为沟通有无，以备百姓的消费。这六种，不是有户口的平民家家都能自己做到的，必须依靠买卖，即使贵几倍，也不得不买。豪民富商，就利用这要挟贫困弱小，前代的圣贤已知道这种情况，所以要主管他们。每一主管设立条例来防患禁止，违反的人处罚至死。”邪恶的官吏和狡猾的百姓一同侵犯平民，广大人民各自不能安定地生活。

五年后，是天凤元年，重新颁布金银龟贝等货币，大幅度地增减它们的价值。废除大小钱，改为货布，长二寸五分，宽一寸，货布首长八分有余，宽八分，它的圆孔直径二分半，足枝长八分，中间宽二分，其正面右边的文字是“货”，左边的文字是“布”，重二十五

wealthy traders. Xue Zizhong and Zhang Changshu of Luoyang and Xing Wei of Linzi and others traveled by post chaise, crisscrossing the nation in pursuit of profits, doing underhand deals with the prefectures and counties, and compiling fraudulent accounts. The official warehouses were no longer full, and the common people were more than ever stressed. When Wang Mang knew of the people's worries, he issued another edict: "Salt is the commander of delicious viands. Wine is the senior of the hundred medicines, and the delight of happy gatherings. Iron is a fundamental in farming. Famous mountains and great lakes are the storehouses for rich and abundant resources. The Equalizing Markets in Five Cases and the system of credits and loans are the means whereby common people can acquire their needs at an equitable price. Cast metal money is the channel between supply and demand, a means of exchange for the people's expenses. These six controlled things are not permissible for common people to make privately. They must necessarily look to the markets. Though the price may be several times higher, there is no option but to buy. Adventurers and rich merchants then coerce the poor and the weak. The sages of old understood this and wished to control them. For each one of the controls let there be formulated legal articles for preventive and prohibitory control; and let those who offend be punished by death." Predatory officials and unscrupulous commoners alike encroached upon the masses to prevent them leading an untroubled life.

Five years later, in the first year of Tianfeng (14 AD), he again issued gold, silver, tortoiseshell, and cowries as media of exchange, greatly increasing or decreasing their values; both large and small cash were demonetized. They were replaced with spade money *huobu*, two inches and five-tenths long and an inch wide, with a head over eight-tenths long, and eight-tenths wide, pierced by a round hole two and a half tenths in diameter. This forked into legs eight-tenths long, two-tenths apart. The obverse read *huo* on the

【原文】

“货”，左曰“泉”，枚直一，与货布二品并行。又以大钱行久，罢之，恐民挟不止，乃令民且独行大钱，与新货泉俱枚直一，并行尽六年，毋得复挟大钱矣。每壹易钱，民用破业，而大陷刑。莽以私铸钱死，及非沮宝货投四裔，犯法者多，不可胜行，乃更轻其法：私铸作泉布者，与妻子没入为官奴婢；吏及比伍，知而不举告，与同罪；非沮宝货，民罚作一岁，吏免官。犯者俞众，及五人相坐皆没入，郡国槛车铁锁，传送长安钟官，愁苦死者什六七。

作货布后六年，匈奴侵寇甚，莽大募天下囚徒人奴，名曰猪突豨

【今译】

铢，相当于二十五货泉。货泉直径为一寸，重五铢，其正面右边的文字是“货”，左边的文字是“泉”，一枚价值是一，同货布两类一并流行。又因为大钱流通很久，废除它，怕百姓挟带使用不停止，就命百姓暂且单独行使大钱，同新货泉都一枚价值是一，同行共六年，不得再挟带大钱。每一次更改钱币，百姓都要破产，而且大批犯法。王莽把私自铸钱的人处死，以及非议诋毁宝货的人迁徙到边远地区，犯法的人太多了，不能完全执行，就更改减轻刑法：私自铸造泉布的，同妻子儿女一同没收进官府当奴婢；官吏以及左邻右舍，知道而不举报，与犯人同罪；非议诋毁宝货者，百姓罚做一年苦工，官员就被免职。犯法的人更多，等到五人相连坐都没入官府，郡国囚车铁锁，押送到长安钟官，痛苦而死的人十之六七。

制作货布后六年，匈奴入侵很厉害，王莽大规模招募天下的囚犯

right and *bu* on the left. Its weight was 25 *zhu* and its value was 25 *huoquan*. The *huoquan* was one inch across, five *zhu* in weight, with the inscription on the right reading *huo* and that on the left, *quan*. Each coin was worth one *huoquan*. These coins and the spade money were the two types put into circulation at the same time. Furthermore, considering that large cash had been in use for a long time, he feared that even if they were no longer legal tender, the people would not cease to use them. Consequently he ordered that for the time being the people could keep on using the large cash which had the same value as one new *huoquan*, but that after a six-year period of dual circulation, large cash would be withdrawn and its possession no longer permitted. With every change in coinage, people were bankrupted, and broke the law in droves. Wang Mang considered that those privately casting coins should die, and that those who criticized the precious wares system should be banished to the far ends of the empire. However, the law breakers were so many, this was not feasible. He made the penalties less draconian. Those who privately cast *quan* and *bu* money would make serfs together with their wives and children, to serve under government authorities. Should a government official or head of a neighborhood unit know of infringement but not denounce it, they were liable to the same punishment as the offender. Common people who criticized the precious wares system were punished by a year of forced labor, whereas officials faced dismissal for the same offense. Law breakers became the more numerous, and together with non-informing heads of mutually responsible neighbor units, they were all made serfs. From prefectures and fiefs, caged and shackled on government carts, they were escorted to the Mint in Changan to do forced labor. Some 60 or 70 percent of them died of their suffering.

Six years after the coinage of *huobu* money, there were extensive attacks and raids by the Huns. Wang Mang, in a general conscription for military service, mobilized those languishing in the

【原文】

勇，壹切税吏官，訾三十而取一。又令公卿以下至郡县黄绶吏，皆保养军马，吏尽复以与民。民摇手触禁，不得耕桑，徭役烦剧，而枯旱蝗虫相因。又用制作未定，上自公侯，下至小吏，皆不得奉禄，而私赋敛，货赂上流，狱讼不决。吏用苛暴立威，旁缘莽禁，侵刻小民。富者不得自保，贫者无以自存，起为盗贼，依阻山泽，吏不能禽而覆蔽之，浸淫日广，于是青、徐、荆楚之地往往万数。战斗死亡，缘边四夷所系虏，陷罪，饥疫，人相食，及莽未诛，而天下户口减半矣。

自发猪突豨勇后四年，而汉兵诛莽。后二年，世祖受命，荡涤烦

【今译】

和奴隶，叫做猪突豨勇，一切税收都来自官民，收取财产税的三十分之一。又命令公卿以下到郡县黄绶官，都要保养军马，官吏把军马全转给百姓令他们来保养。百姓动辄触犯禁令，不能进行耕种采桑，徭役烦杂沉重，而且有旱灾蝗虫相捣乱。又因为制度没有制定，上自公侯，下至小吏，都得不到俸禄，而私自收取赋税，贿赂上级，不处理案情。官吏凭藉苛刻残暴建立威严，藉着王莽的禁令，侵掠弱小百姓。富有的人不能自我保护，贫困的人无法生存，群起而成为盗贼，依据山湖的险阻，官吏不能擒获他们而隐瞒实情，事情越闹越大，于是青、徐、荆楚等地往往有上万数的人。战争死亡的，沿边境一带被少数民族所俘虏的，犯法的，饥饿疾病而死的以及人吃人的，这样到王莽被杀之前，天下的户口已经减少了一半。

从征发猪突豨勇后四年，汉朝的军队诛杀了王莽。两年后，世祖

empire's prisons, its convict laborers, and its male serfs, calling them the "courageous pigs and valiant boars." A general tax was levied on officials and commoners alike, to the tune of one-thirtieth of their estimated assets. Furthermore, he issued orders that from the highest noble and official at court, down to yellow-ribbon officials at local level, all should raise horses for the armed forces. The authorities in turn imposed this requirement on the people. The people could not move a hand without encountering some prohibition or other. They hardly had a chance to work their land or tend their mulberry trees, and public works labor exhausted them. Drought and plagues of insects, moreover, followed each other in turn. In addition, because institutions were not well established, salaries were not received, whether you were a noble of the realm or a lowly official. On the other hand, they were appropriating taxes and levies for themselves, and bribing their superiors. Trivial and complex legal cases went undecided. Officers used extreme tyranny to establish their prestige. Taking advantage of Wang Mang's prohibition measures, they harried the weak and lowly. The rich were unable to protect themselves; the poor had no means of survival at all. They rose up as thieves and robbers, living as outlaws in the mountains and marshes, out of reach of the authorities, who, unable to capture them, kept quiet about the true situation. Day by day they spread, like water gathering behind a dam. In the lands of Qingzhou, Xuzhou, and Jingzhou, there were often groups of 10,000 upwards. They perished in fighting and combating, were captured along the frontiers by the barbarians, and sank into crime. Many died of hunger and sickness, and some resorted to cannibalism. By the time Wang Mang had been put to death, the population had fallen by half.

Four years after the "courageous pigs and valiant boars" were sent forth, Han soldiers put Wang Mang to death. Two years later, Emperor Shizu the founder of the Eastern Han, receiving the mandate, abolished the vexatious and exacting punishment code. He

【原文】

苛，复五铢钱，与天下更始。

赞曰：《易》称“裒多益寡，称物平施”，《书》云“茂迁有无”，周有泉府之官。而《孟子》亦非“狗彘食人之食不知敛，野有饿莩而弗知发”。故管氏之轻重，李悝之平籴，弘羊均输，寿昌常平，亦有从徕。顾古为之有数，吏良而令行，故民赖其利，万国作乂。及孝武时，国用饶给，而民不益赋，其次也。至于王莽，制度失中，奸轨弄权，官民俱竭，亡次矣。

——卷二十四下《食货志》第四下

【今译】

承受天命，扫除烦琐和苛刻的刑法，恢复五铢钱，与天下百姓一道除旧布新。

赞曰：《易》上称“把多的取出来给少的，称量物质的多少然后公平地施与”，《书》上说“交易有无”，周朝有泉府的官职，而《孟子》上照样批评“狗和猪吃人吃的食物时不知道收敛，田野中有饿死的人而不知道开仓赈民”。所以管子关于商品、货币、物价的理论，李悝的平籴之法，桑弘羊的调剂运输平抑物价，耿寿昌的设立常平仓，也都是有缘故的。只是古代干这些事都有节度，官吏好，法令得以行使，所以百姓依赖他们得好处，天下都太平。到孝武帝时，国家费用富足，百姓不增加赋税，这就差一点了。到了王莽时，制度失中，为非作歹的人掌握权利，官民都被榨干了，这就更差了。

restored the five-*zhu* cash. Together with all under Heaven he made a new beginning.

Author's comment: The *Book of Changes* sets forth: "Where there is plenty there should be taken an amount to fill scarcity, to bring about a balance in equal distribution." The *Book of Documents* mentions: "exchanging what they had for what they had not." The Zhou had the fiscal office of treasurer for market taxes. Mencius too deplored: " When dogs and swine eat the food of men, you do not know how to impose restriction; when people die of hunger in the fields, you do not know how to open up your granaries for them." Consequently, Master Guan had his theory of thc light and heavy in merchandise, currency and prices; Li Kui had his balanced prices through purchase of grain; Sang Hongyang the equalizing tax substitution, and Geng Shouchang the equalization of prices. Each policy had its reason for existence. But the ancients applied such things methodically and the officials were virtuous, so that orders were actually implemented. Consequently their people depended upon them for benefits, and the empire enjoyed peace. When it came to the time of Emperor Wudi, the state had ample funds to meet its needs, and taxes on the people did not increase; this was worse than before. When it came to Wang Mang's time, the system lost its balance. Evil doers seized and abused their power. Officials and commoners alike were squeezed dry. No other time was as bad as this.

艺文志序

【原文】

昔仲尼没而微言绝，七十子丧而大义乖，故《春秋》分为五，《诗》分为四，《易》有数家之传。战国从衡，真伪分争，诸子之言纷然淆乱。至秦患之，乃燔灭文章，以愚黔首。汉兴，改秦之败，大收篇籍，广开献书之路。迄孝武世，书缺简脱，礼坏乐崩，圣上喟然而称曰："朕甚闵焉！"于是建藏书之策，置写书之官，下及诸子传说，皆充秘府。至成帝时，以书颇散亡，使谒者陈农求遗书于天下，

【今译】

自从孔子死后精要微妙之言也就中断了。七十弟子死后，经典要义的解释也就出现了分歧。所以解释《春秋》分为《左氏传》、《公羊传》、《谷梁传》、《邹氏传》、《夹氏传》五家，解《诗》的分为《毛诗》、《齐诗》、《鲁诗》、《韩诗》四家，解《易》也分为好几家。战国时合纵联横，真伪争论不休，诸子的学说纷纷混乱不清。到了秦始皇对这种状况感到害怕时，他们便烧毁文章，以愚弄百姓。汉朝建立后，革除秦朝的弊端，大规模征收书籍文章，广开献书的门路。到孝武帝时代为止，书籍残缺，竹简脱落，礼节遭到破坏，乐礼被摧毁。皇上喟然而叹道："朕很悲哀这些事！"于是建立藏书的简策，设置了抄书的官员，一直到诸子传说，都充实到秘府。到成帝的时候，由于书籍散失的特别厉害，就派谒者陈农向天下征求分散

Chapter 6

Preface to Bibliographic Treatise

After the death of Confucius, the subtle essence of words was also cut short. After his 70 disciples died, interpretations of the meaning of the classics also diverged. So there were five schools of explanation of the *Spring and Autumn Annals* (*Zuo's Annals*, *Gongyang's Commentary* and *Guliang's Commentary*, *Zou's Commentary* and *Jia's Annals*). There were four schools of understanding the *Book of Odes* ("Mao's edition of the Book of Odes," "Qi's edition," "Lu's edition," and "Han's edition"); and there were several different schools for unlocking the *Book of Changes*. The truth or otherwise of the political stratagems in the Warring States Period were subject to endless contentious debate, and the doctrines of various schools of philosophers were a confusing mix. In the Qin Dynasty, the First Emperor was afraid of this situation, and so burned the literature to keep the people in ignorance. After the founding of the Han Dynasty, they reversed the abuses of Qin, collecting and organizing books and articles on a large scale, thus opening up avenues for donating books.

By the time of Emperor Wudi, books were incomplete, bamboo slips scattered, the rites lost, and music destroyed. The Emperor sighed: "I am very sad about these things!" Hence the establishment of a book collection policy, and the appointment of transcription officials, until various philosophers' doctrines and legends were added to the secret government library. In the reign of Emperor Chengdi, because of the particularly severe loss of books, Imperial Receptionist Chen Nong was sent to solicit scattered and fragmented books from around the land. Guanglu Grand Master

【原文】

诏光禄大夫刘向校经传诸子诗赋，步兵校尉任宏校兵书，太史令尹咸校数术，侍医李柱国校方技。每一书已，向辄条其篇目，撮其指意，录而奏之。会向卒，哀帝复使向子侍中奉车都尉歆卒父业。歆于是总群书而奏其《七略》，故有《辑略》，有《六艺略》，有《诸子略》，有《诗赋略》，有《兵书略》，有《术数略》，有《方技略》。今删其要，以备篇籍。

《易》曰："宓戏氏仰观象于天，俯观法于地，观鸟兽之文，与地之宜，近取诸身，远取诸物，于是始作八卦，以通神明之德，以类万物之情。"至于殷、周之际，纣在上位，逆天暴物，文王以诸侯顺命而行道，天人之占可得而效，于是重《易》六爻，作上下篇。孔氏为之《彖》、《象》、《系辞》、《文言》、《序卦》之属十篇。故曰《易》道深矣，人更三圣，世历三古。及秦燔书，而《易》为筮卜

【今译】

的书籍。命令光禄大夫刘向校经传诸子诗赋，步兵校尉任宏校兵书，太史令尹咸校占卜的书，侍医李柱国校医药之书。每校完一部书，刘向就整理编目，概括其大意，录下来把它上奏给皇帝。当刘向死后，哀帝又派刘向的儿子侍中奉车都尉刘歆完成父亲的事业。刘歆于是总结所有书籍而把《七略》上奏给皇帝，所以就有了《辑略》，有了《六艺略》，《诸子略》，《诗赋略》，《兵书略》，《术数略》，和《方技略》。现在删去多余部分，只留下主要的。以使所收书篇更完备。

《易》说："伏羲氏仰观天象，俯察地理，观察鸟兽的纹彩和土地的适应性，近的就取自自己的身体，远的就取之于万物，于是创造八卦，以通达神明的德性，以模仿万物的性情。"到了殷、周之际，纣王身居帝位，违背天意，摧残万物，文王作为诸侯顺天命而行天道，天人的预测可以得到并且能显现，于是重叠《易》的六爻，作了上下篇。孔子作了《彖》、《象》、《系辞》、《文言》、《序卦》之类共十篇。所以说《易》的道理是很深刻的，经历了伏羲、文王、孔子三代圣人，经历了上、中、下三个远古时代。到秦始皇烧书时，

Liu Xiang was ordered to collate classics and their annotations, the works of various thinkers, and poetry; Infantry Commandant Ren Hong collated military books; Grand Astrologer Yin Xian collated books on divination; and Attending Physician Li Zhuguo medical books. Every complete book was catalogued by Liu Xiang, and he summarized its gist, recording it in a memorial to the Emperor. After Liu Xiang's death, his son Imperial Chariot Defender Liu Xin was ordered by Emperor Aidi to complete his father's endeavor. Liu Xin then summarized all the books and submitted the *Seven Books of Summary* to the Emperor, so there was the "Series of Book Summary," with "Summary of Classics and History," "Summary of Thinkers," "Summary of Poetry," "Art of War Summary," "Divination Summary," and "Summary of Medical Classics." These days we delete the extra parts, leaving only the main body. Articles included make the books more complete.

According to the *Book of Changes*: "Fu Xi observed astronomical phenomena in the sky and looked down at geographical rules on earth, observing the patterns and colors of birds and animals and the adaptability of the land, taken close from his own body, or far from all things, so as to create eight trigrams to communicate the virtues of gods and parallel the trend of events in all earthly matters." In the era between Yin and Zhou, King Zhou was on the throne, contravening the rule of heaven and destroying the myriad of things; King Wen as a vassal prince practiced the Way according to heaven's mandate, so that heaven could be predicted by man's divination and followed. Then he paired up the trigrams to form the hexagrams in the *Book of Changes*, making two texts for each. Confucius made altogether 10 texts of "summaries," "icons," "treatises attached," "classical words," "trigram sequencing," etc. So the truth of the *Book of Changes* is very deep, experienced by three generations of sages (Fu Xi, King Wen, and Confucius), and in three ancient eras. When the Qin Emperor burned the books, the *Book of*

【原文】

之事，传者不绝。汉兴，田(和)[何]传之。讫于宣、元，有施、孟、梁丘、京氏列于学官，而民间有费、高二家之说。刘向以中《古文易经》校施、孟、梁丘经，或脱去“无咎”、“悔亡”，唯费氏经与古文同。

《易》曰：“河出图，雒出书，圣人则之。”故书之所起远矣。至孔子纂焉，上断于尧，下讫于秦，凡百篇，而为之序，言其作意。秦燔书禁学，济南伏生独壁藏之。汉兴亡失，求得二十九篇，以教齐鲁之间。讫孝宣世，有《欧阳》、《大小夏侯氏》，立于学官。《古文尚书》者，出孔子壁中。武帝末，鲁共王坏孔子宅，欲以广其宫，而得《古文尚书》及《礼记》、《论语》、《孝经》凡数十篇，皆古字也。共王往入其宅，闻鼓琴瑟钟磬之音，于是惧，乃止不坏。孔安国者，孔子后也，悉得其书，以考二十九篇，得多十六篇。安国献

【今译】

《易》因为是讲卜筮的事情的，传授的人没有断绝。汉始皇建立后，田何传授《易》。到了宣帝、元帝之时，有施、孟、梁丘、京氏传授《易》学的被列入官府传授之学，而民间有费直、高相两家的学说。刘向以宫中的《古文易经》校施、孟、梁丘经，有的地方脱漏“无咎”、“悔亡”，只有费氏经与古文相同。

《易》上说：“黄河中的龙马驮河图而出，洛水中的神龟背载赤文绿字而出，伏羲和大禹依照图文分别画出八卦图。”所以《尚书》的起源很久远了，到孔子时就加以撰修，上起于尧，下止于秦，共一百篇，并为它作序，说明他写作的意图。秦始皇焚书禁学，济南的伏生独自把它们藏在墙壁中。到了汉朝建立之时大都散失，只找到了二十九篇，用它们在齐、鲁间传教。到了孝宣帝时代，有《欧阳》、《大小夏侯氏》，被立在官府学宫。《古文尚书》被发现在孔子家的壁中。武帝末年，鲁共王拆毁孔子的住宅，打算扩大他的宫殿，却得到了《古文尚书》以及《礼记》、《论语》、《孝经》共几十篇，都是先秦时代的文字。共王进入孔子的住宅，听到演奏琴瑟钟磬的声音，于是感到害怕了，便停止毁房。孔安国是孔子的后代，全部得到这些书，比原先的二十九篇，多出了十六篇。孔安国把它献给了皇上。

Changes continued to be handed down without interruption because it is about divination. After the founding of Han, Tian He taught the *Book of Changes*. In the reigns of emperors Xuandi and Yuandi, there were official scholars like Shi, Meng, Liangqiu, and Jing. But there were also the doctrines of two private teachers, Fei Zhi and Gao Xiang. Liu Xiang compared the ancient *Book of Changes* in the palace collection against the books of Shi, Meng, and Liangqiu, and found that in some places phrases like "without fault," and "peril eliminated" were missing; only Fei's version was the same as the ancient one.

According to the *Book of Changes*: "The Yellow River gave forth the Map, and the Luohe River the Writing, both of which the sages (Fu Xi and Yu) used to work out the eight trigrams." Therefore, the *Book of Documents* is of very ancient origin, before Confucius compiled it, beginning from the period of Yao until the Qin, with a total of 100 essays. He prepared its preface, clarifying the author's intention. The Qin Emperor burned books to forbid learning, but Mr. Fu in Jinan alone hid them in the wall. By the time the Han Dynasty was established, most of the book was lost, only 29 chapters were to be found, and they were used to teach in Qi and Lu. In Emperor Xuandi's reign, "Ouyang's Documents" and "Senior and Junior Xiahou's Documents," were established in the official schools. The ancient *Book of Documents* was found in Confucius' wall. At the end of Emperor Wudi's reign, Prince Gong of Lu demolished the home of Confucius in order to expand his palace, only to find the ancient *Book of Documents*, and the *Book of Rites*, *The Analects of Confucius*, *The Book of Filial Piety*, altogether dozens of pre-Qin classical texts. When the prince went into the residence, he could hear the sound of the zither being plucked and bells being struck, and became so scared that he stopped the demolition. Kong Anguo was a descendant of Confucius, and he obtained all these books, 16 chapters more than the original 29. Kong Anguo presented them to the

【原文】

之。遭巫蛊事，未列于学官。刘向以中古文校欧阳、大小夏侯三家经文，《酒诰》脱简一，《召诰》脱简二。率简二十五字者，脱亦二十五字，简二十二字者，脱亦二十二字，文字异者七百有馀，脱字数十。《书》者，古之号令，号令于众，其言不立具，则听受施行者弗晓。古文读应尔雅，故解古今语而可知也。

《书》曰："诗言志，(哥)[歌]咏言。"故哀乐之心感，而(哥)[歌]咏之声发，诵其言谓之诗，咏其声谓之(哥)[歌]。故古有采诗之官，王者所以观风俗，知得失，自考正也。孔子纯取周诗，上采殷，下取鲁，凡三百五篇，遭秦而全者，以其讽诵，不独在竹帛故也。汉兴，鲁申公为《诗》训故，而齐辕固、燕韩生皆为之传。或取《春秋》，采杂说，咸非其本义。与不得已，鲁最为近之。三家皆列于学官。又有毛公之学，自谓子夏所传，而河间献王好之，未得立。

【今译】

这时逢巫蛊的事情，没有被学校列入。刘向用宫中古文校欧阳、大小夏侯的三家经文，其中《酒诰》脱落一简，《召诰》脱落两简。大致是一简有二十五字的，脱落的也是二十五个字，简上是二十二字的，脱落的也是二十二个字，文字不同的有七百多字，脱落几十个字。《尚书》是古代帝王的号令，号令对于众人，所说的不能晓然明谕，就会使听的人和做的人不明了。古文宣扬的应接近雅正，所以理解了古今语言就可知道《尚书》的意义了。

《书》上说："诗言志，歌咏言。"所以心中有哀乐之感，就会有歌咏之声。把它用语言表达出来就称为诗，把它用歌声表达出来就称为歌。所以古代有收集诗的官员，君王用它观察风俗了解政治的得失，自我加以稽考修正。孔子精选了周诗，上起殷朝，下到鲁国，共有三百零五篇，虽然经历了秦始皇的焚书还能保存下来，是因为它是讽诗并能背诵，不单靠文字流传。汉朝建立后，鲁申公为《诗》进行解释，齐国的辕固、燕国的韩生都为《诗》作解说。有的取自《春秋》，采用众人的杂论，都不是《诗》的本来意思。如不得已而要用《诗》，只有鲁《诗》最与《诗》本义相近。三家都被列于学校。又有毛公的学说，自称是子夏所传授的，而河间献王喜欢它，就没被列于学校。

Emperor. This occurred in the period of hunting sorcerers, so they were not included in the schools. Liu Xiang compared the ancient *Book of Documents* in the palace collection against the books of Ouyang and the two Xiahous, and found a bamboo slip missing from "Decree on the Banning of Wine," and two bamboo slips missing from "Decree of Mr. Zhao." Generally there were 25 characters on a slip, the missing represented 25 characters, while 22 were missing when a slip contained 22 characters. There were over 700 discrepant characters, with dozens missing. The *Book of Documents* was a collection of ancient kings' orders which affected the masses; their content had to be clear and concise, otherwise neither listeners nor implementers would understand clearly. Classical Chinese should be standard, so if you understand the ancient and modern languages, you can know the meaning of the book.

In the *Book of Documents* it says: "Poetry expresses aspiration in words, and songs vocalize the words." So when the heart feels sad or happy, the voice will sing. Expressed in language, it is poetry, while vocalized, it is a song. So in ancient times, there were poetry collecting officials, and the kings used poetry to observe customs, to understand the pros and cons of political situations, and to further continual self-correction.

Confucius selected the cream of Zhou poetry, starting from Yin Dynasty until Lu, a total of 305 poems, which survived the tyranny of Qin because they could be recited vocally, independent of a written form. After the founding of the Han, Master Shen Pei in Lu annotated the *Book of Odes* with contemporary Chinese; Yuan Gu in Qi and Mr. Han Yan also commented on it. Some borrowed from the *Spring and Autumn Annals*, incorporating everyone's comments, and departing from the original meaning of the *Odes*. If you have to use it, Lu's is closest to the original meaning. These three versions were all included in the official schools. There was also Mr. Mao's doctrine, claiming to have been taught by Zixia, and Prince Xian of

【原文】

《易》曰："有夫妇父子君臣上下，礼义有所错。"而帝王质文世有损益，至周曲为之防，事为之制，故曰："礼经三百，威仪三千。"及周之衰，诸侯将逾法度，恶其害己，皆灭去其籍，自孔子时而不具，至秦大坏。汉兴，鲁高堂生传《士礼》十七篇。讫孝宣世，后仓最明。戴德、戴圣、庆普皆其弟子，三家立于学官。《礼古经》者，出于鲁淹中及孔氏，(学七十)[与十七]篇文相似，多三十九篇。及《明堂阴阳》、《王史氏记》所见，多天子诸侯卿大夫之制，虽不能备，犹瘉仓等推《士礼》而致于天子之说。

《易》曰："先王作乐崇德，殷荐之上帝，以享祖考。"故自黄帝下至三代，乐各有名。孔子曰："安上治民，莫善于礼；移风易俗，莫善于乐。"二者相与并行。周衰俱坏，乐尤微眇，以音律为

【今译】

《易》上说："对于夫妇、父子、君臣上下的区别，礼义有所规定。"但帝王的质朴和文采代代有增有减，到周朝时就规定得极为细致，每一件事都要有制度，所以说："礼经有三百条，礼仪的细节有三千条。"等到周朝衰落后，诸侯超越礼法的限制，厌恶礼法不利于己，都把它们抛弃毁掉了。到孔子时就不完备了，到秦国时，就遭到更大的破坏。到了汉朝，鲁国高堂生传授《士礼》十七篇。到孝宣帝时为止，后仓的最为明晰。戴德、戴圣、庆普都是他的学生，三家都被列在学校。《礼古经》出现在鲁国的淹中和孔氏家中，同十七篇的文章相似，多出了三十九篇。至于《明堂阴阳》、《王史氏记》上所见到的，大多是天子诸侯卿大夫的制度，虽然不能详备，但仍比后仓等人推论《士礼》而向天子陈说的学说多。

《易》上说："前代帝王制作音乐崇尚道德，隆重地进献祭品上帝，供奉祖先。"所以从黄帝以下到三代，乐曲都各自有名称。孔子说："安定国家治理百姓，没有比礼更好的，改变风俗，没有比乐更好的。"礼和乐相辅相成。周朝衰落后，礼和乐都被破坏了，音乐之

Hejian liked it. Even so was not included in the schools.

It says in the *Book of Changes*, "As regards the distinction of superior and inferior between husband and wife, father and son, monarch and subject, rites and morality are somewhat standardized." But the monarchs' character and literary accomplishments increased or decreased from generation to generation, until the Zhou Dynasty when the provisions were very detailed, and there was a system for everything, hence "There are 300 books on the rites, and 3,000 rules of etiquette." After the decline of Zhou, princes went beyond the limits of propriety, so they hated being hide-bound by etiquette, abandoned the rules and destroyed the books. They were no longer complete by the time of Confucius, and under Qin, even worse destruction was wrought. After the rise of Han, Mr. Gaotang in Lu taught "Rites of Gentlemen," in 17 chapters. In the reign of Emperor Xuandi, Hou Cang's teachings were the most illuminating. Dai De, Dai Sheng, and Qing Pu were all his students, and all three were included in the schools. *The Ancient Ceremony Book* came from Yanzhong and Confucius' family in Lu, similar to the 17 chapters, but with 39 extra chapters. As for those found in *Yin and Yang in the Hall of Enlightened Rule* and *The Records of Mr. Wangshi*, they dealt mostly with the system concerning the monarch, princes, chamberlains and grand masters; although not detailed, they were still better than what Hou Cang and others had inferred from "Rites of Gentlemen," and were presented to the Emperor.

According to the *Book of Changes*: "The former kings produced music and exalted virtue, sacrificing it ceremoniously to the Heavenly Emperor, and worshipping his ancestors." Therefore, from the Yellow Emperor to the following three dynasties, music bore individual titles. Confucius said: "For securing the repose of superiors and the good order of the people, there is nothing better than the rules of propriety. For changing their manners and altering their customs, there is nothing better than music." Ritual and music

【原文】

节，又为郑卫所乱，故无遗法。汉兴，制氏以雅乐声律，世在乐官，颇能纪其铿锵鼓舞，而不能言其义。六国之君，魏文侯最为好古，孝文时得其乐人窦公，献其书，乃《周官•大宗伯》之《大司乐》章也。武帝时，河间献王好儒，与毛生等共采《周官》及诸子言乐事者，以作《乐记》，献八佾之舞，与制氏不相远。其内史丞王定传之，以授常山王禹。禹，成帝时为谒者，数言其义，献二十四卷记。刘向校书，得《乐记》二十三篇，与禹不同，其道寖以益微。

古之王者世有史官，君举必书，所以慎言行，昭法式也。左史记言，右史记事，事为《春秋》，言为《尚书》，帝王靡不同之。周室既微，载籍残缺，仲尼思存前圣之业，乃称曰："夏礼吾能言之，杞

【今译】

理尤其精妙，因为它的节奏在音律，又加上被郑、卫之音所扰乱，所以没有遗传下来的规则。汉朝建立后，制氏认为雅乐声律，世代都在乐官，颇能记忆一些音乐的铿锵鼓舞的音节，但不能说出它的含义。六国的君主中，魏文侯最崇尚古乐，孝文帝的时候得到他的乐人窦公，献上他的书，是《周官·大宗伯》中的《大司乐》章。武帝的时候，河间献王喜欢儒术，同毛生等人共同采集《周官》和诸子学说中论说音乐的部分，撰写成《乐记》，献上八佾之舞，同制氏相差不远。内史丞王定传授《乐记》，把它授给常山的王禹。王禹在成帝时任谒者官，几次论说它的意义，献上二十四卷的记载。刘向校书，得到二十三篇的《乐记》，同王禹的不同，这方面的学问越来越衰亡了。

古代帝王世代都有史官，君王的举动一定加以记录，其目的是以此使君主言行谨慎，其言行可为民之法则。左侧史官记其言，右侧史官记其行，行动记下来就是《春秋》，语言记下来就是《尚书》，帝王没有不跟这相同的。周室衰败后，书籍破残损缺，仲尼想保存前代圣人的业绩，就说："夏礼我能说出来，但杞国的就不能全面验

supplemented and complemented each other. After the decline of Zhou, both were destroyed. Since music was especially delicate, as its tempo was regulated by rhythm, and the vulgar sounds of Zheng and Wei disturbed the tradition, there were no rules passed down. When Han was established, Mr. Zhi used elegant music to regulate the sound. The Zhi family had worked for generations in the office of music, so they remembered quite well some of the sonorous syllables of music, if not what they meant. Among the monarchs of the Six States, Marquis Wen of Wei had the most respect for ancient things. His musician Mr. Dou was found in the reign of Emperor Wendi and he presented his book, which was the Musician-in-Chief chapter in "Minister of Rites" in *Ritual of Zhou*. In the reign of Emperor Wudi, Prince Xian of Hejian liked Confucianism, and, together with Mr. Mao, collected information on music in *Ritual of Zhou* and the theory of various philosophers, and compiled it as *Records of Music*. He presented eight-yi dance, quite similar to Mr. Zhi's system. His secretary Wang Ding inherited it and handed it down to Wang Yu of Changshan. Wang Yu, the imperial receptionist in the reign of Emperor Chengdi, talked of its meaning several times, before presenting 24 chapters of *Records*. Liu Xiang collated books, and acquired 23 chapters of the *Records of Music*, different from those of Wang Yu, so the knowledge in this area had declined.

Ancient monarchs kept historians under every ruler, and the king's actions had to be recorded; the purpose of such records being to make the monarch prudent in words and deeds, and to serve as the people's example or warning. The left scribe noted his words; the right one recorded his acts. The documented acts formed the *Spring and Autumn Annals*, while the words were the *Book of Documents*, and the monarchs did not deviate from this. After the House of Zhou declined, the books were damaged or missing, so Confucius wanted to save the cause of previous generations of sages, saying: "I am able to describe the ceremonies of the Xia Dynasty,

【原文】

不足征也；殷礼吾能言之，宋不足征也。文献不足故也，足则吾能征之矣。”以鲁周公之国，礼文备物，史官有法，故与左丘明观其史记，据行事，仍人道，因兴以立功，就败以成罚，假日月以定历数，借朝聘以正礼乐。有所褒讳贬损，不可书见，口授弟子，弟子退而异言。丘明恐弟子各安其意，以失其真，故论本事而作传，明夫子不以空言说经也。《春秋》所贬损大人当世君臣，有威权势力，其事实皆形于传，是以隐其书而不宣，所以免时难也。及末世口说流行，故有《公羊》、《穀梁》、《邹》、《夹》之传。四家之中，《公羊》、《穀梁》立于学官，邹氏无师，夹氏未有书。

《论语》者，孔子应答弟子时人及弟子相与言而接闻于夫子之语也。当时弟子各有所记。夫子既卒，门人相与辑而论纂，故谓之《论语》。

【今译】

证了；殷礼我能说一说，但宋国的就不能全面考证了。这是文献不够的缘故，文献足够的话，我就能加以考证了。”因为鲁国是周公的封国，礼节文采都完备，史官有法度，所以让左丘明观看了他们历史的记载，根据所行的事情，依照人道，用成就来建立功赏，根据失败来加以责罚，藉日月来确定节气的时间，藉诸侯朝见天子来端正礼乐。有所隐讳贬损的事情，不能见之于书籍，就用口传授给弟子，弟子回去后所说的就互不相同了。左丘明怕他的弟子们各自按照自己的见解，以致失去真意，所以研究本来的事实而加以解释，倡明孔子是不用空言来解说经文的。《春秋》所贬损的当代君臣，有权威势力，他们的事情就写进了解释中，因此这本书就被隐藏起来了，没有宣扬，用来避免遭到当时的灾难。等到末世人们口头传说流行开来，便有《公羊》、《穀梁》、《邹》、《夹》的传。这四家之中，《公羊传》、《穀梁传》两家被列在皇家学校讲解，邹氏没有老师，夹氏没有书。

《论语》这部书，是记载孔子回答其弟子及时人提问，以及其门徒相互问答的一部书。当时弟子对于孔子的言行各自有所记录。孔子卒后，门人相互收集并记下来，所以称为《论语》。汉朝建立后，有

but cannot sufficiently attest to those of Qi. I am able to describe the ceremonies of Yin, but cannot sufficiently attest to those of Song. I cannot do so because of the insufficiency of the documents. If those were sufficient, I could adduce them in support of my words." Since the State of Lu was ruled by the Duke of Zhou, its ritual system and sacrificial tools were complete, and its historians were methodical, so they showed Zuo Qiuming their historical records. Based on the things done, in line with humane rightness they established rewards for meritorious achievements and formulated punishments for transgressions. They ascertained their calendar by the sun and the moon, and corrected their ritual and music by the princes' audience with the monarch. Some derogatory or commendatory comments had to be concealed, not be seen in the books, so they were passed on to the disciples verbally, who went back and said different things. Qiuming was afraid that his disciples followed their own opinions, losing the true meaning, so he explained by studying the facts, expounding that Confucius did not explain the classics just by empty words. The targets of derogatory comments in the *Spring and Autumn Annals* were the contemporary monarchs and courtiers, with authoritarian power, so they were written into the explanations. Thus this book was hidden from public view, uncirculated, so as to avoid summary disaster. Oral tradition became popular at the end of the dynasty, circulated as commentaries of Gongyang, Guliang, Zou, and Jia. Of the four, two explanations of Gongyang and Guliang were included in the official schools; Zou's had no teacher, and Jia's had no books.

The Analects of Confucius is a record of the Sage's answers to questions from his disciples and other contemporaries, and a book of questions and his answers recorded from conversations among the disciples. At the time, the disciples recorded the Sage's words and deeds separately. When Confucius died, the disciples collected them from each other and wrote down what we call the "Analects." After

【原文】

汉兴，有齐、鲁之说。传《齐论》者，昌邑中尉王吉、少府宋畸、御史大夫贡禹、尚书令五鹿充宗、胶东庸生，唯王阳名家。传《鲁论语》者，常山都尉龚奋、长信少府夏侯胜、丞相韦贤、鲁扶卿、前将军萧望之、安昌侯张禹，皆名家。张氏最后而行于世。

《孝经》者，孔子为曾子陈孝道也。夫孝，天之经，地之义，民之行也。举大者言，故曰《孝经》。汉兴，长孙氏、博士江翁、少府后仓、谏大夫翼奉、安昌侯张禹传之，各自名家。经文皆同，唯孔氏壁中古文为异。"父母生之，续莫大焉"，"故亲生之膝下"，诸家说不安处，古文字读皆异。

《易》曰："上古结绳以治，后世圣人易之以书契，百官以治，万民以察，盖取诸《夬》。""夬，扬于王庭"，言其宣扬于王者朝廷，其用最大也。古者八岁入小学，故《周官》保氏掌养国子，教

【今译】

《齐论语》和《鲁论语》两家。传授《齐论语》的，有昌邑中尉王吉、少府宋畸、御史大夫贡禹、尚书令五鹿充宗、胶东庸生等人，只有王阳是名家。传授《鲁论语》的，有常山都尉龚奋、长信少府夏侯胜、丞相韦贤、鲁扶卿、前将军萧望之、安昌侯张禹，都是名家。张氏在最后，因而流行于世。

《孝经》是孔子对曾子讲解孝道的著作。孝道，是天经地义之事，是人人应尽之事。从大的方面来说，所以叫《孝经》。在汉朝，有长孙氏、博士江翁、少府后仓、谏大夫翼奉、安昌侯张禹传授《孝经》，各成一家之言。各家经文都相同，只有孔氏壁中的古文不同。"父母生之，续莫大焉"，"故亲生之膝下"，这两句各家的说法都不合适，古文的字和断句都不同。

《易》上说："上古时代用结绳的办法记事，后代圣人改用文字记事，百官用来治事，万民用来辨别事物，这都是取之于《易经》中六十四卦中的《夬》卦。""夬，用于王庭决断事物"，是说它能宣扬在君王的朝廷，用处最大。古代的人八岁进入小学，所以《周官》

the founding of Han, there appeared two schools - "Qi Analects" and "Lu Analects." The scholars who taught "Qi Analects" included princedom officer Wang Ji (alias Yang) of Changyi, Chamberlain for the Palace Revenue Song Ji, Censor-in-Chief Gong Yu, Director of the Imperial Secretariat Wulu Chongzong, and Mr. Yong of Jiaodong, but only Wang Yang was famous. Those who taught "Lu Analects" were Defender of Changshan Gong Fen, Chamberlain for the Changxin Palace Revenue Xiahou Sheng, Prime Minister Wei Xian, Fu Qing of Lu, Front General Xiao Wangzhi, Marquis of Anchang Zhang Yu, all of whom were famous. Zhang Yu was the last of these, so he was very popular in the land.

The Classic of Filial Piety was Confucius' treatise on filial piety directed to his student Zeng Zi. Filial piety is the constant method of Heaven and the righteousness of Earth, and the practical duty of Man. In broad terms, the treatise was called *The Classic of Filial Piety*. In the Han dynasty, there were Mr. Zhangsun, Erudite Jiang Weng, Chamberlain for the Palace Revenues Hou Cang, Grand Master of Remonstrance Yi Feng, and Marquis of Anchang Zhang Yu who taught *The Classic of Filial Piety*. All of these were famous. The various versions were the same, except for the classical version discovered in the wall of Confucius' home. The sentences "The son derives his life from his parents, and no greater gift could possibly be transmitted," and "the feeling of affection grows up at the parents' knees," are discrepant, as are the actual Chinese characters used and the punctuation.

According to the *Book of Changes*: "In remote antiquity, people kept records by tying knots, and later sages shifted to writing as notes, so that officials administered and civilians identified things by them, which was takenfrom 'Guai' or resolution, one of the 64 hexagrams." "'Guai' means decision for things at the royal court," that is, it could be promoted at the king's court, and hence most useful. In ancient times, eight-year-olds entered primary school, so

【原文】

之六书，谓象形、象事、象意、象声、转注、假借，造字之本也。汉兴，萧何草律，亦著其法，曰："太史试学童，能讽书九千字以上，乃得为史。又以六体试之，课最者以为尚书御史史书令史。吏民上书，字或不正，辄举劾。"六体者，古文、奇字、篆书、隶书、缪篆、虫书。皆所以通知古今文字，摹印章，书幡信也。古制，书必同文，不知则阙，问诸故老。至于衰世，是非无正，人用其私。故孔子曰："吾犹及史之阙文也，今亡矣夫！"盖伤其寖不正。《史籀篇》者，周时史官教学童书也，与孔氏壁中古文异体。《苍颉》七章者，秦丞相李斯所作也；《爰历》六章者，车府令赵高所作也；《博学》七章者，太史令胡母敬所作也；文字多取《史籀篇》，而篆体复颇

【今译】

的保氏掌管着教养国君之子的事，教给他们六书，称象形、象事、象意、象声、转注、假借，它们是造字的根本所在。汉朝建立后，萧何创造了律令，也写了这样的条文，说："太史考试学童，能够背诵九千字以上书的人，才能当史。再用六体来考试，成绩最好的任命为尚书御史史书令史。官民上书，字有不端正的，就要揭发举报。"六体，就是古文、奇字、篆书、隶书、缪篆、虫书，都是用来认识古今文字，摹刻印章，书写幡作为信物的。依据古代制度，书一定要同文字，不知道的暂时空缺，然后来求教年老者。到了衰落的时代，是非没有正确答案，人们都根据自己的想法来造字。所以孔子说："我还赶上了史书中的缺疑不写的地方，现在连缺疑不写的地方也没有了！"大概是对字渐渐不正确而感到悲哀。《史籀篇》，是周朝时的史官用来教学童的书，字与孔氏壁中的古文字体相异。《苍颉》七章，是秦朝丞相李斯所作的；《爰历》六章，是车府令赵高所作；《博学》七章，是太史令胡母敬所作；文字大多取自《史籀篇》，但篆体又差别很大，造就是所谓的秦篆。这时候已开始创造隶书，

the Palace Protector of *Ritual of Zhou* was in charge of upbringing the sons of the monarch, teaching them six categories of Chinese characters, i.e. pictographs, self-explanatory characters, associative compounds, onomatopoeia, transfer simulation, phonetic loans; they are the basis of character formation. With the founding of Han, Xiao He created laws, among which was this provision: "The grand astrologer tests children, and those who can read out 9,000 characters or more may become a historian. Then he tests them in six calligraphic styles, and those with the best scores are appointed imperial secretary, censor, and secretary for history books. The officials and people who write reports in poor handwriting will be exposed and impeached." The six calligraphic styles were classical, variant characters, seal script, official script, cursive seal, and insect script, which were used to understand past and contemporary texts, inscribe seals, and write the tally banners. According to the ancient system, books should be written in the same writing system throughout. If one did not know a character, it should be left blank temporarily, until an elder could advise. As to the declining era, there was no correct version to crib from, so people formed characters according to their own ideas. This caused Confucius to lament: "Even in my early days, a historiographer would leave a blank in his text. Now, alas! There are no such things." Probably he was sad that the orthography was getting more and more slipshod. *Historian Zhou's Reader* was a history book for teaching children in the Zhou dynasty, with a calligraphic style different from the classical style found in Confucius' wall. *Cang Jie* in seven chapters was created by the Qin Prime Minister Li Si; *Yuan Li* in six chapters was created by Chief of Livery Zhao Gao; *Erudite* in seven chapters was created by Grand Astrologer Humu Jing; the characters were mostly taken from *Historian Zhou's Reader*, but they varied greatly from seal script, hence the so-called Qin lesser seal script. At this time, they had begun to create the official script, originating in the

【原文】

异，所谓秦篆者也。是时始造隶书矣，起于官狱多事，苟趋省易，施之于徒隶也。汉(书)[兴]，闾里书师合《苍颉》、《爰历》、《博学》三篇，断六十字以为一章，凡五十五章，并为《苍颉篇》。武帝时司马相如作《凡将篇》，无复字。元帝时黄门令史游作《急就篇》，成帝时将作大匠李长作《元尚篇》，皆《苍颉》中正字也。《凡将》则颇有出矣。至元始中，征天下通小学者以百数，各令记字于庭中。扬雄取其有用者以作《训纂篇》，顺续《苍颉》，又易《苍颉》中重复之字，凡八十九章。臣复续扬雄作十(二)[三]章，凡一百二章，无复字，六艺群书所载略备矣。《苍颉》多古字，俗师失其读，宣帝时征齐人能正读者，张敞从受之，传至外孙之子杜林，为作训故，并列焉。

六艺之文：《乐》以和神，仁之表也；《诗》以正言，义之用也；《礼》以明体，明者著见，故无训也；《书》以广听，知之术

【今译】

起源于官府中诉讼案件很多，为了方便省事，这种简便的文字首先用于处理徒隶事务的公文。汉朝建立后，乡间的教师就合集成《苍颉》、《爰历》、《博学》三篇，把六十字断为一章，共有五十五章，合并而成《苍颉篇》。武帝时司马相如作《凡将篇》，没有重字。元帝时黄门令史游作《急就篇》，成帝时将作大匠李长作《元尚篇》，都是《苍颉》中的正字。《凡将篇》则有很大的出入。到元始年中，征召天下懂得文字的人以百计，各命他们在朝廷中记字。扬雄选取其中有用的来作《训纂篇》，顺着连接《苍颉篇》，又换了《苍颉篇》中重复的字，共成八十九章。臣又继承扬雄的作了十三章，共成一百零二章，没有重复的字，六艺和各书所记载的字大致都齐全了。《苍颉篇》中多古字，平庸的教师弄错了它的断句，宣帝时就征召齐国的能纠正断句的人，张敞去接受传授，传到他的外孙的儿子杜林时，他就作了解释，与《苍颉篇》并行。

六艺的文章中：《乐》用来调节精神，是仁的表现；《诗》用来端正言语，是义的运用；《礼》用来明确规矩，明确了就容易见得着，所以没有注释；《书》用来推广道德，是求知的方法；《春秋》

many court cases in government, in order to facilitate proceedings, so this simple calligraphic style was first used in processing the documents of prisoners. After the Han Dynasty was established, the provincial teachers amalgamated three books - *Cang Jie*, *Yuan Li*, and *Erudite* - partitioning 60 characters off as a separate chapter, to make a total of 55 chapters, all combined as *Book of Cang Jie*. In the reign of Emperor Wudi, Sima Xiangru compiled *Book of Fanjiang*, containing not one repeated character. In the reign of Emperor Yuandi, Director of Eunuch Attendants Shi You compiled *Book of Improvisation*, and in the reign of Chengdi, Chamberlain for the Palace Buildings Li Chang compiled *Book of Yuanshang*, both in the same script as *Cang Jie*. But *Book of Fanjiang* contained very different characters. During the Yuanshi reign period (1-5 AD), hundreds of school graduates were recruited from all over the land, and ordered to take notes in the Imperial Court. Yang Xiong selected the useful characters to compile the 89-chapter *Book of Character Explanation*, to supplement *Book of Cang Jie* by replacing its repeated characters. Your humble servant supplemented Yang Xiong's work with 13 further chapters, to make it 102 chapters, with no repeated characters, and the characters recorded in written texts of the six arts are now generally complete. The *Book of Cang Jie* contains many classical characters, and mediocre teachers got the punctuation wrong. So in the reign of Empeor Xuandi, there was a recruitment of Qi people who could read correctly, and Zhang Chang went to learn from them; he then taught his own disciples, down to his great-grandson Du Lin, who explained the texts in a parallel textbook to *Book of Cang Jie*.

The texts of the six arts comprise: *Book of Music* used to adjust the spirit, an expression of benevolence; *Book of Odes* used to correct speech, the application of righteousness; *Book of Rites* used to clarify rules, since what is clear is easy to prove, and no commentary is necessary; *Book of Documents* used to promote

【原文】

也；《春秋》以断事，信之符也。五者，盖五常之道，相须而备，而《易》为之原。故曰"易不可见，则乾坤或几乎息矣"，言与天地为终始也。至于五学，世有变改，犹五行之更用事焉。古之学者耕且养，三年而通一艺，存其大体，玩经文而已，是故用日少而畜德多，三十而五经立也。后世经传既已乖离，博学者又不思多闻阙疑之义，而务碎义逃难，便辞巧说，破坏形体；说五字之文，至于二三万言。后进弥以驰逐，故幼童而守一艺，白首而后能言；安其所习，毁所不见，终以自蔽。此学者之大患也。序六艺为九种。

儒家者流，盖出于司徒之官，助人君顺阴阳明教化者也。游文于六经之中，留意于仁义之际，祖述尧舜，宪章文武，宗师仲尼，以重

【今译】

用来判断处理问题，是信用的标志。这部书，体现仁、义、礼、智、信，相互补充，不可或缺，而《易》又为其本源。所以说"《易》的意义不知道，那么乾坤差不多就要停息了"，这是说同天地共始终的。至于五学，世代有变化，就像五行交替行事。古代的学者边耕种边修养，三年而通晓一艺，保留它的大致内容，研究经文罢了，因此所用的时候少而积累的德行就多。三十五岁经就通了。后代的经和传已经互相矛盾，博学的人又不思考多听多疑的含义，而追求用支离破碎的僻义去逃避别人的诘难，牵强附会，巧为立说，破坏文字的形体；解说五个字的文章，达到二三万言。后来的人相互攀比，所以幼童抱守一艺，到头发白后才能讲说。安于他所学习的，诋毁他所没有见过的，最终自己欺骗了自己。这是学者的大患。总括六艺为九种。

儒家学派，其源头来自掌管教化的司徒，其宗旨是辅助君主顺应阴阳提倡教化。它研习六经，专心于仁义之间，遵循尧舜之道，效法文武，以孔子为宗师，来显示他们言辞的分量，其道最为高深。孔子

knowledge, the way to pursue wisdom; *Spring and Autumn Annals* used to make judgments on matters, a sign of trust. These books reflect the five constant virtues of benevolence, righteousness, propriety, wisdom, and trust, none of which can exist without the other; and the *Book of Changes* was their origin. Hence, "Without understanding the *Book of Changes*, the universe of *qian* and *kun* would almost cease," which means that it starts and ends with heaven and earth. As to the five learning sections of the five books, there are changes from generation to generation, as the five elements act alternately. The ancient scholars cultivated themselves while farming, becoming proficient in an art in three years, but they studied the written texts of the books, retaining their general content at most. This way they could accumulate more virtue in less time. By the time they were 35, they were proficient in the five books. In later generations, since the commentaries were contradictory to the books, scholars were reluctant to ponder the meaning of Confucius' teaching "hearing much and putting aside the points in doubt," but pursued the fragmented meaning to avoid being criticized. They used far-fetched ideas to establish clever opinions that did violence to the form and substance of the texts; they explained five characters with texts of up to 30,000 characters. The later they came to the field, the more persistent they were; so one could come to an art as a child and not be able to say anything about it until one was a graybeard. Content in their scholarship, they maligned what they had not seen, and ultimately fooled themselves. This is the scourge of scholars. All in all, the six arts are a variety of nine.

The Confucian schools originated with ministers in charge of moral education; their purpose is to assist the monarch in conforming to *yin* and *yang* and promoting enlightenment. They include study of the six classics, but concentrate on benevolence and righteousness, following the way of Yao and Shun and the example of Kings Wen and Wu. They look to Confucius as the Master, to

【原文】

其言，于道最为高。孔子曰："如有所誉，其有所试。"唐虞之隆，殷周之盛，仲尼之业，已试之效者也。然惑者既失精微，而辟者又随时抑扬，违离道本，苟以哗众取宠。后进循之，是以《五经》乖析，儒学寖衰，此辟儒之患。

道家者流，盖出于史官，历记成败存亡祸福古今之道，然后知秉要执本，清虚以自守，卑弱以自持，此君人南面之术也。合于尧之克攘，《易》之嗛嗛，一谦而四益，此其所长也。及放者为之，则欲绝去礼学，兼弃仁义，曰独任清虚可以为治。

阴阳家者流，盖出于羲和之官，敬顺昊天，历象日月星辰，敬授民时，此其所长也。及拘者为之，则牵于禁忌，泥于小数，舍人事而任鬼神。

法家者流，盖出于理官，信赏必罚，以辅礼制。《易》曰"先王

【今译】

说："如果要对人有所赞誉，就要对他有所考察。"唐、虞的鼎盛，殷周的兴旺，已经证明行之有效。但不甚明智者已经不知其精妙细微之处，而偏邪的人又随着时代进退，违背偏离道的根本，只是用来博取众人的尊敬。后来的人以他们为榜样，因此《五经》互相矛盾，儒家学说渐渐衰微，这就是见闻寡陋的儒生的弊端。

道家学派，应当是由史官演化而来，道家著作记载历代成败存亡祸福之道，但能秉要执本，清净虚无以保持自我节操，谦卑柔弱以保护自我，这是君王统治之术。与尧的自我约束谦让，《易》的含恨隐忍相合，能一谦而得到天益、地益、神益、人益，这是他们的长处。等到放荡的人来修道，就想全部抛弃礼仪，并放弃仁义，说只要清净虚无就可以太平。

阴阳家学派，出于天文历法之官，他们敬顺上天，观测推算日月星辰的运行，谨慎地告诉给人民以农作的时间，这是他们的长处。等到拘泥的人来实行，就会受到禁忌的牵掣，拘泥于小的技能，放弃人事而从事于迷信鬼神之事。

法家学派，起源于法官，主张有功者必赏，有罪者必罚，以刑法

show the weight of their words, and their Way is the highest and most profound. Confucius said: "If I commend a man, there must be ground for it in my examination of that individual." The prosperity of Tang and Yu, the flourishing of Yin and Zhou, and the feats of Confucius, have effectively been proven. But the not very wise have lost the exquisite nuances, and the prejudiced advance or retreat with the times and, in reversal or deviation from the fundamental way, aiming only to win popular respect through provocative statements. Later people followed their example, so the "Five Classics" became contradictory, and Confucianism gradually declined, creating trouble for the scholars of narrow focus.

Taoism probably evolved via the official historians, recording the Way of success or otherwise, survival or otherwise, good or bad fortune of the ancient dynasties; but the monarch's art of ruling is to grasp the fundamental factor, seek a peaceful and quiet empty mind to keep personal integrity, to protect the self by maintaining weak and humble. Their strength lay in the self-restraint and humility of Yao, forbearance to swallow anger as in the *Book of Changes*, combining to achieve benefit for heaven, earth, gods, and man. Then the dissolute came along, intent on revising the Way, abandoning all rites, and discarding benevolence and righteousness, claiming that they could bring peace and order simply by means of a peaceful, quiet, and empty mind.

The *Yin-Yang* School came from the officials in charge of the astronomical calendar. Their strength was that they revered heaven, observed and predicted the turning of the sun, the moon and the stars, and told people the detailed times for farming activities. As to over-formalistic people implementing this, they would be bogged down by taboos in the detailed skills, concentrating on supernatural matters at the expense of human affairs.

Legalism originated with the judges, and advocates that due rewards and punishment should be meted out without fail, to aid

【原文】

以明罚饬法”，此其所长也。及刻者为之，则无教化，去仁爱，专任刑法而欲以致治，至于残害至亲，伤恩薄厚。

名家者流，盖出于礼官。古者名位不同，礼亦异数。孔子曰：“必也正名乎！名不正则言不顺，言不顺则事不成。”此其所长也。及警者为之，则苟钩(釽)[鈲]析乱而已。

墨家者流，盖出于清庙之守。茅屋采椽，是以贵俭；养三老五更，是以兼爱；选士大射，是以上贤；宗祀严父，是以右鬼；顺四时而行，是以非命；以孝视天下，是以上同：此其所长也。及蔽者为之，见俭之利，因以非礼，推兼爱之意，而不知别亲疏。

从横家者流，盖出于行人之官。孔子曰：“诵《诗》三百，使于四方，不能专对，虽多亦奚以为？”又曰：“使乎，使乎!”言其当

【今译】

辅佐礼制。《易》上说“前代君王以严明的刑罚来整顿法制”，这是他们的长处。等到刻薄的人来施行，就不要教化，放弃仁爱，只施行刑法而想达到太平，以至于残害至亲，恩将仇报。

名家学派，起源于礼官。古代身份地位不同，所行礼仪亦有区别。孔子说：“一定要端正名分！名不正那么言就不通，言不通事就不成。”这是他们的长处。等到那些专门揭发他人隐私的人来从事名家活动，就只能是增添乱子罢了。

墨家学说，起源于看守宗庙之官。这种人住在以柞木作椽子的茅草屋，因而崇尚俭朴；赡养三老五更，因此他们博爱；挑选士子举行大射礼，因此他们尊重贤能的人；祭祀祖宗，尊敬父辈，因此他们迷信鬼神；顺应四季而行，因此他们不信命运；以孝来昭示天下，因此他们对他人则求其同：这是他们的长处。可是愚者对此，就会因节俭的利益来反对礼节，推行博爱，但不知道分别亲疏。

纵横家学派，当出自接待贵客之官。孔子说：“背诵了《诗》三百首，出使四方，不能随机应对，即使背诵的《诗》再多，又有什么用呢？”又说：“使者啊，使者！”是说使者应当权衡事情，见机

the ritual system. According to the *Book of Changes*:"The previous kings used strict penalties to rectify the legal system." This is their strength. When it comes to the unkind people who implement it, they do not educate, they cast aside kindheartedness, intent only on achieving peace through the criminal law, to the extent that they will even harm their loved ones, maltreat and hurt their benefactors.

The School of Logicians originated with the rite ministers. In ancient times, if a name or status was different, the rite was also different. Confucius said: "What is necessary is to rectify names! If names be not correct, then language is not in accordance with the truth of things. If language be not in accordance with the truth of things, affairs cannot be carried on to success." This is their strength. As to the nitpickers, they simply engage in roundabout fragmenting and sophistry, only adding trouble.

Mohism originated with the official guards of the quiet ancestral temples. Such people live in thatched cottages with rafters of oak, which means a frugal life-style. They support the Three Old Folk and Five Retired Officials, so they show universal love. They hold an archery ceremony to select the scholar, so they respect the worthy elite of the people. They worship their ancestors, respect their fathers, so they stand in awe of ghosts. They act by the four seasons, so they do not believe in fate. They declare filial piety to the world, so they seek harmony. This is their strength. But at the less informed end of the scale, they see the benefit of frugality at the expense of what is fitting; they push universal love, but do not distinguish close connections from distant ones.

Strategism came from officials in charge of reception of guests. Confucius said: "Though a man may be able to recite the three hundred *Odes*, yet if, when sent to any quarter on a mission, he cannot give his replies unassisted, notwithstanding the extent of his learning, of what practical use is it?" He also said: "Messenger, messengers!" meaning that a messenger should weigh the matter,

【原文】

权事制宜，受命而不受辞，此其所长也。及邪人为之，则上诈谖而弃其信。

杂家者流，盖出于议官。兼儒、墨，合名、法，知国体之有此，见王治之无不贯，此其所长也。及荡者为之，则漫羡而无所归心。

农家者流，盖出于农稷之官。播百谷，劝耕桑，以足衣食，故八政一曰食，二曰货。孔子曰“所重民食”，此其所长也。及鄙者为之，以为无所事圣王，欲使君臣并耕，誖上下之序。

小说家者流，盖出于稗官。街谈巷语，道听涂说者之所造也。孔子曰：“虽小道，必有可观者焉，致远恐泥，是以君子弗为也。”然亦弗灭也。闾里小知者之所及，亦使缀而不忘。如或一言可采，此亦刍荛狂夫之议也。

诸子十家，其可观者九家而已。皆起于王道既微，诸侯力政，时君世主，好恶殊方，是以九家之(说)[术]蠭出并作，各引一端，崇其

【今译】

行事，接受使命但不接受言辞，这是他们的长处。等到邪恶的人来加以从事，就会重在弄虚作假而抛弃诚信。

杂家学派，当出于议事之官。兼有儒家、墨家，融合了名、法，懂得国家体制有这些家和派，预见治国没有不贯通，这是他们的长处。等到放纵的人来参与，就会漫无边际而无所依托。

农家学派，当起源于主管农业之官。播种百谷，致力耕作和蚕桑，以求丰富衣和食，所以八政中一是食，二是货。孔子说“所重视的是百姓的食物”，这是他们的长处。等到鄙陋的人来主办此事，认为不用事奉圣王，想让君臣一同耕作，打乱了上下等级的秩序。

小说家学派，应当出于收集民间传说的小官。是由街谈巷语，道听途说的人所制造的。孔子说：“即使是小道，也一定有可观的地方，向深远处发展，恐怕就会拘泥，因此君子不干。”但也没有消灭。民间有小智慧的人来进行传播，也使它连续不被遗忘。如果有时有一句话可采用，这也是草野狂夫的议论。

诸子十家，其中可观的只有九家罢了。都兴起在王道衰微，诸侯主持政治的时候，当世君主，好恶相当悬殊，因这九个学派群起并

use his discretion, accept the mission but do not accept the rhetoric. This is their strength. As to the evil people engaged in this, they will abandon trust and focus on fraud.

The Eclectics School comes from the officials of remonstration. Synthesizing Confucianism and Mohism, combining the logician and legalist schools, they understand that all exist in the state system, and foresee that all reigns are permeated with them. This is their strength. As to those who are too indulgent, they will be without ideological boundaries or bedrock.

The Agriculturist School originated among officials in charge of agriculture. They grow various grains, encourage farming and sericulture, in order to enrich clothing and food; so, of the eight political affairs, the first is food, and the second is commodities. Confucius said: "The thing to prioritize is people's food." That is their strength. As to the vulgar people who engage in this, they think it unnecessary to serve the sage kings, intent on having both ruler and subjects work the land, thereby disrupting the upper and lower levels of hierarchy.

The Gossipist School probably emerged from minor officials collecting folklore and legends. It is fashioned from street gossip and hearsay. Confucius said: "Even in inferior studies and employments there is something worth looking at, but if one carries them too far, there is a danger of getting grounded in worldly matters. Therefore, the superior man does not practice them." But they should not be eliminated. Vernacular folk wisdom may spread and be taken up and continued in more formal speech, so it is not forgotten without trace. If occasionally such words can be used, it is bound to be a rough haymaker's argument.

Only nine of the ten schools of philosophy are worth looking at. They all rose when the monarch's Way was on the decline and the vassal kings were powerful and combating each other; the then masters of the world had quite different likes and dislikes, so the

【原文】

所善，以此驰说，取合诸侯。其言虽殊，辟犹水火，相灭亦相生也。仁之与义，敬之与和，相反而皆相成也。《易》曰："天下同归而殊涂，一致而百虑。"今异家者各推所长，穷知究虑，以明其指，虽有蔽短，合其要归，亦《六经》之支与流裔。使其人遭明王圣主，得其所折中，皆股肱之材已。仲尼有言："礼失而求诸野。"方今去圣久远，道术缺废，无所更索，彼九家者，不犹瘉于野乎？若能修六艺之术，而观此九家之言，舍短取长，则可以通万方之略矣。

传曰：不歌而诵谓之赋，登高能赋可以为大夫。言感物造耑，材知深美，可与图事，故可以为列大夫也。古者诸侯卿大夫交接邻国，以微言相感，当揖让之时，必称《诗》以谕其志，盖以别贤不肖而观

【今译】

立，各自坚持自己的学说，崇尚他们好的一面，以用来游说各国君主，希望取得诸侯王支持。这些学说虽然有差别，就像水火一样，相灭也能相生。仁与义，敬与和，相反也都能相互补充促进。《易》上说："天下归宿相同而道路各异，思想一致但思考不同。"现在不同学派各自推崇自己的长处，深究事物的始末，以懂得它的要旨，即使有弊端，综合他们的要领，也是《六经》的支和流的关系。假使这个人遇到明王圣主，得到他的公正对待，就都能成为辅佐君王的大臣之才。仲尼曾说："礼制失去了就向民间寻求。"现在距离圣王久远，道德缺乏，没有地方再去寻求，这九家，不就比民间学说有所超越吗？如果能学习六艺学术，再钻研这九家的言论，扬长避短，就可以通晓各方的谋略了。

古书上说："不能歌唱而只朗诵就叫做赋，爬到高处能作赋可以当大夫。"是说能够触景生情发为文辞，才智出众可与共商大事者为大夫。古时候诸侯卿大夫同邻国交涉谈判，用精微的言语来相互交谈，在宾主相见的外交场合，一定要引用《诗》来表达自己的志向，不外乎以此来判别贤能和不肖并观察对方的盛衰。所以孔子说"不学

nine schools emerged side by side, each one sticking to its doctrine, advocating what it deemed good, using it to lobby the monarchs in the hope of winning their support. Although there are differences between these theories, like fire and water, they can generate as well as inhibit each other. Benevolence and righteousness, respect and harmony, they can complement and promote each other even though contrary in their orientation. According to the *Book of Changes*: "They all come to the same (successful) issue, though by different paths under heaven; there is one result, though there might be a hundred anxious schemes." Now the different schools promote their strong points, getting to the bottom of things to understand their gist; even if there are drawbacks, when you integrate their essentials, you find them to be branches of the mainstream of the Six Classics. If such a person were to encounter a sage king, and his views got a good reception, he might become the king's right-hand man. Confucius said: "The rites lost in the towns had to be sought after among country people." Nowadays, we are remote from the sages, lack the Way and its rules, and have nowhere else to look. Are these nine schools not superior to folk theory? If one can learn the rules of the six arts, and then delve into these nine doctrines, discard their weaknesses and select their strengths, one can be familiar with the strategy of all of the parties.

The old writings say: "Reading without singing is poetic prose; if one can climb a great height and writes poetic prose in response, he can make a grand master." This means that he who can be moved by the occasion to a creative act distinguishes himself from the horde, and can be trusted with major affairs as a grand master. The princes and high officials in ancient times used to move each other with subtle words in negotiations with neighboring countries. During diplomatic greetings, the two sides always expressed their aspirations by reference to the *Odes*, which was no more than a way to distinguish between the elite and the unworthy and observe

【原文】

盛衰焉。故孔子曰“不学《诗》，无以言”也。春秋之后，周道寖坏，聘问歌咏不行于列国，学《诗》之士逸在布衣，而贤人失志之赋作矣。大儒孙卿及楚臣屈原离谗忧国，皆作赋以风，咸有恻隐古诗之义。其后宋玉、唐勒，汉兴枚乘、司马相如，下及扬子云，竞为侈丽闳衍之词，没其风谕之义。是以扬子悔之，曰：“诗人之赋丽以则，辞人之赋丽以淫。如孔氏之门人用赋也，则贾谊登堂，相如入室矣，如其不用何！”自孝武立乐府而采歌谣，于是有代赵之讴，秦楚之风，皆感于哀乐，缘事而发，亦可以观风俗，知薄厚云。[序]诗赋为五种。

权谋者，以正守国，以奇用兵，先计而后战，兼形势，包阴阳，用技巧者也。

形势者，雷动风举，后发而先至，离合背乡，变化无常，以轻疾制敌者也。

【今译】

习《诗》，就没有话可说”。春秋后，周朝王道逐渐被破坏，诸侯之间通问修好时歌咏不再出现在各国，学《诗》的人隐逸在民间，贤能失志的人就去创作赋了。大儒孙卿和楚国的大臣屈原遭到谗言而为国担忧，就都创作赋来进行讽谏，都有古诗哀伤的意味。这之后有宋玉、唐勒，汉朝涌现出枚乘、司马相如，一直到扬子云，争着写出华丽繁冗的文辞，淹没了讽劝的意义。因此扬子云对此很悔恨，说：“诗人的赋华丽有原则，辞人的赋华丽无度。就像孔氏的门人使用赋一样，就有贾谊登堂，相如入室了，如果他们不用赋又怎样呢！”从孝武帝设立乐府并采集歌谣后，于是有代国、赵国的歌曲，秦国、楚国的风格，都是对于事物有哀乐之感，因事而作，可以藉此以观察风俗，知道政治的得失。编排诗赋的次序，分为五种。

权谋学派，用正规的办法守卫国家，对敌作战则主张出奇制胜，先计划后作战，有形势家雷厉风行的气势，也兼有阴阳家的神秘莫测，是注重使用心思计谋的一派。

兵形势家，其用兵主张像迅雷疾风一样，攻势凌厉，行动迅速，后发而先至，进退聚散，变化无常，用轻快来制服敌人。

each other's rise and fall. So Confucius said: "If you do not learn the *Odes*, you will not be fit to converse with." After the Spring and Autumn Period, when the Zhou's Way was destroyed gradually, singing no longer appeared during inter-state visits, the *Odes* learners were lost among the commoners, and the worthy learned were demoralized, and thus resorted to creating poetic prose. The great Confucian Xun Qing and the Chu minister Qu Yuan were victims of slander, and thus concerned for their state, they created allegorical poetic prose as vehicles for their criticism, both with the melancholic mood of the ancient odes. After them, there were Song Yu, Tang Le, and in the Han Dynasty, Mei Sheng, Sima Xiangru, down to Yang Xiong, trying to outdo each other with ornate, cumbersome phrase-making, and thereby drowning the critical message. This upset Yang Xiong enormously: "There is a principle behind gorgeousness in poetic prose written by a poet; but in the hands of a prose writer such gorgeousness is excessive. Like the poetic prose used by Confucian disciples, there were the proficient Jia Yi and Sima Xiangru, but what if they had not used it so!" Since Emperor Wudi established the Music Bureau and collected folk songs and ballads, we have had the songs of Dai and Zhao, ballads of Qin and Chu, all of which are sentimental, composed for a purpose, and they give insights into customs, and the ups and downs of politics. Poetry and prose arranged in order are divided into five categories.

The Military Tactics School safeguards the kingdom by keeping rules, but advocates beating the enemy by surprise tactics. They plan first before engaging battle, and combine intimidating drive-and-sweep tactics together with the mysterious ways of the *Yin-Yang* school. It is a school that sets great store by careful planning.

The Military Situation School moves like thunder and rises like the wind. They start late but reach the goal first, change unpredictably in advance and retreat, gathering and parting, using speed to subdue the enemy.

【原文】

阴阳者，顺时而发，推刑德，随斗击，因五胜，假鬼神而为助者也。

技巧者，习手足，便器械，积机关，以立攻守之胜者也。

兵家者，盖出古司马之职，王官之武备也。《洪范》八政，八曰师。孔子曰为国者"足食足兵"，"以不教民战，是谓弃之"，明兵之重也。《易》曰"古者弦木为弧，剡木为矢，弧矢之利，以威天下"，其用上矣。后世耀金为刃，割革为甲，器械甚备。下及汤武受命，以师克乱而济百姓，动之以仁义，行之以礼让，《司马法》是其遗事也。自春秋至于战国，出奇设伏，变诈之兵并作。汉兴，张良、韩信序次兵法，凡百八十二家，删取要用，定著三十五家。诸吕用事而盗取之。武帝时，军政杨仆捃摭遗逸，纪奏兵录，犹未能备。至于孝成，命任宏论次兵书为四种。

【今译】

兵阴阳家，主张顺应天时而用兵，推测刑罚与德化，观察星斗转移而知吉凶，依据五行之相生相克，假藉鬼神而用兵。

兵技巧家，主张练习手足的灵活，使用器械则得心应手，熟用弓弩，以求攻守之胜。

兵家学派起源于古代司马之官，是王官的军备。《洪范》八种政事中，第八是军事。孔子说治理国家的人"要有丰富的粮食和充足的军队"，"因为不教育老百姓懂得作战，就等于抛弃了他们"，这是表明军队的重要性。《易》说"古代的人用弦木制造为弓，把木削为箭，弓箭的锐利，可以威行天下"，它的用处很大。后代销金为刀，割掉皮革作为铠甲，器械很完备。到了汤武承受天命，用军队战胜动乱而帮助百姓，用仁义来感动他们，用礼让来行动，《司马法》是他们遗留下来的事情。从春秋到战国，出奇招设伏兵，变化狡诈的战争时常发生。汉朝建立后，张良、韩信编排兵法，共有一百八十二家，删去没用的，选取重要可用的，确定了三十五家。吕姓专权后就盗取了它。武帝的时候，军政杨仆拾取遗文散籍，记录下来上奏兵录给皇上，仍没有全面。到了孝帝、成帝时，命任宏评议编次兵书为四种。

The Military *Yin-Yang* School advocates deploying troops according to points in time, calculating the inhibition and enhancement,following astrology, using the interactions of the five elements. They make use of spirits and gods as their help.

The Military Craftsmanship School advocates exercising the flexibility of hands and feet, to achieve dexterous wielding of arms, and skilled bowmanship; the aim is to win in offense and defense.

The Military School originated among the ancient military strategists, in charge of the princely armaments. Among the eight political affairs in *The Great Norms*, the eighth is the military. Confucius said, in order to govern the country one should "have sufficiency of food and sufficiency of military equipment" and "To lead an uninstructed people to war is to throw them away," which is an indication of the importance of the military. According to the *Book of Changes*: "The ancient people used wood and string to form bows, and sharpened wood to make arrows; with these things they produced awe across the land." It was very useful. Later, they smelted metal for knives, cut leather as armor and their equipment became quite complete. When Kings Tang and Wu received the mandate, using their armies they overcame the turmoil to help the people. They moved them with benevolence and righteousness and used the rites to affect behavior. Their legacy is *Sima's Art of War*. From the Spring and Autumn period to the time of the Warring States, surprise attacks and ambushes were rife, as wars of cunning were frequent. After the founding of the Han Dynasty, Zhang Liang and Han Xin arranged the arts of warfare, a total of 182 varieties; deleting the useless, they selected 35 important ones. After the Lü family came in power, they stole them. In the reign of Emperor Wudi, military politician Yang Pu gathered together the scattered books, and recorded a list of military books in his memorial to the Emperor, but it was still far from comprehensive. Under Emperor Chengdi, Ren Hong was ordered to compile the arts of war into four

【原文】

天文者，序二十八宿，步五星日月，以纪吉凶之象，圣王所以参政也。《易》曰："观乎天文，以察时变。"然星事殉悍，非湛密者弗能由也。夫观景以谴形，非明王亦不能服听也。以不能由之臣，谏不能听之王，此所以两有患也。

历谱者，序四时之位，正分至之节，会日月五星之辰，以考寒暑杀生之实。故圣王必正历数，以定三统服色之制，又以探知五星日月之会。凶厄之患，吉隆之喜，其术皆出焉。此圣人知命之术也，非天下之至材，其孰与焉！道之乱也，患出于小人而强欲知天道者，坏大以为小，削远以为近，是以道术破碎而难知也。

五行者，五常之形气也。《书》云"初一曰五行，次二曰羞用五

【今译】

天文学家排列二十八宿的顺序，推算金木水火土五星和日月，用来记录吉凶的征象，圣王用来作为政治的参考。《易》上说："观察日月星辰在宇宙间分布运行的现象，来考察时世的变化。"然而星事凶险，不是精细之人不能加以运用。观察景象来责问形体，不是英明的君王也不能归顺听命。用不能运用星事的大臣，来规劝不能接纳的君王，这就是两边都有危害的缘故。

历谱是排列四季日行之方法，确定春秋、秋分、夏至和冬至的节气，推合日月和金、木、水、火、土五星的时辰，以考察寒暑杀生的实际情况的。所以圣王一定要端正推算节气的度，以确定三统服色的制度，又以探索五星日月交会的时间。凶险的忧患，吉祥的喜悦，它们的方术都由这里产生。这是圣人知晓天命的方法，不是天下最高才能的人，谁能够参预这件事！道德败坏后，担心历谱出于小人而强自想知道天道的人，破坏大的用来作为小的，削减远的用来作为近的，因此规律和方法遭到破坏而难以知晓了。

金、木、水、火、土五行是仁、义、礼、智、信五常的外在形气。《尚书》上说"初一叫五行，初二叫羞用五事"，是说进用五事

varieties, comment and provide a commentary.

Divination astronomers arranged the order of 28 zodiac constellations, calculated the revolution of the five planets, the sun and the moon, to record the auspicious and ominous signs, to be used by the sage kings as a political reference. According to the *Book of Changes*: "The observation of the brilliant phenomena of the heavens is to examine when the world changes." However, astrology is a dangerous thing, not to be utilized except by a meticulous person. To question the gain and loss in political affairs by observing the signs, this cannot convince anyone except the wise king. That is why there are hazards for both when a minister who does not know much about astrology tries to persuade an incredulous king.

Divination calendar makers arranged the four seasons and identified the equinoxes and solstices, to correlate the celestial bodies of the sun, the moon and the five planets, so as to observe the actual situation of engendering and exterminating in summer and winter. So the sage kings were sure to correct the calendar, to determine the system of Three-Entity Calendar dates and imperial color, and to explore the intersection of the planets, the sun and the moon. Their formulas could cover the disaster of famine, and the joy of good harvest. This is the method by which the sages knew the destiny, and who but they, the most talented people in this world, could comprehend such mysterics! With the decline of morality, calendar divination fell into the hands of low persons who wanted to use the Way of Heaven for their own purposes, when they destructed the great to make it small and the distant to make it close. Hence the disciplines and methods became damaged and hard to fathom.

Five-elements Divination. The five elements of metal, wood, water, fire and earth are the external forms or *qi* of the five constant virtues of benevolence, righteousness, propriety, wisdom and good faith. According to the *Book of Documents*: "The first day was called the five elements, and the next day proceeded with the five things

【原文】

事”，言进用五事以顺五行也。貌、言、视、听、思心失，而五行之序乱，五星之变作，皆出于律历之数而分为一者也。其法亦起五德终始，推其极则无不至。而小数家因此以为吉凶，而行于世，寖以相乱。

蓍龟者，圣人之所用也。《书》曰：“女则有大疑，谋及卜筮。”《易》曰：“定天下之吉凶，成天下之亹亹者，莫善于蓍龟”，“是故君子将有为也，将有行也，问焉而以言，其受命也如向，无有远近幽深，遂知来物。非天下之至精，其孰能与于此！”及至衰世，解于齐戒，而娄烦卜筮，神明不应。故筮渎不告，《易》以为忌；龟厌不告，《诗》以为刺。

杂占者，纪百事之象，候善恶之征。《易》曰：“占事知来。”

【今译】

来顺应五行。貌、言、视、听、思中心失去了，金、木、水、火、土的次序就混乱，五星的变化就开始发作，这些都是出于律历的数而分化为一部分。它的方法也是起源于五德终始，推演它到极致就会没有不能达到的地方。而小数家因此以它作为吉凶的象征，流行在世间，逐渐变得混乱。

蓍龟是圣人用来占卜吉凶的。《尚书》上说：“你如果有很大的疑问，就用卜筮来决定。”《周易》上说：“确定天下的吉凶，促使天下的兴旺发达，没有比蓍龟更好的了。”“因为君子将有所作为，有所行动，就用他的言语来询问《易》，《易》很快就会告诉他吉凶，不分远近幽深，便知道将要发生的事情。除了天下最精诚的人，还有谁能成为这样呢！”等到了衰落的时代，对于斋戒就懈怠了，屡次使用卜筮，神明就不再显灵了。所以卜筮时轻慢，神灵就不会加以预告。《易》把这作为忌讳；龟神感到厌烦了就不会显灵，《诗》以此作为警戒。

杂占是记录各种事物的表象，观测好坏的征兆的。《周易》上说：

of self-cultivation," meaning proceeding to fit to the five elements the five things; namely, appearance, speech, visual, hearing, and thinking. When the heart for the five things was lost, then the order of the five elements was disrupted, and perturbation of the planets began to occur. These all came out of the numbers in the calendar and differentiated into a separate part. Its method was also derived from the circulation of the quality of the five elements, which reached anywhere when extrapolated to the limit. The small diviners thus used it as a symbol of good and bad omen, popularized it in the world, and gradually brought it to chaos.

Divination of yarrow stalks and tortoise shells. Yarrow stalks and tortoise shells were used by sages for divination. According to the *Book of Documents*: "If you have a great doubt, use divination to decide." According to the *Book of Changes*: "Determining the issues of good or ill luck in the world, and making all men under heaven full of strenuous endeavors, there is nothing greater than the methods of yarrow stalks and the tortoise shells." "Therefore, when a superior man is about to take action of a more private or public character, he asks the *Changes*, making his inquiry in words. The answer comes quickly, telling him whether there will be good fortune or bad. Be the subject remote or near, mysterious or deep, he forthwith knows the nature of the coming result. If the *Changes* were not the most exquisite thing under heaven, would it be concerned in such an operation as this?" As to the age of decline, because of slackness in fasting, and over-use of fortune telling, the gods no longer appeared. So when the divination is slap-dash, no prognostication is given. In the *Book of Changes*, this is taken as a taboo. The tortoise gods, thus offended, will not manifest. This was taken as a warning in the *Book of Odes*.

Miscellaneous divination is a record of the appearance of all things, forecasting signs benign and malignant. According to the *Book of Changes*: "The future can be known through divination."

【原文】

众占非一，而梦为大，故周有其官。而《诗》载熊罴虺蛇众鱼旐旟之梦，著明大人之占，以考吉凶，盖参卜筮。《春秋》之说訞也，曰："人之所忌，其气炎以取之，訞由人兴也。人失常则訞兴，人无衅焉，訞不自作。"故曰："德胜不祥，义厌不惠。"桑谷共生，大戊以兴；鸲雉登鼎，武丁为宗。然惑者不稽诸躬，而忌訞之见，是以《诗》刺"召彼故老，讯之占梦"，伤其舍本而忧末，不能胜凶咎也。

形法者，大举九州之势以立城郭室舍形，人及六畜骨法之度数、器物之形容以求其声气贵贱吉凶。犹律有长短，而各征其声，非有鬼神，数自然也。然形与气相首尾，亦有有其形而无其气，有其气而无其形，此精微之独异也。

数术者，皆明堂羲和史卜之职也。史官之废久矣，其书既不能

【今译】

"占卜可以知道将来。"各人所占的都不一致，就以梦为准，所以周朝设有这占卜之官。《诗经》上所记载的熊罴虺蛇众鱼旐旟的梦，写明是大人的占卜，用来考察吉凶，大致参照卜筮。《春秋》解说妖说："人们所忌讳的东西，它的气焰招来灾害，妖是由人兴起的。人失去常态那么妖孽就兴起，人没有空隙可钻，妖孽不会自行产生。"所以说："道德太胜就不吉祥，仁义太繁琐就不顺。"桑和谷一同生长，大戊因此兴盛；鸲和雉跳到鼎上，武丁就成为宗主。但迷惑的人不从自身加以考察而忌讳妖孽的出现，因此《诗》上讽刺说"召来他们的老人，询问占梦的吉凶"，对他们舍本忧末，不能战胜灾祸感到痛心。

形法家研究相地、相宅、相人之法术，其大者可以相九州之地势以建立城郭屋舍，又可相人及六畜之骨法，以及器物之形状以求其吉凶贵贱的。就像律管有长短，各自发出自己的声音一样，这不是有鬼神，而是数的自然体现。但形和气首尾相连贯，也有有形但没有气，有气没有形的，这就是精妙细微的独特之处。

数术家包括天文、历法、五行、占卜之类的法术，都是掌握祭祀

Different diviners had different methods, so dreams were made the standard, and the Zhou appointed officials for this. The *Book of Odes* recorded dreams about bears, snakes, fishes, and human throngs, explaining the gentleman's divination. It was used to examine for good and bad omens, generally referring to tortoise and yarrow divination. The *Spring and Autumn Annals* comments on the supernatural: "What people take as taboo, whose flames of *qi* provoke disasters, so the rise of the supernatural is caused by people. When people lose the five constant virtues, then the supernatural will be on the rise; the supernatural will not self-generate if people are not at fault." So it is said: "Excessive virtue is not auspicious, while over-tight righteousness is a hindrance." When mulberry and millet grew together, King Dawu was so prosperous; when a mynah and pheasant jumped on the tripod, Wuding became the ancestral sovereign. However, people in perplexities did not increase their self-examination, but avoided the emergence of the supernatural as taboo, so the *Book of Odes* mocks that "The old courtiers were summoned to expound dreams," bemoaning that they care about trifles to the neglect of essentials, not able to overcome their distress.

Divination of forms exists as geomancy and physiognomy. On a large scale it can take the general terrain of the country to project the forms of towns and houses. It can also measure the bones in people and domestic animals, and the shape of objects to ascertain whether they are noble or cheap, auspicious or unlucky. Each gives off its particular sound and tone, rather as different lengths of bamboo pitch-pipes possess different tones, not because of ghosts and spirits, but from the natural expression of numbers. However, when forms and *qi* are connected tail-to-head, there are scenarios of form without *qi*, or *qi* without form, which are the subtle nuances of the unique.

The Divination School includes the divination arts of astrology, calendar and five elements: they were in the charge of officials in charge of Hall of Enlightened Rule. Since the post of official

【原文】

具，虽有其书而无其人。《易》曰：“苟非其人，道不虚行。”春秋时鲁有梓慎，郑有禆灶，晋有卜偃，宋有子韦。六国时楚有甘公，魏有石申夫。汉有唐都，庶得粗觕。盖有因而成易，无因而成难，故因旧书以序数术为六种。

医经者，原人血脉经(络)[落]骨髓阴阳表里，以起百病之本，死生之分，而用度箴石汤火所施，调百药齐和之所宜。至齐之得，犹慈石取铁，以物相使。拙者失理，以瘉为剧，(以死为生)[以生为死]。

经方者，本草石之寒温，量疾病之浅深，假药味之滋，因气感之宜，辩五苦六辛，致水火之齐，以通闭解结，反之于平。及失其宜者，以热益热，以寒增寒，精气内伤，不见于外，是所独失也。故谚曰：“有病不治，常得中医。”

房中者，(性情)[情性]之极，至道之际，是以圣王制外乐以禁内

【今译】

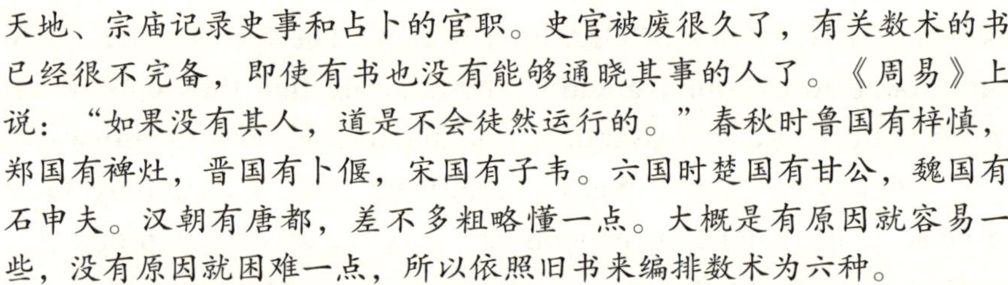

天地、宗庙记录史事和占卜的官职。史官被废很久了，有关数术的书已经很不完备，即使有书也没有能够通晓其事的人了。《周易》上说：“如果没有其人，道是不会徒然运行的。”春秋时鲁国有梓慎，郑国有禆灶，晋国有卜偃，宋国有子韦。六国时楚国有甘公，魏国有石申夫。汉朝有唐都，差不多粗略懂一点。大概是有原因就容易一些，没有原因就困难一点，所以依照旧书来编排数术为六种。

医学著作是探求人的血脉、经络和骨髓、阴阳、表里的，以此来找出百病的根源所在和死生的界限，使用时度量石针以及热汤与烈火所产生的影响，再来调整百药相配所适宜的情况。等到达到调和状态，就像磁石取铁，用一物来役使另一物。笨拙的人失去了分寸，就把病愈的当作病重的，把要活的当作要死的。

古代医学的方剂是本着草和石的寒温性质，测量疾病的深浅，藉着药味的作用，顺应气感适宜，辨别五苦六辛，达到水火调融，以沟通闭塞解除症结，使它恢复到平衡。等到它失去平衡，用热更加热，用寒更加寒，使精气内部受到伤害，不显现在外，这是它惟一的过失。所以谚语说：“有病不治理好，经常生病就会成为医师。”

男女房中之事是情性的极端，达到道的极点，因此圣王主张以音

historian was abolished a long time ago, the books of divination are not complete, and even if they were available, there are not persons able to use them. According to the *Book of Changes*: "But if there be not the proper men to carry this out, the Way cannot be pursued without them." In the Spring and Autumn Period, there were Zi Shen in the State of Lu, Pi Zao in the State of Zheng, Bu Yan in Jin, and Zi Wei in Song. In the Warring States Period, there were Mr. Gan in Chu, Shi Shenfu in Wei. In the Han Dynasty, there was Tang Du, with a modicum of expertise. Probably it was easier when some tradition existed, but more difficult without it, so the variety of divination school amounts to six in accordancc with the old books.

Medical classics explore a man's blood, channel system, bone marrow, *yin* and *yang*, exterior and interior, in order to identify the root cause of sicknesses and the demarcation of life and death. They combine the impact of stone needles, decoction and fire, and adjust various medicaments appropriate to the condition. As to the efficacy of the medicaments, it is like the action of a magnet on iron - applying one thing to create an effect on another. Clumsy practitioners have lost a sense of proportion, regarding the cured as seriously ill, and the alive as dying.

Classical medical prescriptions measure the depth of the disease based on the chill or warmth of herbs and stone; and by the function of medicinal flavors, conform to the changes in temperature of the environment; they identify the five bitter herbs and six pungent herbs, and make preparations with water and fire, so as to free the channel of blockage and restore it to equilibrium. As to those extreme practitioners, they increase heat with more heat, and add cold to cold, so that the primordial energy is internally damaged but without showing on the outside. This is its fault alone. So a saying goes: "When a sick person does not seek medical treatment, he may still recover through the self-regulating functions of his body."

Sex art deals in the extremes of passion, to the boundary of the

【原文】

情，而为之节文。传曰：“先王之作乐，所以节百事也。”乐而有节，则和平寿考。及迷者弗顾，以生疾而陨性命。

神仙者，所以保性命之真，而游求于其外者也。聊以荡意平心，同死生之域，而无怵惕于胸中。然而或者专以为务，则诞欺怪迂之文弥以益多，非圣王之所以教也。孔子曰：“索隐行怪，后世有述焉，吾不为之矣。”

方技者，皆生生之具，王官之一守也。太古有岐伯、俞拊，中世有扁鹊、秦和，盖论病以及国，原诊以知政。汉兴有仓公，今其技术晻昧，故论其书，以序方技为四种。

——卷三十《艺文志》第十

【今译】

乐以禁情欲，因而叫做节制修饰。传说：“先王创作音乐，用来节制百事。”欢乐而有节制，那么就会心平气和，长命百岁。等到迷惑的人无所顾忌，就会产生疾病而丢掉性命。

所谓神仙之术是追求人的长生不老而想超脱凡尘的。暂且用来净化安定心灵，视死生没有分界，没有惊惧在胸中。然而有的人专门来从事这些事，就会使荒诞不实怪异迂阔的文章日益增多，不是圣王所用来作为教化的东西。孔子说：“寻求事物的隐蔽之理和行为怪诞，后代将有所记载，我不干这样的事。”

方技都是安于生命自然的工具，是天子之官的一个主持。太古时候有岐伯、俞拊，中世纪时有扁鹊、秦和，都是议论病理而涉及国家的治理，探求病症来知道政事。汉朝建立后有仓公。现在他的技巧方法模糊不清，所以评论他的书籍，编排方技为四种。

mystic principle. So the sage kings advocated music to guard against lust, and formulated a rite which called for moderation. According to *Zuo's Annals*: "The previous kings composed music, in order to be moderate in everything." When there was moderate restraint in pleasure (music), it would result in peace of mind and long life. As to the lascivious and shameless people they will catch disease and perish.

The so-called "Immortal Arts" is the pursuit of transcending the mundane world and achieving eternal life. They were used to purify the soul and pacify the mind, thus equalizing life and death, putting an end to fearful tremors in the chest. However, some people gave themselves over to these things entirely, and more and more weird, absurd and boasting articles appeared, not at all what the sage kings intended as moral education. Confucius said: "To live in obscurity and practice wonders, in order to be mentioned with honor in future age - this is what I do not do."

Mystic techniques are all natural tools for prolonging life; they are a support for the monarch's officials. In remote antiquity, there were Qi Bo, Yu Fu, and in the middle ages there were Bian Que and Qin He. Their theories on pathology went into the realm of governance, they explored diseases to know the conduct of political affairs. In the Han Dynasty, we had the Magistrate of Taicang. Now his skills are indistinct, so the comments on his books are arranged into four types.

萧何传

【原文】

萧何，沛人也。以文毋害为沛主吏掾，高祖为布衣时，数以吏事护高祖。高祖为亭长，常佑之。高祖以吏繇咸阳，吏皆送奉钱三，何独以五。秦御史监郡者，与从事辨之。何乃给泗水卒史事，第一。秦御史欲入言征何，何固请，得毋行。

及高祖起为沛公，何尝为丞督事。沛公至咸阳，诸将皆争走金帛财物之府分之，何独先入收秦丞相御史律令图书臧之。沛公具知天下厄塞，户口多少，强弱处，民所疾苦者，以何得秦图书也。

初，诸侯相与约，先入关破秦者王其地。沛公既先定秦，项羽后

【今译】

萧何，沛地人。因能写文书没有疵病而为沛主吏掾。高祖为平民时，萧何多次在吏事上袒护高祖。高祖作了亭长，又常帮助他。高祖以吏的身份到咸阳服役，小吏们都出钱三百为高祖送行，只有萧何出了五百钱。秦御史监郡的人，和从事考察其职事，萧何于是被授予泗水郡卒吏一职，考课最优等。秦御史打算言于朝廷，征用萧何，萧何坚决请求，才得以未去。

等到高祖起事做了沛公，萧何曾经任丞督事。沛公到了咸阳，诸位将领都争相跑到储存金帛财物的府库去瓜分。只有萧何先进去收藏起秦丞相御史的律令图书。沛公之所以详细地知道天下要塞，户口多少；强弱分布，人民痛恨忧苦的事情，就是因为萧何收得了秦的图书。

起初，诸侯们互相约定，先进入函谷关击破秦的就在其地称王。

Chapter 7

Biography of Xiao He

Xiao He, a man of Pei, was made Chief Secretary of Pei County on account of his flawless calligraphy and fair administration. When the future Gaozu was still a commoner, Xiao shielded him many things as an official, and when Gaozu was made a village chief, he often helped Xiao. Before Gaozu went to Xianyang to serve as a drafted official, other officials gave him 300 cash; Xiao was the only one to give him 500. The Qin censor who supervised the prefecture, and his assistants, examined Xiao He on his administrative track record, and he was made prefecture clerk of Sishui as a result, having achieved the highest score. The censor intended to report to the Court recommending that Xiao be drafted there, but Xiao firmly requested to be excused, and was ultimately successful in this.

When Gaozu rebelled as Magistrate of Pei, Xiao was appointed Aide de camp. The Magistrate of Pei conquered Xianyang, and his generals all hurried to the treasuries and strong-rooms where gold, silk and other riches were stored, to divide them up among themselves. But Xiao He headed straight to the offices of Qin's prime minister and censor-in-chief to collect up books on precepts and laws and maps. The Magistrate of Pei acquired detailed knowledge about the empire's fortresses, population and household numbers, the distribution of strongholds and vulnerable points, the things people hated and suffered from, all because Xiao obtained all Qin's books and maps.

Initially, the vassal kings agreed a covenant that the first of them to break into the Hangu Pass and conquer Qin should be King of Guanzhong, the lands within the Pass. The Magistrate of Pei was

【原文】

至，欲攻沛公，沛公谢之得解。羽遂屠烧咸阳，与范增谋曰："巴蜀道险，秦之迁民皆居蜀。"乃曰："蜀汉亦关中地也。"故立沛公为汉王，而三分关中地，王秦降将以距汉王。汉王怒，欲谋攻项羽。周勃、灌婴、樊哙皆劝之，何谏之曰："虽王汉中之恶，不犹愈于死乎？"汉王曰："何为乃死也？"何曰："今众弗如，百战百败，不死何为？《周书》曰'天予不取，反受其咎'。语曰'天汉'，其称甚美。夫能诎于一人之下，而信于万乘之上者，汤武是也。臣愿大王王汉中，养其民以致贤人，收用巴蜀，还定三秦，天下可图也。"汉王曰："善。"乃遂就国，以何为丞相。何进韩信，汉王以为大将军，说汉王令引兵东定三秦。语在《信传》。

何以丞相留收巴蜀，填抚谕告，使给军食。汉二年，汉王与诸侯

【今译】

沛公已经先平定了秦，项羽后到，要攻打沛公，沛公向他谢罪，才得以解脱。项羽于是在咸阳城进行屠杀焚烧，和范增谋划说："巴蜀道路险阻，秦的移民都居住在蜀。"于是说："蜀、汉也是关中的地盘。"于是立沛公为汉王，把关中地分为三份，把秦的降将封王来抗拒汉王。汉王很生气，要策划攻打项羽。周勃、灌婴、樊哙都鼓励汉王，萧何劝谏说："虽然在汉中为王不好，但不是比死好些吗？"汉王说："怎么就会死呢？"萧何说："现在兵士不如人家多，百战百败，除了死还能怎样？《周书》说'天给予却不去接受，反会遭受其害'。俗语说'天汉'，以汉配天，名称非常美好。能够在一人之下受委屈，却在万乘诸侯之上伸张其志的，是商汤、武王。为臣希望大王在汉中称王，休养百姓，招致贤才，收用巴蜀的财力，回军平定三秦，就可以谋取天下了。"汉王说："好。"于是去封国即位，任命萧何为丞相。萧何举荐韩信，汉王任命他为大将军，说服汉王使他领兵东进平定三秦，其事迹记载在《信传》里。

萧何以丞相身份接管留守巴、蜀，镇抚、谕告境内百姓，使其供

first to conquer Qin, and Xiang Yu arrived after him, so he wanted to attack the Magistrate of Pei, who immediately apologized and was able to escape. Xiang Yu then burned down the city of Xianyang, massacring its inhabitants, and planned with Fan Zeng: "Ba and Shu [present-day Sichuan] are difficult to reach, and the Qin emigrants should live in Shu." So he said: "Shu and Han are also the territory of Guanzhong." Thus he made the Magistrate of Pei the King of Han, dividing Guanzhong into three parts, and elevating the former Qin generals to the status of kings there so as to resist King of Han. King of Han was incensed, and planned to attack Xiang Yu. Whereas Zhou Bo, Guan Ying and Fan Kuai encouraged him, Xiao remonstrated: "It is indeed no good thing to be King of Han, but is it not better than death?" "Why would I die?" came his retort, to which Xiao responded: "You have fewer soldiers than others, so you'll lose every battle. What could happen except death? According to *Book of Zhou*: 'If you do not accept what is given by heaven, you are liable to suffer instead.' As the saying goes: 'In heaven there is the Milky Way [note: a homophone for Han]'; the Han affixed to heaven, is indeed a beautiful name. King Tang of the Shang Dynasty and King Wu of Zhou were able to bow under one person, so as to hold their heads high over the country. Your servant hopes that you consent to be King in Han, letting the people rest so we can recruit more worthy men, and taxing Ba-Shu's resources so we can bring our army back to recover the three Qin kingdoms. Then we could reap the empire." The king agreed, went to his fief, ascended the throne, and appointed Xiao He as his prime minister. Xiao He recommended Hann Xin, whom the King appointed as general-in-chief; Hann Xin then persuaded the King to order the troops east to subjugate the three Qin kingdoms. For details, see the chapter "Biography of Hann Xin."

Xiao He stayed behind in Ba-Shu as prime minister, collecting the local revenue, and keeping the local people in line and notified

【原文】

击楚，何守关中，侍太子，治栎阳，为令约束，立宗庙、社稷、宫室、县邑，辄奏，上可许以从事；即不及奏，辄以便宜施行，上来以闻。计户转漕给军，汉王数失军遁去，何常兴关中卒，辄补缺。上以此剸属任何关中事。

汉三年，与项羽相距京、索间，上数使使劳苦丞相。鲍生谓何曰："今王暴衣露盖，数劳苦君者，有疑君心。为君计，莫若遣君子孙昆弟能胜兵者悉诣军所，上益信君。"于是何从其计，汉王大说。

汉五年，已杀项羽，即皇帝位，论功行封，群臣争功，岁余不决。上以何功最盛，先封为酂侯，食邑八千户。功臣皆曰："臣等身被坚执兵，多者百余战，少者数十合，攻城略地，大小各有差。今

【今译】

给军食。汉二年，汉王和诸侯攻打楚，萧何守在关中，侍卫太子，治理栎阳。制定法令规约，建立宗庙、社稷、宫室、县邑，经常上奏，皇上许可的就去执行。如果来不及上奏，就按适宜的方式施行，皇上回来后再告诉皇上。计算户口转运粮饷供给军需，汉王多次丧师逃跑，萧何经常征发关中兵士，立即加以补充，皇上因此把关中事务专门交给萧何。

汉三年，和项羽在京、索之间对峙，皇上多次派使者慰劳丞相。鲍生对萧何说："现在大王日晒衣裳，露湿车盖，却多次慰劳您，这是对您有疑心。为您着想，不如把您的子孙兄弟中能打仗的都派到军队中去，皇上就更信任您了。"于是萧何听从了他的计策，汉王非常高兴。

汉五年，已杀掉项羽，登了帝位，按功劳封赐，群臣争功，一年多难以决定，皇上因萧何功劳最大，先封为酂侯，食邑八千户。功臣们都说："我们亲自披着铠甲，拿着兵器，多的经历百余战，少的也有几十回合，攻城略地，多少不等。现在萧何没有汗马功劳，只是

them to supply the military with food. In year two of Han, the King and his vassal king allies attacked Chu, while Prime Minister Xiao defended Guanzhong, attended to the Crown Prince, and governed in Yueyang. He established laws and statutes, in addition to the Imperial Ancestral Temple, Altar of the Land and Grain, palaces, county and town walls. He often sent memorials to his lord and implemented what the lord approved. If there was no time for a memorial, he carried it out at his own discretion only informing the King on his return. He counted the population, transferred food supply, and military pay. The King of Han lost his troops and escaped alone several times, but Xiao regularly sent replenishments by mobilizing soldiers in Guanzhong. So the King delegated to him all the affairs of Guanzhong.

In year three of Han, while in military stand-off with Xiang Yu between Jing and Suo, the King frequently sent messengers to the prime minister with gifts of appreciation. Mr. Bao said to Xiao: "Now the King, himself undergoing the hardships of campaigning, has kept sending you rewards. This means he is suspicious of you. For your own sake, I would advise you to send to the army all those of your children, grandchildren and brothers capable of taking arms, and then His Majesty will trust you the more." Xiao He followed this plan, to the great joy of the King.

By year five, Xiang Yu had been killed, and the King was now enthroned as Emperor, and so was dispensing titles according to services rendered. The courtiers competed for recognition of their deeds and it took more than a year before he decided Xiao He was the most deserving, ennobling him as Marquis of Zan, with a fief of 8,000 households. The meritorious ministers who remained to be rewarded grumbled: "We, dressed in armor and bearing weapons, have fought over a hundred battles or dozens of skirmishes at least; we have attacked towns and seized territories, large or small. Now Xiao has no valorous exploits in battle, just phrase-making and not

【原文】

萧何未有汗马之劳，徒持文墨议论，不战，顾居臣等上，何也？”上曰：“诸君知猎乎？”曰：“知之。”“知猎狗乎？”曰：“知之。”上曰：“夫猎，追杀兽者狗也，而发纵指示兽处者人也。今诸君徒能走得兽耳，功狗也；至如萧何，发纵指示，功人也。且诸君独以身从我，多者三两人；萧何举宗数十人皆随我，功不可忘也！”群臣后皆莫敢言。

列侯毕已受封，奏位次，皆曰：“平阳侯曹参身被七十创，攻城略地，功最多，宜第一。”上已桡功臣多封何，至位次未有以复难之，然心欲何第一。关内侯鄂(千)秋时为谒者，进曰：“群臣议皆误。夫曹参虽有野战略地之功，此特一时之事。夫上与楚相距五岁，失军亡众，跳身遁者数矣，然萧何常从关中遣军补其处。非上所诏令召，而数万众会上乏绝者数矣。夫汉与楚相守荥阳数年，军无见粮，萧何转漕关中，给食不乏。陛下虽数亡山东，萧何常全关中待陛下，

【今译】

舞文弄墨发表议论，不去打仗，地位却在我们之上，为什么？”皇上说：“各位知道打猎的事吧？”都说：“知道。”又问：“知道猎狗吗？”回答说：“知道”。皇上说：“打猎，追杀野兽的是狗，而发纵指示野兽所处的是人。现在各位只能追逐获得野兽，功劳和猎狗类似；至于萧何，发纵指示，功劳与猎人一样。而且各位只是以己身跟随我，多的三两个人，萧何全族几十人都跟随我，功劳不可忘记！”以后群臣都不敢说了。

列侯受封完毕，上奏位次，都说：“平阳侯曹参受伤七十处，攻城略地，功最多，应列为第一。”皇上已经使功臣屈从而多封了萧何，至于位次没有办法再为难他们，然而心里想让萧何位居第一。当时关内侯鄂秋为谒者，进言说：“群臣的议论都不对。曹参虽然有野战略地的功劳，这只是一时的事。皇上与楚相持五年，损兵折将，多次轻身逃跑，然而萧何常从关中派军队来补充。不是皇上诏令召来士卒，却有数万人在皇上乏绝时赶到。汉与楚在荥阳相守多年，军中没有现存的粮食，萧何从关中转运粮饷，供给不缺。陛下虽多次丢失山

war-making. Why then is he positioned above us?" The Emperor asked: "You know about hunting, I suppose?" "Yes," they replied. Then came the follow-up question: "You know about dogs?" "Yes," they responded. The Emperor said: "In hunting, it is the dogs that pursue the quarry, but it is the human who directs the pack as to where the beast is. Now you gentlemen only chased the beast, and your contributions can be compared with the hunting dogs. Whereas Xiao He, giving directions, has the same credit as the hunter. Furthermore, you gentlemen just followed me by yourselves, bringing at most two or three relatives, whereas Xiao's clan of dozens of people have followed all the way, and his contribution cannot be forgotten!" After this, the ministers dared not say anything.

When the process of enfeoffment was completed, they all lobbied about ranking, saying: "Cao Can the Marquis of Pingyang was injured in 70 places. He attacked towns and seized territories, amassing the best merit. He should rank as the first." The Emperor had managed to quell the warriors' complaints and reward Xiao more than them, so he did not cross them again in the matter of ranking, but in his heart he wanted Xiao to have the highest rank. At that time, Marquis of Guannei E Qiu put in a word: "The ministers' arguments are wrong. Although Cao Can has battlefield exploits, and has seized territory, these were all one-off feats. Your Majesty and Chu were locked in stalemate for five years, and you suffered heavy losses of soldiers, escaping with your light horse many times, but Xiao repeatedly replenished your military forces from Guanzhong. These soldiers were not summoned by imperial edict, but on several occasions tens of thousands rushed to Your Majesty's aid when you were *in extremis*. Han and Chu spent many years in Xingyang in military stalemate, without ready food for the army, but Xiao He transferred a never failing supply from Guanzhong. Your Majesty lost land east of the Mountain many times, but Xiao He always

【原文】

此万世功也。今虽无曹参等百数，何缺于汉？汉得之不必待以全。奈何欲以一旦之功(而)加万世之功哉！萧何当第一，曹参次之。”上曰：“善。”于是乃令何第一，赐带剑履上殿，入朝不趋。上曰：“吾闻进贤受上赏，萧何功虽高，待鄂君乃得明。”于是因鄂(千)秋故所食关内侯邑二千户，封为安平侯。是日，悉封何父母兄弟十馀人，皆食邑。乃益封何二千户，“以尝繇咸阳时何送我独赢钱二也”。

陈豨反，上自将，至邯郸。而韩信谋反关中，吕后用何计诛信。语在《信传》。上已闻诛信，使使拜丞相为相国，益封五千户，令卒五百人一都尉为相国卫。诸君皆贺，召平独吊。召平者，故秦东陵侯。秦破，为布衣，贫，种瓜长安城东，瓜美，故世谓“东陵瓜”，从召平始也。平谓何曰：“祸自此始矣。上暴露于外，而君守于内，

【今译】

东，萧何常保全关中以待陛下，这是万世的功劳。现在即使没有曹参这样的人一百个，汉又能损失什么呢？汉的获得不一定非等待他们才能保全。为什么要以一旦之功加于万世之功之上呢！萧何应当第一，曹参次之。”皇上说：“好。”于是令萧何为第一，恩赐佩剑穿履上殿，进朝廷不必小步急行。皇上说：“我听说进贤要受上赏，萧何功劳虽高，有了鄂君才得以彰明。”于是在鄂秋原来所食关内侯邑二千户之上，又加封为安平侯。这天，全部封赏萧何的父母兄弟十几人，都有食邑。又加封萧何二千户，“用来报答在咸阳服役时惟独萧何多送我二百钱。”

陈豨反叛，皇上亲自率军，到了邯郸。韩信在关中谋反，吕后采用萧何的计策杀了韩信。在《信传》有记载。皇上听说已杀了韩信，派使者拜丞相为相国，加封五千户，命令士卒五百人和一个都尉为相国护卫。诸君都庆贺，只有召平表示哀悼。召平，是原来秦的东陵侯。秦灭亡后，成为平民，很穷，在长安城东种瓜，瓜非常甜美，所以世间所谓“东陵瓜”，就是从召平开始的。召平对萧何说：“灾祸从此开始了。皇上露营在外，而您在朝中留守，没有遭受箭石之苦，

preserved the territory of Guanzhong waiting for Your Majesty; this was service and honor lasting a thousand generations. And now even without a hundred persons like Cao Can, how could the Han have fared the worse? What Han had obtained would not have been necessarily kept intact by waiting for them. Why should momentary credit outrank immortal credit! Xiao He should be the first, followed by Cao." The Emperor said: "Good." In the end he decreed that Xiao was the highest ranking, was allowed to enter Court wearing shoes and sword, without having to shuffle in quick small steps. The Emperor said: "I heard that those who recommend the virtuous deserve the best reward. Xiao's merit may be high, but it was Mr. E's exposition that made that clear." Then in addition to the original 2,000 households that E Qiu enjoyed as Marquis of Guannei, he was made Marquis of Anping. That day, Xiao's parents and brothers, a dozen in all, received fiefdoms. Xiao He was granted an additional 2,000 households, "in repayment of the 200 extra cash that Xiao alone presented before I was drafted to serve in Xianyang."

When Chen Xi rebelled, the Emperor personally led his army to Handan to put down the rising. When Hann Xin planned to rebel in Guanzhong, Empress Lü killed him by following Xiao He's plan, as is recorded in the "Biography of Hann Xin." Receiving the news of Hann Xin's death, the Emperor sent an emissary to promote his prime minister to councilor-in-chief, with 5,000 households added to his fief. He also ordered him a guard of 500 soldiers and a defender. All the gentlemen congratulated Xiao He: Zhao Ping alone sent condolences. Zhao Ping had been Marquis of Dongling under Qin. After the fall of the Qin regime, he became a commoner, scraping a living by growing melons east of Chang'an. His melons tasted very sweet, so the so-called "Dongling melon" originated from him. Zhao Ping told Xiao: "For you this is the beginning of disaster. While the Emperor is camping out, being subjected to the attacks of stones and arrows, you remain safe at Court. However, the reason he increased

【原文】

非被矢石之难，而益君封置卫者，以今者淮阴新反于中，有疑君心。夫置卫卫君，非以宠君也。愿君让封勿受，悉以家私财佐军。”何从其计，上说。

其秋，黥布反，上自将击之，数使使问相国何为。曰：“为上在军，拊循勉百姓，悉所有佐军，如陈豨时。”客又说何曰：“君灭族不久矣。夫君位为相国，功第一，不可复加。然君初入关，本得百姓心，十馀年矣，皆附君，尚复孳孳得民和。上所谓数问君，畏君倾动关中。今君胡不多买田地，贱贳贷以自汙？上心必安。”于是何从其计，上乃大说。

上罢布军归，民道遮行，上书言相国强贱买民田宅数千人。上至，何谒。上笑曰：“今相国乃利民！”民所上书皆以与何，曰：“君自谢民。”后何为民请曰：“长安地狭，上林中多空地，弃，愿令民得入田，毋收稾为兽食。”上大怒曰：“相国多受贾人财物，

【今译】

而给您加封置卫，是因为现在淮阴侯刚在内部反叛，对您有疑心。给您配置守卫护卫您，不是用来恩宠您的。希望您辞谢封赏不受，以全部家产资助军队。”萧何听从了召平的计策，皇上很高兴。

这年秋天，黥布造反，皇上亲自率军攻打，多次派使者问相国在做什么。回答说：“因为皇上在军中，所以相国安抚勉励百姓，倾家所有资助军事，像陈豨造反时那样。”门客又劝说萧何道：“您不久就会被灭族了。您位为相国，功劳第一，无以复加。然而您刚入关时，本来很得民心，已有十几年了。都已亲附您了，您仍孜孜不倦以得民和。皇上之所以多次问您，是怕您倾动关中。现在您为什么不多买田地，低息借贷以自损声名，皇上一定会安心。”于是萧何听其计策，皇上于是很高兴。

皇上平定黥布后归来，百姓在路上拦住皇上，上书说相国强行贱买百姓田宅数千人。皇上回朝后，萧何去谒见。皇上笑道：“现在相国竟向百姓取利！”把百姓上的书都给了萧何，说：“您自己向百姓谢罪吧！”之后萧何为百姓请求说：“长安地窄，上林中有很多空地，丢弃不用，希望能让百姓进去耕种，不要收了稾秸做兽食。”皇

your fief and gave you a guard is because the Marquis of Huaiyin just rebelled at Court and you are now an object of mistrust. The guard he sent to escort you is not for your gratification. I would advise you to decline the fief, and dedicate all your family property to financing the military." Xiao He followed this plan and the Emperor was pleased.

That autumn, Tattooed Bu rebelled, and the Emperor personally led his army to attack him, and he sent messengers several times to ask what the councilor-in-chief was doing. The reply was: "Because the Emperor is soldiering so I comfort and encourage the people, contributing all my belongings to fund the military, as when Chen Xi rebelled." One of Xiao He's entourage persuaded him: "Your entire clan may soon be exterminated. You are Councilor-in-Chief, with the highest merit and honor, to which no more can be added. But it is more than 10 years since you came inside the Pass and won the very hearts of the people. The people are attached to Your Honor, but you still tirelessly try to win them over. The reason that the Emperor keeps on asking you is because he is afraid of you toppling his authority in Guanzhong. My suggestion is that you buy much land on low-interest credit, and thereby sully your own reputation? That way the Emperor will feel at ease." Xiao adopted the plan, and the Emperor was delighted.

When the Emperor returned after putting down Tattooed Bu, people stopped him on the road, protesting against the Councilor-in-Chief's forcible purchase of thousands of people's land and houses for a song. When the Emperor reached Court, Xiao went for an audience. The Emperor laughed: "Now the Councilor-in-Chief has actually benefited from the people!" He gave Xiao all the petitions received, saying: "You shall apologize to the people on your own!" Xiao afterwards petitioned in the interest of the people: "Chang'an is narrow in area, but there is much open space in the Imperial Forest Park that lies unused. Please allow the people to work the land in the

【原文】

为请吾苑！”乃下何廷尉，械系之。数日，王卫尉侍，前问曰：“相国胡大罪，陛下系之暴也？”上曰：“吾闻李斯相秦皇帝，有善归主，有恶自予。今相国多受贾竖金，为请吾苑，以自媚于民。故系治之。”王卫尉曰：“夫职事苟有便于民而请之，真宰相事也。陛下奈何乃疑相国受贾人钱乎！且陛下距楚数岁，陈豨、黥布反时，陛下自将往，当是时相国守关中，关中摇足，则关西非陛下有也。相国不以此时为利，乃利贾人之金乎？且秦以不闻其过亡天下，夫李斯之分过，又何足法哉！陛下何疑宰相之浅也！”上不怿。是日，使使持节赦出何。何年老，素恭谨，徒跣入谢。上曰：“相国休矣！相国为民

【今译】

上大怒道：“相国接受了商人的很多贿赂，替他们请求我的林苑！”于是把萧何下交给廷尉，带上刑具拘禁起来。数日后，王卫尉侍奉皇上，上前问道：“相国犯了什么大罪，陛下那么粗暴地拘禁他？”皇上说：“我听说李斯为秦皇帝作丞相，有善行就归于主上，有过错就归于自己。现在相国受了商人贿赂，为他们请求我的林苑，来自己讨好于百姓，所以拘捕治罪。”王卫尉说：“供职办事有利于民的就向上请求，是真正的宰相的责任。陛下怎么能怀疑相国接受了商人的钱呢！况且陛下抗拒楚军数年，陈豨、黥布反叛时，陛下亲自率军前往，那时相国守在关中，关中稍有举动关西就不归陛下所有了。相国不在此时图利，难道会贪图商人的钱吗？而且秦因为听不进说自己的过错而丢掉了天下，李斯的与君分过，又何足效法！陛下何至于把宰相看得如此浅薄！”皇上不高兴。这一天，派使者拿着符节赦免放出了萧何。萧何年纪已老，一向恭谨，光着脚入朝谢罪。皇上说：“相国不要这样！相国为百姓请求我的林苑未得允许，我不过是桀

park, instead of reaping the straw for animal fodder." The Emperor thundered: "The Councilor-in-Chief has accepted great bribes from the merchants, and now he is asking for my park on their behalf!" So he handed over Xiao in chains to the Chamberlain for Law Enforcement. A few days later, Chamberlain for the Palace Garrison Mr. Wang served the Emperor. He came up and asked: "What is the Councilor-in-Chief's felony that causes Your Majesty to detain him violently?" The Emperor replied: "I heard that when Li Si served as Councilor-in-Chief of the Qin Emperor, he attributed all good deeds to his lord and evil deeds to himself. Now the Councilor-in-Chief has accepted the merchants' bribes, and asked me for the Forest Park to please the common people, so I arrested him as punishment." Wang said: "It is a prime minister's real responsibility to request anything that might be convenient to the people. How can Your Majesty suspect that the Councilor-in-Chief has accepted the merchants' money? Moreover, when Your Majesty resisted the Chu army for years, or personally led your army to attack the rebels Chen Xi and Tattooed Bu, the Councilor-in-Chief defended Guanzhong. If there had been the slightest movement in Guanzhong, Your Majesty would not now own all area to the west of the Pass. The Councilor-in-Chief took no advantage at that time, but now you think he's greedy for the merchants' money? Qin was overthrown because the Qin Emperor would not hear his own fault spoken of, and Li Si's sharing of the fault is not worthy of emulation! How can Your Majesty suspect the prime minister of being so shallow!" The Emperor was unhappy and that same day he sent a messenger with his tally to pardon and release Xiao from custody. Xiao He was an old man by now, and was always respectful, so he entered Court barefoot, not wearing the shoes to which he was entitled. The Emperor remonstrated: "This is not fitting for the Councilor-in-Chief! You petitioned for my forest park for the people and I did not approve it. So I am only a Lord like King Jie and King Zhou, while you are the virtuous Councilor-in-

【原文】

请吾苑不许，我不过为桀纣主，而相国为贤相。吾故系相国，欲令百姓闻吾过。”

高祖崩，何事惠帝。何病，上亲自临视何疾，因问曰：“君即百岁后，谁可代君？”对曰：“知臣莫如主。”帝曰：“曹参何如?”何顿首曰：“帝得之矣。何死不恨矣！”

何买田宅必居穷辟处，为家不治垣屋。曰：“令后世贤，师吾俭；不贤，毋为势家所夺。”

孝惠二年，何薨，谥曰文终侯。子禄嗣，薨，无子。高后乃封何夫人同为酂侯，小子延为筑阳侯。孝文元年，罢同，更封延为酂侯。薨，子遗嗣。薨，无子。文帝复以遗弟则嗣，有罪免。景帝二年，制诏御史：“故相国萧何，高皇帝大功臣，所与为天下也。今其祀绝，朕甚怜之。其以武阳县户二千封何孙嘉为列侯。”嘉，则弟也。薨，子胜嗣，后有罪免。武帝元狩中，复下诏御史：“以酂户

【今译】

纣之主，而相国是贤相。我之所以拘捕相国，是想让百姓知道我的过错。”

高祖崩，萧何事奉惠帝。萧何病重，皇上亲自去探望他，于是问道：“您百岁之后，谁可以代替您呢？”回答说：“没有比主上更了解臣下的了。”皇帝说：“曹参怎么样？”萧何顿首说：“皇上得到贤才了，我死而无憾了！”

萧何买田宅一定在贫穷偏僻之地，治家不修有院墙的房屋，说：“假使后代贤能，将学习我的俭朴；不贤，也不会被权势之家所侵夺。”

孝惠二年，萧何薨，谥号文终侯。其子萧禄继承他，薨，没有儿子。高后于是封萧何夫人同为酂侯，小子萧延为筑阳侯。孝文元年，罢免同，改封萧延为酂侯。薨，其子萧遗继承他。萧遗薨，没有儿子。文帝又让萧遗的弟弟萧则继承，因为有罪而罢免。景帝二年，诏令御史：“已故相国萧何，是高皇帝的大功臣，参与过争取天下的大事。现在他的后代绝灭，朕很怜惜他。可把武阳县二千户封给萧何孙萧嘉为列侯。”萧嘉，是萧则的弟弟。薨，其子萧胜继承，后来有罪罢免。武帝元狩中，又下诏御史：“把酂地两千四百户封萧何曾孙萧

Chief. The reason I arrested you was to demonstrate my fault to the people."

After the death of Emperor Gaozu, Xiao He served Emperor Huidi. When Xiao was seriously ill, the Emperor went in person to visit him, and asked: "When you are not here, who can replace you?" Xiao replied: "Nobody has better understanding of his subjects than my Lord." The Emperor asked: "How about Cao Can?" Xiao kowtowed and said: "Your Majesty has made the worthy choice and I can die without regret!"

When Xiao bought land and houses they were sure to be located in some poor remote area, and when he built a house, it never had courtyard walls. He said: "If my descendants are virtuous and talented, they will learn from my frugality; if not worthy, they will not be taken by powerful people."

In the second year of Emperor Huidi's reign, Xiao died, and was posthumously honored as Marquis of Wenzhong. His son Xiao Lu inherited his title, but died without a son and heir. So the Empress Dowager made Xiao He's widow Tong Marquis of Zan and his nephew Xiao Yan Marquis of Zhuyang. In the first year of Emperor Wendi's reign, Tong was removed and Xiao Yan replaced her as Marquis of Zan. He was succeeded by his son Xiao Yi, who died sonless. The Emperor allowed Xiao Yi's younger brother Xiao Ze to inherit the title, but dismissed him for a crime. In year two of Emperor Jingdi's reign, he decreed to the censor: "Xiao He the late Prime Minister was Gaozu's courtier, a man who gave outstanding service, one of our founding fathers. Now that he is heirless, I pity him. I hereby make his grandson Xiao Jia adjunct marquis, with a fief of 2,000 households in Wuyang County." Xiao Jia was the younger brother of Xiao Ze, and was succeeded by his son Xiao Sheng, who was subsequently dismissed for a crime.

In the Yuanshou reign period (122-117 BC), Emperor Wudi also decreed to the censor: "I hereby make Xiao He's great grandson

【原文】

二千四百封何曾孙庆为酂侯，布告天下，令明知朕报萧相国德也。”庆，则子也。薨，子寿成嗣，坐为太常(仪)[牺]牲瘦免。宣帝时，诏丞相御史求问萧相国后在者，得玄孙建世等十二人，复下诏以酂户二千封建世为酂侯。传子至孙获，坐使奴杀人减死论。成帝时，复封何玄孙之子南䜌长喜为酂侯。传子至曾孙，王莽败乃绝。

——卷三十九《萧何曹参传》第九

【今译】

庆为酂侯，布告天下，使天下明知朕报答萧相国的恩德。”萧庆，是萧则的儿子。薨，其子寿成继承，因为献给太常的牺牲瘦瘠获罪罢免。宣帝时，诏令丞相御史查询萧相国后代尚存的人，找到玄孙建世等十二人，又下诏把酂二千户封建世为酂侯。传子至孙萧获，因指使奴仆杀人而以减死论罪。成帝时，又封萧何玄孙之子南䜌长萧喜为酂侯。传子至于曾孙。王莽失败后就绝灭了。

Xiao Qing Marquis of Zan with a fief of 2,400 households in Zan. Let it be known to the world that I repay the kindness of Councilor-in-Chief Xiao." Xiao Qing was the son of Xiao Ze. He was succeeded by his son Xiao Shoucheng, who was dismissed for the offense of presenting a scrawny animal for the imperial sacrifice. Emperor Xuandi ordered his prime minister and censor to inquire about surviving descendants of Councilor-in-Chief Xiao He. Twelve were discovered, including his great-great-grandson Xiao Jianshi, whom he also made Marquis of Zan with a fief of 2,000 households. The title was inherited by the son and then the grandson Xiao Huo. The latter was sentenced to death for ordering his servant to murder, but his penalty was reduced. Under Emperor Chengdi the title went to the son of Xiao He's great-great-grandson Xiao Xi, the Magistrate of Nanqiang. The title then went to his son, down to his great-grandchildren. After the downfall of Wang Mang, the line died out.

贾谊传

【原文】

贾谊，雒阳人也，年十八，以能诵诗书属文称于郡中。河南守吴公闻其秀材，召置门下，甚幸爱。文帝初立，闻河南守吴公治平为天下第一，故与李斯同邑，而尝学事焉，征以为廷尉。廷尉乃言谊年少，颇通诸家之书。文帝召以为博士。

是时，谊年二十馀，最为少。每诏令议下，诸老先生未能言，谊尽为之对，人人各如其意所出。诸生于是以为能。文帝说之，超迁，岁中至太中大夫。

谊以为汉兴二十馀年，天下和洽，宜当改正朔，易服色制度，定官名，兴礼乐。乃草具其仪法，色上黄，数用五，为官名悉更，奏之。

【今译】

贾谊，洛阳人，十八岁时，就因能够背诵诗书和会写文章闻名当地。河南郡守吴公听到他才学优异，把他召到门下，非常器重他。汉文帝即位不久，听说河南郡守吴公政绩为全国第一，过去与李斯同乡，曾经向李斯学习过，于是征召他做廷尉。廷尉就推荐说贾谊年纪虽小，但很能通晓诸子百家之书。汉文帝就召贾谊做了博士。

这时，贾谊二十多岁，在博士中是最年轻的。汉文帝每次下令讨论的问题布置下来，年长的博士们不能说上什么，而贾谊能够一一回答，并且人人都觉得说出了他们的意思。博士们于是认为贾谊才能出众。汉文帝喜欢他，破格提拔，一年之内提升到太中大夫。

贾谊认为汉朝建立二十多年了，国家太平和洽，应当改订历法，改变车马服饰的颜色，订立法令制度，确定官职名称，振兴礼乐。于是起草各项仪式的法度，车马服饰的颜色用黄色，官印数字用“五”，确定官职名称，全部改变旧制，贾谊上奏皇上。汉文帝谨慎

Chapter 8

Biography of Jia Yi

Jia Yi, born in Luoyang, was known throughout his prefecture at the age of 18 for being able to recite classics and poetry and write essays. The Governor of Henan Mr. Wu heard about his excellent scholarship, and summoned him to his official residence as a protege, thinking very highly of him. On ascending the throne, Emperor Wendi heard that Henan Governor Mr. Wu was ranked No.1 in the empire for the quality of his administration. Wu came from the same area as Li Si and had learned political affairs under him, so the Emperor recruited him as Chamberlain for Law Enforcement. Wu, in turn, recommended young Jia Yi as being well versed in the books of various schools of philosophers. The Emperor then summoned Jia Yi as an Erudite.

Jia Yi, in his early twenties at the time, was the youngest of the Erudites. Whenever the Emperor ordered discussion of his edicts, the older Erudites could not say anything, but Jia Yi was able to answer everything, and could put into words what everyone was thinking. The scholars therefore believed that Jia Yi was a rising star, of exceptional talent. The Emperor was pleased with him, ordering his promotion outside of the norms; within a year he rose to be Superior Grand Master of the Palace.

It was Jia Yi's opinion, that since 20-plus years had passed since the Han Dynasty was established, and that now all was peace and harmony, therefore they should revise the calendar, change the color of clothes, rectify the constitution, determine the official titles, and revitalize ritual and music. Then he drafted a system of rites, and memorialized the Emperor about his suggested changes to the

【原文】

文帝谦让未皇也。然诸法令所更定，及列侯就国，其说皆谊发之。于是天子议以谊任公卿之位。绛、灌、东阳侯、冯敬之属尽害之，乃毁谊曰：“雒阳之人年少初学，专欲擅权，纷乱诸事。”于是天子后亦疏之，不用其议，以谊为长沙王太傅。

谊既以適去，意不自得，及度湘水，为赋以吊屈原。屈原，楚贤臣也，被谗放逐，作《离骚赋》，其终篇曰：“已矣！国亡人，莫我知也。”遂自投江而死。谊追伤之，因以自谕。其辞曰：

恭承嘉惠兮，竢罪长沙。仄闻屈原兮，自湛汨罗。造托湘流兮，敬吊先生。遭世罔极兮，乃陨厥身。乌虖哀哉兮，逢时不祥！鸾凤伏窜兮，鸱鸮翱翔。阘茸尊显兮，谗谀得志；贤圣逆曳兮，方正倒植。谓随、夷溷兮，谓跖、蹻廉；莫邪为钝兮，铅

【今译】

从事，来不及实行。然而各项法令的更改确定，以及各个诸侯都住到自己的封国里去，这些主张都是贾谊提出的。于是汉文帝与大臣商议，让贾谊担任公卿的职位。绛侯、灌侯、东阳侯、冯敬这些人嫉妒他，就诋毁说：“洛阳这个少年，年纪轻轻，学识浅薄，一心想独揽大权，给许多事情造成混乱。”由于这样，汉文帝后来也疏远了他，不采纳他的意见，让他做长沙王太傅。

贾谊因为贬官离开了，意志没有得到施展，在渡湘水时，写了一篇赋吊念屈原。屈原是楚国一位贤明的臣子，遭受谗言而被放逐，写作《离骚赋》，在篇末写道：“算了吧！国家无人，没有了解我的。”于是投江而死。贾谊追念哀伤他，因此以屈原自喻。他的赋写道：

我禀承皇帝恩旨，到长沙去上任。曾以谦恭的心情听别人说屈原投汨罗江自尽的事。如今我来到湘江岸边用湘江水来寄托我对屈原的哀思与祭吊。大量的世俗谗言秽语泼向先生，您只能投江自尽毁灭自己的身体。呜呼悲哀呀！您生不逢时，没有遇到一个好的年代。神奇的大鸟隐藏或者飞离，而鸥鹰却在天空中飞翔。无德无能的小人却能够名声显赫，地位高贵，惯于阿谀奉承的小人都能得志得意。贤良的正人君子竟遭到不测的悲惨命运。正直的人不得顺正道而行被颠倒了位置。世上竟有人说不贪天下而投水身亡的卞随和不食周粟而饿死的伯夷贪婪，反而说大盗跖、蹻是廉洁的；他们竟说古代十分锋利的名剑莫邪钝缓，

old system, among them using the color yellow on the Emperor's carriage, the figure "five" in seals, and determining the official titles. But Wendi, being ultra-cautious, did not implement the ideas. However, it was following Jia Yi's proposal that they revised the laws, and all vassal lords went back to their own fiefs. So the Emperor discussed with his ministers, in an attempt to promote Jia Yi to a top position as a great noble of the realm, or as chief minister of state. The Marquis of Jiang, Guan Ying, the Marquis of Dongyang, Feng Jing and others were jealous of Jia Yi, and slandered him: "This whippersnapper from Luoyang is just a beginner, but bent on power, causing confusion to many things." Influenced by their animosity, the Emperor later also drew away from Jia Yi, rejecting his advice, and sending him away as Grand Mentor of the King of Changsha.

Banished from the court, Jia Yi was disconsolate. Crossing the Xiang River, he wrote a prose poem in memory of Qu Yuan. Qu Yuan was a worthy courtier of the Kingdom of Chu, a victim of slander and exile, who wrote a prose poem *The Lamenti*, which ended, "That's an end to it! My country is unpeopled. No one there to know me." Then he jumped into the river and died. Yi's commemoration was sorrowful, identifying with Qu Yuan. He wrote:

I humbly accepted the imperial grace, to wait for imperial judgment in office in Changsha. I heard that Qu Yuan committed suicide by drowning himself in Miluo River. Today I came to the Xiang River and to commit my verse to water, mourning the master reverently. Having been slandered to the utmost, you had to destroy yourself. Alas! How wretched. You did not encounter a good age! Phoenixes hide or flee, but hawks are soaring in the sky. Mean villains win distinction, and servile flatterers proud success. Virtuous gentlemen are forced to withdraw, the frank and upright are toppled. Hermits Bian Sui and Boyi are besmirched, where the Robbers Zhi and Zhuang Jue are cleaned; the famous sword Moye is blunt, though common

【原文】

刀为铦。于嗟默默，生之亡故兮！斡弃周鼎，宝康瓠兮。腾驾罢牛，骖蹇驴兮；骥垂两耳，服盐车兮。章父荐屦，渐不可久兮；嗟(若)[苦]先生，独离此咎兮！

谇曰：已矣！国其莫吾知兮，子独壹郁其谁语？凤缥缥其高逝兮，夫固自引而远去。袭九渊之神龙兮，沕渊潜以自珍；偭蟂獭以隐处兮，夫岂从虾与蛭螾所贵圣之神德兮，远浊世而自臧。使麒麟可系而羁兮，岂云异夫犬羊？般纷纷其离此邮兮，亦夫子之故也！历九州而相其君兮，何必怀此都也？凤皇翔于千仞兮，览德辉而下之；见细德之险(微)[徵]兮，遥增击而去之。彼寻常之污渎兮，岂容吞舟之鱼！横江湖之鳣鲸兮，固将制于蝼蚁。

谊为长沙傅三年，有服飞入谊舍，止于坐隅。服似鸮，不详鸟也。谊既以适居长沙，长沙卑湿，谊自伤悼，以为寿不得长，乃为赋

【今译】

而普通铅铁刀都十分锋利。唉！您如此默默不得志无缘无故遭遇迫害。放弃传国的周鼎宝物而不要，却把破烂的瓦罐当宝贝。驾车用疲惫不堪的牛来驾辕，用跛腿的驴来拉车边套；骏马垂着双耳，拉着超重的盐车。用殷人的礼帽来垫鞋，这种混乱的局面还能维持很久吗？嗐！受苦受难的屈原先生啊！惟独您遭受到这些灾难。

宣示说：得了吧！在国内能有谁了解您，先生您一个人在这生闷气，心里的话又能向谁讲呢？没有人理解，就应当像凤凰鸟一样飘缈高飞消逝在远方，自我引退。效法隐藏在深渊里的蛟龙，要深藏在水中珍爱自己，神龙怎能和水虫、鱼、虾、蛤蟆、蚂蟥、蚯蚓之类为伍？要远离污浊的境界而自我珍藏，就要珍贵圣人流传下来的美德啊！假如骏马能叫人拴住，任人驾驭使唤，那它又与狗羊有什么不同呢？您遭遇到各种各样的迫害与不幸，也是您没有洁身自好，远离这污浊的尘世的缘故啊！您完全可以云游中国大地，选择一个明君去辅佐他，何必一定要怀念楚国呢？像凤凰一样的君子能飞上万里长空，当看到有光辉德性的明君时才肯下来。当看到德行短浅卑劣有危险的征兆，便马上拍打着双翅远走高飞而去。在长宽只有十几尺的死水坑里，怎能容下可以吞掉船的大鱼。在江湖中来回游的鳣鲸大鱼，一旦游入死水坑中必然要受到蝼蛄和蚂蚁的侵袭。

贾谊做长沙王太傅的第三年，有一只猫头鹰飞入贾谊的房间里，停在座位的旁边。猫头鹰像鸮，是一种不吉祥的鸟。贾谊已因被贬来居长沙，长沙低洼潮湿，贾谊常常哀伤，以为寿命不可能长，就作赋

knives feign sharpness. Alas! Your silence, no reason for living. Giving up the inherited Zhou Tripod, to treasure broken jars instead. Driving a chariot with tired cattle, with help from lame donkeys; strong horses with hanging ears, to pull overladen salt carts. Formal caps are used as shoe padding: can this chaos last so long!. Hai! Suffering master Qu Yuan! Only you suffered from these disasters.

So be it! In the country none can know you, but in your melancholy thoughts, to whom could you say that? The phoenix drifting away on high retires, to disappear into the yonder, like the the dragon hidden in the abyss, who goes deep down in the water for self-love; the dragon stays in its own water away from others, and how could it befriend shrimps, leeches, and earthworms? Precious are the divine virtues handed down from the sages, and you preserve yourself far off from the polluted world. If the kirin could be harnessed, would it be any different from dogs or sheep? In this chaotic world, it also befell the master to encounter this fault and misfortune! You could have traveled all over China to assist a wise ruler, so why must you cherish Chu? The phoenix soars thousands of yards in the sky, alighting only at the sight of an enlightened ruler with great virtue. When it sees the dangerous signs of despicable morals, it will fly far away on flapping wings. How could such a measly ditch of stagnant water accommodate a fish large enough to swallow a ship! If sturgeons and whales that rule the rivers and lakes enter the ditch, they will be attacked and harried by mole crickets and ants.

In the third year that Jia Yi was Grand Mentor in Changsha, an owl-like bird flew into the room where he was, stopping next to his seat. That fowl, an inauspicious bird, looked like an owl. Since he had been banished to Changsha, which is low-lying and humid, Jia Yi was often sentimental, thinking that his life could not be long. So

【原文】

以自广。其辞曰：

单阏之岁，四月孟夏，庚子日斜，服集余舍，止于坐隅，貌甚闲暇。异物来崒，私怪其故，发书占之，谶言其度。曰“野鸟入室，主人将去”。问于子服：“余去何之？吉乎告我，凶言其灾。淹速之度，语余其期。”

服乃太息，举首奋翼，口不能言，请对以意。万物变化，固亡休息。斡流而迁，或推而还。形气转续，变化而嬗。沕穆亡间，胡可胜言！祸兮福所倚，福兮祸所伏；忧喜聚门，吉凶同域。彼吴强大，夫差以败；粤栖会稽，句践伯世。斯游遂成，卒被五刑；傅说胥靡，乃相武丁。夫祸之与福，何异纠缠！命不可说，孰知其极？水激则旱，矢激则远。万物回薄，震荡相转。云烝

【今译】

来安慰自己，赋写道：

丁卯年夏季的第一个月二十三日这天傍晚，太阳就要西下时，一只猫头鹰停栖在我的居室里，停留在座位的一角，神态十分悠闲从容不迫。这只奇怪的鸟停栖在我的家中，看到猫头鹰飞进我的居室，便暗自猜测它飞来是什么原因。我打开占卜吉凶的书，以书中预言吉凶的话核对吉凶的定数。书上说：“野生的飞鸟飞入屋内，屋主人将要离开此地。”我向猫头鹰发问：“我将要到什么地方去？如果有吉利的事，你就告诉我，即使将有凶事，也请把灾祸是什么对我说明。我的寿命是长是短，请告诉我一个定期。”

猫头鹰于是叹息了一声，然后抬起头，奋力拍打翅膀，它虽然嘴里不能说人语，却能用示意的方式来作答，根据它的表情来猜测它的心情。它的意思说：世间万种物种循环变化万千，原本就没有止境停息，旋转流动，推移变化，有时运转而消失，有时推移而回还。形和气的转化连续而不断，变化无穷无尽，有如蝉之蜕化。精大深奥微妙之处说也说不完，简直就是无法用语言表达。祸中含有福因，福中隐藏着祸根，祸福彼此相因相随，往往会因祸生福，福中藏祸。忧喜同聚在同一家之门，吉凶共在同一个地域。春秋时期的吴国曾经是个强大的国家，而吴王夫差却因此而战败。越国曾经被吴国战败，越王勾践被吴王夫差围困在会稽山中，而越王勾践卧薪尝胆，经过充分准备又一举灭掉吴国。李斯成功地游说秦国，做了秦国丞相，后被赵高所害，竟然身受五刑而死。傅说原是一名一个接一个捆在一起服劳役的囚徒，而最后却位居殷高宗武丁的丞相。所以福与祸之间的关系与两三股绳子绞合拧在一起有什么不同呢？天命是无法解说清楚的，谁知道它的终极止境在哪里！水受到激发便迅猛奔流，箭受到激发便能射得很远。万物往返回荡相激，

he wrote prose poems to comfort himself. Here is one:

When the sun slanted on the afternoon of the 23rd of the fourth moon of the year of the rabbit, an owl came to perch in my living room, next to my seat. Calm and relaxed it looked. A strange bird perching in my abode, I secretly wondered why. I opened the divination book to check it with the augury. The book says: "Wild birds flying into the room, then the owner will want to leave." I asked Mr. Owl: "Where will I go? If it is a lucky thing, do tell me it. Even if there is misfortune, please explain to me what evil it is. As to the span of my life, please tell my days."

The owl sighed, and raised his head, beating his wings. Although he had not words, he was poised to indicate his meaning. All matter changes, without stop. The rotating flow changes over time, dispersing and sometimes coming back also. Form and vital energy shift into each other continuously, evolving and substituting. The subtleties are inexhaustible, thus simply inexpressible. 'Good fortune lies within bad, while bad fortune lurks within good.' Worry and happiness gather inside the same door, while good or ill luck are in the same area. Wu was once a powerful state, but its king Fuchai was defeated. King Goujian of Yue was confined in Kuaiji Mountains, but in the end prevailed. Li Si successfully lobbied the state of Qin, and became its premier, but sustained a death of the fifth kind of punishment. Fu Yue was once a tied slave laborer, but eventually became prime minister of King Wuding. Therefore, the relationship between good fortune and bad, is it different from the twisted strands of a rope! Destiny cannot be explained clearly, and who knows where is its ultimate end? Flowing water when excited will be torrential, while arrows stimulated can be shot very far. Everything circles around, vibrating on and back. Water vaporizes into clouds, and cold clouds return

【原文】

雨降，纠错相纷。大钧播物，坱圠无垠。天不可与虑，道不可与谋。迟速有命，乌识其时？

且夫天地为炉，造化为工；阴阳为炭，万物为铜，合散消息，安有常则？千变万化，未始有极。忽然为人，何足控揣；化为异物，又何足患！小智自私，贱彼贵我；达人大观，物亡不可。贪夫徇财，列士徇名；夸者死权，品庶每生。怵迫之徒，或趋西东；大人不曲，意变齐同。愚士系俗，僒若囚拘；至人遗物，独与道俱。众人惑惑，好恶积意；真人恬漠，独与道息。释智遗形，超然自丧；寥廓忽荒，与道翱翔。乘流则逝，得坻则止；

【今译】

不断变化转化。水受热上蒸为云，云受冷又从天而降为雨，事物的变化自然现象错综复杂无法分清。自然界形成万物好像用制陶转轮运转造物，变化多端，范围广大无边无际。天和道，其理深远，不可人为思虑谋度。人的寿命长短，生死迟速自有天命，哪能预知它的期限呢！

况且上天与大地就好像是一个冶炼金属的炉子，造化万物的造物主就像是冶金工匠。以阴阳当做冶炼炉中的炭火，自然界中的万物当做被冶炼的铜矿石料。聚灭生息，毁灭生存，这一切怎么会有一定的规律呢？自然界万物的千变万化，没有开始也没有终止极限。偶然生而成人，也不值得过分地珍爱；死后变为鬼神又何必过分地忧伤！眼光短浅耍小聪明的人总是自私自利，以他物为贱，以自己为贵。通达的人目光心胸远大，对万物一视同仁没有不适宜的地方。贪婪无厌的人以身殉财，重义轻生之士为名节而死；谋求虚名重视权势的人为争权夺利而死。平民百姓大多都是贪生怕死。为名利所引诱，为贪财所逼迫的人整天东奔西跑到处钻营。道德修养高深的人不为物欲所屈服，万物再怎么变化都等量齐观一视同仁。愚笨的人为世俗所累所牵系，其窘迫的形态如同被囚禁的犯人一样。有至高的道德的人，抛弃了身外之物的拖累，惟独与大道共存。人们慌恐疑惑不可终日，头脑中聚集了很多可爱和可憎的事物。而得天地之道的真人却十分恬静淡漠，独与大道共存同处。放弃智慧思虑，遗弃形体，做到心如死灰，形如槁木达到人生修养的最高境界。在寥阔恍惚深远的世界中，得天地之道的真人无所依附，惟与大道共翱翔。人生像浮在水上的木头顺水而流漂向远方，只是在碰到水中小洲才停止。把自己的身躯任凭命运来支配，不把身躯看成是自己私有之物。

as rain; things crisscross in indistinguishable complexity. The formation of all things by Heaven, like a potter operating his wheel shows a limitless immensity. Heaven is beyond reasoning, and the Way beyond measuring. The length of human life is destined. How can you predict its duration?

Moreover, heaven and earth is like a metal smelting furnace, and the Creator of all things like a metallurgist, using yin and yang as charcoal, and all things in nature as the copper ore. Combination and decomposition, prosperity and decline, how can all this have a law? Ever-changing, there is no beginning or end. Occasionally one is born as human, which is nothing to be conceited about; when one is incarnated as another creature, why should one show grief! Short-sighted, puny people are always selfish, making themselves important at the expense of others. Broad-minded people are magnanimous, accepting everything no matter what. Greedy people sacrifice their lives to wealth, martyrs die for their reputation; and ambitious people die of struggle for power, while most commoners cling to life. The lure of profit and greed to possess force people to run from pillar to post. Superior people do not yield for material desires, and remain the same no matter how things change. Stupid people are bound by usage, as trapped as prisoners in confinement. People of high morality abandon material possessions, only to join the Way. The people are bewildered, and in their desperate minds are gathered lovely or odious things. True people live a quiet and indifferent life, and co-exist alone with the Way. Releasing their intelligence and leaving their form, in transcendental abandon; in the deep trance worldwide, they soar with the Way. They drift downstream to the distance, only stopping when they hit a sandbank. They leave their own bodies to fate, not as their own private things. Alive, they float along, to be laid to rest

【原文】

纵躯委命，不私与己。其生兮若浮，其死兮若休？澹乎若深渊之靓，泛乎若不系之舟。不以生故自保，养空而浮。德人无累，知命不忧。细故蒂芥，何足以疑！

后岁馀，文帝思谊，征之。至，入见，上方受釐，坐宣室。上因感鬼神事，而问鬼神之本。谊具道所以然之故。至夜半，文帝前席。既罢，曰："吾久不见贾生，自以为过之，今不及也。"乃拜谊为梁怀王太傅。怀王，上少子，爱，而好书，故令谊傅之，数问以得失。

是时，匈奴强，侵边。天下初定，制度疏阔。诸侯王僭儗，地过古制，淮南、济北王皆为逆诛。谊数上疏陈政事，多所欲匡建，其大略曰：

臣窃惟事势，可为痛哭者一，可为流涕者二，可为长太息者六，若其它背理而伤道者，难遍以疏举。进言者皆曰天下已安已

【今译】

活着的时候就好像将自己的生命托附人间，死后就如同永久地安息。淡泊的人生就像死一般宁静的深渊，而推波助澜的思想波涛就如同没有拴住的航船。不应因为生在人世间而过于珍惜自己的生命，最好是养其空虚之性，以浮游于人世之间。有修养有德性的人无所牵累，居无思行无虑，不藏是非美恶，因为他们知天命而不会自寻忧愁。像猫头鹰飞入室内这样琐细之事有什么值得疑虑的呢！

一年多以后，汉文帝想念贾谊，征召他回京城长安。贾谊到了，进入朝廷求见，汉文帝正在承受神灵的降福，坐在宣室里接见贾谊。汉文帝因对鬼神之事有所感触，就向贾谊询问鬼神的原本。贾谊详细讲述其中的道理。一直谈到深夜，汉文帝听得不觉移坐到席的前端。谈论完了，汉文帝说："我很久没看到贾生了，自以为超过他了，今天看来，还比不上他啊。"于是任命贾谊作梁怀王的太傅。梁怀王，是汉文帝的小儿子，很受宠爱，又喜欢读书，所以叫贾谊作他的老师，他多次向贾谊请教成败得失。

这一时期，匈奴强盛，常常侵犯汉朝边疆。汉朝刚刚建立，法规制度粗疏而不严明。诸侯王超越本身的权力范围，占据的土地超过古代制度的规定，淮南王、济北王都因为谋反而被诛灭。贾谊多次上疏陈述政事，他的意见大多是想改变和建立新制度，其大意是：

我私下考虑了当前的国家形势，认为可以为之痛哭的有一件，可以为之流涕的有二件，可以为之长叹的有六件，至于其他违背事理而伤害正道的，难以分条列举。向陛下进言的人都说国

after death. Indifferent as the quiet abyss, their thoughts billow like a ship set loose. They are not too jealous of their lives in this world, they prefer to nurture emptiness, the better to float among men. The virtuous people have nothing to tie them down, because they are happy with their fate. So trivial a matter as the owl, what cause is it for worry?

By the time a year had passed, the Emperor missed Jia Yi, and recalled him to the capital. When he arrived he sought an audience with the Emperor, who was just taking the sacrifice meat as blessing; he received Jia Yi sitting in the Palace Chamber. The Emperor, touched by the gods and otherworldly matters, asked about their origin, and Jia Yi explained the truth of them in detail. They talked deep into the night, and Wendi unconsciously moved to sit at the front of the seat. The talk over, he said: "I did not see Mr. Jia for a long time, and thought I had surpassed him; but today it seems I do not come up to his level." So he named Jia Yi Grand Mentor to Prince Huai of Liang. The prince was the Emperor's youngest and favorite son, an avid reader; Jia Yi became his teacher, and he was repeatedly asked about success or failure in government.

During this period, the Huns grew strong, often invading the frontier. The empire had just been subjugated and the rules and regulations were incomplete. Vassal kings overstepped their authority, and their territories exceeded the ancient system of land tenure. The kings of Huainan and Jibei had been exterminated for conspiracy to rebel. Jia Yi presented several memorials on political affairs. His views were mostly aimed to change and establish the new system, as shown below:

I humbly considered the current situation in the country. One can weep over one thing, cry over two, and sigh over six. As to other things that are contrary to common sense and hurting the Way, they are difficult to list. The advisors mostly say that the world has become peaceful and well-governed, but

【原文】

治矣，臣独以为未也。曰安且治者，非愚则谀，皆非事实知治乱之体者也。夫抱火厝之积薪之下而寝其上，火未及燃，因谓之安，方今之势，何以异此！本末舛逆，首尾衡决，国制抢攘，非甚有纪，胡可谓治！陛下何不壹令臣得孰数之于前，因陈治安之策，试详择焉！

夫射猎之娱，与安危之机孰急？使为治劳智虑，苦身体，乏钟鼓之乐，勿为可也。乐与今同，而加之诸侯轨道，兵革不动，民保首领，匈奴宾服，四荒乡风，百姓素朴，狱讼衰息，大数既得，则天下顺治，海内之气，清和咸理，生为明帝，没为明神，名誉之美，垂于无穷。《礼》祖有功而宗有德，使顾成之庙称为太宗，上配太祖，与汉亡极。建久安之势，成长治之业，以承祖庙，以奉六亲，至孝也；以幸天下，以育群生，至仁也；立经

【今译】

家已经安宁已经治理好了，我独认为国家远未治理好。说国家安定并治理好的人，不是愚蠢就是阿谀奉承，都不是从事实出发知道治乱的根本的人。这如同把火种放在柴堆下而自己睡到上面，柴堆没有被点燃，就说很平安，当前国家的形势，跟这种情况有什么两样呢！本与末被颠倒了，前后的堤防被破坏了，国家制度混乱，并不是很有纲纪，怎么可以说治理好了呢。陛下为何不让我在您面前获得机会，来深入细致地陈述国家政治修明、社会安定的策略，试让您来仔细选择呢。

打猎这种娱乐，与掌握国家安危的关键哪一个紧要？如果认为去治理国家就要伤脑筋，苦身体，缺少钟鼓的娱乐，这是不对的。娱乐与现在一样，再加上诸侯遵守法纪，国家没有战乱，民众得到安定，匈奴表示臣服，边远地区的人归顺朝廷，百姓简朴无华，纠纷诉讼逐步消失。治国的大计掌握了，就能使天下顺治，社会气象清平和谐，都很合理，活在世上就做贤明的帝王，去世了则做明神，美好的名誉，流传千古。《周礼》上说，作为开国的君主要有功，做为继业的君主要有德，使陛下您的帝业功德，上与高祖刘邦相配，并和汉朝统治一起流芳百世。建立永久安定的局势，成就长久统治的基业，以此继承祖业，奉养六亲，这是最孝的了；以此造福天下，养育万物，这是最仁的了；确立

I alone beg to differ. Those who talk about peace and order are either dolts or flatterers; not the people who actually know the basic facts of government. It is akin to someone inserting kindling under the pyre while he sleeps above it, calling it safe while the pyre is not lit. The current situation is no different! This is a reversal of cause and effect, the head severed from the tail, with the state system in confusion, without morality and law. How can it be said to be good government! Why does Your Majesty not let me put before you the in-depth and detailed statement of the strategic options of the political and social stability, so that you could carefully choose.

Which is more urgent, to amuse oneself hunting, or the key to national security? To govern the country, if it is necessary to rack the brain and strain the body, it is not right to do so without the ritual music of bells and drums. Music remains the same now, as with the princes who comply with the law, the state not at war, the people with body and soul together, the Huns obedient, the people in remote areas in allegiance, folk customs simple and litigation gradually disappearing. With the master plan in place, you can rule the world smoothly, the social atmosphere peaceful and harmonious. You live as a wise emperor, and die an enlightening god, with a good reputation inherited down to infinity. According to the Rites of Zhou, *the founding father must have the merit of creation and his successors should do virtuous deeds. Your Temple of Gucheng should be known as the Grand Temple, to match the temple of Emperor Gaozu, and endure eternally with the immortal Han rule. It is the most filial of the emperors that establishes a permanent stable situation and long-term success of the regime, so as to preserve the ancestral temple and care for all imperial siblings; it is the most benevolent that benefits the world and nurtures all living things; it is the most*

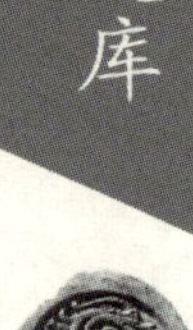

【原文】

陈纪，轻重同得，后可以为万世法程，虽有愚幼不肖之嗣，犹得蒙业而安，至明也。以陛下之明达，因使少知治体者得佐下风，致此非难也。其具可素陈于前，愿幸无忽。臣谨稽之天地，验之往古，按之当今之务，日夜念此至孰也，虽使禹舜复生，为陛下计，亡以易此。

夫树国固必相疑之势，下数被其殃，上数爽其忧，甚非所以安上而全下也，今或亲弟谋为东帝，亲兄之子西乡而击，今吴又见告矣。天子春秋鼎盛，行义未过，德泽有加焉，犹尚如是，况莫大诸侯，权力且十此者乎！

然而天下少安，何也？大国之王幼弱未壮，汉之所置傅相方握其事。数年之后，诸侯之王大抵皆冠，血气方刚，汉之傅相称病而赐罢，彼自丞尉以上偏置私人，如此，有异淮南、济北之为

【今译】

准则，颁布纲纪，轻重缓急处理得宜，而后可以成为万世的法式，即使有愚笨不成器的后代，还能承受祖业得到安定，这是最英明的了。靠陛下这样的英明通达，只要让稍许懂得治国道理的人在下面辅佐，做到这样不是什么难事。这些办法可以原原本本摆在您的前面，希望不要忽视。我谨慎地考察自然和社会，用历史加以验证，研究当前必须解决的事情，日夜思念这套治国安邦的办法已经很成熟了。即使禹、舜再生，为陛下计谋，也不会改变这个办法。

诸侯王国的力量强大了，必然会造成与朝廷互相猜疑对立的局势，民众因此屡次遭受灾祸，朝廷也常为此而忧虑，这实在不是安定朝廷、保全民众的办法。如今有你的亲弟图谋在东部地区称帝，亲兄的儿子也向西面进攻朝廷，同时，吴王谋反的事又报上来了。陛下正当壮年，行事合乎道义，没有过错，对诸侯王的恩泽又不断增加，他们尚且如此，更何况那些最大的诸侯，权力比他们还要强大十倍呢！

然而，天下还稍微安定，这是什么原因呢？因为那些大诸侯国的国王还未成年，朝廷派去的太傅、丞相正掌握着王国的大权。几年以后，诸侯王大都加冠成人，精力旺盛，朝廷委派的太傅、丞相则不得不称病免官，那些诸侯王就会把丞尉以上的官员，都安插上自己的亲信，像这样，他们的所作所为与淮南王、济北王

intelligent that establishes guidelines, issues discipline and prioritizes all processes fairly, so that they become the example for all generations; even if there would be unworthy stupid descendants, they would still inherit the ancestral property safely. It is not difficult to do this for such a wise monarch as Your Majesty, with the humble assistance of those who know just a little how to govern a country. This can be laid bare in front of you, and I hope not to be ignored. I carefully checked this with heaven and earth, verified it with historical events and examined it in the current affairs, to be pondered on day and night until it has become very mature. Even if Kings Yu and Shun came back to plan for Your Majesty, they would not change this.

The establishment of fiefs among the vassal lords will surely lead to mutual competition and antagonism, so that the subjects suffer disaster and Your Majesty often suffers from worries about this. This is no way to achieve reassurance at Court, or security for your subjects. Just now your younger brother attempted to be emperor in the east, and your nephew also attacked you to the west; the Prince of Wu is also reported to have rebelled. The Son of Heaven is in the prime of life, righteous and very gracious, never at fault, but they behave like this nonetheless, not to mention the vassal lords, ten times more powerful than they!

That said, the empire is somewhat peaceful, but why? Because the vassal lords are still young and weak, and their grand mentors and prime ministers appointed by the Court exercise power in their stead. In a few years, most princes will be crowned as energetic adults, and they will dismiss the Court appointees on the pretext of illness. They will appoint only their cronies to positions above the aides and commandants. Thus, how will their behavior differ from the rebellious kings of

【原文】

邪！此时而欲为治安，虽尧舜不治。

黄帝曰："日中必熭，操刀必割。"今令此道顺而全安，甚易，不肯早为，已乃堕骨肉之属而抗刭之，岂有异秦之季世乎！夫以天子之位，乘今之时，因天之助，尚惮以危为安，以乱为治，假设陛下居齐桓之处，将不合诸侯而匡天下乎？臣又以知陛下有所必不能矣。假设天下如曩时，淮阴侯尚王楚，黥布王淮南，彭越王梁，韩信王韩，张敖王赵，贯高为相，卢绾王燕，陈豨在代，令此六七公者皆亡恙，当是时而陛下即天子位，能自安乎？臣有以知陛下之不能也。天下殽乱，高皇帝与诸公并起，非有仄室之势以豫席之也。诸公幸者，乃为中涓，其次廑得舍人，材之不逮至远也。高皇帝以明圣威武即天子位，割膏腴之地以王诸公，多者百余城，少者乃三四十县，惪至渥也，然其后十年之间，反者九起。陛下之与诸公，非亲角材而臣之也，又非身

【今译】

有什么不同呢！到了那时，要想使国家长治久安，即使唐尧虞舜也是办不到的。

黄帝说："太阳正中时一定要晒东西，拿着刀子就要赶快去切割东西。"现在按照这个道理去做，使国家巩固，民众安全，是很容易的。假如不趁早采取措施，就会伤害骨肉之情，以致要杀他们的头，这难道和秦朝末年还有什么不同吗？现在您凭着天子的权位，趁着当今的有利时机，靠着上天的保佑，还对转危为安、改乱为治的措施有顾虑；假如陛下处于当年齐恒公的地位，还能联合诸侯恢复天下的秩序吗？我知道陛下一定不能这样做。假如国家的形势还像从前那样，淮阴侯韩信还统治楚国，黥布统治淮南，彭越统治梁国，韩王信统治韩国，张敖统治赵国，贯高做赵国的相，卢绾统治燕国，陈豨还在代国，假如这六七人都还活着，而这时陛下即天子位，自己能觉得安全吗？我有理由认为是不能的。那时，天下混乱，高皇帝和这些人一同起兵，起初并没有亲族的势力可以依靠。这些人中的幸运者才做了中涓，差一点的只当舍人，他们的才能比高皇帝差得很远。高皇帝凭着他的圣明威武登上了天子之位，把肥沃的土地分封给这些人做诸侯王，多的有一百多座城池，少的也有三、四十个县，恩德是极深厚的了。可是在以后的十年当中，反叛的事件发生了九起。陛下

Huainan and Jibei! When this comes about, not even Yao and Shun could stabilize the country.

The Yellow Emperor said: "When the sun is at the meridian, this is the time to dry things; when holding a knife, this is the time to cut things." Now is the time when it is relatively easy to consolidate the country and safeguard the people. If we do not act as early as possible, it will hurt the kinship, or end up in their beheading, and how would that be any different from the last days of the Qin Dynasty? You, with the power of Son of Heaven, taking advantage of the current favorable opportunity, relying on heaven's blessing, still have misgivings about transforming danger to safety and changing chaos to governance. Suppose Your Majesty were in the position of Duke Huan of Qi, would you be able to unite the vassal lords to bring back order? I know that this would be beyond Your Majesty. Suppose the situation was as before, when the Marquis of Huaiyin ruled Chu, Tattooed Bu ruled Huainan, Peng Yue ruled Liang, Hann Xin ruled Hann, Zhang Ao ruled Zhao with Guan Gao as its prime minister, Lu Wan ruled Yan, and Chen Xi ruled Dai; if those six or seven people were still alive, would Your Majesty have felt safe when you ascended the throne? I have reason to believe that you could not. At that time, the world was chaotic. The founding emperor Gaozu and these people revolted together, having no relatives supplying troops to rely on at first. The more fortunate of these heroes only worked as attendants, the rest were merely hangers-on, and far less capable. Gaozu became emperor on account of his august wisdom and grandeur, and ceded fertile land to make these people vassal kings, with fiefs ranging from 30-40 counties to over a hundred towns. What favor was that. But in the following decade, there were nine cases of rebellious events. As to Your Majesty's relations with these people, you did not

【原文】

封王之也，自高皇帝不能以是一岁为安，故臣知陛下之不能也。然尚有可诿者，曰疏，臣请试言其亲者。假令悼惠王王齐，元王王楚，中子王赵，幽王王淮阳，共王王梁，灵王王燕，厉王王淮南，六七贵人皆亡恙，当是时陛下即位，能为治乎？臣又知陛下之不能也。若此诸王，虽名为臣，实皆有布衣昆弟之心，虑亡不帝制而天子自为者。擅爵人，赦死罪，甚者或戴黄屋，汉法令非行也。虽行不轨如厉王者，令之不肯听，召之安可致乎！幸而来至，法安可得加！动一亲戚，天下圜视而起，陛下之臣虽有悍如冯敬者，适启其口，匕首已陷其匈矣。陛下虽贤，谁与领此？故疏者必危，亲者必乱，已然之效也。其异姓负强而动者，汉已幸胜之矣，又不易其所以然。同姓袭是迹而动，既有征矣，其势尽又复

【今译】

与这些人的关系，并不是亲自同他们较量过才使他们甘心臣服的，也不是亲自封他们当诸侯王的。在这种情况下，高皇帝也不能得到一年的安宁，所以我知道陛下也是不能得到安宁的。然而，还有一个可以推托的藉口，说与他们的关系疏远，那就让我说说那些关系亲近的同姓王吧。假如悼惠王还在齐国称王，元王还在楚国称王，中子在赵国称王，幽王在淮阳称王，共王在梁国称王，灵王在燕国称王，厉王在淮南称王，假如这六七位贵人都还健在，这时陛下即位为天子，能把国家治理好吗？我又知道陛下是不能的。这些同姓诸侯王，虽然名义上是臣子，实际上都认为自己和皇帝是一般的兄弟关系，他们没有一个不想采用皇帝的礼仪制度让自己做皇帝的。他们擅自封爵，赦免死罪的人，甚至有人乘坐皇帝专用的黄绸车盖的车，汉朝的法令在那里不能推行。即使能推行，对于图谋不轨如厉王那样的人，命令他都不肯听从，召见他又怎么会来呢？侥幸来了，法律又怎么能施加到他的身上去呢？如果制裁了一个亲戚，天下的诸侯王就会瞪着眼起来反抗。陛下的臣子当中虽然有冯敬那样勇敢的人，但刚要开口告发诸侯王，刺客的匕首就已经刺进他的胸膛了。陛下虽然英明，但谁能辅佐您来一起治理这些诸侯王呢？所以说关系疏远的异姓王必然危害国家，关系亲近的同姓王也一定会反叛，这已经被事实证明了。那些自恃实力强大而反叛的异姓诸侯王，汉朝已经幸运地战胜他们了，可是并没有改变造成混乱的原因。同姓诸侯王又沿着这条老路发动叛乱，已经有征兆了，这种局势又完全

fight alongside them before they became your subjects, nor did you personally make them princes. In this case, Gaozu himself could not have got a year of peace, still less Your Majesty. However, there is an excuse for their estrangement, so let me talk about those close relations. If Prince Daohui was still in Qi, Prince Yuan in Chu, the middle son in Zhao, Prince You in Huaiyang, Prince Gong in Liang, Prince Ling in Yan, Prince Li in Huainan; if these six or seven nobles were still alive when Your Majesty ascended the throne, could you govern well? The answer must, again, be no. If these same-surname princes, although nominally your subjects, in fact, believed themselves to have an ordinary fraternal relationship with the emperor, I fear there is not one among them who would not want to use the Emperor's ritual system to make himself Emperor. They would arbitrarily confer knighthoods, pardon capital offenses, or even ride carriages with the imperial yellow silk awning, and Han laws would not be implemented. Even if they were, when lawless people such as Prince Li refused to obey your commands, how would he come when summoned? Even if he was by luck to come, how could the law be applied to his body? If you touched a relative, the vassal lords of the empire would rise up with Your Majesty in their sights. Even if your courtiers included brave men like Feng Jing, an assassin's dagger would pierce his chest as he started to speak his accusation. Although Your Majesty is wise, who will assist you to control these princes? Thus, as estranged princes are bound to be dangerous, so close relations of the same surname will certainly rebel, which has already been proven. Han was lucky enough to defeat those princes with different surnames who controlled strong armies and rebelled, but the underlying cause was not changed. Princes with the same surname act along this old track in rebellion, and we have already seen signs thereof, absolutely along the

【原文】

然。殃既之变，未知所移，明帝处之尚不能以安，后世将如之何！

屠牛坦一朝解十二牛，而芒刃不顿者，所排击剥割，皆众理解也。至于髋髀之所，非斤则斧。夫仁义恩厚，人主之芒刃也；权势法制，人主之斤斧也。今诸侯王皆众髋髀也，释斤斧之用，而欲婴以芒刃，臣以为不缺则折。胡不用之淮南、济北？势不可也。

臣窃迹前事，大抵强者先反。淮阴王楚最强，则最先反；韩信倚胡，则又反；贯高因赵资，则又反；陈豨兵精，则又反；彭越用梁，则又反；黥布用淮南，则又反；卢绾最弱，最后反。长沙乃在二万五千户耳，功少而最完，势疏而最忠，非独性异人也，亦形势然也。曩令樊、郦、绛、灌据数十城而王，今虽以残亡可也；令信、越之伦列为彻侯而居，虽至今存可也。然则天

【今译】

和过去一样。灾祸的变化，还不知要演变到什么地方。像您这样英明的皇帝处在这种情况下，尚且不能使国家安宁，后世的人又将怎么办呢！

屠牛坦一个早晨宰十二头牛，可是锋利的刀刃没有变钝，这是因为他拍击剥割的地方都在肌肉和骨头的缝隙之间。至于对付大腿骨的地方，不是用砍刀就是用斧头。仁义恩厚好比皇上的利刃，权势和法制好比皇上的砍刀和斧子。如今诸侯王都像一些大腿骨，对他们不用砍刀斧子，而想用利刃去切割，我认为不是碰出缺口就是被折断。为什么不用仁义厚恩去对待淮南王、济北王呢？因为形势不允许了。

我私下考察以前发生的事情，大都是势力强大的诸侯王先反叛。淮阴侯韩信称王于楚，势力最强，就最先反叛；韩王信依靠匈奴的势力，继续反叛；贯高依靠赵国的优越条件，又反叛；陈豨军队精悍，又反叛；彭越利用梁国的力量，又反叛；黥布依靠淮南的力量，又反叛；卢绾势力最弱，最后一个反叛。长沙王的封地内人口才二万五千户，功劳小但保存得最完善，势力弱而对朝廷最忠诚，这不是由于性格独特与其他诸侯王不同，而是形势使他这样的。如果从前把樊哙、郦商、周勃、灌婴等人封为占据几十个城池的诸侯王，即使现在他们的势力已经削弱了，也是不可以的。如果让韩信、彭越这些人只居于彻侯地位，即使现在还存在，也是可以的。既然这样，治理国家的大计就可以知道

same lines as in the past. Changes in disaster know not where to evolve to. If a wise emperor such as my Lord is still unable to make the country peaceful, who in future will know how to deal with it!

Tan the cattle-butcher slaughtered 12 head of cattle in a morning, but did not blunt his sharp edge, because he beat, cut and stripped according to their anatomical features. For the femurs, he would use a machete or an ax. Virtue and grace are the lord's sharp edge, while power and the rule of law are his machete and ax. Now the vassal kings are all femurs. If you do not use the machete and ax on them, preferring to use the knife, I think you will probably twist the blade or probably even break it. Why was it not used on the princes of Huainan and Jibei? Because the situation did not allow it.

When your servant humbly looked into historical precedent, it was generally the more powerful princes who rebelled first. The Marquis of Huaiyin Hann Xin had been King in Chu, with the strongest influence, so he was the first to rebel; as King Hann Xin he continued to rebel, supported by the Huns; Guan Gao rebelled because of favorable conditions in Zhao; Chen Xi's elite army then rebelled; Peng Yue rebelled with the forces of Liang; Tattooed Bu rebelled on the strength of Huainan; Lu Wan being the weakest, was the last to rebel. The King of Changsha had a fief of only 25,000 households, with few glorious deeds to his credit, and little influence; but his loyalty to the throne was the most total. This was not because his character was unique, different from the lords, but because the situation made him so. If Fan Kuai, Li Shang, Zhou Bo and Guan Ying had been made kings of dozens of towns, in today's situation, their power would have evaporated. If Hann Xin, Peng Yue, and the like had been made to live as mere ordinary marquises or grandees of the twentieth order,

【原文】

下之大计可知已。欲诸王之皆忠附，则莫若令如长沙王；欲臣子之勿菹醢，则莫若令如樊、郦等；欲天下之治安，莫若众建诸侯而少其力。力少则易使以义，国小则亡邪心。令海内之势如身之使臂，臂之使指，莫不制从，诸侯之君不敢有异心，辐凑并进而归命天子，虽在细民，且知其安，故天下咸知陛下之明。割地定制，令齐、赵、楚各为若干国，使悼惠王、幽王、元王之子孙毕以次各受祖之分地，地尽而止，及燕、梁它国皆然。其分地众而子孙少者，建以为国，空而置之，须其子孙生者，举使君之。诸侯之地其削颇入汉者，为徙其侯国及封其子孙也，所以数偿之；一寸之地，一人之众，天子亡所利焉，诚以定治而已，故天下咸知陛下之廉。地制壹定，宗室子孙莫虑不王，下无倍畔之心，上

【今译】

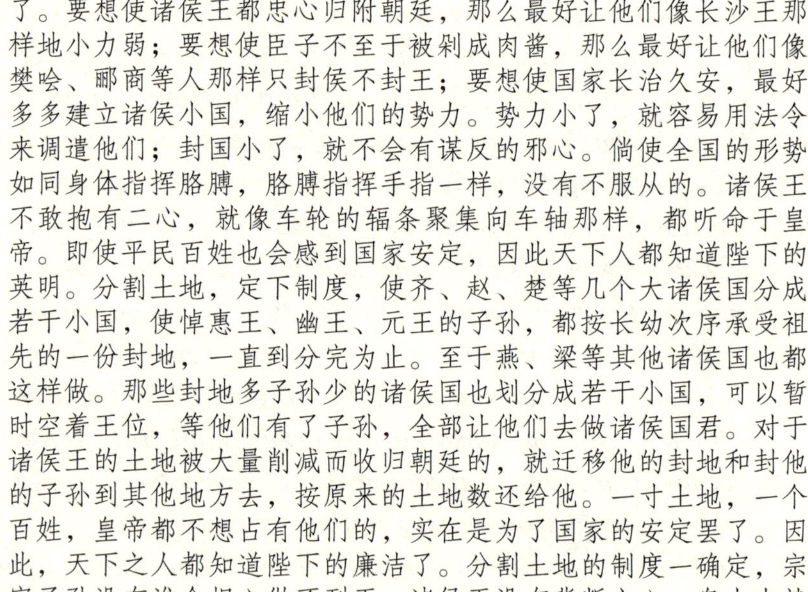

了。要想使诸侯王都忠心归附朝廷，那么最好让他们像长沙王那样地小力弱；要想使臣子不至于被剁成肉酱，那么最好让他们像樊哙、郦商等人那样只封侯不封王；要想使国家长治久安，最好多多建立诸侯小国，缩小他们的势力。势力小了，就容易用法令来调遣他们；封国小了，就不会有谋反的邪心。倘使全国的形势如同身体指挥胳膊，胳膊指挥手指一样，没有不服从的。诸侯王不敢抱有二心，就像车轮的辐条聚集向车轴那样，都听命于皇帝。即使平民百姓也会感到国家安定，因此天下人都知道陛下的英明。分割土地，定下制度，使齐、赵、楚等几个大诸侯国分成若干小国，使悼惠王、幽王、元王的子孙，都按长幼次序承受祖先的一份封地，一直到分完为止。至于燕、梁等其他诸侯国也都这样做。那些封地多子孙少的诸侯国也划分成若干小国，可以暂时空着王位，等他们有了子孙，全部让他们去做诸侯国君。对于诸侯王的土地被大量削减而收归朝廷的，就迁移他的封地和封他的子孙到其他地方去，按原来的土地数还给他。一寸土地，一个百姓，皇帝都不想占有他们的，实在是为了国家的安定罢了。因此，天下之人都知道陛下的廉洁了。分割土地的制度一确定，宗室子孙没有谁会担心做不到王，诸侯王没有背叛之心，皇上也就

they would have existed even today. This being the case, the plan to govern the country can be understood. To make all the princes allegiant to the Court, it is best that they be as weak as the King of Changsha; to have the courtiers avoid being cut into mincemeat as punishment, it is best to have them do as Fan Kuai, Li Shang, etc, enfeoffing as marquis but not king. In order to bring long-term peace and order in the country, it is best to establish a multitude of princedoms to reduce their power. The smaller their domains, the less likely the ambition to supplant you. Let the situation in the country correspond to the body in command of its arms, its arms in command of its fingers, which obey invariably. The princes dare not harbor disloyalty; just as the spokes of the wheels move with the axle, so they must follow orders from the Son of Heaven. Thus, even commoners will be aware of national stability, and the world will know Your Majesty's wisdom. Divide up the territories, and finalize the system, so that Qi, Zhao, and Chu are each divided into several small fiefs, and princes Daohui, You and Yuan's descendants would all share their ancestors' fiefs by seniority order until the land is all apportioned. As for Yan, Liang and other princes, they would be expected to do the same. Those vast fiefdoms with few descendants should also be divided into several princedoms, left empty temporarily, until their children and grandchildren can all be made princes. As regards the land of the princes that were forfeited to Han as a punitive measure, you simply give their descendants fiefdoms elsewhere, compensating them according to the quantity of the original land. Their Emperor wants to profit not one whit by this, which is purely in the interest of national stability. Thus, all will know the unsullied character of His Majesty. A definite land system will reassure the imperial clan descendants, who will not be jealous of their princedoms; the vassal lords will not want to

【原文】

无诛伐之志，故天下咸知陛下之仁。法立而不犯，令行而不逆，贯高、利幾之谋不生，柴奇、开章之计不萌，细民乡善，大臣致顺，故天下咸知陛下之义。卧赤子天下之上而安，植遗腹，朝委裘，而天下不乱，当时大治，后世诵圣。壹动而五业附，陛下谁惮而久不为此？

天下之势方病大瘇。一胫之大几如要，一指之大几如股，平居不可屈信，一二指搐，身虑亡聊。失今不治，必为锢疾，后虽有扁鹊，不能为已。病非徒瘇也，又苦𨂂盭。元王之子，帝之从弟也；今之王者，从弟之子也。惠王，亲兄子也；今之王者，兄子之子也。亲者或亡分地以安天下，疏者或制大权以偪天子，臣故曰非徒病瘇也，又苦𨂂盭。可痛哭者，此病是也。

【今译】

没有讨伐的念头，因此，天下人都知道陛下的仁爱了。法制建立而没有人触犯，政令推行而没有人违抗。像贯高、利己之类的阴谋不会发生，柴奇、开章那样的诡计也不会出现，百姓都趋向善良，大臣都表示顺从，因此，天下人都知道皇上的正义了。这样，即使让幼儿当皇帝，国家也是安宁的；即使立遗腹子为皇帝，让臣下朝拜先帝遗留下来的衣物，天下也不会混乱。这样，当代能大治，后代也会称颂陛下的圣明。实行这一措施，就能建树这样五项功业，陛下还顾虑什么而迟迟不这样做呢？

目前，天下的形势好像一个人正患着脚肿病一样。一条小腿肿得差不多跟腰一样粗，一个脚趾头肿得差不多像大腿一样粗。平时不能屈伸，一两个脚趾抽动，全身都感到疼痛难忍。如果现在不及时治疗，必然成为难治之症，以后即使有扁鹊也无能为力了。况且患的不仅仅是脚肿病，而且还苦于脚掌扭折。元王的儿子是陛下的堂弟；现在当楚王的是陛下堂弟的儿子。惠王的儿子是陛下亲哥哥的儿子，现在做齐王的是陛下哥哥的孙子。现在，陛下近亲当中有的还没有封地来保持天下的安定局面，而疏远的人有的执掌着大权来威胁皇上。所以，我说不但患脚肿病，同时还苦于脚掌扭折。可以为之痛哭的，就是这种病啊。

rebel, and the Emperor will not hanker to suppress them, so the world knows the benevolence of His Majesty. The rule of law will be established and none will violate it, and decrees will be implemented that none will disobey; the conspiracy of Guan Gao or Li Ji would not occur, nor the tricks of Chai Qi and Kaizhang. The common people will incline to goodness, the courtiers will become obedient, and all will know the justice of the Emperor. Thus, even if a young baby ruled as Emperor, the world would be peaceful; if a posthumous child of the Emperor reigned, with the courtiers worshipping the fur robe left behind by the late Emperor, even then there would not be chaos. In this way, peace and order will reign in our own times, and future generations will praise the sagacity of the Emperor. With the adoption of that measure, the above five meritorious achievements can follow. What is there to consider more? Why does Your Majesty delay in taking this course?

Currently, our situation is like a man suffering from a swollen foot. A swollen shank is almost as thick as the waist and a swollen toe is almost as thick as the thigh. Usually you cannot bend or stretch when you are sleeping or sitting, and the body hurts unbearably when one or two toes twitch. If not treated in time, it will inevitably become an intractable disease, one beyond the power of even Bian Que to cure. Moreover, you not only suffer from a swollen foot, but also from foot deformation. The son of Prince Yuan is the Lord's cousin; and the present Prince of Chu is the son of your cousin. The son of Prince Hui is your elder brother's son, and the present Prince of Qi is your brother's grandson. Now, some of your close relations have no fiefs to maintain stability in the world, whereas some estranged people have power enough to threaten Your Majesty. So, I talk about not only suffering from a swollen foot, but also from foot deformity. This malady is cause for weeping.

【原文】

天下之势方倒县。凡天子者，天下之首，何也？上也。蛮夷者，天下之足，何也？下也。今匈奴嫚娒侵掠，至不敬也，为天下患，至亡已也，而汉岁致金絮采缯以奉之。夷狄征令，是主上之操也；天子共贡，是臣下之礼也。足反居上，首顾居下，倒县如此，莫之能解，犹为国有人乎？非亶倒县而已，又类辟，且病痱。夫辟者一面病，痱者一方痛。今西边北边之郡，虽有长爵不轻得复，五尺以上不轻得息，斥候望烽燧不得卧，将吏被介胄而睡，臣故曰一方病矣。医能治之，而上不使，可为流涕者此也。

陛下何忍以帝皇之号为戎人诸侯，势既卑辱，而祸不息，长此安穷！进谋者率以为是，固不可解也，亡具甚矣。臣窃料匈奴之众，不过汉一大县，以天下之大困于一县之众，甚为执事者羞之。

【今译】

现在，天下的形势正好上下颠倒。天子是天下的头，为什么呢？因为在上面。蛮夷是天下的脚，为什么呢？因为在下面。现在匈奴对汉朝肆意侮辱，侵扰掠夺，不敬到了极点，成为天下的祸害，没有止境，而汉王朝每年却还向它赠送大量的金钱、丝绵和各种彩色的丝织品。匈奴对汉朝发号施令，掌的是皇上的权柄；皇上向匈奴纳贡，行的是臣下的礼节。现在脚反而到上面，头反而在下面，如此颠倒，不能解救，还能说有治国的人才吗？不但上下颠倒而已，又像得了足病，还患了风病。足病只是局部性的病，风病则是一大片地方疼痛。现在在西部边境上，即使爵位很高的人也不能轻易免除兵役，儿童以上的人都因为战备而得不到休息，哨兵日夜了望烽火不得安睡，将官都披戴着铠甲睡觉。所以我说这是一方得了病。这种病，医生能够治疗，但皇上没有让他治。可以为之流泪的，就是这件事啊。

陛下怎能忍受以堂堂的皇帝的称号去作匈奴的诸侯，地位既卑下屈辱，又祸患无穷，长此下去，哪有穷尽？出谋献策的人都认为这样做是对的，这实在让人不可理解，这些人简直无能到了极点。我私下估计匈奴的人口只不过是汉朝的一个大县，以这么大的天下，而受困于只相当于一县人口的匈奴，我真为执政的大臣们羞愧。

Now, the world situation is upside down. The Son of Heaven is the head of the world, and why? Because he is on the top. Barbarians are the feet of the world, and why? Because they are below. Now the Huns wantonly insult us, harassing and plundering, disrespectful in the extreme; they have become our relentless scourge, but every year Han presents them with quantities of silver money and varieties of colored silks. When barbarians give orders, they are wielding the Lord's authority and when the Lord pays tribute to the barbarians, he is acting like a subject paying his courtesy. Now instead of head coming first, the feet are raised to the top, making it impossible to solve this upside-down situation. Can we say that there is rule by talents? Not only is it upside down, it looks lame too, also paralyzed. Foot malady is only a localized problem, but paralysis is a disease causing suffering across a wide area. Now in the western and northern border prefectures, even the highest nobility cannot easily be exempted from military service, young boys are rarely relieved, scouts get no sleep watching the beacon towers day and night, while generals and officials sit sleeping in their armor. Therefore, I say one side of our territory is sick.

The doctors can cure this disease, but the Emperor will not let them. This is cause for tears.

How can Your Majesty endure to be a vassal prince to the Huns whilst bearing the dignified title of Emperor? How endure this humiliation and endless scourge? Will there ever be an end to it? All the advisors think this policy correct, but it is hard to understand; these people are simply resourceless in the extreme. I personally estimate that the population of the Huns equates to just one large county under Han, and for our vast empire to be trapped by such a meanly peopled land makes me blush on behalf of the ruling ministers. Why does Your

【原文】

陛下何不试以臣为属国之官以主匈奴？行臣之计，请必系单于之颈而制其命，伏中行说而笞其背，举匈奴之众唯上之令。今不猎猛敌而猎田彘，不搏反寇而搏畜菟，玩细娱而不图大患，非所以为安也。德可远施，威可远加，而直数百里外威令不信，可为流涕者此也。

今民卖僮者，为之绣衣丝履偏诸缘，内之闲中，是古天子后服，所以庙而不宴者也，而庶人得以衣婢妾。白縠之表，薄纨之裹，緁以偏诸，美者黼绣，是古天子之服，今富人大贾嘉会召客者以被墙。古者以奉一帝一后而节适，今庶人屋壁得为帝服，倡优下贱得为后饰，然而天下不屈者，殆未有也。且帝之身自衣皂绨，而富民墙屋被文绣；天子之后以缘其领，庶人孽妾缘其履：此臣所谓舛也。夫百人作之不能衣一人，欲天下亡寒，胡可得也？一人耕之，十人聚而食之，欲天下亡饥，不可得也。饥寒切于民之肌肤，欲其亡为奸邪，不可得也。国已屈矣，盗贼直须时

【今译】

陛下为什么不任命我为属国之官去掌管匈奴呢？实行我的计策，必定可以捉住单于，掌握他的生死命运，制服中行说而鞭打他的脊背，使整个匈奴都听从陛下的命令。现在不去打击凶猛的敌人而去打野猪，不捕捉叛臣而去捕捉兔子，贪图娱乐而不考虑解除国家的大祸患，这不是使天下安定的做法啊。皇上的恩德本来可以施行到很远的地方，而现在仅仅在数百里以内就行不通了。可以为之流泪的，就是这件事啊。

现在民间贩卖奴婢的人，给奴婢穿上镶了花边的绣花衣和丝鞋，圈在木栅栏内，这些奴婢穿的都是古代皇后的服饰，而且皇后平时不穿，也只是在祭祀时穿，而现在一般人却用来给婢妾穿了。用白色绉纱做面子，细薄熟绢做衬里，又镶上花边，更漂亮的还绣上花纹，这是古代帝王的服饰，现在富商大贾在宴会上招待客人时，却用来挂在墙壁上。古代这些服饰只用来侍奉一帝一后，是节制、适宜的。现在一般人的屋壁挂上了皇帝的服饰，下贱的倡优也用皇后的服饰，这样天下财力不枯竭，恐怕是不会有的吧。况且皇帝自己穿的是黑色粗厚的丝织品，而富民的墙壁上披挂着华丽的刺绣；皇后用来镶衣领的花边，一般人的婢妾却用来镶在鞋口上，这就是我所讲的错乱的事。一百个人做衣，不能满足一人穿，要想使天下之人不受冻，怎么可能做到呢？一个人种地收获的粮食，十个人聚集起来吃它，要想使天下之人不挨饿，是不可能做到的。饥饿寒冷关系到人的身体，要想使他们不做奸邪的事，也是不可能的。国家的财力已经枯竭了，盗贼兴起

Majesty not appoint me as the officer in charge of vassal states to be master of the Huns? If you follow my plan, we will surely catch the Chanyu by the neck as master of his fate; harness Zhonghang Yue and give his back a whipping; thus we could bring the Huns to heel and make them submit to your command. Today you do not go out attacking the enemy Hun, or arresting treacherous ministers; rather you go out hunting rabbits, and seek fine entertainment instead of freeing the people of the major scourge. The Lord's kindness and might could have been spread afar to distant places, but it will not work now even within hundreds of li *around. This is cause for lamentation.*

Now private slave traders provide their young slaves with robes in embroidered lace and silk shoes, to be penned behind the rails; these were the costumes of ancient queens, usually worn only for sacrificial rituals, but now the common people can clothe their petty concubines in them. White crepe lined with fine silk, and bordered in lace, the more beautiful also in embroidered ax patterns; this was the ancient imperial costume, but now rich merchants entertaining guests at parties hang them on the wall. These ancient costumes served one King and Queen only, in moderate and fitting restraint. Now common people hang their walls with kingly costumes and degraded actresses use queenly garb - how can our empire's finances not become depleted? Moreover, the Lord wore his black thick silk, while rich commoners have their walls wrapped in gorgeous embroidery; the Empress wore the lacey collar, but commoners have lace set in their concubines' shoes; this is what I call things in disorder. What a hundred persons make cannot clothe one person; how could it be done to make the world free from cold? One person's harvest, ten people gather together to eat; it is impossible to make the world free from hunger. It is impossible to make people free of evil when cold and hunger

【原文】

耳，然而献计者曰“毋动”，为大耳。夫俗至大不敬也，至亡等也，至冒上也，进计者犹曰“毋为”，可为长太息者此也。

商君遗礼义，弃仁恩，并心于进取，行之二岁，秦俗日败。故秦人家富子壮则出分，家贫子壮则出赘。借父耰锄，虑有德色；母取箕帚，立而谇语。抱哺其子，与公併倨；妇姑不相说，则反唇而相稽。其慈子耆利，不同禽兽者亡几耳。然并心而赴时，犹曰蹶六国，兼天下。功成求得矣，终不知反廉愧之节，仁义之厚。信并兼之法，遂进取之业，天下大败；众掩寡，智欺愚，勇威怯，壮陵衰，其乱至矣。是以大贤起之，威震海内，德从天下。曩之为秦者，今转而为汉矣。然其遗风馀俗，犹尚未

【今译】

只是需要时间罢了。然而献计的人却说：“不变动为上策。”社会风气已经到了对长上极不尊敬的地步，简直是没有尊卑等级，简直是冒犯皇上，而献计的人却说：“不要去改变这种状况。”可以为之深深叹息的，就是这样的事啊。

商君抛弃礼义，舍弃仁恩，一心一意变法图强，他的变法主张推行了两年，秦朝的风俗渐渐衰败。所以秦朝人家庭富裕儿子成年了就分家，家庭贫寒儿子成年了就到女方家去成婚。借给父亲农具，就流露出恩赐的脸色；母亲取用一下畚箕和扫帚，立即遭到责骂。儿媳抱着孩子喂奶，与公公一同伸开腿坐着；婆媳之间一不高兴，就顶嘴吵架。他们宠爱儿子贪图利益，不同禽兽的地方没有多少了。然而商君顺应时势一心进取，还可以说是为了挫败六国，统一天下。功成名就了，最终不知道违背了廉耻羞愧的节操，违背了仁义的厚德。推行兼并的办法，成就了进取的事业，却败坏了天下。势力大的压倒势力小的，聪明的欺侮愚笨的，勇猛的威吓胆怯的，强壮的欺凌衰弱的，真是乱到了极点。因此大贤汉高祖刘邦出来扶持天下的危乱，声威震荡四海，恩德遍布天下。过去是秦朝的天下，如今转为汉朝的天下了。但是秦朝遗留下来的风俗习惯，还没有改变。当今社会上人们都竟相追

close in on their bodies. Our financial resources having dried up, it is just a matter of time before thieves and brigands rise. However, the advisors said: "No change is the best policy." When social customs have reached extremes of disrespect, with hardly any hierarchy, this is simply offensive to the Emperor. But the advisors still said: "Do not change this situation." This is cause for deep sighing.

Lord Shang abandoned ritual and righteousness, discarded benevolence and grace, and focused single-mindedly on state building, but the customs of Qin deteriorated after two years of advocating this. The result was the son of a wealthy family in Qin had a separate family on coming of age, while the adult son of a poor family went to live with his wife's family. With a look of condescension, he lent his rakes and hoes to his father; he immediately rebuked his mother for using his dustpan and broom. Holding her baby at breast, she sat by her father-in-law with her legs stretched out; she talked back to her mother-in-law when they disagreed. They doted on their sons and sought profit, not much different from beasts. Lord Shang, however, focused single-mindedly on riding the trend of times, namely defeating the six other states for a unified world. But after they succeeded in achieving what they desired, they ended up not knowing a return to moral integrity, sense of shame and the virtue of benevolence and righteousness. The policy of annexation made the mission forge ahead, but it ruined the world. The strong overwhelmed the weak, the smart bullied the stupid, the ferocious intimidated the timid and the strong humiliated the weak: it was chaos epitomized. Therefore, Han Emperor Gaozu, great and worthy, came in the hour of need, shaking the whole world and spreading his virtue. The empire of Qin became that of Han. But the legacy of Qin customs has not changed. Though people compete with each other in luxury

【原文】

改。今世以侈靡相竞，而上亡制度，弃礼谊，捐廉耻，日甚，可谓月异而岁不同矣。逐利不耳，虑非顾行也，今其甚者杀父兄矣。盗者剟寝户之帘，搴两庙之器，白昼大都之中剽吏而夺之金。矫伪者出几十万石粟，赋六百馀万钱，乘传而行郡国，此其亡行义之(先)[尤]至者也。而大臣特以簿书不报，期会之间，以为大故，至于俗流失，世坏败，因恬而不知怪，虑不动于耳目，以为是适然耳。夫移风易俗，使天下回心而鄉道，类非俗吏之所能为也。俗吏之所务，在于刀笔筐箧，而不知大(礼)[体]。陛下又不自忧，窃为陛下惜之。

夫立君臣，等上下，使父子有礼，六亲有纪，此非天之所为，人之所设也。夫人之所设，不为不立，不植则僵，不修则坏。《筦子》曰："礼义廉耻，是谓四维；四维不张，国乃灭亡。"使筦子愚人也则可，筦子而少知治体，则是岂可不为寒心

【今译】

求奢侈豪华，而上面又没有建立制度，这种抛弃礼义，摒弃廉耻的风气一天比一天厉害，可以说是每年每月都不一样了。只注重追逐名利，而不顾行为的好坏，到了今天，严重的发展到杀害自己的父亲兄弟了。盗贼割取皇帝宗庙后室的门帘，拿起汉高祖、汉惠帝两庙的祭器，白天在大都城中抢夺官吏的钱财。作伪的人骗出近十万石粮食，征收六百多万钱财，乘坐官车周游郡国，这真是没有道义到了极点。而大臣只把不上报公文和期会的中断当作大事。至于社会风俗的败坏，却安然处之不以为怪，无动于衷，以为是理所当然的事。移风易俗，使天下人心归向正道，这些不是平庸的官吏所能做到的。平庸的官吏所能干的，只在于写写公文，收收钱财，不懂得治国的根本。陛下您又不为此忧虑，我私下为陛下惋惜。

确立君臣上下之间的等级关系，使父子之间有礼可遵，六亲之间有法度可循，这不是上天所为，而是人们设立的。人们设立的制度，不做的事不设立，不建立制度就维护不了人际关系，不维护制度就会破坏人际关系。《管子》说："礼义廉耻是治国的四个纲，这四个纲不张，国家就要灭亡。"假使管子是个愚蠢的人那就罢了，假使管子是稍微知道治国的根本道理的，那么，怎

in today's society, there is no established constitution above. Increasingly, they abandon propriety and sense of shame and things change by the month and year. They focus only on the pursuit of fortune, regardless of good or bad behavior; even patricide and fratricide is not off-limits. Thieves cut door curtains from the imperial mausoleums, lifted the sacrificial utensils from the temples of Gaozu and Huidi, and robbed money from officials in the Great Metropolis in broad daylight. Counterfeiters cheated nearly 100,000 piculs of millet, levied more than six million cash, traveling in the prefectures and princedoms on official carriages; this is moral decay in the extreme. The ministers only deem important a failure to submit documents or breaking an appointment. Indifferent to the decay of social customs, they do not think it extraordinary, rather a matter of course. In fact, it is beyond such mediocre officials to transform established traditions and customs, so that people come back to the Way. These mediocrities are competent only at writing documents and collecting money; they do not understand the fundamentals of rule. Since Your Majesty does not care about this either, your subject grieves for you.

Establishing the hierarchical relationship between the monarch above and the subjects below, so that courtesy exists between father and son, and rules of conduct between relatives: this was not something willed by heaven, but set up by people. A system that man establishes does not stand up without man acting; without a system, relationships cannot be safeguarded, without maintaining the system relationships may be destroyed. Master Guanzi said: "Propriety, righteousness, honesty and sense of shame are the four social bonds, and without extending the four, the State will perish." If Guanzi had been stupid, it would have been passable then, but if Guanzi had known a little about the rule of government, then how it not break his

【原文】

哉！秦灭四维而不张，故君臣乖乱，六亲殃戮，奸人并起，万民离叛，凡十三岁，[而]社稷为虚。今四维犹未备也，故奸人幾幸，而众心疑惑。岂如今定经制，令君君臣臣，上下有差，父子六亲各得其宜，奸人亡所幾幸，而群臣众信，上不疑惑！此业壹定，世世常安，而后有所持循矣。若夫经制不定，是犹度江河亡维楫，中流而遇风波，船必覆矣。可为长太息者此也。

夏为天子，十有馀世，而殷受之。殷为天子，二十馀世，而周受之。周为天子，三十馀世，而秦受之。秦为天子，二世而亡。人性不甚相远也，何三代之君有道之长，而秦无道之暴也？其故可知也。古之王者，太子乃生，固举以礼，使士负之，有司齐肃端冕，见之南郊，见于天也。过阙则下，过庙则趋，孝子之

【今译】

能不为此寒心呢？秦朝舍弃四个纲而不张，所以君臣的等级关系错乱，六亲遭殃被杀，奸邪的人一同起来，万民叛离朝廷，一共十三年，而整个国家成为一片废墟。现今四个纲还没有齐备，所以奸人有机可乘，而人心疑惑不定。哪如在现在确定等级制度的原则，让君是君臣是臣，上下有差别，父子与六亲各得其所，奸人没有机会可乘，而群臣都讲忠信，皇上不疑惑！这样的法度一建立，世世代代得到安宁，而后代就有法可遵循了。假如等级制度的原则没有确定，就像渡江时没有缆绳和船桨一样，到中流遇到风波，必定要翻船。我认为可为之叹息的就是这样的事啊。

夏朝统治天下，有十多代，而殷商承接它。殷商统治天下，有二十多代，而周朝承接它。周朝统治天下，有三十多代，而秦朝承接它。秦朝统治天下，两代就灭亡了。人的性情相差不是很远，为什么夏商周三代的君主政治清明统治长久，而秦朝没有德政暴虐残酷呢？这当中的原因可以知道。古代的帝王，太子刚生下来，就用礼来教养，让士人背着他，有关的官员整洁身心显示庄重，端正衣冠，到南郊祭天。过宫阙就下车马步行，过宗庙就俯着身小步快走，这是孝子之道。所以在婴孩时教育就已经进

heart? Qin discarded the four bonds, so they disappeared; the hierarchical relationship of monarch and subjects was disrupted, relatives close and distant suffered and got killed, evildoers rose everywhere, the populace left as renegades. In a matter of 13 years, the entire country became a wasteland. And today the four bonds are still not reunited, so treacherous people take advantage, and the people are uncertain and unsettled. What better now than to identify the principle of hierarchy, so that the monarch and his subjects are well positioned, to distinguish between the top and the bottom, until father, sons and relatives can get what they think appropriate, treacherous people can take no chances, the ministers are all faithful, and the Emperor harbors no suspicion! Once the system is established, you will get constant peace from generation to generation, and future reigns will have an example to follow. If the principle of hierarchy is not settled, just like crossing a river without paddles or ropes we shall surely capsize mid-stream when encountering a storm. This is cause enough to sigh deeply.

The Xia Dynasty ruled the world for more than a dozen reigns, and Shang took it. Shang ruled the world for more than 20 reigns, and Zhou took it. Zhou ruled the world for more than 30 reigns, and Qin took it. But Qin met its demise in just two generations. Human nature had not changed greatly, so why did the Xia, Shang and Zhou monarchs rule a long time with good principles, only to be followed by the cruel tyranny of unprincipled Qin? The reason can be known. The ancient monarchs exemplified the Crown Prince in the use of propriety when he was just born, by carrying him on a scholar's back, and the relevant officials with clean body and mind, in correct code of dress, accompanied him to the southern suburbs to worship heaven. It was the Way of a filial child to walk over to the palace instead of riding a chariot, and to shuffle over

【原文】

道也。故自为赤子而教固已行矣。昔者成王幼在襁抱之中，召公为太保，周公为太傅，太公为太师。保，保其身体；傅，傅之德(意)[义]；师，道之教训：此三公之职也。于是为置三少，皆上大夫也，曰少保、少傅、少师，是与太子宴者也。故乃孩提有识，三公、三少固明孝仁礼义以道习之，逐去邪人，不使见恶行，于是皆选天下之端士孝悌博闻有道术者以卫翼之，使与太子居处出入。故太子乃生而见正事，闻正言，行正道，左右前后皆正人也。夫习与正人居之，不能毋正，犹生长于齐不能不齐言也；习与不正人居之，不能毋不正，犹生长于楚之地不能不楚言也。故择其所耆，必先受业，乃得尝之；择其所乐，必先有习，乃得为之。孔子曰："少成若天性，习贯如自然。"及太子少长，知妃色，则入于学。学者，所学之官也。《学礼》曰："帝

【今译】

行了。过去，周成王还在襁褓之中，召公做太保，周公做太傅，太公做太师教育他。保，保护他的身体；傅，传授给他道德、行为的道理；师，教育训导：这就是三公的职责。于是又设三少，都是上大夫级别，叫少保、少傅、少师，这是同太子生活在一起的人。所以当太子刚懂事，三公、三少就给他讲明孝、仁、礼、义，并引导他去做，驱逐奸邪之人，不让太子见到不好的行为。由于这样，都选拔天下行为端正，讲求孝悌，见识广博，有道德学术的人护卫辅助他，让这些人跟太子居住一处，同出同入。所以太子刚生下来见到的是正事，听到的是正言，推行的是正道，左右前后都是品行端正的人。习惯于同品行端正的人相处，品行就不会不端正，如同生长在齐国不能不讲齐国话；习惯于同品行不端正的人相处，品行就不会端正，如同生长在楚国不能不讲楚国话。所以选择天子的嗜好，必须先使他接受教育，然后才能去试行。选择天子的爱好，必须先使他有了习惯，然后才能去做。孔子说："小时养成的习惯好像是自然的天性。"等到太子稍稍长大，知道女色，就让他进入学校学习。学，就是朝廷里的学馆。《学礼》说："帝入东学，懂得尊敬亲属，重视仁爱，于是

the ancestral temple in quick steps. Thus they were educated since infancy. In the past, when yet a baby, King Cheng of Zhou had Duke of Shao as his Grand Guardian, Duke of Zhou as his Grand Mentor and Jiang Taigong as his Grand Preceptor. His Guardian was to protect his body; his Mentor was to teach him the moral truth; and his Preceptor to guide him with experiences: these were the responsibilities of Three Excellencies. Then Three Juniors, all senior grand masters, were established. They were called Junior Guardian, Junior Mentor and Junior Preceptor, all living together with the Prince. So when the Prince just began to learn as a boy, the Three Excellencies and Three Juniors elucidated the principles of filial piety, benevolence, propriety and righteousness, and guided him in practice, expelling treacherous persons, so that the Prince witnessed no bad behavior. As such, well-behaved, knowledgeable personages with filial piety and ruling skills were selected from the realm to assist him, so that these people lived alongside the Prince. The Prince was born to see the right things, to hear the right words and to go the right way, being surrounded by the right people on all sides. Those used to consorting with people of good character and conduct will not be incorrect, just like those who grow up in Qi speak no dialect other than Qi; those used to consorting with incorrect people will not have correct behavior, just as those who grow up in Chu speak only Chu dialect. So in choosing the Son of Heaven's hobbies, it was first essential that he be educated before trying it; in selecting his favorite, it was first essential to accustom him before doing it. As Confucius said: "The habit formed in one's childhood seems to be instinct and what is habitually done becomes a natural thing." When the Prince grew up a little and understood about sex, they let him enter the school. The school was where he learned in the palace. According to the

【原文】

入东学，上亲而贵仁，则亲疏有序而恩相及矣；帝入南学，上齿而贵信，则长幼有差而民不诬矣；帝入西学，上贤而贵德，则圣智在位而功不遗矣；帝入北学，上贵而尊爵，则贵贱有等而下不踰矣；帝入太学，承师问道，退习而考于太傅，太傅罚其不则而匡其不及，则德智长而治道得矣。此五学者既成于上，则百姓黎民化辑于下矣。”及太子既冠成人，免于保傅之严，则有记过之史，彻膳之宰，进善之旌，诽谤之木，敢谏之鼓。瞽史诵诗，工诵箴谏，大夫进谋，士传民语。习与智长，故切而不愧；化与心

【今译】

亲、疏有了序别而恩德都能施加到了；帝入南学，懂得尊敬老年人，注重信义，于是长幼有了区别而民众互相不欺骗；帝入西学，懂得尊敬贤良，注重道德，于是圣贤聪明的人得到任用而有功之人不被遗漏；帝入北学，懂得尊敬有地位的人，崇尚爵禄，于是贵贱之分有了等级而卑下的人不超越自己的身份；帝入太学，从师请教治国的道理，回来练习并接受太傅的考核，太傅惩罚他不合标准的地方，而改正不足之处，于是，德行和智慧增长了，治国的办法也学到了。这五学在上面学成了，那么百官和平民在下面就会受感化而和睦相处了。”等到太子加冠成年，免去太保、太傅的管束，就有记载过失的官员，用减膳食的办法进行规劝的官员，还竖起旌旗招引人们进善言，在路旁竖起木牌记载过失，在官府门口设进谏时敲的鼓。瞽史用诗来规劝，乐工朗诵进谏的文章来规劝，大夫进献计谋，士传诵民间警语。智慧和学习一起增长，所以做事就能切合准则；教化和思想一起形成，所以行为合乎道理就像出自本性一样。夏商周三代之礼：春天的早

Rites of Learning*: "When the monarch went to the East School, he learned how to respect his family and cherish benevolence, so the order of affinity among relatives ensued, and kindness could be applied; when he went to the South School, he learned how to respect the elderly and focus on faith, so the young and old were distinguished, and the people did not cheat; when he went to the West School, he learned how to respect the able and virtuous, and focus on moral integrity, so wise sages were given office, and the meritorious were not passed over; when he went to the North School, he learned how to respect the distinguished and entitled, so the status of high or low people was stratified and the lower people did not go beyond their own status. When he went to the Imperial College, he followed his teachers to investigate the Way. He came back practicing and was examined by his Grand Mentor, who punished him for his substandard actions, and corrected his inadequate behavior, so that his virtues and wisdom grew, achieving the Way of ruling. These five being finished by the ruler above, then the civilians and officials of all ranks and descriptions below became civilized and lived in harmony." When the Prince came of age at 20, he was freed from the constraints of the Grand Guardian and Grand Mentor; but he was accompanied by historians who documented his mistakes, butlers who tried to persuade him to reduce imperial diets, banners put up to attract potential advisors, roadside boards recording his faults, and drums in front of the official residence that encouraged daring admonishers. Historians used poetry to persuade, musicians recited articles to persuade, grand masters offered advice, and scholars conveyed folk epigrams. Intelligence and learning grew together, so he would be able to meet the standards with a clear conscience; education and mind formed together, so he would conform to the Way as if by nature.*

【原文】

成，故中道若性。三代之礼：春朝朝日，秋暮夕月，所以明有敬也；春秋入学，坐国老，执酱而亲馈之，所以明有孝也；行以鸾和，步中《采齐》，趣中《肆夏》，所以明有度也；其于禽兽，见其生不食其死，闻其声不食其肉，故远庖厨，所以长恩，且明有仁也。

夫三代之所以长久者，以其辅翼太子有此具也。及秦而不然。其俗固非贵辞让也，所上者告讦也；固非贵礼义也，所上者刑罚也。使赵高傅胡亥而教之狱，所习者非斩劓人，则夷人之三族也。故胡亥今日即位而明日射人，忠谏者谓之诽谤，深计者谓之妖言，其视杀人若艾草菅然。岂惟胡亥之性恶哉？彼其所以道之者非其理故也。

鄙谚曰："不习为吏，视已成事。"又曰："前车覆，后车诫。"夫三代之所以长久者，其已事可知也；然而不能从者，是

【今译】

上去祭日，秋天的傍晚去祭月，以此表示敬重天地；春秋入学的时候，请国老上座，太子捧着肉酱亲自送给他，以此表示孝敬长老；乘车出行，速度快慢要适合车上的铃声，走路时，慢步要合乎《采齐》的节奏，快步要合乎《肆夏》的节拍，以此表明懂得礼节；对于禽兽，活的时候见过它，听见过它的叫声，死了以后就不吃它的肉，所以要远庖厨，以此加深恩惠，而且表明有仁爱之心。

夏商周三代之所以统治长久，是因为他们辅助太子有这些办法。到了秦朝就不是这样。他们的社会风气本来就不是讲究谦让，他们崇尚的是揭发人家隐私；他们本来就不是讲究礼义，他们崇尚的是刑罚。赵高辅助秦二世，教他的是刑戮之法，所练习的不是杀人割鼻子，就是灭门三族。所以秦二世今天登上皇帝位而明天就杀人，把忠心进谏的话说成是诽谤，深远的计谋当成妖言，把杀人看作是割草一样。难道只是秦二世的性恶吗？那是由于教育他的东西不合理的缘故。

俗语说："不熟悉做官的事，看看以前官吏做过的事。"又说："前面的车颠覆了，后面的车作好戒备。"夏商周三代的统治之所以长久，看过去的事就可知道了；然而不能依从的，是不

The Rite of the Three Former Dynasties was this: on a spring morning he worshipped the sun, on an autumn evening he worshipped the moon, thus showing his respect for nature. When he began school in spring and autumn, he yielded the seat of honor to the country's senior, feeding him personally with ground meat, thus showing his filial piety and respect for age; when riding a carriage his pace suited to the rhythm of the bells on the rig; he walked gently to rhythm of "Gathering Shepherd's Purse," and trotted to the rhythm of "Four Xia,"thus showing his knowledge of propriety; as for beasts and fowl, if he had seen them alive, he would not eat their bodies, or if he had heard them cry he would not eat their flesh, so he kept far from the kitchen, deepening his compassion and showing his benevolent heart.

The Xia, Shang and Zhou ruled a long time, because they aided the Prince with these approaches. It was not the case with Qin. Their social customs did not emphasize humbleness, but advocated denouncing people's weaknesses; they did not emphasize rite and righteousness, but advocated penalties. They made Zhao Gao teach Prince Huhai, and indoctrinated him about penalties. When he was not having the noses of criminals cut off, he was practicing triple-clan family extermination (killing the clans of the father, mother and wife). So Huhai was enthroned today and tomorrow he was shooting arrows at people, describing loyal reprimands as slander, visionary plans as make-believe, and regarding killing as akin to mowing grass. Did all this stem just from Huhai's evil nature? It was because the things he was taught were wrong.

The old adages say:"If you are not experienced as an official, just see what officials have done before," and, "the overturned cart ahead is a warning to those behind." The reason the Xia, Shang and Zhou dynasties ruled so long is that

【原文】

不法圣智也。秦世之所以亟绝者，其辙迹可见也，然而不避，是后车又将覆也。夫存亡之变，治乱之机，其要在是矣，天下之命，县于太子；太子之善，在于早谕教与选左右。夫心未滥而先谕教，则化易成也；开于道术智谊之指，则教之力也。若其服习积贯，则左右而已。夫胡、粤之人，生而同声，耆欲不异，及其长而成俗，累数译而不能相通，行者[有]虽死而不相为者，则教习然也。臣故曰选左右早谕教最急。夫教得而左右正，则太子正矣，太子正而天下定矣。《书》曰："一人有庆，兆民赖之。"此时务也。

凡人之智，能见已然，不能见将然。夫礼者禁于将然之前，而法者禁于已然之后，是故法之所用易见，而礼之所为生难知也。若夫庆赏以劝善，刑罚以惩恶，先王执此之政，坚如金石，行此之令，信如四时，据此之公，无私如天地耳，岂顾不用哉？

【今译】

效法圣贤的聪明。秦朝之所以迅速灭亡，有痕迹留下可以看出；然而如果不避免，后面的车又将倾覆了。存与亡的变化，治与乱的关键，其要旨就在这里了。天下的命运，决定于太子；太子治国能力的强弱，在于早期开导教育，在与选拔辅助护卫太子的左右人。在思想还没有放开时就先开始教育，那么教化就容易成功；领悟治国道理和知识道义的要旨，则是教育的力量了。至于习惯的养成，则是左右的任务了。北方人和南方人，生下时声音相同，嗜好欲望也没有什么差异，等长大养成习惯了，他们之间的语言经过多次翻译也不能相通，行为习惯有到死也不能互相改变的，那是教育和习惯造成的结果。所以我说选好左右辅佐的人和进行早期教育是最重要的。教育得当而且左右的人品行端正，那么太子就正派，太子正派了，天下也就安定了。《尚书》说："天子一人有庆幸的事，亿万民众依赖他得好处。"这是当前急于办的事。

大凡人的智慧，能见到的已经是这样，不能见到的也想这样。礼是用在禁止人们的行为将要发生之前，而法律是用在行为已经发生之后，所以法律的功能容易看到，而礼的功效却难知晓。假如庆赏用来劝善，刑罚用来惩恶，先王执掌这样的政权，会坚硬如同金石，推行这样的命令，会得到长久信从，掌握这种方法的人，

they knew what officials had done in the past; however, this cannot be imitated because we do not have the same intelligence of the sages. The demise of the Qin was so rapid that its traces can still be seen, but if we do not avoid them, the carts behind will overturn. The key to survival or demise, order or anarchy lies here. The destiny of the empire hinges on the Prince; the good Prince comes from early moral education and choice of the people beside him. Teaching before his mind is liberated will lead to easy indoctrination; instilling comprehension of how to govern, inculcating the gist of ruling through righteousness is credited to the power of education; forming his habits is the task of those around him. The northern barbarians and southern Yue people, born with the same voice, and similar likes and lusts, grow into their habits; they cannot communicate despite every effort and multiple translations; even if they died they could not adapt their behavior; this comes from education and habit. So I say that the priority is to choose good people around him and early moral education. With the right education plus decent people around him, the Prince will be upright, and in turn there will be stability in the world. According to the Book of Documents*: "When one person is but fortunate, millions of people depend on him." This is our most pressing priority.*

People with no uncommon intelligence can see what has already happened, but cannot see what will happen. The purpose of a rite is to stop something happening, and the law is used to ban something after the event, so its legal function is easy to see, whereas the effectiveness of the rite is difficult to know. As to the practice of rewards to encourage good and penalties to punish evil, the former Kings were rock-firm in implementing such a policy, as faithful as the seasons in administering this command, and as selfless as heaven and earth in complying with this method; so why is it not used

【原文】

然而曰礼云礼云者，贵绝恶于未萌，而起教于微眇，使民日迁善远罪而不自知也。孔子曰："听讼，吾犹人也，必也使毋讼乎！"为人主计者，莫如先审取舍；取舍之极定于内，而安危之萌应于外矣。安者非一日而安也，危者非一日而危也，皆以积渐然，不可不察也。人主之所积，在其取舍，以礼义治之者，积礼义；以刑罚治之者，积刑罚。刑罚积而民怨背，礼义积而民和亲。故世主欲民之善同，而所以使民善者或异。或道之以德教，或欧之以法令。道之以德教者，德教洽而民气乐；欧之以法令者，法令极而民风哀。哀乐之感，祸福之应也。秦王之欲尊宗庙而安子孙，与汤武同，然而汤武广大其德行，六七百岁而弗失，秦王治天下，十馀岁则大败。此亡它故矣，汤武之定取舍审而秦王之定取舍不审矣。夫天下，大器也。今人之置器，置诸安处则

【今译】

像天地一样无私，难道还不使用吗？然而说礼之于礼，重要的是杜绝坏事在没有发生以前，而教育放在细微的地方，使老百姓一天天接近善良远离罪恶而自己不知道。孔子说："审理诉讼，我同别人一样，一定要使诉讼事件消灭才好！"为国君谋划的人，不如先审定要选择和弃置的东西；取舍的标准定于朝廷，而安危的开始应验在社会上。平安不是一天能够平安的，危险也不是一天就危险了的，都是积蓄以后才逐渐发生的，不可不仔细考察。国君所积蓄的，在取舍方面。用礼义来治理国家的人，积蓄的是礼义；用刑罚来治理国家的，积蓄的是刑罚。刑罚多而老百姓就要埋怨反抗，礼义多而老百姓就会和睦相亲。所以国君希望老百姓从善的想法相同，而使老百姓行善的方法是不同的。有人教导他们德行，有人用法令来逼迫他们。用德行教导他们的，德行被推广而民众和气快乐；用法令来威逼他们的，法令到了极点而民众的风气哀怨。哀乐之感，便是祸福的应证。秦王想尊崇宗庙而安定子孙的想法，与商汤、周武王相同，然而商汤、周武王扩大了他们的德行，六七百年而不失败，秦王治理天下，十多年就大败了。这没有别的缘故，商汤、周武王确定取舍审慎而秦王确定取舍不审慎。天下，是重要的工具。现在人们把器物放在安稳的

at all? For people who uphold the rite, however, it is more important to cut out bad things before they emerge, and to initiate education in a small point, causing the people gradually to move closer to good and stay away from crimes without being conscious of doing so. Confucius said: "In hearing law suits, I am like any other person. The point is to ensure there is no need for law suits!" For Your Majesty's strategists, it is better first to examine what to accept or reject; the criteria are set within the Imperial Court, but it is out in society that stability or risk are confirmed. Stability is not achieved overnight, nor does risk appear in a day; both accumulate gradually, so must not be neglected. The Lord accumulates what he chooses or rejects. Ruling with courtesy and righteousness, he accumulates courtesy and righteousness; whereas governing the country by penalty, he accumulates penalty. Accumulated penalty will lead to people's discontent and hatred, while accumulated courtesy and righteousness will make people harmonious and attached. So the monarchs were like-minded in wishing their people to be virtuous, but they took different approaches in trying to make them so. Some of them guided the people with virtuous teaching, and others drove them with decrees. The former let virtue permeate and the atmosphere among the people was joyous; the latter were extreme in their decrees and made a mood of misery. Feelings of joy and lamentation are the proofs of fortune and misfortune. The King of Qin wanted to honor his ancestral temple to stabilize his descendants, in the same way as King Tang of Shang and King Wu of Zhou. But these had expanded their virtue, lasting six or seven centuries without failing, whereas the King of Qin ruled the empire for a mere dozen years before he was destroyed. The reason is that King Tang and King Wu made their choices carefully and the King of Qin imprudently. The empire is an important implement.

【原文】

安，置诸危处则危。天下之情与器亡以异，在天子之所置之。汤武置天下于仁义礼乐，而德泽洽，禽兽草木广裕，德被蛮貊四夷，累子孙数十世，此天下所共闻也。秦王置天下于法令刑罚，德泽亡一有，而怨毒盈于世，下憎恶之如仇雠，祸几及身，子孙诛绝，此天下之所共见也。是非其明效大验邪！人之言曰："听言之道，必以其事观之，则言者莫敢妄言。"今或言礼谊之不如法令，教化之不如刑罚，人主胡不引殷、周、秦事以观之也？

人主之尊譬如堂，群臣如陛，众庶如地。故陛九级上，廉远地，则堂高；陛亡级，廉近地，则堂卑。高者难攀，卑者易陵，理势然也。故古者圣王制为等列，内有公卿大夫士，外有公侯伯子男，然后有官师小吏，延及庶人，等级分明，而天子加焉，故其尊不可及也。里谚曰："欲投鼠而忌器。"此善谕也。鼠近于

【今译】

地方就安稳，放在危险的地方就危险。天下的情况与器物没有什么不同，在于天子怎么放置它。商汤周武王把天下放于仁、义、礼、乐的位置，而恩德广被四方，禽兽、草木茂盛，恩德加于蛮貊四夷，接连子孙几十代，这是天下人都知道的。秦王把天下放在法令刑罚的位置，恩德一点没有，而埋怨仇恨遍布社会，平民百姓憎恨他如仇敌，祸害差一点临身，后来子孙诛死断绝，这是天下人都看到的。这不是很明显的效验吗！有人说："听人说话，一定要看他的行动，这样他就不敢胡说八道了。"今天有人说礼义不如法令，教化不如刑罚，国君为何不援引商、周、秦朝的事来让他们看呢？

国君的高贵譬如殿堂，群臣譬如台阶，百姓譬如地。所以台阶在九级以上，地基离地面远，那么殿堂就高；台阶没有级，离地面近，殿堂就低下。高的难以攀登，低的易于跨上，这是理所当然的。所以古代圣王制定等级，朝廷有公、卿、大夫、士，地方封国有公、侯、伯、子、男，然后有大小官吏，一直排到平民，等级分明，而天子的地位在最上面，所以他的尊贵是至高无

Now if we are to put the implement in a secure place, it will be safe, but at risk if put in somewhere dangerous. The situation in the empire is no different; its security depends on where the Son of Heaven places it. King Tang and King Wu placed the world in benevolence, righteousness, propriety, and music, and their virtue and grace permeated to make the animals and plants flourish and benefit the barbarous tribes in the four border areas, continuing to successive descendants of dozens of generations, as is known all over. The King of Qin put the world to his decrees and punishments, with scarcely any virtue and grace; discontent and hatred was universal, so that his subjects resented him as an enemy, he was almost assassinated, and later his descendants were killed off. People everywhere saw this. Clearly this was only to be expected! Some people say: "The way to hear what people say is to watch what they actually do, so that they will not dare to talk nonsense." Some people may say that courtesy and righteousness are not as good as decrees, and education less effective than punishments. Why does not the Lord invoke the facts of the Shang, Zhou, and Qin Dynasties for them to look at?

The sovereignty of the monarch is like a palace hall, the courtiers like its steps, and the people like the ground. So if there are more than nine steps, the walls are well off the ground, and the palace is high; if the step is level, the walls are near to the ground, then the palace is low. It stands to reason that a high palace is difficult to climb, and a low-sited one easy to overcome. Thus, the ancient sage kings developed hierarchies, so that the Imperial Court included dukes and ministers, grand masters, and literati; local nobles included dukes, marquises, earls, viscounts and barons; then came leading officials and clerks, down to the civilian population, in clear-cut grades, and the Son of Heaven's position was at the top, so his honor was

【原文】

器，尚惮不投，恐伤其器，况于贵臣之近主乎！廉耻节礼以治君子，故有赐死而亡戮辱。是以黥劓之罪不及大夫，以其离主上不远也。礼不敢齿君之路马，蹴其刍者有罚；见君之几杖则起，遭君之乘车则下，入正门则趋；君之宠臣虽或有过，刑戮之罪不加其身者，尊君之故也。此所以为主上豫远不敬也，所以体貌大臣而厉其节也。今自王侯三公之贵，皆天子之所改容而礼之也，古天子之所谓伯父、伯舅也，而令与众庶同黥劓髡刖笞伌弃市之法，然则堂不亡陛乎？被戮辱者不泰迫乎？廉耻不行，大臣无乃握重权，大官而有徒隶亡耻之心乎？夫望夷之事，二世见当以重法者，投鼠而不忌器之习也。

臣闻之，履虽鲜不加于枕，冠虽敝不以苴履。夫尝已在贵宠之位，天子改容而体貌之矣，吏民尝俯伏以敬畏之矣，今而有

【今译】

上的。里巷流行的谚语说："要投掷东西打老鼠却又顾忌损坏器物。"这是很好的比喻。因为老鼠距离器物近，人们尚且害怕损坏器物而不敢打，何况显贵之臣距主上太近了呢！用廉耻节礼治理君子，所以有赐死而没有杀戮侮辱。因此，脸上刺字割掉鼻子的罪行不加到大夫头上，因为他们离主上不远啊。礼规定不能计算拉国君坐的车的马的年龄，踢踩马的草料要受惩罚；看到国君的案桌拐杖就肃立，遇到国君的车马就去到低处，进入正门就小步快走；国君的宠臣即使有人有了过错，杀戮的罪行不加在他身上，这样做是为了尊敬国君。这是为了使皇上预先避开对他不尊敬的事情，而用礼貌来鼓励大臣保持节操。今天自王侯三公这些贵人起，都是天子所要敬重以礼相待的人，就是古代的天子称作伯父、伯舅的人，而对他们与民众同样施用各种刑罚，那么殿堂不是失去台阶了吗？被杀戮侮辱的人不是太迫近天子吗？廉耻不被推行，大臣岂不就会掌握过重的权力，大官不就会有囚徒的无耻之心了吗？望夷宫这件事，秦二世被判处重刑，这是投鼠而不忌器造成的。

我听说，鞋子即使很新也不能放到枕头上，帽子即使破旧也

paramount. A popular saying goes: "He hesitates to strike a rat for fear of smashing dishes." This is a very good analogy. Just as people fear damaging the dishes that are so close to the rat, and thus refrain from striking it, so it is with the noble officials so close to the ruler! For governance of gentlemen through their sense of shame and moral integrity, there is "suicide with imperial order" that spares them the indignity of execution. Therefore, the punishment of cutting off the nose or tattooing the face is not applied to the grand masters, because they are not far from the lord. Propriety prohibits calculating the age of horses pulling the imperial carriages, and to kick the imperial horse fodder is to invite punishment; all stand when we see the imperial bench or stick, all step down when we encounter the imperial wagons; all shuffle in quick steps when we enter the front entrance; even if a favorite of the monarch commits a fault, out of respect for the monarch the offender is exempt from execution or imprisonment. This is to enable the monarch to preclude any disrespect to him, and politely encourage the courtiers to maintain their moral integrity. Now nobles above princes, marquises and the Three Excellencies are all met with courtesy by the Son of Heaven; the ancient monarchs called them elder uncles, but now they too are subject to commoners' penalties, like having the face tattooed, the nose cut-off, the beard cut-off, the foot cut-off, beating, denunciation, public execution. Is this not a case of the palace losing its steps? Are the people killed or insulted not too close to the ruler? When sense of shame is not present, will not the ministers appropriate excessive powers, and will not high-ranking officials have a prisoner's shameless heart? As to the incident at Wangyi Palace, the second Qin Emperor was sentenced to death, which came about because of striking a rat regardless of taboos.

I hear that shoes, even if very new, should never be placed

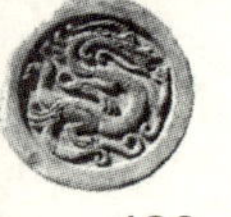

【原文】

过，帝令废之可也，退之可也，赐之死可也，灭之可也；若夫束缚之，系绁之，输之司寇，编之徒官，司寇小吏詈骂而榜笞之，殆非所以令众庶见也。夫卑贱者习知尊贵者之一旦，吾亦乃可以加此也，非所以习天下也，非尊尊贵贵之化也。夫天子之所尝敬，众庶之所尝宠，死而死耳，贱人安宜得如此而顿辱之哉！

豫让事中行之君，智伯伐而灭之，移事智伯。及赵灭智伯，豫让衅面吞炭，必报襄子，五起而不中。人问豫子，豫子曰："中行众人畜我，我故众人事之；智伯国士遇我，我故国士报之。"故此一豫让也，反君事仇，行若狗彘，已而抗节致忠，行出乎列士，人主使然也。故主上遇其大臣如遇犬马，彼将犬马自为也；如遇官徒，彼将官徒自为也。顽顿亡耻，奊诟亡节，廉耻不立，且不自好，苟若而可，故见利则逝，见便则夺。主上有

【今译】

不能用来垫鞋。曾经处在被尊宠地位的人，天子对他以礼相待，官吏民众曾对他表示过敬畏。今天有了过错，皇帝下令废黜爵位可以，罢除官职可以，赐他死可以，灭了他的家族可以；至于把他捆绑起来，牵着押送给司寇，编在徒官的管辖之下，让司寇小吏咒骂和鞭打他，这恐怕是不能让一般民众看到的吧！卑贱的人熟知被尊宠的人一旦有了过错，我也可以同样对待他，这不是教习天下的办法，也不符合尊尊贵贵的教化。天子曾经敬重过，民众曾经尊崇过，让他死了就死了，卑贱人怎么可以这样折磨侮辱他呢！

豫让事奉中行氏之君，在智伯攻灭中行氏之后，转而事奉智伯。等到赵襄子灭掉智伯，豫让就毁坏容貌，吞炭使声音嘶哑，一定要报复赵襄子，为智伯报仇，但多次没有成功。有人问豫子，豫子回答说："中行氏像对一般人那样对待我，我也像一般人那样事奉他；智伯像国士一样待我，我就像国士一样报答他。"所以同一个豫让，起初背叛自己的主人去事奉他的仇敌，行为像猪狗，后来又持节尽忠，行为像烈士，这是主上使他这样的。所以国君对待他的大臣如同对待犬马，他们就甘愿做犬马。如果对待他们如同对待犯人，他们就甘愿做犯人。顽固愚笨无耻，胸无大志没有节操，没有廉耻之心，并且不自爱，马马虎虎就可以了，所以他们见利便向往，见利便争夺。遇到主上失利，

on a pillow, and that a hat, no matter how shabby, cannot be used as an insole. Now if someone who has been in a respected position, been treated by the Emperor with courtesy, respected by officials and people kneeling down to him in awe, if that person transgresses the Emperor can now depose him, dismiss him, order him to commit suicide, exterminate his whole family. As to having him bundled up, led with a rope to the minister of justice, under the official jurisdiction of prison wardens, to be cursed and whipped by its petty clerks... this is not for the eyes of commoners! Once the lowly person knows a high-born is at fault, he feels entitled to also treat him thus: this is no way to teach the world, nor in line with instilling respect for the nobles. He enjoyed the Emperor's respect, and was revered by the common people. If he had to die, just let him die; how can you allow him to be insulted by common torturers!

Yu Rang initially served the lord of Zhonghang, but moved to serve the Earl of Zhi after the latter attacked and destroyed Zhonghang. When Zhao Xiangzi exterminated Zhi, Yu Rang smeared his face and swallowed charcoal, determined to take revenge on Zhao, but he failed five times. Someone asked Yu, and Yu said: "Zhonghang treated me as an ordinary person, so I served him like most people; Zhi treated me like a statesman, so I thanked him like a statesman." So the same Yu, who first betrayed his lord to serve his enemy, behaving like a cur or swine, later remained loyal out of integrity, like a martyr, since his lord had made him like that. So if the lord treats his courtiers like a dog or a horse, they will become a dog or a horse. If he treats them like criminals, they will act the part. Stupid, timid, shameless, unambitious, without courage or sense of shame, not self-loving, muddling along, so they crave after prospective profits, and compete for opportunities. When the lord encountered difficulty, they would seize the opportunity to

【原文】

败，则因而挺之矣；主上有患，则吾苟免而已，立而观之耳；有便吾身者，则欺卖而利之耳。人主将何便于此？群下至众，而主上至少也，所托财器职业者粹于群下也。俱亡耻，俱苟妄，则主上最病。故古者礼不及庶人，刑不至大夫，所以厉宠臣之节也。古者大臣有坐不廉而废者，不谓不廉，曰"簠簋不饰"；坐污秽淫乱男女亡别者，不曰污秽，曰"帷薄不修"；坐罢软不胜任者，不谓罢软，曰"下官不职"。故贵大臣定有其罪矣，犹未斥然正以謼之也，尚迁就而为之讳也。故其在大谴大何之域者，闻谴何则白冠氂缨，盘水加剑，造请室而请罪耳，上不执缚系引而行也。其有中罪者，闻命而自弛，上不使人颈盭而加也。其有大罪者，闻命则北面再拜，跪而自裁，上不使捽抑而刑之也，曰："子大夫自有过耳！吾遇子有礼矣。"遇之有礼，故群臣自憙；婴

【今译】

就乘机篡权；遇到主上有了患难，就只顾自己苟且偷生，袖手旁观；有利于自己的，就欺诈出卖主人而从中谋利。这样对主上有什么好处呢？群臣众多，而主上只有一人，主上委托的财器职业等权力都集中在群臣之手。全都无耻，全都胡作非为，主上就最担心了。所以古人说："礼不及庶人，刑不至大夫"，这样做是为了勉励宠臣守节。古代有大臣因为不廉洁之罪要被废黜的，不说不廉洁，说"簠簋不整洁"；因为淫乱肮脏男女无别的，不说肮脏，说"帷薄不修"；因为软弱无能不能胜任官职的，不说软弱无能，说"下官不职"。所以对有地位的大臣定罪时，不仅不以斥责的口吻正面宣布他的罪行，还迁就地为他隐讳。所以那些处于应被大声谴责呵斥的地位的人，听到谴责呵斥就穿上丧服，磐水加剑，到请罪的房间去请罪，皇上不叫人捆绑起来牵着走。犯有中等罪行的人，听到命令便自毁容仪认罪，皇上不使人把刀架到他的脖子上。犯有大罪的人，听到命令便朝北跪拜认罪，跪下自杀，皇上不派人揪住他的头发往下按把他处死，说："你大夫是自己有罪啊！我待你是有礼的。"对待他有礼，所以群臣自

usurp power; when the lord encountered trouble, they would live just for the sake of remaining alive, stand by and look on; when there was opportunity to benefit themselves, they would betray the master for profit. What good does this do to the lord? Courtiers are the vast majority, while the lord is the extreme minority, so entrusted funds, implements, and responsibilities are concentrated in the hands of courtiers. If all of them are shameless, and act outrageously, it would be most difficult for the lord. For this is why the ancients said: "Courtesy does not cover the common people, while punishment does not reach the grand masters," a policy intended to encourage the integrity of the favorite courtiers. In ancient times, when ministers were removed on grounds of corruption, they did not mention corruption, but "untidy sacrificial utensils," when men and women were indecently promiscuous, there was no mention of indecency, but "inadequate curtains"; when weak officials were incompetent, they did not say weaknesses, but "unprofessional inferior officials." Therefore, when the distinguished ministers were convicted, they were still not rebuked but announced positively, and their crimes obligingly concealed. So those who were liable to loud condemnation, on hearing the condemnation hoot, put on penal white caps with yak-tail tassels, and carrying a dish of water with a sword lying on it, went to the petition room to admit their crimes. But the Emperor did not have them tied up and led away. Officials who had committed moderate crimes disfigured their faces when they heard the order; the Emperor did not have a sword laid on their necks. Those guilty of a felony knelt down northward, repeatedly kowtowing at the command, in admission of guilt, and committed suicide; and the Emperor did not have men grab them by the hair and push down their heads for execution. He said: "You yourself is guilty! But I treat you courteously." Treated with courtesy,

【原文】

以廉耻，故人矜节行，上设廉耻礼义以遇其臣，而臣不以节行报其上者，则非人类也。故化成俗定，则为人臣者主耳忘身，国耳忘家，公耳忘私，利不苟就，害不苟去，唯义所在。上之化也，故父兄之臣诚死宗庙，法度之臣诚死社稷，辅翼之臣诚死君上，守圄扞敌之臣诚死城郭封疆。故曰圣人有金城者，比物此志也。彼且为我死，故吾得与之俱生；彼且为我亡，故吾得与之俱存；夫将为我危，故吾得与之皆安。顾行而忘利，守节而仗义，故可以托不御之权，可以寄六尺之孤。此厉廉耻行礼谊之所致也，主上何丧焉！此之不为，而顾彼之久行，故曰可为长太息者此也。

是时丞相绛侯周勃免就国，人有告勃谋反，逮系长安狱治，卒亡事，复爵邑，故贾谊以此讥上。上深纳其言，养臣下有节。是后大臣

【今译】

爱；以廉耻待人，所以人们就注重节操和德行。皇上设立廉耻礼义来对待他的臣子，而臣子不以节操和德行报答他的主上，那他就不是人啊。所以教化成、风俗定，那么作为臣子的人，就会想到主上便忘了自己，想到国家便忘了自己的家庭，想到公事便忘了私事，见利不随便谋取，见害不苟且逃避，只按照道义办事。皇上施行教化，所以父兄之臣忠诚于祖业而死，制定和推行法度的大臣忠诚于国家而死，辅助保护君主的大臣忠诚于君主而死，守边御敌的大臣忠诚于城郭疆界而死。所以说圣人拥有金城，就是用金城这样的物来比喻众臣的这种意志的。他尚且为我而死，所以我必须与他共生死；他尚且为我而亡，所以我必须与他共存亡；他将为我去冒危险，所以我必须与他一起平安。顾全德行而忘记利益，守住节操而主持正义，所以可以托付给他不加约束的大权，可以寄养未成年而父已死的皇帝。这是勉励廉耻推行礼义所应该达到的，主上何必要失去这些呢！这些事不做，反而长久地顾及不该做的事，所以我说可以为之叹息的就是这些事啊。

这时丞相绛侯周勃免职回到封国，有人告发周勃谋反，把周勃捆绑押解到长安下狱治罪，结果没有反事，又恢复了他的爵位，所以贾谊用周勃的事来规劝汉文帝处罚大臣要慎重。汉文帝深深地接受了他的意见，对待臣下有了分寸。这以后大臣犯了罪，都自杀，没有处以

the courtiers love themselves; given a sense of shame, people focus on integrity and virtue. If the Emperor treats his courtiers with sense of shame, propriety and righteousness, they would not be human if they do not repay him with integrity and virtue. With moral education fulfilled and customs settled, the courtier officials would think of the lord and forget themselves, dedicate themselves to the country and forget their own family, devote themselves to public service and forget their private interest; they would act only in accordance with moral principle, without myopically seeking benefit and dodging damage. When the Emperor practices moral education, the elder officials indeed die for the ancestral temple, the bureaucrats die loyal to the country, the official aides die loyal to the monarch, and the officers who defend borders and resist the enemy die for the city walls. Therefore, the sages have a golden city, a term to describe the will of public officials. He is going to die for me, so I have to stand with him, and he will die for me, so I have to stay alive with him; he would take the risk for me, so I must be safe with him. They focus on good behavior at the expense of benefit, keep high moral principle to uphold justice; thus you can trust him with unbridled power, and ask him to foster the underage orphaned emperor. This is achieved by encouraging sense of shame and implementing rite and righteousness; what would the lord lose in this! But instead of this, unacceptable things have long prevailed. This merits a deep sigh.

At the time, Prime Minister Zhou Bo, Marquis of Jiang, was dismissed back to his fief, and someone informed against Zhou Bo for conspiracy to rebel. Zhou was arrested and detained in prison in Changan, but ultimately he was acquitted and restored to his peerage and fief. Jia Yi admonished the Emperor for this. Wendi took his ideas to heart, and fostered his courtiers from propriety. After that,

【原文】

有罪，皆自杀，不受刑。至武帝时，稍复入狱，自甯成始。

初，文帝以代王入即位，后分代为两国，立皇子武为代王，参为太原王，小子胜则梁王矣。后又徙代王武为淮阳王，而太原王参为代王，尽得故地。居数年，梁王胜死，亡子。谊复上疏曰：

陛下即不定制，如今之势，不过一传再传，诸侯犹且人恣而不制，豪植而大强，汉法不得行矣。陛下所以为蕃扞及皇太子之所恃者，唯淮阳、代二国耳。代北边匈奴，与强敌为邻，能自完则足矣。而淮阳之比大诸侯，廑如黑子之著面，适足以饵大国耳，不足以有所禁御。方今制在陛下，制国而令子适足以为饵，岂可谓工哉！人主之行异布衣。布衣者，饰小行，竞小廉，以自托于乡党，人主唯天下安社稷固不耳。高皇帝瓜分天下以王功臣，反者如猬毛而起，以为不可，故蕲去不义诸侯而虚其国。

【今译】

死刑的。到了汉武帝时，从甯成开始，才逐渐有大臣犯罪入狱的。

起初，汉文帝以代王的身份即皇帝位。后来把代国分为两国，立皇子刘武为代王，刘参为太原王，小儿子刘胜为梁王。后来又调代王刘武为淮阳王，而太原王刘参做代王，得到原先代王的全部封地。过了几年，梁王刘胜死了，没有儿子。贾谊又上疏说：

陛下如果不订立制度，如今的形势，只不过是一二世罢了，诸侯王国尚且没有管束，势力建起并逐步强大，汉王朝的法令就得不到推行了。陛下用来保持自己和皇太子所依赖的，只不过是淮阳和代两国罢了。代国北面靠近匈奴，与强敌为邻，能够保全自己就差不多了。而淮阳同大诸侯相比，仅仅如同小小的黑痣长在脸上，只适合被大国所吞食，而不足以抵御大国。现在制度在于陛下制定，编制诸侯国而让自己的儿子适合作大国的食饵，难道可以说是工于心计吗！主上行为与平民百姓不同。平民百姓，注重小德行，讲究小廉洁，以此托付于乡里，主上注重的是统一天下，安定社会。高皇帝瓜分天下给有功之臣做诸侯王，反对的人如同猬毛一样起来，认为不可以，所以除去不义的诸侯而空着

when his courtiers committed crimes, they were all allowed to commit suicide, rather than being executed. In the reign of Emperor Wudi, imprisonment was gradually reinstated, starting from Ning Cheng.

Emperor Wendi had been Prince of Dai before being enthroned. Subsequently Dai was divided into two, with Prince Liu Wu becoming Prince of Dai, and Liu Can becoming Prince of Taiyuan; his youngest son Liu Sheng became Prince of Liang. Later, Liu Wu was transferred as Prince of Huaiyang, and Prince of Taiyuan, Liu Can as Prince of Dai, restoring the fiefdom to its original form. Several years later, Prince Liu Sheng died without sons. Jia Yi submitted this memorial:

> *If Your Majesty does not set up a new system, continuing what we have today, after but one or two generations, the vassal kings will defy the Court's control, gradually nurturing powerful forces until the writ of Han can run no longer. The only sure thing Your Majesty can depend on to defend yourself and the Crown Prince are the two princedoms of Huaiyang and Dai. Dai borders on the Huns in the north, neighboring a powerful enemy, and is barely able to sustain itself. As for Huaiyang, compared to the great princes it is just like a small mole on the face, only enough to be swallowed by the big powers; it could not withstand them. Now the system is developed by Your Majesty, and the way you are arranging the princedoms will only make your sons juicy prey for big powers; can this be calculation on your part? Imperial behavior is different from that of the civilian population: they focus on small operations, and are meticulous over small matters of integrity, which benefit the local community; but what the lord focuses on is the unification of the whole country, stability in all society. When Emperor Gaodi carved up the empire to reward the meritorious officers as vassal kings, opponents rose up like*

【原文】

择良日，立诸子雒阳上东门之外，毕以为王，而天下安。故大人者，不牵小行，以成大功。

今淮南地远者或数千里，越两诸侯，而县属于汉。其吏民徭役往来长安者，自悉而补，中道衣敝，钱用诸费称此，其苦属汉而欲得王至甚，逋逃而归诸侯者已不少矣。其势不可久。臣之愚计，愿举淮南地以益淮阳，而为梁王立后，割淮阳北边二三列城与东郡以益梁；不可者，可徙代王而都睢阳。梁起于新郪以北著之河；淮阳包陈以南楗之江，则大诸侯之有异心者，破胆而不敢谋。梁足以扞齐、赵，淮阳足以禁吴、楚，陛下高枕，终亡山东之忧矣，此二世之利也。当今恬然，适遇诸侯之皆少，数岁之后，陛下且见之矣。夫秦日夜苦心劳力以除六国之祸，今陛下力

【今译】

他的国家。选择良辰吉日，在洛阳上东门外立他的几个儿子，全都做了诸侯王，这样天下安定了。所以干大事的人，不被小的行动所牵累，最后成就大功业。

现在淮南这个诸侯国跨越的土地，远的有达到几千里的，超过梁和淮阳两个诸侯，而作为县属汉王朝统辖。淮南的官吏和老百姓因为徭役往来长安的人，拿出全部家财添补衣服，但半路上衣服就破了，钱大多用在这项费用的开支上，他们苦于隶属于汉而非常想得一个诸侯王，逃跑而归附于诸侯的已经不少了。这种形势不能让它长久。我有一个愚笨的计谋，希望拿出淮南之地加给淮阳，而在立了梁王以后，割淮阳北边二三县和东郡加给梁国；不行的话，可调代王建都睢阳。梁国的土地从新郪起向北靠近黄河，淮阳取陈国以南土地接着长江，这样，大诸侯国有野心的，也会吓破胆而不敢图谋。梁国足以防御齐国、赵国，淮阳足以抵挡吴国、楚国。陛下可高枕而卧，没有崤山以东的忧患了，这是两代人的利益啊。当今国家安定，正好遇上诸侯都年少，几年以后，陛下将看到危机了。秦朝日夜苦心积虑消除六国的祸患，现在陛下以权力控制天下，只用面颊表情示意人，想要达到

the spines of a hedgehog. For them it was unacceptable, so the unrighteous kings were removed and their states evacuated. On an auspicious day, the Emperor established all his sons as vassal kings, outside the Upper East Gate in Luoyang. When they all had this status, the empire's stability was secured. So great people are not to be tied down by small operations, so they may ultimately achieve great things.

Distant Huainan is thousands of li *away, across the two princedoms of Liang and Huaiyang, but governed remotely by Han. Its officials and commoners who journey between there and Changan for corvee exhaust the family wealth to finance the trips, but their clothes are torn halfway, so most of the money is spent on these expenses. They suffer acutely from belonging to Han and want very much a vassal king; many are those who escaped, attaching themselves to the princes. This situation cannot be allowed to persist. In my humble opinion you should transfer some land of Huainan to Huaiyang; after establishing the Prince of Liang, we would cede two or three counties in the north of Huaiyang and Dongjun Prefecture to Liang. If this does not work, we could move the Prince of Dai to his new capital Suiyang. Liang's territory would start from Xinqi to the north near the Yellow River, while Huaiyang would cover the land south of Chen down to its border on the Yangtze River, so that the disloyal vassals would be deterred from plotting for it. Liang would be strong enough to guard against Qi and Zhao, while Huaiyang could resist Wu and Chu. Your Majesty might sit back and relax, with no further concerns about the East of Mountains, which would benefit two generations. Today, the country is settled, just when the princes are young; but in a few years, Your Majesty will see the dangers. The Qin Dynasty exerted its heart and strength day and night to eliminate the scourge of those six countries, but now Your Majesty controls*

【原文】

制天下，颐指如意，高拱以成六国之祸，难以言智。苟身亡事，畜乱宿祸，孰视而不定，万年之后，传之老母弱子，将使不宁，不可谓仁。臣闻圣主言问其臣而不自造事，故使人臣得毕其愚忠。唯陛下财幸！

文帝于是从谊计，乃徙淮阳王武为梁王，北界泰山，西至高阳，得大县四十馀城；徙城阳王喜为淮南王，抚其民。

时又封淮南厉王四子皆为列侯。谊知上必将复王之也，上疏谏曰："窃恐陛下接王淮南诸子，曾不与如臣者孰计之也。淮南王之悖逆亡道，天下孰不知其罪？陛下幸而赦迁之，自疾而死，天下孰以王死之不当？今奉尊罪人之子，适足以负谤于天下耳。此人少壮，岂能忘其父哉？白公胜所为父报仇者，大父与伯父、叔父也。白公为乱，非欲取国代主也，发愤快志，剡手以冲仇人之匈，固为俱靡而已。淮

【今译】

的就能如意，如果陛下高拱两手酿成六国的祸患，就难以说聪明不聪明。苟全自身没有滋事，蓄留祸乱，仔细看看而不决定，万年之后，传给老母弱子，将使他们不得安宁，不可以说是仁爱。我听说圣主要说话时，先问臣子而不自己先说。因此使臣子们能够尽表愚忠。希望陛下采纳我的话。

汉文帝于是采纳了贾谊的计策，就调淮阳王刘武为梁王，梁国北面以泰山为界，西面到达高阳，得大县四十多个；调城阳王刘喜为淮南王，安抚他的老百姓。

当时，又封淮南厉王刘长的四个儿子都当列侯。贾谊知道皇上一定要恢复诸侯王的爵位，上疏进谏说："我私下担心陛下将要封淮南厉王的几个儿子为王，这是没有同臣下仔细计议过啊。淮南王反叛作乱，天下谁不知道他的罪行？陛下幸而宽大放逐他，他自杀而死，天下谁认为他死得不应该呢？今天重用罪人的儿子，恰好辜负了天下人对厉王的谴责！厉王的儿子稍稍长大，难道能忘了他父亲的仇恨吗？白公胜为父报仇，就是针对祖父和伯父、叔父的。白公胜发动政变，不是夺权篡位，而是发泄心中的愤恨之气，手持尖刀刺向仇人胸膛，

the world, your power so great that you achieve what you want by a gesture. But if Your Majesty adopts a hands-off approach to the six countries, this is brewing up disaster, and could hardly be called smart. Preserving yourself in an uneventful state at all costs, you are storing up trouble and calamity for the future; to concentrate on minutia is to avoid decisions. In 10,000 years, you will be succeeded by a weak son and an old mother, who will have no rest. This can hardly be called benevolent. I heard that when the sage kings wished to say something, they asked their courtiers to speak first, so that they were able to show their blind devotion. I hope that Your Majesty will accept my humble advice.

Emperor Wendi adopted Jia Yi's strategy, moving the Prince of Huaiyang Liu Wu to the Princedom of Liang, with more than 40 large counties, which on the north was bounded by Mount Tai, and on the west by Gaoyang; then he moved Prince of Chengyang Liu Xi to Huainan, to appease his people.

At that time, Prince Li of Huainan Liu Chang's four sons were all made adjunct marquises, and Jia Yi knew that the Emperor would surely restore the title of princes to the vassal lords, so he admonished: "I fear Your Majesty will wish the Prince Huainan's sons to succeed, but you have not carefully deliberated on it with your courtiers. The Prince of Huainan was known for his disloyalty and behavior against the Way, so who in the world does not know of his crimes? Fortunately, Your Majesty was lenient and expelled him only, allowing him to commit suicide. But who in the world thinks he should not have died? Today you elevate this criminal's sons, just to bear the blame of the world! The sons have barely grown up. How can they forget their father? Magistrate of Bai Sheng took revenge for his father on his own grandfather and uncles; his coup was not meant to usurp power, but to vent the anger in his heart. Holding his dagger against his enemy's breast, he was ready to perish along

【原文】

南虽小，黥布尝用之矣，汉存特幸耳。夫擅仇人足以危汉之资，于策不便。虽割而为四，四子一心也。予之众，积之财，此非有子胥、白公报于广都之中，即疑有剸诸、荆轲起于两柱之间，所谓假贼兵为虎翼者也。愿陛下少留计！”

梁王胜坠马死，谊自伤为傅无状，常哭泣，后岁馀，亦死。贾生之死，年三十三矣。

后四岁，齐文王薨，亡子。文帝思贾生之言，乃分齐为六国，尽立悼惠王子六人为王；又迁淮南王喜于城阳，而分淮南为三国，尽立厉王三子以王之。后十年，文帝崩，景帝立，三年而吴、楚、赵与四齐王合从举兵，西乡京师，梁王扞之，卒破七国。至武帝时，淮南厉王子为王者两国亦反诛。

孝武初立，举贾生之孙二人至郡守。贾嘉最好学，世其家。

赞曰：刘向称“贾谊言三代与秦治乱之意，其论甚美，通达国

【今译】

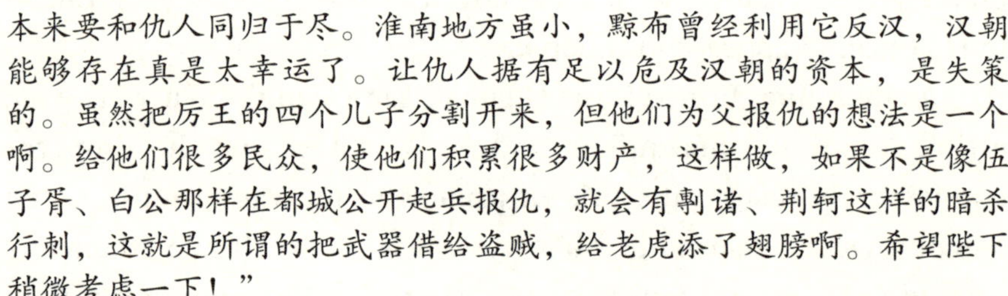

本来要和仇人同归于尽。淮南地方虽小，黥布曾经利用它反汉，汉朝能够存在真是太幸运了。让仇人据有足以危及汉朝的资本，是失策的。虽然把厉王的四个儿子分割开来，但他们为父报仇的想法是一个啊。给他们很多民众，使他们积累很多财产，这样做，如果不是像伍子胥、白公那样在都城公开起兵报仇，就会有剸诸、荆轲这样的暗杀行刺，这就是所谓的把武器借给盗贼，给老虎添了翅膀啊。希望陛下稍微考虑一下！”

梁王刘胜坠马而死，贾谊感伤自己作为太傅失了职，常常哭泣。过了一年多，也死了。贾谊死时，年三十三岁。

后来的四年，齐文王死了，没有儿子。汉文帝想起贾谊的话，于是把齐国分成六个小国，分别立悼惠王的六个儿子为王；又调淮南王刘喜到城阳，把淮南分成三个小国，分别立厉王的三个儿子为王。以后十年，汉文帝驾崩，汉景帝继位，景帝三年，吴、楚、赵与四个齐王联合起兵反叛，向西直逼汉京城长安，梁孝王刘武保卫长安，最后打败七国。到汉武帝时，淮南厉王的儿子做了王的也有两国谋反而被诛灭。

汉武帝即位，任贾谊的孙子二人为郡太守。其中贾嘉最好学，继承书香门第。

赞曰：刘向称“贾谊谈论夏商周三代和秦朝治乱的意义，他的论

with his foe. Huainan is small in area, but Tattooed Bu used it to fight against Han, and the Dynasty was lucky to survive. Letting an enemy possess means enough to endanger Han is a policy mistake. Although separated into four areas, the four sons are of the same mind, and it is a mind bent on revenge. Giving them a lot of people will mean that they accumulate much property; to do this is like allowing Wu Zixu and Magistrate of Bai to openly declare revenge in the capital; it is like preparing the ground for assassins like Zhuan Zhu or Jing Ke to rise between the columns. It is called 'lending weapons to a brigand' or 'giving wings to a tiger.' I hope Your Majesty will ponder on this a while!"

The Prince of Liang Liu Sheng fell off a horse and died, and Jia Yi felt guilty of his own misconduct in office and often wept. After a year, he too died, at the age of 33.

Four years later, King Wen of Qi died without a son. Wendi remembered Jia Yi's advice, so he divided Qi into six smaller princedoms, one apiece for each of Prince Daohui's six sons; he moved Prince of Huainan Liu Xi to Chengyang, dividing Huainan into three smaller princedoms, one apiece for each of Prince Li's three sons. Ten years later, Wendi died, and was succeeded by Emperor Jingdi. In year three of his reign, Wu, Chu, and Zhao jointly declared rebellion with four Princes of Qi, marching westward toward the capital. The Prince of Liang defended Chang'an, and in the end defeated the seven princes. In the reign of Emperor Wudi, two of Prince Li of Huainan's sons also rebelled and got killed as princes.

Soon after Wudi ascended, he appointed Jia Yi's two grandsons as prefect governors. Jia Jia was the more eager to learn, and inherited the family tradition.

Author's note: Liu Xiang said: "In his talk about the significance of stability and turmoil in Xia, Shang and Zhou dynasties and Qin dynasty, Jia Yi's exposition is very beautiful. He

【原文】

体，虽古之伊、管未能远过也。使时见用，功化必盛。为庸臣所害，甚可悼痛。”追观孝文玄默躬行以移风俗，谊之所陈略施行矣。及欲改定制度，以汉为土德，色上黄，数用五，及欲试属国，施五饵三表以系单于，其术固以疏矣。谊(以夭)[亦天]年早终，虽不至公卿，未为不遇也。凡所著述五十八篇，掇其切于世事者著于传云。

——卷四十八《贾谊传》第十八

【今译】

述十分优美，他通晓国家典章制度，即使是古代的伊尹、管仲也不能超过他。假如当时他的主张得以实行，功业教化必定显著。但他被庸臣陷害，实在让人痛心”。回过头去看看汉文帝沉静无为，身体力行来移风易俗，贾谊所陈述的主张被略微施行了。等到想改定制度，因为汉是土德，就崇尚黄色，官印的数字使用“五”，等到想试着拥有属国，就施用贾谊的“五饵”、“三表”来紧紧拴住单于，他的办法因此取得了效果。贾谊英年早逝，他做官虽然没到公卿，但不是没有机遇。他的著述共五十八篇，摘取其中切于时事的内容写在他的传中。

was familiar with national institutions, even Yi Yin and Guan Zhong in the ancient times could not surpass him much. If his ideas had been implemented, his achievements and role in moral education would have been fabulous. But he was framed by mediocre officials, much to our grief." Looking back to Emperor Wendi's silence inaction and earnest practice to reform social mores, Jia Yi's ideas were implemented to a degree. As to his aspiration to revise the constitution, his approach was effective: Han took earth as its virtue, it advocated the color yellow, used the digit "five" in official seals, and did try to keep the Chanyu tied up via the vassal states, applying his "five baits" and "three strategies" idea. Jia Yi died young, but he had his opportunities even though he did not become a top official. Of his writings in 58 volumes, those concerning current events were summarized in his biography.